# Financial Reporting Analysis and Planning

# Financial Reporting Analysis and Planning

### Mary Bishop
F.C.C.A., BA. Hons

### Jonathan Evans
ACA

### Mervyn Hughes
F.C.C.A., A.T.I.I.

### Margaret M. Woods
M.Sc., A.C.C.A.

Apart from any fair dealing for the purpose of research or private study, or criticism or review, as permitted under the Copyright, Designs and Patents Act 1988, this publication may only be reproduced, stored or transmitted, in any form or by any means, with the prior permission in writing of the publisher, or in the case of reprographic reproduction in accordance with the terms and licences issued by the Copyright Licensing Agency. Enquiries concerning reproduction outside those terms should be addressed to the publishers' agents at the undermentioned address:

CIB Publishing
c/o The Chartered Institute of Bankers
Emmanuel House
4–9 Burgate Lane
Canterbury
Kent CT1 2XJ

CIB Publications are published by The Chartered Institute of Bankers, a non-profit making registered educational charity, and are distributed exclusively by CIB mail order.

The Chartered Institute of Bankers believes that the sources of information upon which the book is based are reliable and has made every effort to ensure the complete accuracy of the text. However, neither CIB, the author nor any contributor can accept any legal responsibility whatsoever for consequences that may arise from errors or omissions or any opinion or advice given.

ISBN 0-85297-532-5

First Edition
Copyright © Chartered Institute of Bankers 1996

Second Edition
Copyright © Chartered Institute of Bankers 1999

**Typeset by Leech Design, Preston**

# Contents

| | | Page |
|---|---|---|
| INTRODUCTION | | 1 |
| UNIT 1 | The Conceptual Framework | 7 |
| UNIT 2 | The Regulatory Framework | 25 |
| UNIT 3 | The Legal Framework | 37 |
| UNIT 4 | Valuation of Assets | 55 |
| UNIT 5 | Accounting for Liabilities | 89 |
| UNIT 6 | Financial Statements | 113 |
| UNIT 7 | Taxation | 147 |
| UNIT 8 | Accounting for Investments | 167 |
| UNIT 9 | Capital Reorganisation | 209 |
| UNIT 10 | Business Valuations | 231 |
| UNIT 11 | Ratio Analysis | 245 |
| UNIT 12 | Cash Flow Statement (1) | 273 |
| UNIT 13 | Cash Flow Statement (2) | 289 |
| UNIT 14 | Cost Behaviour | 297 |
| UNIT 15 | Capital Investment Appraisal | 321 |
| UNIT 16 | Plans, Forecasts and Budgets | 345 |
| UNIT 17 | FRS8 'Related Party Disclosures' | 365 |
| Appendix | | 369 |
| Glossary | | 433 |
| Index | | 441 |

# Introduction

## The Concept of the Course

This is a practical course written for students studying for banking and finance qualifications and also for practitioners in the financial services who are looking for a practical refresher. The framework of this study text is structured so that many will find it to be the most coherent way of learning the subject.

Each chapter or Unit of the Study Text is divided into sections and contains:

- learning objectives
- an introduction, indicating how this subject area relates to others to which the reader may have cause to refer
- clear, concise topic-by-topic coverage
- examples and exercises to reinforce learning, confirm understanding and stimulate thought
- often a recommendation on illustrative questions to try for practice.

**Exercises**

Exercises are provided throughout to enable you to check your progress as you work through the text. These come in a variety of forms; some test your ability to analyse material you have read, others see whether you have taken in the full significance of a piece of information. Some are meant to be discussed with colleagues, friends or fellow students.

A suggested solution is usually given, but often in abbreviated form to help you avoid the temptation of merely reading the exercise rather than actively engaging your brain. We think it is preferable on the whole to give the solution immediately after the exercise rather than making you hunt for it at the end of the chapter, losing your place and your concentration. Cover up the solution with a piece of paper if you find the temptation to cheat too great!

Examples can also often be used as exercises, if not the first time you read a passage then certainly afterwards when you come to revise.

Each of the main Units consists of study notes designed to focus attention upon the key aspects of the subject matter. These notes are divided into convenient sections for study purposes. Following each small group section there is a 'Student Activity' session, which is intended to encourage students to think about what they have studied in the preceding few sections and to consolidate their knowledge. In many cases, these Student Activity sessions comprise a series of short questions for each of which a reference is given to the precise part of the preceding text where the answer may be found. Students are strongly encouraged to use these Study Activity sessions in order to test their understanding of the material. They should also note their areas of weakness and re-read the relevant parts of the text.

At the end of each Unit there are self-assessment questions. These comprise a number of short answer questions and multiple-choice questions and a full specimen examination question. The answers to all these questions are to be found in the Appendix at the back of the book. Students should remain aware of the fact that the examination itself will comprise questions drawn from across the whole Chartered Institute of Bankers syllabus; the key sections of which for this subject are:

Financial Reporting Framework

Financial Reporting – The Practical Aspects

Capital Structures

Interpretation of Financial Reports

Management Control

Although the workbook is designed to stand alone, as with most topics, certain aspects of this subject are constantly changing. Therefore it is of great importance that students should keep up to date with these key areas.

It is anticipated that the student will study this course for one academic year, reading through and studying approximately two Units every three weeks. However, it should be noted that as topics vary in size and as knowledge tends not to fall into uniform chunks, some Units in this workbook are unavoidably longer than others.

The masculine pronoun 'he' has been used in this Workbook to encompass both genders and to avoid the awkwardness of the constant repetition of 'he and/or she'.

# INTRODUCTION

# Study Guide

In the next few pages, we offer some advice and ideas on studying, revising and approaching examinations.

**Studying**

As with any examination, there is no substitute for preparation based on an organised and disciplined study plan. You should devise an approach which will enable you to get right through this Study Text and still leave time for revision of this and any other subject you are taking at the same time. Many candidates find that about six weeks is the right period of time to leave for revision, enough time to get through the revision material, but not so long that it is no longer fresh in your mind by the time you reach the examination.

This means that you should plan how to get to the last Unit by, say, the end of March for a May sitting or the end of August for an October sitting. This includes not only reading the text, but making notes and attempting the bulk of the illustrative questions.

We offer the following as a starting point for approaching your study.

- Plan time each week to study a part of this Study Text. Make sure that it is 'quality' study time: let everyone know that you are studying and the you should not be disturbed. If you are at home, unplug your telephone or switch the answerphone on; if you are in the office, put your telephone on 'divert'.

- Set a clearly defined objective for each study period. You may simply wish to read through a Unit for the first time or perhaps you want to make some notes on a Unit you have already read a couple of times. Don't forget the illustrative questions.

- Review your study plan. Don't panic if you fall behind, but do think how you will make up for lost time.

- Look for examples of what you have covered in the 'real' world. If you work for a financial organisation, this should be a good starting point. If you do not, then think about your experiences as an individual bank or building society customer or perhaps about your employer's position as a corporate customer of a bank. Keep an eye on the quality press for reports about banks and building societies and their activities.

*Revising*

- The period which you have earmarked for revision is a very important time. Now it is even more important that you plan time each week for study and that you set clear objectives for each revision session.

- Use time sensibly. How much revision time do you have? Remember that you still need to eat, sleep and fit in some leisure time.

- How will you split the available time between subjects? What are your weaker subjects? You will need to focus on some topics in more detail than others. You will also need to plan your revision around your learning style. By now, you should know whether, for example, early morning, early evening or late evening is best.

- Take regular breaks. Most people find they can absorb more this way than if they attempt to revise for long uninterrupted periods of time. Award yourself a five minute break every hour. Go for a stroll or make a cup of coffee, but do not turn the television on.
- Believe in yourself. Are you cultivating the right attitude of mind? There is absolutely no reason why you should not pass this exam if you adopt the correct approach. Be confident, you have passed exams before so you can pass this one.

### *The day of the exam*

- Passing professional examinations is half about having the knowledge, and half about doing yourself full justice in the examination. You must have the right technique.
- Set at least one alarm (or get an alarm call) for a morning exam.
- Having something to eat but beware of eating too much; you may feel sleepy if your system is digesting a large meal.
- Don't forget pens, pencils, rulers, erasers and anything else you will need.
- Avoid discussion about the exam with other candidates outside the exam hall.

### *Tackling the examination paper*

First, make sure that you satisfy the examiner's requirements

*Read the instructions on the front of the exam paper carefully.* Check that the exam format hasn't changed. It is surprising how often examiners' reports remark on the number of students who attempt too few - or too many - questions, or who attempt the wrong number of questions from different parts of the paper. Make sure that you are planning to answer the right number of questions.

*Read all the questions on the exam paper before you start writing.* Look at the weighting of marks to each part of the question. If part (a) offers only 4 marks and you can't answer the 12 marks part (b), then don't choose the question.

*Don't produce irrelevant answers.* Make sure you answer the question set, and not the question you would have preferred to have been set.

*Produce an answer in the correct format.* The examiner will state in the requirements the format in which the question should be answered, for example in a report or memorandum. If a question asks for a diagram or an example, give one. If a question does not specifically asks for a diagram or example, but it seems appropriate, give one.

Second, observe these simple rules to ensure that your script is pleasing to the examiner.

*Present a tidy paper.* You are a professional and it should always show in the presentation of your work. Candidates are penalised for poor presentation and so you should make sure that you write legibly, label diagrams clearly and lay out your work professionally. Markers of scripts each have dozens of papers to mark; a badly written scrawl is unlikely to receive the same attention as a neat and well laid out paper.

# INTRODUCTION

*State the obvious.* Many candidates look for complexity which is not required and consequently overlook the obvious. Make basic statements first. Plan your answer and ask yourself whether you have answered the main parts of the question.

*Use examples.* This will help to demonstrate to the examiner that you keep up-to-date with the subject. There are lots of useful examples scattered through this study text and you can read about others if you dip into the quality press or take notice of what is happening in your working environment.

Finally, Make sure that you give yourself the opportunity to do yourself justice.

*Select questions carefully.* Read through the paper once, then quickly jot down any key points against each question in a second read through. Reject those questions against which you have jotted down very little. Select those where you could latch on to 'what the question is about' - but remember to check carefully that you have got the right end of the stick before putting pen to paper.

*Plan your attack carefully.* Consider the order in which you are going to tackle questions. It is a good idea to start with your best question to boost your morale and get some easy marks 'in the bag'.

*Read the question carefully and plan your answer.* Read through the question again very carefully when you come to answer it.

*Gain the easy marks.* Include the obvious if it answers the question and do not spend unnecessary time producing the perfect answer. As suggested above, there is nothing wrong with stating the obvious.

*Avoid getting bogged down in small parts of questions.* If you find a part of a question difficult, get on with the rest of the question. If you are having problems with something the chances are that everyone else is too.

*Don't leave the exam early.* Use your spare time checking and rechecking your script.

*Don't worry if you feel you have performed badly in the exam.* It is more likely that the other candidates will have found the exam difficult too. Don't forget that there is a competitive element in exams. As soon as you get up and leave the exam hall, forget the exam and think about the next - or , if it is the last one, celebrate!

*Don't discuss an exam with other candidates.* This is particularly the case if you still have other exams to sit. Put it out of your mind until the day of the results. Forget about exams and relax.

# FINANCIAL REPORTING, ANALYSIS AND PLANNING

# Unit 1

## The Conceptual Framework

> **Objectives**
>
> After studying this Unit you should be able to:
>
> - describe the objectives of financial statements and the fundamental accounting concepts
> - identify the desirable characteristics of accounting reports
> - understand the different approaches to calculating an entity's surplus income, and
> - explain the limitations of historic cost accounts.

### 1 Introduction

1.1 The objective of financial statements is to provide users with useful information. While this is merely a statement of the obvious it provides us with a guide as to what should or should not be included in financial statements.

1.2 Corporate reports are usually readily available and are a convenient point for communicating information to the world at large. In this Unit we will be examining who the company communicates with and how this can best be achieved.

1.3 We will then go on to discuss the conceptual problems in preparing accounts and the problems associated with historic cost accounts.

### 2 The corporate report

2.1 In 1975 the Accounting Standards Committee produced a discussion paper, 'The Corporate Report'. The paper stated that:

> 'the fundamental objective of corporate reports is to communicate economic measurements of and information about resources and performance of the reporting entity useful to those having reasonable rights to such information.'

2.2 The paper identified the following parties who have a reasonable right to information about the reporting entity:

- shareholders (existing and potential shareholders)
- loan creditors

# FINANCIAL REPORTING, ANALYSIS AND PLANNING

- employees
- analysts and advisers (stockbrokers, journalists, etc.)
- business contacts (trade creditors, competitors, etc.)
- the government
- the public.

2.3 Shareholders and potential shareholders need information in order to decide whether to buy or sell the company's shares and how to vote at the company's annual general meeting. In order to make these decisions they need information on the company's performance and on its dividend policy.

2.4 Loan creditors will be concerned with the safety of their interest payments and the future repayment of their capital. They will therefore need to know the company's recent cashflows and the likely future cashflows. They will also be concerned that any covenants associated with their loans have not been breached.

2.5 Employees require information on the security of their employment and on their likely future wage levels.

2.6 Analysts and advisers need information on the stability and performance of companies to advise their clients – stockbrokers for potential investors and credit-rating agencies for potential creditors of the company.

2.7 Business contacts include the following:

(a) suppliers, who need to know that they will be paid and that the company will be a reliable long-term customer; and

(b) customers, who need to know that their supplies will continue and that the company will not cease to trade.

2.8 The government, in addition to possibly being a customer or supplier of the company, takes an interest in:

(a) the current and prospective contribution of the company to the economic well being, and employment in the area/country

(b) the ability of the company to pay taxes

(c) the company's compliance with company and tax law.

2.9 The public may have wide and varied requirements. 'The Corporate Report' recognised that it would be impossible to meet all these general purpose needs. However the public should have access to the information available to the other groups.

2.10 Having identified the users of corporate reports the paper then identified the characteristics of the information contained in the reports which made them useful. These were:

- relevance
- comprehensibility
- reliability
- completeness
- objectivity

# THE CONCEPTUAL FRAMEWORK

- timeliness
- comparability.

2.11 Relevance: the information provided is pertinent to the users of the report. The type of information will vary between the user groups and over time.

2.12 Comprehensibility: the report can be readily understood. The information provided is neither too detailed nor insufficient to make an informed judgment.

2.13 Reliability: users must have confidence that the figures and information are accurate and free from bias. This is usually achieved by an independent audit.

2.14 Completeness: the paper stated that 'Reports should present a rounded picture of the economic activities of the reporting entity' i.e. the report should be balanced and not give greater emphasis to some aspects of the entity's performance at the expense of others.

2.15 Objectivity: several items in the financial statements are necessarily subjective. The application of accounting standards should help ensure that these items are treated in a consistent manner which is free from bias.

2.16 Timeliness: the longer it takes for the information to reach the users the less useful it becomes.

2.17 Comparability: in order to judge a company's performance it is necessary to have some benchmark with which to compare it i.e. previous years' accounts or the accounts of similar companies. For those comparisons to be valid the accounts must be produced in the same manner. This is achieved by the application of consistent accounting concepts and policies.

## 3 The ASB's Statement of Principles

3.1 Accounting standards in the UK have historically been set as a matter of expediency. This has led to some conceptual inconsistencies between the standards. To date there has been no conceptual framework for the preparers of accounts or the bodies which issue accounting standards.

3.2 The ASB recognised the need for such a framework and published an Exposure Draft (ED) of its *Statement of Principles* in November 1995. The statement contains seven chapters.

(1) The objective of financial statements

(2) The qualitative characteristics of financial information

(3) The elements of financial statements

(4) Recognition in financial statements

(5) Measurement in financial statements

(6) Presentation of financial information

(7) The reporting entity.

3.3 The ASB gave the following as their main reasons for developing the *Statement of Principles*.

# FINANCIAL REPORTING, ANALYSIS AND PLANNING

- To assist the ASB by providing a basis for reducing the number of alternative accounting treatments permitted by accounting standards and company law.
- To provide a framework for the future development of accounting standards.
- To assist auditors in forming an opinion as to whether financial statements conform with accounting standards.
- To assist users of accounts in interpreting the information contained in them.
- To provide guidance in applying accounting standards.
- To give guidance on areas which are not yet covered by accounting standards.
- To inform interested parties of the ASB's approach in formulating accounting standards.

We will look at each of the seven chapters in sections 4 – 10 of this Unit.

## 4 The objective of financial statements

4.1 The first chapter states that

>'The objective of financial statements is to provide information about the financial position, performance and financial adaptability of an enterprise that is useful to a wide range of users for assessing the stewardship of management and for making economic decisions.'

4.2 The chapter gives the same list of users as 'The Corporate Report'. It acknowledges that although the information needs of all users cannot be met there are needs that are common for all users. These needs will usually be met if the financial statements meet the needs of the providers of risk capital to the enterprise.

4.3 It also states that all three components of the financial statements (balance sheet, profit and loss account and cash flow statement) are interrelated as they reflect different aspects of the same transaction.

4.4 The chapter emphasises the ways financial statements provide information about the financial position of an enterprise. The main elements which affect the position of a company are:

(a) the economic resources it controls

(b) its financial structure

(c) its liquidity and solvency

(d) its financial adaptability, i.e. its ability to adapt to changes in its environment.

The importance of these elements and their disclosure is stressed.

# THE CONCEPTUAL FRAMEWORK

## 5 Qualitative characteristics of financial information

5.1 The 1995 ED examines the various characteristics and their relationships with each other in the following diagram:

**Diagram 1.1**
**The Qualitative characteristics of financial information**

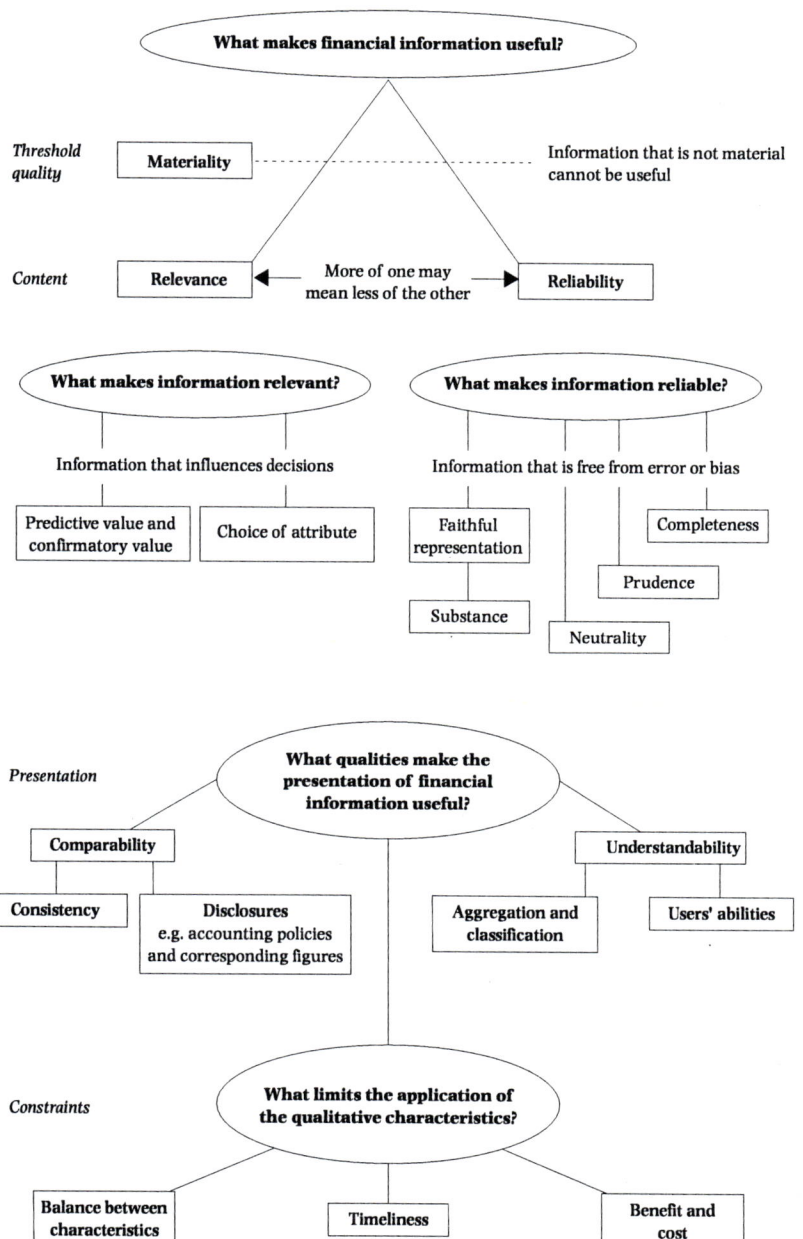

5.2 The diagram is reasonably self explanatory. You should note how a distinction is made between the primary characteristics of relevance and reliability and the secondary characteristics given in the lower part of the diagram.

FINANCIAL REPORTING, ANALYSIS AND PLANNING

## 6 Elements of financial statements

6.1 The chapter lists the elements that should be included in financial statements. Any item not listed should not be included. The elements are defined as follows.

6.2 *Assets* are rights or other access to future economic benefits controlled by an entity as a result of past transactions or events.

6.3 *Liabilities* are obligations of an entity to transfer economic benefits as a result of past transactions or events.

6.4 *Ownership* interest is the residual amount found by deducting all the entity's liabilities from all the entity's assets.

6.5 *Gains* are increases in ownership interest, other than those relating to contributions from owners.

6.6 *Losses* are decreases in ownership interest, other than those relating to distributions to owners.

6.7 *Contributions from owners* are increases in ownership interest resulting from investments made by owners in their capacity as owners.

6.8 *Distributions to owners* are decreases in ownership interest resulting from transfers made to owners in their capacity as owners.

## 7 Recognition in financial statements

7.1 This chapter discusses the three stages of recognition of assets and liabilities. It describes the criteria used to determine each of the stages which are given as:

(a) initial recognition

(b) subsequent remeasurement and

(c) derecognition.

7.2 *Initial recognition* An element should be recognised if there is sufficient evidence that the change in assets or liabilities inherent in the element has occurred. This includes, where appropriate, evidence that a future inflow or outflow of benefit will occur and that it can be measured at a monetary amount with sufficient reliability.

7.3 *Subsequent remeasurement* A change in the amount at which an asset or liability is recorded should be recognised if there is sufficient evidence that the amount of an asset or liability has changed and the new amount of the asset or liability can be measured with sufficient reliability.

7.4 *Derecognition* An asset or liability should cease to be recognised if there is no longer sufficient evidence that the entity has access to future economic benefits or an obligation to transfer economic benefit. This includes, where appropriate, evidence that a future inflow or outflow of benefit will occur.

7.5 The chapter also states the criteria for recognising gains and losses linking them with the treatment of assets and liabilities given above as follows.

# THE CONCEPTUAL FRAMEWORK

'At any stage in the recognition process, where a change in total assets is not offset by an equal change in total liabilities or a transaction with owners, a gain or loss will arise.

'The recognition of gains involves consideration of whether there is sufficient evidence that an increase in net assets (i.e. in ownership interest) had occurred before the end of the reporting period.

'The recognition of losses involves consideration of whether there is sufficient evidence that a decrease in ownership interest had occurred before the end of the reporting period. Prudence has the effect that less evidence of occurrence and reliability of measurement is required for the recognition of a loss than for a gain.'

## 8 Measurement in financial statements

8.1 This chapter places great emphasis on current values and has been criticised by several interested parties.

8.2 Its chosen approach is as follows.

(a) When an asset is purchased or a liability incurred it is recorded at the transaction cost. This is historic cost which at the time is also the current replacement cost.

(b) When the recognition criteria for a change are met the asset/liability may be remeasured. The monetary amount at which the asset/liability is recorded is changed.

(c) The use of current values is suggested with the chapter stating that:

'Practice should develop by evolving in the direction of greater use of current values to the extent that this is consistent with the constraints of reliability and cost.'

(d) The current value to be used for assets is 'value to business' i.e. the lower of replacement cost and recoverable amount. The recoverable amount is the higher of net realisable value and value in use.

(e) Market values may be used as an effective measure of value to the business for liabilities.

(f) The chapter does concede that historic cost has the merits of familiarity and, to some extent, objectivity.

## 9 Presentation of financial statements

9.1 The chapter commences by observing that financial information is presented in the form of a structured set of financial statements comprising primary statements and supporting notes, which are in some instances accompanied by supplementary information.

9.2 The primary financial statements are the:

- profit and loss account

- statement of total recognised gains and losses (SORG)
- balance sheet
- cash flow statement.

9.3 The notes to the financial statements provide additional information to 'amplify and explain' the primary statements. Disclosure in the notes is not sufficient to correct or justify non-disclosure or misrepresentation in the primary statements.

9.4 Supplementary information relates to voluntary disclosures and information which is too subjective to be disclosed in the primary statements and notes.

9.5 The profit and loss account and the statement of total recognised gains and losses are statements of financial performance. In order to assess an entity's overall performance it is necessary to consider all the gains and losses that arise during a period.

9.6 The gains and losses in the statement of total recognised gains and losses are those that relate to assets and liabilities whose primary function is to enable the entity's operations to be carried out, i.e. its fixed assets, and so on. All other gains and losses are reported in the profit and loss account.

9.7 The chapter discusses the usefulness of the balance sheet, but recognises that it does not purport to show the value of the enterprise. The balance sheet's function is described as follows:

> **'The balance sheet (together with related notes) provides information about an entity's assets and liabilities and its ownership interest and shows their relationships to each other at a point of time. The balance sheet delineates the entity's resource structure (major classes and amounts of assets) and its financial structure (major classes and amounts of liabilities and ownership interest).'**

> **'The financial position of an entity is determined by the economic resources it controls, its financial structure, its liquidity and solvency, and its capacity to adapt to changes in the environment in which it operates.'**

9.8 The cash flow statement provides useful information concerning how an entity's activities generate and use cash. It does this by showing an entity's cash inflows and outflows during a period, distinguishing between those that are the result of operations and those that result from other activities. This assists users in assessing the entity's liquidity, solvency, financial adaptability and the relationship between profits and cash flow.

9.9 Throughout the Exposure Draft great emphasis is placed on financial adaptability which it defines as:

> **'the ability of an entity to take effective action to alter the amounts and timing of cash flows so that it can respond to unexpected needs or opportunities.'**

9.10 Thus financial adaptability comes from the ability to:

- raise new capital
- obtain cash by selling assets without disrupting continuing operations

# THE CONCEPTUAL FRAMEWORK

- achieve a rapid improvement in the net cash inflows generated by operations.

The primary statements provide information to assist the user to assess an entity's financial adaptability.

9.11 The chapter closes by discussing the use of highlights and summary indicators and the different kinds of supplementary information that might be included alongside the primary statements, including:

(a) an operating and financial review

(b) information prepared from a different perspective from that adopted in the financial statements

(c) statistical information

(d) highlights and summary indicators.

## 10 The reporting entity

10.1 This chapter discusses the entity that is preparing the corporate report. It is mainly concerned with group structures and how investments in other companies should be accounted for.

10.2 It states that:

> **'The classification of investments needs to reflect the way in which they are used to further the business of the investor and the consequent effect on the investor's financial position, performance and financial adaptability. The two key factors for this purpose are the degree of influence of the investor and the nature of the investor's interest in the results, assets and liabilities of its investee.'**

10.3 This chapter is broadly consistent with the principles of group accounting discussed in later Units of this book. The basic principle is that the financial statements show all the assets and liabilities under the control of the reporting entity and their combined performance.

10.4 Therefore if an enterprise controls the assets of a business by owning the equity of another enterprise, as opposed to owning the assets and liabilities directly, consolidated financial statements must be prepared. Consolidation is a process that aggregates the total assets, liabilities and results of the parent and its subsidiaries.

## 11 SSAP2

11.1 Prior to the ASB formulating the *Statement of Principles*, which has proved highly controversial, SSAP2 was the main guide in formulating accounting policies. The standard contained the following fundamental accounting concepts:

- going concern
- accruals

# FINANCIAL REPORTING, ANALYSIS AND PLANNING

- consistency
- prudence.

11.2 The *going concern* concept assumes that the enterprise will continue in operational existence for the foreseeable future.

11.3 Under the *accruals* concept revenue and costs are recognised as they are earned and incurred and not as money is paid or received. Revenues and costs are matched with one another so far as their relationship can be established or justifiably assumed. They are dealt with in the profit and loss account of the period to which they relate.

11.4 The *consistency* concept requires that there is consistency of accounting treatment of like items within each accounting period and from one period to the next.

11.5 The *prudence* concept requires that revenue and profits are not anticipated, but are recognised by inclusion in the profit and loss account only when realised in the form of either cash or other assets of which the ultimate cash realisation can be assessed with reasonable certainty. It also requires that provision is made for all known liabilities (expenses and losses) whether the amount of these is known with certainty or is a best estimate in the light of the information available.

11.6 The other concepts which have been widely accepted and used are *materiality* and *substance over form*.

11.7 *Materiality* is based on the relevance of information to users. If the financial statements contained a large amount of small inconsequential items these could easily conceal the larger more significant items. Therefore only items of significance need to be highlighted or disclosed. The Financial Accounting Standards Board defined materiality as follows:

> **'The magnitude of an omission or misstatement of accounting information that, in the light of surrounding circumstances, makes it probable that the judgment of a reasonable person relying on the information would have been changed or influenced by the omission or misstatement.'**

11.8 *Substance over form* requires that the economic substance of a transaction is reported as opposed to its legal form. For example under a hire purchase agreement the legal title to the asset does not pass until the final payment is made. However, the economic reality is not that the asset was hired until the last payment was made, but that the asset was purchased using loan finance. The transaction is therefore reported in the financial statements as such with the asset being included in the balance sheet and depreciated. The loan is shown as a liability and implicit rate of interest is accrued to the profit and loss account.

THE CONCEPTUAL FRAMEWORK

## Student Activity 1

Before reading the next section of text, answer the following questions and check your answers against the paragraphs indicated.

1. List the users of corporate reports. *Paragraph 2.2*

2. List the desirable characteristics of corporate reports distinguishing between primary and secondary characteristics. *Paragraphs 2.10 & 5.1*

3. List the seven chapters of the *Statement of Principles*. *Paragraph 3.2*

4. How does the statement define assets and liabilities? *Paragraphs 6.2 & 6.3*

5. Which gains and losses should be reported in the statement of total recognised gains and losses? *Paragraph 9.6*

If your answers are basically correct, then proceed to the next section. If significant parts of your answers are wrong, then study the whole of the relevant sections again in detail. Note your areas of weakness and be prepared for further questions on these areas at the end of this Unit.

## 12 Approaches to profit measurement

12.1 Traditionally, profits in accounts have been calculated by deducting costs from revenues. This fits neatly with the accounting equation where the opening capital plus profit less drawings equals the closing capital.

12.2 Whereas the accountant's model measures capital by reference to the values of individual assets, economists have produced different measures of capital.

12.3 In *The Theory of Interest* (1930), Fisher defined income as the psychological enjoyment which an individual obtains from spending money on the consumption of goods and services. An individual's capital is therefore his stock of future consumption which represents his stock of future enjoyment that gives the capital value.

12.4 Fisher's definition is difficult to implement in practice. Sir John Hicks produced a more useful definition when he defined income as:

> **'the maximum value a man can consume during a week and still expect to be as well off at the end of the week as he was at the beginning'.**

12.5 This leaves the problem of deciding what we mean by 'well off'. We could define this as our capacity to consume. Our capacity to consume would be our future income stream. This would mean that our capital today is the discounted present value of our future net receipts. Hence Hicks' model is usually expressed numerically as follows:

$$Y = C + (K_e - K_s)$$

where:

$Y$ = Income
$C$ = Consumption
$K_e$ = Capital at the end of the period
$K_s$ = Capital at the start of the period

FINANCIAL REPORTING, ANALYSIS AND PLANNING

**Example 1.1**

On 1.1.X1 Alan buys a security which will pay an annual dividend of £2,000 at the end of the next three years with no repayment of capital. His cost of capital is 10%.

Thus the capital value of this investment will be:

$$\frac{2{,}000}{1.1} + \frac{2{,}000}{(1.1)^2} + \frac{2{,}000}{(1.1)^3} = £4{,}974$$

On 1.1.X2 it will be:

$$\frac{2{,}000}{1.1} + \frac{2{,}000}{(1.1)^2} = £3{,}471$$

On 1.1.X3 it will be:

$$\frac{2{,}000}{1.1} = £1{,}818$$

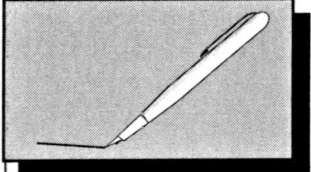

## Student Activity 2

Before reading the next section of text, answer the following question and check your answer carefully.

Work out the income according to the formula for each year.

*(See Appendix for answer)*

If your answer is basically correct, then proceed to the next section. If your answer is wrong, then study the whole of the relevant sections again in detail. Note your areas of weakness and be prepared for further questions on these areas at the end of this Unit.

## 13 Methods of capital maintenance

13.1 Accounts are usually prepared on a historic cost basis. Under this method the capital of the business is maintained at its historic level.

13.2 However in times of rising prices the accruals concept means that yesterday's costs are deducted from today's revenues. The profit is therefore overstated in times of inflation, and if distributed by way of dividend payments would deplete the capital of the business in 'real' terms.

13.3 For example, say a trader sets up in business selling caravans. He has £10,000 initial capital with which he purchases his first caravan which he sells three months later for £15,000. At the time of the sale it would cost the trader £11,000 to buy another caravan for resale.

It would appear that the trader has made £5,000 profit. However, if he were to withdraw this amount from the business he would be unable to continue trading as there would be insufficient funds available to purchase a further caravan for resale. The trader has made a 'holding gain' by owning the caravan while its price rose.

We can draw up a trading account as follows.

# THE CONCEPTUAL FRAMEWORK

|  | £ | £ |
|---|---:|---:|
| Sale proceeds |  | 15,000 |
| Historic cost |  | 10,000 |
| Historic cost profit |  | 5,000 |
|  |  |  |
| Less holding gain: |  |  |
| Replacement cost | 11,000 |  |
| Historic cost | (10,000) |  |
|  |  | (1,000) |
| Operating gain |  | 4,000 |

The operating gain can be withdrawn from the business without impairing its operating capacity.

The holding gain of £1,000 would normally be transferred to a capital maintenance reserve.

13.4 Hicks' formula can therefore be used to calculate a business' profit. That profit is the amount which can be distributed or withdrawn from the business without reducing the capital which existed at the start of the period.

13.5 The problem is then the measurement of capital. There are a number of methods available, namely:

(a) historic cost

(b) adjusted historic cost

(c) replacement costs (entry values)

(d) net realisable value (exit values)

(e) the present value of future receipts from an asset.

13.6 Historic cost only maintains a business' capital in nominal pounds and as we have seen this fails to protect the business' operating capacity in times of rising prices. However, modified historic cost accounts where fixed assets are revalued are widely used and have stood the test of time.

13.7 Adjusted historic cost accounts recognise the change in the level of prices. The historic cost accounts are adjusted to reflect the change in the general level of prices. The financial statements are restated in terms of the value of money as at the business' year end.

13.8 The capital at the start of the year is maintained in terms of 'real' pounds. For example assume that Alpha Ltd made an historic cost profit of £20,000 and that its opening capital was £100,000. During the year the general level of prices rose 5%. In order to maintain the company's capital £100,000 × 5% must be transferred to the capital maintenance reserve increasing the non-distributable capital to £105,000.

The adjusted historic cost profit would be:

|  | £000 |
|---|---:|
| Historic cost profit | 20,000 |
| Less: transfer to capital maintenance reserve | 5,000 |
| | 15,000 |

13.9 Although adjusted historic cost accounts have the virtue of relative simplicity and are objectively based on historic cost accounts they do not necessarily lead to the business maintaining its operating capacity. The assets the business uses and goods it trades may be increasing in price at a rate in excess of the general increase in prices.

13.10 Replacement cost accounting is an attempt to overcome this drawback. The business' assets are valued at their replacement cost. Thus the holding gains on individual assets are recognised and retained in the business. Often specific price indices are used for groups of assets to reduce the work involved in obtaining the relevant replacement costs.

13.11 However, the use of replacement costs does have the following disadvantages:

- the replacement costs can be subjective
- technological change may mean that the asset is obsolete
- the business may not intend to replace the asset
- replacement cost accounts are difficult for users to understand.

13.12 An alternative is to measure the business' capital using the net realisable value (NRV), or exit value, of its assets. The net realisable value of an asset is the cash which would be obtained if an asset were sold, i.e. the sale proceeds less the costs incurred in making the sale.

13.13 Current cost accounts using exit values recognise holding gains on the assets in the same way as entry values. The use of exit values has practical problems due to the difficulty in obtaining the realisable values. Consequently it can be highly subjective, and on a theoretical basis it would seem to be contrary to the going concern concept.

13.14 However, it does have the following advantages:

- it recognises the opportunity cost of holding the assets
- the asset values are realistic and easy to understand
- exit values are currently applied in practice to some extent, (monetary assets, stock, land and buildings).

13.15 Valuing assets using the net present value of the receipts they will generate is theoretically the most accurate method of measuring capital. However the difficulty in estimating these future cash flows makes it impractical in most instances.

13.16 Adjusted historic cost accounts maintain the owner's purchasing power and this is known as the *proprietary* concept. The maintenance of the business' purchasing power, or operating capacity, is known as the *entity* concept.

13.17 In the UK the first standard dealing with changing prices proposed a system of adjusted historic cost accounts (Current Purchasing Power). This was

# THE CONCEPTUAL FRAMEWORK

widely criticised and was open to the theoretical objection that it failed to maintain a company's operating capacity.

13.18 A second standard, SSAP16, was issued requiring the use of current costs. This was very complicated, widely ignored and subsequently abandoned.

13.19 In recent years technological change and diversification by businesses has again focused attention on adjusted historic cost accounts. Specific price increases have less relevance as assets currently in use no longer have equivalent replacements available. It is also possible to compare one year with another using adjusted historic cost accounts, whereas this is not possible with current cost accounts.

## Student Activity 3

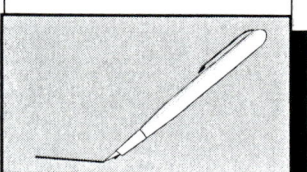

Before reading the next section of text, answer the following questions and check your answers against the paragraphs indicated.

1. How did Sir John Hicks define income? *Paragraph 12.4*
2. Distinguish between holding gains and operating gains. *Paragraph 13.3*
3. Current cost accounting maintains a business' operating capacity. True/False
4. What are entry and exit values? *Paragraph 13.5*

The answer to 3 is: true

If your answers are basically correct, then proceed to the next section. If significant parts of your answers are wrong, then study the whole of the relevant sections again in detail. Note your areas of weakness and be prepared for further questions on these areas at the end of this Unit.

## 14 Limitations of historic cost accounts

14.1 Despite their longevity historic cost accounts have been recognised as limited in the information which they provide. They provide a record of the stewardship of the company's management during the period just ended. However many users of financial statements are more concerned with how the company will perform in the future.

14.2 Forecast information would enable users to compare management's expected and actual performance. Historic cost accounts lack this predictive quality which provides a benchmark against which a company's performance can be measured.

14.3 When the fixed assets are stated at historic cost and prices subsequently rise the company's capital employed will be understated. The depreciation charge will also be understated and the company's earnings overstated.

14.4 This results in the earnings per share being overstated and apparent return on capital employed (ROCE) being higher than it actually is.

14.5 When a company's fixed assets are undervalued shareholders' funds will also be understated. Therefore if the company uses loan capital its gearing ratio will be adversely affected. In practice this means that companies will consider

# FINANCIAL REPORTING, ANALYSIS AND PLANNING

the impact on the ratios mentioned when deciding whether to revalue their fixed assets.

14.6 This leads to a situation where company accounts are not comparable, as some companies will revalue their assets whereas others will not. This inconsistency has arisen due to the lack of a conceptual framework for the preparation of accounts.

14.7 Over the years, accounting standards have been issued in a piecemeal fashion to combat the possibility of creative accounting. A common ruse used by companies is effectively to purchase an asset using a loan, but by structuring the transaction in a certain way, both the asset and the loan are left off the balance sheet. This has the effect of increasing return on capital employed and reducing the gearing ratio.

14.8 SSAP21 recognised that the use of finance leases, where legal ownership of the asset does not pass to the lessee, is one method used by companies to achieve the above result. Hence SSAP21 requires that these leases be accounted for according to the substance of the transaction as opposed to their legal form.

14.9 However as one loop-hole is closed others are found. FRS5 was introduced on the more general principle that all transactions should be accounted for according to their economic substance as opposed to their legal form to try and circumvent the manipulation of financial statements in this way.

14.10 While much has been done to ensure that financial statements give a 'true and fair' view of a company's performance and financial position it is impossible to prevent companies showing their accounts in the best light. For example, a large sale can be postponed until after the year end or perhaps be completed quickly for inclusion in this year's results. The choice of year end will affect the balance sheet position for seasonal companies which may have high borrowings for most of the year which are reduced, say, just after Christmas.

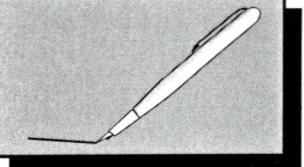

## Student Activity 4

Before moving on, answer the following questions and check your answers in the paragraphs indicated and the appendix.

1. A company's balance sheet represents the fair value of its net assets.
   True/false

2. Only assets legally owned by a company should be included on its balance sheet.
   True/false

3. Name three ratios which are affected when a company revalues its fixed assets.
   *Paragraphs 14.4 & 14.5*

4. Which accounting concept forms the basis for SSAP 21 and FRS 5?

   *(See Appendix for answers to 1., 2. and 4)*

If your answers are basically correct, then proceed to the next section. If parts of your answers are wrong, then study the whole of the relevant sections again in detail. Note your areas of weakness and be prepared for further questions on these areas at the end of this unit.

# THE CONCEPTUAL FRAMEWORK

## Summary

Now that you have completed this Unit you should be able to:

- describe the objectives of financial statements and the fundamental accounting concepts;
- identify the desirable characteristics of accounting reports;
- understand the different approaches to calculating an entity's surplus income; and
- explain the limitations of historic cost accounts.

## Self-assessment questions

1. What is the fundamental objective of corporate reports?
2. Why did the ASB develop the *Statement of Principles*?
3. How does the *Statement of Principles* define gains and losses?
4. What are the primary financial statements?
5. What is 'financial adaptability'?
6. XYZ Ltd is a wine wholesaler. The company buys a consignment of 100 bottles for £300. It then sells these bottles for £600 and purchases another consignment for £350.

   What was the company's operating gain?
7. List four ways of measuring a company's capital.
8. Adjusted historic cost maintains a company's operating capacity.  TRUE/FALSE
9. Give three disadvantages of using replacement costs.
10. Historic cost accounts are objectively prepared and therefore impossible to manipulate.  TRUE/FALSE

*(Answers are given in the Appendix)*

# Unit 2

## The Regulatory Framework

### Objectives

After studying this Unit you should be able to:

- describe the standard setting process and its limitations
- explain the need for an audit and the true and fair view
- understand the implications of the Cadbury Report and the responsibilities of directors
- calculate distributable profits in accordance with the Companies Act provisions
- list the current SSAPs and FRSs.

## 1 Introduction

1.1 In this Unit we will be examining how the methods used by companies for accounting for their operations are established. We will look at the framework for enforcing these accounting methods and the role of the auditor.

1.2 In recent years corporate governance has been taken more seriously and we will discuss the Cadbury Report which was the first major set of recommendations on the subject.

1.3 The accounting methods used affect a company's distributable profits and at the end of this chapter we will examine the Companies Act regulations on distributable profits.

## 2 The background to the standard setting process

2.1 Often there are many different ways of accounting for a transaction. Even after considering the fundamental concepts of accruals and prudence the preparer of accounts may still be left with a number of options.

2.2 During the 1960s there were a number a scandals as apparently healthy companies collapsed. This led to a call for a tighter accounting regime where company accounts would be comparable and the choice of accounting treatments would be less subjective.

2.3 This resulted in the Accounting Standards Committee (ASC) which was established and run by the six main accountancy bodies. However, creative

# FINANCIAL REPORTING, ANALYSIS AND PLANNING

accounting and a flexible interpretation of the accounting standards meant that there was still a deep-seated dissatisfaction with the ways in which accounts were prepared.

2.4 Thus, in the 1980s, Sir Ron Dearing was appointed to lead a committee to report on the standard setting process in the UK. This resulted in the current regime.

## 3 The standard setting process

3.1 The following bodies are involved in the issuing and enforcement of accounting standards in the UK today.

(a) The Financial Reporting Council (FRC)

(b) The Accounting Standards Board (ASB)

(c) The Urgent Issues Task Force (UITF)

(d) The Review Panel.

3.2 On 1 August 1990, the Financial Reporting Council became responsible for obtaining the finance to operate the standard setting process in the UK and ensuring that the system functions efficiently. The council is currently funded by the accountancy profession (CCAB), the Stock Exchange, the Bank of England and the Government.

3.3 The Council consists of members of the accountancy profession and other parties who are concerned with the use or preparation of accounting information.

3.4 Under the new system there are two new bodies that are directly responsible to the FRC. These are:

- the Accounting Standards Board [ ASB ], and
- the Review Panel

3.5 The Accounting Standards Board's stated aims are to establish and improve standards of financial accounting and reporting, for the benefit of users, preparers and auditors of financial information. These aims will be achieved by:

(a) developing principles to guide it in establishing standards and to provide a framework within which others can exercise judgment in resolving accounting issues;

(b) issuing new accounting standards, or amending existing ones, in response to evolving business practices, new economic developments and deficiencies being identified in current practice;

(c) addressing urgent issues promptly.

3.6 This last aim should be achieved by an ASB committee, the Urgent Issues Task Force (UITF). The UITF tackles urgent issues not covered by existing standards and for which the normal standard setting process is neither practical or appropriate. The UITF seeks a consensus on an appropriate accounting treatment for any particular issue within the framework of the law and the principles established in the accounting standards and other

# THE REGULATORY FRAMEWORK

statements issued or adopted by the ASB. Once a consensus is reached by the UITF, the ASB issues a 'UITF Abstract' on the issue addressed. The accounting treatments contained in the UITF Abstract are applicable to all financial statements which are intended to give a true and fair view of the reporting entity's state of affairs at the balance sheet date and of its profits or loss for the period ending on that date.

3.7 Thus we have the following structure.

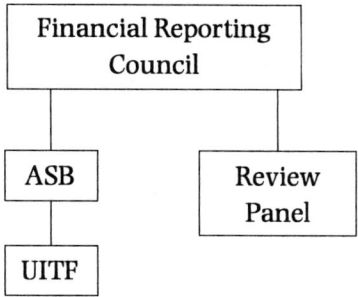

3.8 The ASB has picked up the mantle of the ASC and its main role is that of setting accounting standards. The ASB's original stated intention was to have fewer accounting standards and that these should deal with matters of principle. It was hoped that companies would comply with the spirit of these standards and avoid the need for a large number of detailed accounting treatments.

3.9 However, recent experience has indicated that this may not be possible. Professor Tweedie, head of the ASB, has stated that if companies continue to use elaborate schemes that comply with the letter of the standards but not the spirit, then self regulation may be replaced by a statutory body.

3.10 The ASB has issued a set of guidelines which it intends to follow. These are as follows.

(a) To be objective and to ensure that the information resulting from the application of accounting standards faithfully represents the underlying commercial activity. Such information should be neutral, in that it is free from any form of bias intended to influence users in a particular direction and should not be designed to favour any particular group of users or preparers.

(b) To ensure that accounting standards are clearly expressed and supported by a reasoned analysis of the issues.

(c) To determine what should be incorporated in accounting standards based on research, public consultation and careful deliberation about the usefulness of the resulting information.

(d) To ensure that through a process of regular communication accounting standards are produced with due regard to international developments.

(e) To ensure that there is consistency both from one accounting standard to another and between accounting standards and company law.

(f) To issue accounting standards only when the expected benefits exceed the perceived costs. The board recognises that reliable cost/benefit calculations are seldom possible. However, it will always assess the need

# FINANCIAL REPORTING, ANALYSIS AND PLANNING

for standards in terms of the significance and the extent of the problem being addressed and will choose the standard which appears to be most effective in cost/benefit terms.

(g) To take account of the desire of the financial community for evolutionary rather than revolutionary change in the reporting process where this is consistent with the objectives outlined above.

3.11 The Review Panel acts as the FRC's watch-dog and its aim is to ensure that companies comply with accounting standards. The Panel does not actively seek out companies to investigate, but looks at cases drawn to its attention, e.g. by press comment. The companies concerned are given a chance to explain the accounting treatments used and even if these do appear to be contrary to a particular accounting standard the Panel may regard it as acceptable.

3.12 For example the accounts of Forte Hotels were recently investigated. Forte have never depreciated their freehold hotels (as required by SSAP12) arguing that they are constantly being refurbished and effectively have an indefinite life. The Panel accepted this argument and Forte can continue to prepare its accounts in this way.

3.13 When the Review Panel does not accept a company's arguments it can, following the 1989 Companies Act, apply to the court for an order requiring the company to revise its accounts. At the time of writing the Panel has investigated over one hundred cases. Whenever it has instructed a company to revise its accounts, the instructions have always been complied with and there has been no need for any legal action.

3.14 There is a major incentive to comply with the Review Panel's rulings because the court can order that all or part of the costs of any application to it, and any reasonable expenses incurred by the company due to its need to prepare and distribute revised accounts, shall be borne by those directors who were responsible for issuing the original accounts. In addition the company's auditors would face disciplinary action if they had given the original accounts an unqualified audit report.

3.15 Following the 1989 Companies Act large companies are required to state whether their accounts have been prepared in accordance with accounting standards. If not, any material departures must be disclosed along with the reasons for the treatment used.

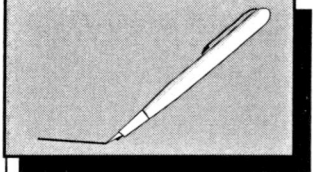

## Student Activity 1

Before reading the next section of text, answer the following questions and then check your answers against the paragraph(s) indicated.

1. How is the FRC financed? (Paragraph 3.2)
2. What are the ASB's stated aims? (Paragraph 3.5)
3. Which body enforces accounting standards?
4. What does the Urgent Issues Task Force do? How? (Paragraph 3.6)

The answer to question 3 is the Review Panel. If your answers are basically correct, then proceed to the next section. If significant parts of your answers are wrong,

# THE REGULATORY FRAMEWORK

then study the whole of the relevant sections again in detail. Note your areas of weakness and be prepared for further questions on these areas at the end of this Unit.

## 4 The need for an audit and the true and fair view

4.1 The Auditing Practices Board has proposed that the purpose of the audit should be defined as being:

> 'to provide an independent opinion to those with an interest in a company that they have received from those responsible for its direction and management an adequate account of:
>
> (a) the proper conduct of the company's affairs – a role which is now widely expected of auditors but is not part of the conventional definition of an audit;
>
> (b) the company's financial performance and position – the traditional role of reporting on financial stewardship;
>
> (c) future risks attaching to the company – a newly defined role, recognising that it is not the purpose of financial statements to predict the future.'

4.2 The auditor's ethical guidelines require the auditor to be both independent and objective. A user's confidence in the financial statements should be enhanced by the knowledge that an independent auditor has examined the company's records and financial statements.

4.3 The Companies Act contains provisions requiring the directors to make information available to the auditor and make it impossible to remove the auditor without the auditor being able to make a statement concerning his or her removal to the company's shareholders.

4.4 Once an audit has been completed the auditor reports on whether, in his or her opinion, the financial statements give a true and fair view. The user can refer to this report to see if there are any areas that gave the auditor concern.

4.5 The Companies Act requires that a company's financial statements give a true and fair view of the company's state of affairs. There is no precise definition of what a true and fair view is. However, the requirement was included in the EEC's 4th Directive and many EEC members had to amend their earlier requirement that accounts should be true and correct.

4.6 The subjective nature of accounts makes it difficult to say that one treatment is correct as opposed to an alternative. Hence the more vague 'true and fair' requirement.

4.7 For practical purposes a company's financial statements give a true and fair view when:

(a) the requirements of the Companies Act are complied with;

(b) all applicable accounting standards have been complied with;

(c) if no accounting standard is available, accepted industry accounting principles are followed;

(d) all material items have been adequately disclosed; and

(e) the presentation of the accounts is appropriate with regard to the information needed by the user of those accounts.

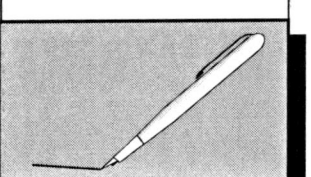

### Student Activity 2

Before reading the next section of text, answer the following questions and then check your answers against the paragraphs indicated.

1. What is the purpose of an audit? *(Paragraph 4.1)*

2. An auditor is employed by a company's directors and has no authority without their co-operation. TRUE/FALSE *(Paragraph 4.3)*

3. Accounts that are correct give a true and fair view. TRUE/FALSE *(Paragraph 4.5)*

4. The UK is the only country in Europe that requires accounts to give a true and fair view. TRUE/FALSE *(Paragraph 4.5)*

If your answers are basically correct, then proceed to the next section. If significant parts of your answers are wrong, then study the whole of the relevant sections again in detail. Note your areas of weakness and be prepared for further questions on these areas at the end of this Unit.

## 5   The Cadbury Report

5.1   The Cadbury Committee was set up in May 1991 in response to a growing lack of confidence in financial reports and in the auditors' ability to give assurance to the users of those reports.

5.2   The Committee's terms of reference were:

> **'To consider the following issues in relation to financial reporting and accountability and to make recommendations on good practice:**
>
> **(a) the responsibilities of executive and non-executive directors for reviewing and reporting on performance to shareholders and other financially interested parties; and the frequency, clarity and form in which information should be provided;**
>
> **(b) the case for audit committees of the board, including their composition and role;**
>
> **(c) the principle responsibilities of auditors and the extent and value of the audit;**
>
> **(d) the links between shareholders, boards and auditors;**
>
> **(e) any other relevant matters.'**

5.3   The Committee aimed to set out the roles and responsibilities of each group involved in the reporting process and identified the following groups.

(a) The directors are responsible for the corporate governance of the company. (Corporate governance was defined as 'the system by which companies are directed and controlled.')

# THE REGULATORY FRAMEWORK

(b) The shareholders are linked to the directors via the financial reporting system.

(c) The auditors provide the shareholders with an external objective check on the directors' financial statements.

(d) Other concerned users, particularly employees (to whom the directors owe some responsibility) are indirectly addressed by the financial statements.

5.4 The Code of Practice issued by the Cadbury Committee applies to all listed companies. However directors of all companies are encouraged to refer to it for guidance. Directors are required to provide a statement contained in the published accounts that the report and accounts comply with the code, or give reasons why this is not so. This statement can only be published after a review by the auditors.

5.5 One of the major recommendations in the Code is that all listed companies establish effective audit committees. These are compulsory in the USA.

5.6 The duties of the audit committee should include:

(a) recommendations to the board on the appointment, resignation or dismissal of the auditor and the audit fee;

(b) review the interim and annual statements before they are submitted to the board;

(c) undertake discussions with the auditors, without the presence of executive directors, at least once a year;

(d) review the internal audit programme and any significant findings;

(e) review the external auditors' management letter and the company's statement on the internal control system.

5.7 The chairman of the audit committee should also be present at the company's AGM in order to answer questions about the committee's work.

5.8 The Code also required that the directors:

(a) report on the effectiveness of their system of internal control;

(b) ensure that an objective and professional relationship is maintained with the auditors;

(c) present a balanced and understandable assessment of their company's position, which means that setbacks should be dealt with as well as successes (the need for a readily understandable report emphasises that words are as important as figures);

(d) explain their responsibility for preparing accounts next to a statement by the auditors about their reporting responsibilities;

(e) should state in their report that the business is a going concern, with supporting assumptions or qualifications if necessary.

5.9 There are two other important recommendations that affect the auditor.

(a) Full disclosure of fees paid to auditors for non-audit work. This is designed to try and ensure objectivity. The report also recommends that the partners in charge of the audit should be rotated, again with a view to enhancing objectivity. However, the rotation of audit firms is not recommended.

(b) The report also recommends a change in the legislation relating to the auditors of companies so that they can report reasonable suspicion of fraud to the appropriate authorities.

### Student Activity 3

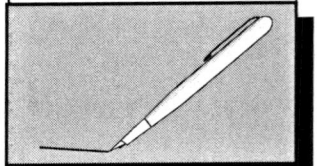

Before reading the next section of text, answer the following questions and then check your answers against the paragraphs indicated.

1. Why was the Cadbury Committee established? *(Paragraph 5.1)*

2. The Code of Practice only applies to listed companies. TRUE/FALSE *(Paragraph 5.4)*

3. Who does the Code require to report on a company's internal controls?

4. Who is responsible for preparing a company's accounts?

The answer to questions 3 and 4 is 'the directors' in both cases. If your answers are basically correct, then proceed to the next section. If significant parts of your answers are wrong, then study the whole of the relevant sections again in detail. Note your areas of weakness and be prepared for further questions on these areas at the end of this Unit.

## 6 Distributable profits

6.1 Section 263 of the Companies Act defines distributable profits as accumulated realised profits, so far as they have not been distributed or capitalised, less accumulated realised losses, so far as they have not been previously written off in a reduction or reorganisation of capital.

6.2 Section 262(3) states:

> **'references to realised profits and realised losses, in relation to a company's accounts, are to such profits or losses of the company that fall to be treated as realised in accordance with principles generally accepted, at the time when the accounts are prepared, with respect to the determination for accounting purposes of realised profits or losses.'**

Therefore if accounts are prepared in line with generally accepted accounting practice the realised reserves shown should equate to the company's distributable profits.

6.3 The rules are more stringent for public companies. A public company cannot make a distribution if at the time:

(a) the amount of its net assets is less than the combined total of its called-up share capital plus its undistributable reserves; or

(b) the distribution will reduce the amount of its net assets to below the combined total of its called-up share capital plus its undistributable reserves.

# THE REGULATORY FRAMEWORK

6.4 Undistributable reserves are:

(a) the share premium account;

(b) the capital redemption reserve;

(c) any accumulated surplus of unrealised profits over unrealised losses; and

(d) any other reserve which cannot be distributed, whether by statute, or by the company's memorandum or articles of association.

## Student Activity 4

Before reading the next section of text, answer the following questions and then check your answer in the Appendix.

As at 31 December 19X7 a company had the following balance sheet:

|  | £'000 | £'000 |
|---|---|---|
| Net assets | | 730 |
| Ordinary share capital | | 600 |
| Share premium account | | 120 |
| Unrealised losses on asset revaluations | | (50) |
| Realised profits | 100 | |
| Realised losses | (40) | |
| | | 60 |
| | | 730 |

What is the maximum distribution the company can make:

(a) if it is a private company?

(b) if it is a public company?

*(Answers are given in the Appendix)*

## 7 Accounting Standards and Financial Reporting Standards that may be examined

7.1 The following is a list of the current Accounting Standards which you may be examined on. Items marked (q) could form the basis of either a quantitative or an essay/note question.

Items not so marked will only form the basis for an essay/note type question.

### Statements of Standard Accounting Practice (SSAPs)

SSAP2 Disclosure of Accounting Policies (q)

SSAP3 Earnings Per Share (As amended by FRS3) (q)

SSAP4 Accounting for Government Grants (q)

SSAP8 The Treatment of Taxation under the Imputation System in the Accounts of Companies (q)

SSAP9 Stocks and Long-Term Contracts (q)

# FINANCIAL REPORTING, ANALYSIS AND PLANNING

SSAP12 Accounting for Depreciation (q)

SSAP13 Accounting for Research and Development (q)

SSAP15 Accounting for Deferred Tax

SSAP17 Accounting for Post Balance Sheet Events (q)

SSAP18 Accounting for Contingencies (q)

SSAP19 Accounting for Investment Properties (q)

SSAP21 Accounting for Leases and Hire Purchase Contracts (q)

SSAP23 Accounting for Acquisitions and Mergers

SSAP24 Accounting for Pension Costs

SSAP25 Segmental Reporting (q)

## *Financial Reporting Standards*

FRS 1    (revised) Cash Flow (q)

FRS 2    Accounting for Subsidiary Undertakings (q)

FRS 3    Reporting Financial Performance (q)

FRS 4    Capital Instruments

FRS 5    Reporting the Substance of Transactions

FRS 6    Acquisitions and Mergers (q)

FRS 7    Fair Values in Acquisition Accounting (q)

FRS 8    Related Party Transactions

FRS 9    Associates and Joint Ventures (q)

FRS 10   Goodwill and Intangible Assets (q)

FRS 11   Impairment of Fixed Assets and Goodwill

FRS 12   Provisions, Contingent Liabilities and Contingent Assets

FRS 13   Derivatives and other Financial Instruments

FRS 14   Earnings per share

FRS15: tangible fixed ands

THE REGULATORY FRAMEWORK

> **Summary**
>
> Now that you have completed this Unit you should be able to:
> - [ ] describe the standard setting process and its limitations
> - [ ] explain the need for an audit and the true and fair view
> - [ ] understand the implications of the Cadbury Report and the responsibilities of directors
> - [ ] calculate distributable profits in accordance with the Companies Act provisions
> - [ ] list the current SSAPs and FRSs.

## Self-assessment questions

1. Name the four bodies which are responsible for issuing and enforcing accounting standards in the UK.

2. List the guidelines the ASB follows when issuing Financial Reporting Standards.

3. How does the Review Panel choose companies to investigate?

4. How does the Review Panel make a company amend its accounts?

5. Define the 'true and fair' view.

6. How did the Cadbury Report define the auditor's role?

7. The auditors provide a statement to say whether the company's annual report complies with the Code of Practice.  TRUE/FALSE

8. What is the role of the audit committee?

9. The Code of Practice requires that the directors and the auditors make statements next to each other concerning their respective responsibilities. What are those responsibilities?

10. How does the Companies Act define distributable profits?

*(Answers are given in the Appendix)*

FINANCIAL REPORTING, ANALYSIS AND PLANNING

# Unit 3

## The Legal Framework

> **Objectives**
>
> After studying this Unit you should be able to:
>
> - describe the accounting requirements of the 1985 and 1989 Companies Acts
> - present accounts in the Companies Act format
> - explain the impact of the 4th, 7th and 8th European directives.

### 1 Introduction

1.1 Limited liability places a company's creditors at risk and therefore companies have a legal obligation to provide them with sufficient information to assess its credit-worthiness. Quoted companies are rarely managed directly by their shareholders and company law also tries to ensure that they are provided with sufficient information.

1.2 In order to harmonise accounting practice throughout the European Community (EC), the European Commission has issued directives in an attempt to aid comparability throughout the Community.

1.3 In this Unit we will be examining the statutory accounting requirements and impact of the European directives.

### 2 The Companies Acts accounting requirements

2.1 SSAP2 is now enshrined in the Companies Act which requires that the fundamental accounting concepts of *going concern*, *accruals*, *consistency* and *prudence* are followed. In line with SSAP2 it also requires the following.

(a) Accounting policies should be applied consistently from one financial period to the next.

(b) If accounts are prepared on the basis of assumptions which differ in material respects from any of the generally accepted fundamental accounting concepts the details, reasons for and effect of the departure from the fundamental concepts must be given in a note to the accounts.

(c) The accounting policies adopted by a company in determining the amounts to be included in the balance sheet and in determining the profit or loss for the year must be stated by a note to the accounts.

# FINANCIAL REPORTING, ANALYSIS AND PLANNING

2.2 Companies must prepare annual accounts and these must be laid before its members at a general meeting. The accounts must be filed with the Registrar of Companies either within either seven months of the year end (for public companies) or within ten months (for private companies).

2.3 Section 221 of the Companies Act requires that every company's accounting records must:

(a) be sufficient to show and explain a company's transactions;

(b) disclose with reasonable accuracy at any time the financial position of the company at that time;

(c) enable the directors to ensure that any profit and loss account or balance sheet gives a true and fair view of the company's financial position.

2.4 The section also requires that the accounting records should contain:

(a) day-to-day entries for money received and paid, with an explanation of why the receipts and payments occurred (the nature of the transactions);

(b) a record of the company's assets and liabilities;

(c) where the company deals in goods:

   (i) statements of stocks at the financial year end;

   (ii) statements of stock-takings on which the figures in (c)(i) are based;

   (iii) with the exception of goods sold on retail, statements of all goods bought and sold identifying the suppliers or customers for each item.

## Student Activity 1

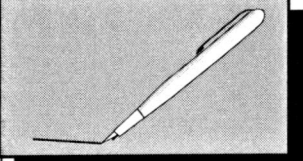

Before reading the next section of text, answer the following questions and then check your answers against the paragraphs indicated.

1. Name the fundamental accounting concepts given in the Companies Act.
   *(Paragraph 2.1)*

2. If the assumptions used in preparation of the accounts differ materially from the fundamental concepts, what action should be taken? *(Paragraph 2.1)*

3. By what date must a company file its annual accounts with the Registrar of Companies? *(Paragraph 2.2)*

4. Which books of prime entry must a company maintain in order to comply with company law? *(Paragraph 2.4)*

In question 4 above the company needs to maintain the following: cash book, containing bank and cash transactions; a fixed asset ledger; sales day book and sales ledger; and a purchase day book and purchase ledger.

If your answers are basically correct, then proceed to the next section. If significant parts of your answers are wrong, then study the whole of the relevant sections again in detail. Note your areas of weakness and be prepared for further questions on these areas at the end of this Unit.

THE LEGAL FRAMEWORK

## 3 The form and content of the balance sheet

3.1 The Companies Act sets out two balance sheet formats, one horizontal and the other vertical. In the UK the vertical format is almost invariably used and this is the format you should use in your examinations.

3.2 Each item in the balance sheet is referenced by letters and roman and arabic numerals. The Companies Act requires that:

(a) Any item preceded by letters or roman numerals must be shown on the face of the balance sheet, unless it has a nil value for both the current and previous year.

(b) Items preceded by arabic numbers may be amalgamated:

  (i) if their individual amounts are not material; or

  (ii) if amalgamation facilitates the assessment of the company's state of affairs (but then the individual items must be disclosed by a note).

(c) Items preceded by arabic numerals may be:

  (i) adapted (i.e. the titles can be altered); or

  (ii) rearranged (their position altered);

  where the special nature of the company's business requires such an alteration.

3.3 Any item required to be shown may be shown in greater detail than required by the prescribed format.

3.4 A company's balance sheet or profit and loss account may include an item not otherwise covered by any of the items listed, except that the following must not be treated as assets in the company's balance sheet:

(a) preliminary expenses;

(b) expenses of and commission on any issue of shares or debentures;

(c) research costs.

3.5 Assets and liabilities may not be set off against each other.

3.6 The vertical balance sheet is shown on the following pages.

**Proforma balance sheet (vertical format)**

|   |   |   | £ | £ | £ |
|---|---|---|---|---|---|
| a) | Called up share capital not paid * | | | X | |
| b) | Fixed assets | | | | |
|    | i Intangible assets | | | | |
|    |   | 1 Development costs | X | | |
|    |   | 2 Concessions, patents, licences, trade marks and similar rights and assets | X | | |
|    |   | 3 Goodwill | X | | |
|    |   | 4 Payments on account | X | | |
|    |   |   |   | X | |
|    | Carried forward | | | | X |

Brought forward                                                                X
   ii  Tangible assets
       1  Land & buildings                                       X
       2  Plant & machinery                                      X
       3  Fixtures, fittings, tools and equipment                X
       4  Payments on account and assets in course
          of construction                                     X
                                                      X

   iii  Investments
       1  Shares in group undertakings                           X
       2  Loans to group undertakings                            X
       3  Participating interests                                X
       4  Loans to undertakings in which the company
          has a participating interest                        X
       5  Other investments other than loans                     X
       6  Other loans                                            X
       7  Own shares                                             X
                                                                    X
                                                                             X
                                                                             X

c)  *Current assets*
   i  Stocks
       1  Raw materials                                          X
       2  Work in progress                                       X
       3  Finished goods and goods for resale                    X
       4  Payments on account                                    X
                                                                    X

   ii  Debtors
       1  Trade debtors                                          X
       2  Amounts owed by group undertakings                     X
       3  Amounts owed by undertakings in which the
          company has a participating interest                X
       4  Other debtors                                          X
       5  Called up share capital not paid*                      X
       6  Prepayments and accrued income**                       X
                                                                    X

   iii  Investments
       1  Shares in group undertakings                           X
       2  Own shares                                             X
       3  Other investments                                      X
                                                                    X

   iv  Cash at bank and in hand                                                   X
                                                                                X

d)  *Prepayments and accrued income***                                          X
Carried forward                                                                X    X

## THE LEGAL FRAMEWORK

|  |  | £ | £ | £ |
|---|---|---|---|---|
| Brought forward | | | X | X |

e) *Creditors: amounts falling due within one year*
   1. Debenture loans — X
   2. Bank loans and overdrafts — X
   3. Payments received on account — X
   4. Trade creditors — X
   5. Bills of exchange payable — X
   6. Amounts owed to group undertakings — X
   7. Amounts owed to undertakings in which the company has a participating interest — X
   8. Other creditors including taxation and social security — X
   9. Accruals and deferred income*** — X
   
   (X)

f) *Net current assets (liabilities)* — X

g) *Total assets less current liabilities* — X

h) *Creditors: amounts falling due after more than one year*
   1. Debenture loans — X
   2. Bank loans and overdrafts — X
   3. Payments received on account — X
   4. Trade creditors — X
   5. Bills of exchange payable — X
   6. Amounts owed to group undertakings — X
   7. Amounts owed to undertakings in which the company has a participating interest — X
   8. Other creditors including taxation and social security — X
   9. Accruals and deferred income*** — X
   
   (X)

i) *Provisions for liabilities and charges*
   1. Pensions and similar obligations — X
   2. Taxation, including deferred taxation — X
   3. Other provisions — X
   
   (X)

j) *Accruals and deferred income*** — (X)

(X)

X

k) *Capital and reserves*
   i  Called up share capital     X
   ii  Share premium account     X
   iii  Revaluation reserve     X
   iv  Other reserves
       1  Capital redemption reserve    X
       2  Reserve for own shares    X
       3  Reserves provided for by the articles
          of association    X
       4  Other reserves    X
                    X
   v  Profit and loss account     X
                                  X

\*/\*\*/\*\*\* These items may be shown in either of the positions indicated.

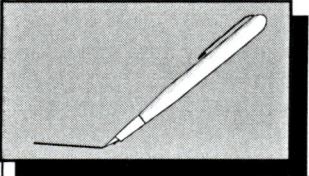

## Student Activity 2

Before reading the next section of text, do the following Activity and then check your answer against the text above.

From memory, reproduce a vertical balance sheet according to the Companies Act format, using made up figures.

If your answer is basically correct, then proceed to the next section. If significant parts of your answer are wrong, then study the whole of the relevant section again in detail. Note your areas of weakness and be prepared for further questions on these areas at the end of this Unit.

## 4   The form and content of the profit & loss account

4.1   The Companies Act gives four profit and loss account formats, two horizontal and two vertical. Once again you should use the vertical format in your examinations. Two formats are given because of the different nature of companies engaged in manufacturing.

4.2   The formats are given on the following pages. Note that turnover is defined by the Companies Act as:

> **'the amounts derived from the provision of goods and services, falling within the company's ordinary activities, after deduction of:**
>
> **(a) trade discounts;**
>
> **(b) value added tax;**
>
> **(c) any other taxes based on the amounts so derived.'**

Neither cost of sales nor distribution costs or administrative expenses are defined. The allocation of costs to the three categories is based on accepted practice and must be applied consistently from one year to the next.

4.3   In addition every profit and loss account must show:

     (a) the company's profit or loss on ordinary activities before taxation, no matter what format is used nor how much it might be amended to suit the

# THE LEGAL FRAMEWORK

    circumstances of a particular case;

(b) amounts to be transferred to or from reserves;

(c) the amount of dividends paid and proposed. The aggregate amount of dividends proposed must be shown in the notes or on the face of the profit and loss account.

4.4 Amounts representing income may not be set off against items representing expenditure.

4.5 Corresponding amounts for the previous financial year must be given for every item shown in a company's balance sheet or profit and loss account. Where a corresponding amount for the previous year is not properly comparable with an amount disclosed for the current year, the previous year's amount should be adjusted and details of the adjustment given in a note.

**Proforma profit and loss account: Format 1**

|     |                                                                              |   £   |   £   |
| --- | ---------------------------------------------------------------------------- | ----- | ----- |
| 1   | Turnover                                                                     |       | X     |
| 2   | Cost of sales *                                                              |       | (X)   |
| 3   | Gross profit or loss                                                         |       | X     |
| 4   | Distribution costs*                                                          | (X)   |       |
| 5   | Administration expenses*                                                     | (X)   |       |
|     |                                                                              |       | (X)   |
|     |                                                                              |       | X     |
| 6   | Other operating income                                                       |       | X     |
|     |                                                                              |       | X     |
| 7   | Income from shares in group undertakings                                     | X     |       |
| 8   | Income from shares in undertakings in which the company has a participating interest | X     |       |
| 9   | Income from other fixed asset investments                                    | X     |       |
| 10  | Other interest receivable and similar income                                 | X     |       |
|     |                                                                              |       | X     |
| 11  | Amounts written off investments                                              | (X)   |       |
| 12  | Interest payable and similar charges                                         | (X)   |       |
|     |                                                                              |       | (X)   |
|     | Profit or loss on ordinary activities before taxation                        |       | X     |
| 13  | Tax on profit or loss on ordinary activities                                 |       | (X)   |
| 14  | Profit or loss on ordinary activities after taxation                         |       | X     |
| 15  | Extraordinary income                                                         | X     |       |
| 16  | Extraordinary charges                                                        | (X)   |       |
| 17  | Extraordinary profit or loss                                                 | X     |       |
| 18  | Tax on extraordinary profit or loss                                          | (X)   |       |
|     |                                                                              |       | X     |
|     |                                                                              |       | X     |
| 19  | Other taxes not shown under the above items                                  |       | (X)   |
| 20  | Profit or loss for the financial year                                        |       | X     |

    *These figures will all include depreciation.

FINANCIAL REPORTING, ANALYSIS AND PLANNING

**Proforma profit and loss account: Format 2**

|    |                                                                                    | £   | £   | £     |
|----|------------------------------------------------------------------------------------|-----|-----|-------|
| 1  | Turnover                                                                           |     |     | X     |
| 2  | Change in stocks of finished goods and work in progress                            |     |     | (X)/X |
| 3  | Own work capitalised                                                               |     |     | X     |
| 4  | Other operating income                                                             |     |     | X     |
|    |                                                                                    |     |     | X     |
| 5  | (a) Raw materials and consumables                                                  | (X) |     |       |
|    | (b) Other external charges                                                         | (X) |     |       |
|    |                                                                                    |     | (X) |       |
| 6  | Staff costs:                                                                       |     |     |       |
|    | (a) wages and salaries                                                             | (X) |     |       |
|    | (b) social security costs                                                          | (X) |     |       |
|    | (c) other pension costs                                                            | (X) |     |       |
|    |                                                                                    |     | (X) |       |
| 7  | (a) Depreciation and other amounts written off tangible and intangible fixed assets ** | (X) |     |       |
|    | (b) Exceptional amounts written off current assets                                 | (X) |     |       |
|    |                                                                                    |     | (X) |       |
| 8  | Other operating charges                                                            |     | (X) |       |
|    |                                                                                    |     |     | (X)   |
|    |                                                                                    |     |     | X     |
| 9  | Income from shares in group undertakings                                           |     | X   |       |
| 10 | Income from shares in undertakings in which the company has a participating interest |     | X   |       |
| 11 | Income from other fixed asset investments                                          |     | X   |       |
| 12 | Other interest receivable and similar income                                       |     | X   |       |
|    |                                                                                    |     |     | X     |
| 13 | Amounts written off investments                                                    |     | (X) |       |
| 14 | Interest payable and similar charges                                               |     | (X) |       |
|    |                                                                                    |     |     | (X)   |
|    | Profit or loss on ordinary activities before taxation                              |     |     | X     |
| 15 | Tax on profit or loss on ordinary activities                                       |     |     | (X)   |
| 16 | Profit or loss on ordinary activities after taxation                               |     |     | X     |
| 17 | Extraordinary income                                                               |     | X   |       |
| 18 | Extraordinary charges                                                              |     | (X) |       |
| 19 | Extraordinary profit or loss                                                       |     | X   |       |
| 20 | Tax on extraordinary profit or loss                                                |     | (X) |       |
|    |                                                                                    |     |     | X     |
|    |                                                                                    |     |     | X     |
| 21 | Other taxes not shown under the above items                                        |     |     | (X)   |
| 22 | Profit or loss for the financial year                                              |     |     | X     |

**This figure will be disclosed by way of a note in Format 1.

THE LEGAL FRAMEWORK

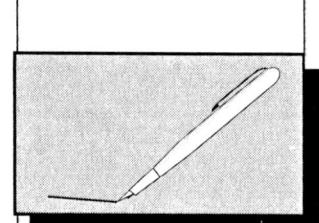

## Student Activity 3

Before reading the next section of text, do the following Activity and then check your answer against the text above.

From memory, reproduce both vertical profit and loss accounts according to the Companies Act formats, using made up figures.

If your answer is basically correct, then proceed to the next section. If significant parts of your answer are wrong, then study the whole of the relevant sections again in detail. Note your areas of weakness and be prepared for further questions on these areas at the end of this Unit.

## 5 Limited Company published accounts – accompanying notes

5.1 The Companies Act requires that the accounts are accompanied by notes on the following:

(a) Particulars of turnover

(b) Particulars of staff

(c) Directors' emoluments

(d) Charges which must be disclosed

(e) Income from listed investments

(f) Rents receivable from land after deducting outgoings

(g) Taxation

(h) Extraordinary and exceptional items and prior year adjustments

(i) Redemption of shares and loans

(j) Earnings per share (listed companies only)

(k) Statement showing movement on reserves.

5.2 Particulars of turnover; turnover must be analysed into:

(a) each class of business;

(b) geographical markets.

The directors can withhold this information if they believe that disclosure would be prejudicial to the best interests of the company and the fact of non-disclosure is stated.

5.3 Particulars of staff; the following facts must be disclosed.

(a) Average number employed by the company (or by the group in consolidated accounts), divided between categories of workers, i.e. between manufacturing and administration.

(b) (i) Wages and salaries paid to staff.

(ii) Social security costs of staff.

(iii) Other pension costs for employers.

# FINANCIAL REPORTING, ANALYSIS AND PLANNING

(c) Number of employees (excluding those working wholly or mainly overseas) earning over £30,000 per annum, analysed under successive multiples of £5,000 excluding pension contributions.

5.4 Directors' emoluments; the following must be disclosed.

(a) The aggregate amounts of:

  (i) emoluments, including pension contributions and benefits in kind; distinction should be made between those emoluments paid as fees and those for executive duties;

  (ii) pensions for past directors;

  (iii) compensation for loss of office.

(b) The chairman's emoluments and those of the highest paid director, if paid more than the chairman, excluding the pension contributions in both cases.

(c) The number of directors whose emoluments, excluding pension contributions, fall within each bracket of £5,000.

(d) Total amounts waived by directors and numbers concerned.

5.5 *A typical note on directors' emoluments would be as follows.*

Directors' remuneration: the amounts paid to directors were as follows:

| | |
|---|---|
| Fees as directors | £50,000 |
| Other emoluments including pension contributions | £638,000 |

Emoluments of the chairman, excluding pension contributions, amounted to £80,000 and those of the highest paid director to £126,000.

The number of directors whose emoluments, excluding pension contributions, fell within the following bands:

| | |
|---|---|
| £25,001 – £30,000 | 3 |
| £30,001 – £35,000 | 1 |
| £35,001 – £40,000 | 6 |
| £60,001 – £65,000 | 2 |
| £75,001 – £80,000 | 1 |
| £125,001 – £130,000 | 1 |

5.6 The charges which must be disclosed are:

(a) auditors' remuneration including expenses;

(b) hire of plant and machinery;

(c) interest payable on:

  (i) bank loans, overdrafts and other loans repayable by instalments or otherwise within five years;

  (ii) loans of any other kind

(d) depreciation:

  (i) amounts of provisions for both tangible and intangible assets;

  (ii) the effect on depreciation of a change in depreciation method;

  (iii) the effect on depreciation of a revaluation of assets.

## THE LEGAL FRAMEWORK

5.7 Taxation should be split between:

(a) UK corporation tax showing the basis of computation;

(b) UK income tax showing the basis of computation;

(c) irrecoverable VAT;

(d) tax attributable to franked investment income.

5.8 If relevant the taxation should be split between that attributable to ordinary activities and that attributable to extraordinary activities. The charge for deferred tax should be shown as a component part of the total tax charge. Any other special circumstances affecting the tax charge should also be disclosed.

5.9 Extraordinary and exceptional items and prior year adjustments will be covered later in the Unit 6 on FRS3.

5.10 Redemption of loans and shares – the amounts set aside for these purposes must be disclosed.

5.11 Earnings per share will be dealt with in Unit 6 on SSAP3 and FRS3.

5.12 The Companies Act also requires that a Directors' Report is included with the accounts. The purpose of the report is to assist the users in obtaining a clearer picture of the company's state of affairs. The Companies Act does not give a formal layout but requires the report to include the following.

(a) A fair review of the development of the business of the company (and its subsidiaries) during the financial year and of the position at the end of the year. The proposed dividends and transfers to reserves should be stated.

(b) The principal activities of the company and any changes that have occurred.

(c) Post balance sheet events when significant events affecting the company have occurred since the end of the year.

(d) Likely future developments of the business.

(e) An indication of the research and development undertaken by the company.

(f) Significant changes in fixed assets and, where significant, an estimate of the difference between the book value of land held as fixed assets and its realistic market value.

(g) Political and charitable contributions; if, taken together, these exceed £200 there must be shown:

(i) separate totals for each classification; and

(ii) where political contributions exceeding £200 have been made, the names of recipients and amounts.

(h) Details of own shares purchased.

(i) With regard to employees:

(i) a statement concerning health, safety and welfare at work of the company's employees;

# FINANCIAL REPORTING, ANALYSIS AND PLANNING

      (ii) for companies with an average workforce exceeding 250, details of employment of disabled people.

  (j) With regard to the directors:

    (i) the names of all persons who had been directors during any part of the financial year;

    (ii) their interests in contracts;

    (iii) for each director, their name and:

- the number of shares held at the start of the year;
- the number of shares held at the end of the year;
- for each director elected in the year there shall also be shown the shares held when elected;
- all the above should be shown as nil where appropriate.

5.13 The various statements of accounting practice also contain detailed disclosure requirements which will cover in subsequent chapters.

## 6 The impact of the 4th, 7th and 8th European Directives

6.1 The 4th European Directive required companies to adopt a standard format for their published accounts throughout the European Community. The preceding formats were included in the 1981 Companies Act, which was consolidated into the 1985 Companies Act, to comply with the Directive.

6.2 Although to date there have only been three Directives affecting accounting practice they have all had a great impact. The 4th Directive obviously affected every company throughout the UK and the European Community.

6.3 The 7th Directive concerned the entities that should be included in consolidated accounts. In the UK consolidated accounts were already standard practice, unlike the practice in many other European companies. However the new definitions of what constitutes a subsidiary undertaking radically tightened the rules, making it harder for companies to keep some of their operations outside their published accounts.

6.4 The 7th Directive was incorporated in the 1989 Companies Act and FRS2 was introduced to assist in the preparation of accounts in compliance with the new rules. This is discussed in further detail in Unit 8 which covers group accounts.

6.5 The 8th Directive was also included in the 1989 Companies Act. The 8th Directive concerned the education, training and monitoring of statutory auditors. The effect of the new rules on the audit profession was very significant.

6.6 One result of the tighter regulatory regime was to increase auditors' overheads; indirectly it also seems to have led to an overhaul of the whole auditing process. This has resulted in an increase in audit costs which may have been recognised by the government who, in an effort to cut red tape, have abolished the audit requirement for companies with a turnover below £350,000.

THE LEGAL FRAMEWORK

## Student Activity 4

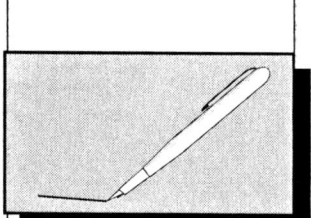

Before reading the next section of text, do the following Activity and then check your answer against the answer given below.

Christmas Plc's trial balance as at 31 December 19X8 was as follows:

|  | Dr £000 | Cr £000 |
|---|---|---|
| Administrative expenses | 420 |  |
| £1 Ordinary shares – fully paid |  | 1,075 |
| 10% Debentures repayable 19Y5 |  | 1,000 |
| Debtors | 940 |  |
| Cash at bank | 80 |  |
| Distribution costs | 840 |  |
| Fixed asset investments | 1,120 |  |
| Franked investment income amount received |  | 150 |
| Plant & machinery: |  |  |
|   At cost | 1,500 |  |
|   Accumulated depreciation |  |  |
|   (at 31 December 19X8) |  | 440 |
| Profit and loss Account |  | 365 |
| Purchases | 1,920 |  |
| Stock (at 1 January 19X8) | 280 |  |
| Trade creditors |  | 520 |
| Turnover |  | 3,900 |
| Dividend paid | 200 |  |
| ACT on dividend paid | 50 |  |
| Interest paid | 100 |  |
|  | 7,450 | 7,450 |

Additional information.

1 Stock at 31 December 19X8 was valued at £300,000.

2 *The following items are included in the above balances:*

|  | Distribution Costs £000 | Administrative Expenses £000 |
|---|---|---|
| Depreciation for the year | 57 | 10 |
| Hire of plant and machinery | 40 | 30 |
| Auditors remuneration | – | 60 |
| Directors' emoluments | – | 90 |

3 The following rates of taxation are applicable:

|  | % |
|---|---|
| Corporation tax | 33 |
| Income tax | 25 |

# FINANCIAL REPORTING, ANALYSIS AND PLANNING

4   The corporation tax charge in the profit and loss account is made up as follows:

|  | £000 |
|---|---|
| Corporation tax | 104 |
| Tax credit on dividends received | 50 |

5   There was no proposed dividend.

6   The corporation tax creditor as at 31 December 19X8 is £54,000.

7   50% of turnover was in the UK and 50% in the rest of the EC.

Turnover was split as to 30% relating to retailing and 70% relating to the manufacture of car parts.

8   There were no additions or disposals of fixed assets during the year.

9   The fixed asset investments were in unquoted shares and none of the companies invested in were group companies.

### Required

Insofar as the information permits, prepare the company's published profit and loss account for the year ended 31 December 19X8 and balance sheet as at that date in accordance with the Companies Act.

Complete this Activity before looking at the following answer.

*Christmas plc profit and loss accounts for the year ended 31 December 19X8*

|  | Notes | £000 | £000 |
|---|---|---|---|
| Turnover | 1 |  | 3,900 |
| Cost of sales |  |  | 1,900 |
| Gross profit |  |  | 2,000 |
| Distribution costs |  | 840 |  |
| Administration expenses |  | 420 |  |
|  |  |  | 1,260 |
|  | 2 |  | 740 |
| Income from fixed asset investments |  |  | 200 |
|  |  |  | 940 |
| Interest payable | 3 |  | 100 |
| Profit or loss on ordinary activities before taxation |  |  | 840 |
| Tax on profit or loss on ordinary activities | 4 |  | 154 |
| Profit or loss on ordinary activities after taxation |  |  | 686 |
| Interim dividend paid |  |  | 200 |
| Retained profit for the year |  |  | 486 |
| Retained profit brought forward |  |  | 365 |
| Retained profit carried forward |  |  | 851 |

# THE LEGAL FRAMEWORK

*Christmas plc balance sheet as at 31 December 19X8*

|  | Notes | £000 | £000 | £000 |
|---|---|---|---|---|
| *Fixed assets* | | | | |
| Tangible assets | 5 | | | 1,060 |
| Investments | 6 | | | 1,120 |
| | | | | 2,180 |
| *Current assets* | | | | |
| Stocks | | | 300 | |
| Debtors | | | 940 | |
| Cash at bank and in hand | | | 80 | |
| | | | 1,320 | |
| *Creditors: amounts falling due within one year* | | | | |
| Trade creditors | | 520 | | |
| Corporation tax | | 54 | | |
| | | | 574 | |
| *Net current assets* | | | | 746 |
| *Total assets less current liabilities* | | | | 2,926 |
| *Creditors: amounts falling due after more than one year* | | | | |
| 10 % Debenture loans | | | 1,000 | |
| | | | | 1,000 |
| | | | | 1,926 |
| *Capital and reserves* | | | | |
| £1 Ordinary shares – fully paid | | | | 1,075 |
| Profit and loss Account | | | | 851 |
| | | | | 1,926 |

*Notes to the accounts*

1. Turnover

   Turnover represents amounts derived from the provision of goods and services falling within the company's ordinary activities net of value added tax.

   | Principle activities | Turnover £000 |
   |---|---|
   | Retailing | 1,170 |
   | Manufacture of car parts | 2,730 |
   | | 3,900 |

   | Geographical analysis | |
   |---|---|
   | UK | 1,950 |
   | Rest of EC | 1,950 |
   | | 3,900 |

2. Operating profit

   Operating profit is stated after charging:

   |  | £000 |
   |---|---|
   | Depreciation | 67 |
   | Hire of plant and machinery | 70 |
   | Auditors' remuneration | 60 |
   | Directors' emoluments | 90 |

3. Interest payable

   |  | £000 |
   |---|---|
   | Interest payable on debenture loans | 100 |

4. Tax on profits on ordinary activities

   |  | £000 |
   |---|---|
   | UK corporation tax (at 33%) | 104 |
   | Tax credit on dividends received | 50 |
   |  | 154 |

5. Tangible fixed assets

   |  | Plant and machinery £000 |
   |---|---|
   | Cost as at 1 January 19X8 and 31 December 19X8 | 1,500 |
   | Depreciation |  |
   | At 1 January 19X8 | 373 |
   | Charge for the year | 67 |
   | At 31 December 19X8 | 440 |
   | Net book value 31 December 19X8 | 1,060 |
   | Net book value 31 December 19X7 | 1,127 |

6. Fixed assets investments

   |  | Investments other than loans in non-group companies £000 |
   |---|---|
   | At 1 January 19X8 and 31 December 19X8 | 1,120 |
   | Unlisted | 1,120 |

# THE LEGAL FRAMEWORK

> **Summary**
>
> Now that you have completed this Unit you should be able to:
> - describe the accounting requirements of the 1985 and 1989 Companies Acts
> - present accounts in the Companies Act format
> - explain the impact of the 4th, 7th and 8th European directives.

## Self-assessment questions

1. The Companies Act contains four balance sheet and two profit and loss account formats. TRUE/FALSE

2. Items in the statutory format preceded by a roman numeral must be shown on the face of the accounts. TRUE/FALSE

3. Items in the statutory format preceded by an arabic numeral must be shown on the face of the accounts. TRUE/FALSE

4. List three items which must not be treated as assets in a company's balance sheet.

5. Turnover should be shown before trade discounts are deducted. TRUE/FALSE

6. The inclusion of the previous year's corresponding figures in the accounts is best practice but not a statutory requirement. TRUE/FALSE

7. List the items that the Companies Act requires to be included in the notes which accompany the statutory accounts.

8. List the particulars of staff which must be disclosed in the notes to the statutory accounts.

9. List the details concerning directors' emoluments that must be disclosed.

10. Which European directives relate to:

    (a) group accounts?

    (b) auditors' qualifications and training?

    (c) the statutory format of accounts?

### Notes

It would assist your studies if could obtain some copies of the annual reports issued by quoted companies. The simplest method of obtaining these is through the *Financial Times* annual reports service. The details of this are given in the Saturday edition on the pages showing the current share prices. The reports are sent free of charge.

# Unit 4

## Valuation of Assets

### Objectives

After studying this chapter you should be able to:

- define a fixed asset and identify the components of its cost
- discuss the merits of capitalising interest and enhancement costs
- apply the principles of SSAP12 'Accounting for depreciation'
- examine various bases of valuation for fixed assets
- understand the factors affecting the carrying value of fixed assets
- explain the methods of accounting for revaluations of fixed assets
- identify and account for investment properties in accordance with SSAP19 'Accounting for investment properties'
- calculate the valuation of stock in the financial statements in accordance with SSAP9 'Stocks and long-term contracts'
- account for long term contracts in accordance with SSAP9 'Stocks and long-term contracts'
- account for research and development expenditure in accordance with SSAP13 'Accounting for research and development'
- understand the characteristics of goodwill and apply FRS10 'Accounting for goodwill' in accounting for the asset
- consider the attributes of other intangible assets and discuss their merits for balance sheet inclusion.

## 1 Introduction

1.1 This Unit covers the valuation of key balance sheet assets. The first part of the Unit looks at tangible assets comprising fixed assets, including investment properties; and stock, including long-term work-in-progress. The second part of the Unit covers accounting for intangible fixed assets, including research and development expenditure, goodwill and brands.

1.2 These categories of asset normally comprise the majority in value of an enterprise's asset base. Thus their accounting and valuation are of importance in preparing the complete financial statements of an enterprise.

FINANCIAL REPORTING, ANALYSIS AND PLANNING

## 2 Tangible fixed assets

**Definition**

2.1 The Companies Act defines fixed assets as those intended to be held on a 'continuing basis'. A fuller definition is given in FRS 11 'Impairment of fixed assets and goodwill'.

2.2 Tangible fixed assets are those that have physical substance and are held for use in the production or supply of goods or services, for rental to others, or for administrative purposes on a continuing basis in the reporting entity's activities. Intangible assets are non-financial fixed assets that do not have physical substance but are identifiable and controlled by the entity through custody or legal rights.

2.3 Thus it is not the nature of the asset that is important, but the intended *use* of that asset. For example, a motor car is usually accounted for as a fixed asset, as the business intends to keep it for use in the business over the following accounting periods. However, for a car dealer it is likely to be a current asset—stock. Or consider a freehold building—if the company intends to dispose of a building in the near future, it should be classified as a *current* asset, rather than the expected fixed asset.

**Valuation**

2.4 Fixed assets, with certain exceptions (see below), are valued at cost less accumulated depreciation. 'Cost' comprises costs incurred in getting the asset to its present location and condition. Thus the purchase price is included along with delivery and installation costs, import duties (if applicable) and similar costs incurred in bringing the asset to its present state. Therefore identical assets can have different costs. A machine imported from France will have a different cost than one imported from Taiwan, owing to the differing transport costs and import duties.

2.5 Some fixed assets are not purchased, but are constructed by the company. In this case, the Companies Act 1985 extends the definition of cost to include the purchase price of raw materials together with 'costs incurred by the company which are directly attributable to the production of the asset'.

2.6 Further certain extra items may be included in the production cost of the asset:

(a) a reasonable proportion of the costs incurred by the company which are only indirectly attributable to the production of that asset, but only to the extent that they relate to the period of production; and

(b) interest on capital borrowed to finance the production of the asset, to the extent that it accrues in respect of the period of production.

2.7 Effectively the company can capitalise directly and indirectly attributable overheads incurred in producing a fixed asset. The allocation of overheads and distinguishing between attributable and non-attributable overheads is a tricky area. Thus as a banker, a greater degree of analysis is necessary when interpreting and comparing the results of companies who have constructed their own fixed assets.

VALUATION OF ASSETS

## Capitalisation of interest

2.8 As can be seen above, the Companies Act permits the capitalisation of interest costs when calculating the production cost of fixed assets. There is no UK accounting standard in this area. Generally the Act is interpreted as allowing this policy if funds have actually been borrowed to finance the construction of the asset and an interest cost is incurred. The Act requires that any capitalised interest should be disclosed. The argument for capitalisation is twofold. First, that the cost of borrowing funds to construct a fixed asset is an intrinsic part of the overall cost of that asset and should not be written off to profit and loss account, any more than the purchase price of a fixed asset should be. Secondly, capitalisation enhances comparability between companies constructing assets and companies purchasing assets. This is because the purchase price of an asset will normally include interest as the seller will take into account *all* costs incurred when pricing the asset.

2.9 Once again though, care is needed in interpreting the accounts where interest has been capitalised. The effect of interest capitalisation is to defer the interest cost, to spread it over future periods, rather than charging it to the accounts during asset construction. Thus in contrasting a company which does capitalise interest with one which does not; in comparison the former will have higher profits initially followed by lower profits later over the asset's life.

## Enhancement costs

2.10 It is often difficult to distinguish whether expenditure on fixed assets represents an enhancement of the asset or whether it is simply routine maintenance. In substance, the question is whether to classify the expenditure as capital or revenue. The effect of classifying enhancement costs as capital is similar to that seen when capitalising interest above. Current period profits are higher with profits over the asset's life lower.

2.11 As mentioned, actually classifying the expenditure can be problematic. For example, painting the outside of a factory can be relatively easily seen as ongoing revenue expenditure. However, fitting replacement windows could be treated as capital expenditure.

2.12 The Accounting Standards Committee (ASC) when examining the area of fixed assets looked at this very issue. Exposure Draft ED 51 released in 1990, suggested that expenditure should be capitalised when the expenditure increases the expected future benefits from the asset *beyond its previously assessed standard of performance*. Examples of such benefits included:

(a) a significant lengthening of the asset's useful economic life (UEL), beyond that conferred by routine repairs or maintenance;

(b) an increase in the asset's capacity;

(c) a substantial improvement in the quality of the asset's output or a reduction in the asset's previously assessed operating costs; or

(d) a significant increase in the value of the asset.

2.13 Note the caveats 'beyond its previously assessed standard of performance' and 'beyond that conferred by routine maintenance'. Judgment needs to exercised, but the over-riding prudence concept may apply. For example, to

FINANCIAL REPORTING, ANALYSIS AND PLANNING

prudently write off the repair expenditure because of uncertainties as to whether the expected reduction in operating costs will actually occur.

## 3 Depreciation

3.1 Depreciation is the method used to write off the cost of the asset over its useful working life—called its useful economic life (UEL). SSAP12 'Accounting for Depreciation' defines depreciation as follows.

> '**Depreciation is the measure of the wearing out, consumption, or other reduction in the useful life of a fixed asset whether arising from use, effluxion of time or obsolescence through technological or market changes.**'

3.2 Deducting depreciation from a fixed asset's cost is not intended to be a valuation exercise. For example, an expensive car may lose 15% of its value immediately it is driven out of the showroom. However, as it has not yet been used in the business, no depreciation would yet be charged. Depreciation is based on the matching concept: matching the asset's cost to the periods expected to benefit from the use of the asset.

### Depreciation methods

3.3 There are several methods of calculating depreciation. The two main methods are *straight line* and *reducing balance*. Straight line depreciation writes off the cost of the fixed asset in equal instalments over the UEL of the asset. Thus for example a five-year lease costing £200,000 would be written off at £40,000 (£200,000/5) per annum. If the asset has an anticipated *residual value*, then this is deducted from the original cost of the asset to give the *depreciable amount*. For example, a piece of machinery costing £40,000 might have an estimated scrap value of £1,000. The Depreciable amount is therefore £39,000 (£40,000 less £1,000)

3.4 The reducing balance method writes off a proportion of the net book value (NBV) of the asset each year. The NBV is the cost of the asset less accumulated depreciation to date. For example, a car costing £10,000 may be written off using a 20% reducing balance rate. At the end of Year 1, the car will be depreciated down to £8,000 (£10,000 less 20% × £10,000). At the end of Year 2 its net book value will be £6,400 (£8,000 brought forward less 20% × £8,000). This method never actually writes off the whole cost of the asset. In practice the asset is often written down to a £1.

3.5 Other methods of calculating depreciation include the following.

- Usage-based methods, e.g. writing off the cost of a machine over its productive capacity.

    For example, Galton Limited purchases a widget making machine for £200,000 in 19X1. The capacity of the machine over its life is estimated at two million widgets. Using the usage based method for depreciating the asset, the machine will be written off at the rate of 10p per widget produced (£200,000 / 2m widgets). Thus if in 19X1 Galton produces 300,000 widgets using the machine, depreciation of £30,000 (300,000 × 10p) will be charged.

# VALUATION OF ASSETS

- Extractive based methods, e.g. in the case of a coal mine.
- 'Sum of the digits method'. This method is related to the reducing balance method; it writes off the cost of the fixed asset in ever decreasing segments.

### Example 4.1

Cuttings Limited purchased a digger on 1 January 19X1 for £15,400. The company intends to keep the digger for eight years, when it will have an estimated scrap value of £1,000. Calculate the depreciation charges over the asset's useful life.

**Solution**

Depreciable amount: £15,400 less £1,000 = £14,400.

Sum of the digits

8 + 7 + 6 + 5 + 4 + 3 + 2 + 1 = 36

Thus in the first year, depreciate by 8/36ths; in the second year depreciate by 7/36ths etc.

|  | 19X1 | 19X2 | 19X3 | 19X4 | 19X5 | 19X6 | 19X7 | 19X8 |
|---|---|---|---|---|---|---|---|---|
| Depreciation | 8/36 × £14,400 | 7/36 × £14,400 | 6/36 × £14,400 | 5/36 × £14,400 | 4/36 × £14,400 | 3/36 × £14,400 | 2/36 × £14,400 | 1/36 × £14,400 |
| Year end | 3,200 | 2,800 | 2,400 | 2,000 | 1,600 | 1,200 | 800 | 400 |
| Net Book Value | £12,200 | 9,400 | 7,000 | 5,000 | 3,400 | 2,200 | 1,400 | 1,000 |

3.6 Different depreciation methods give different depreciation charges in the accounts. However over the life of the asset the total depreciation charged will be the same—but charged to different accounting periods. In general, compared to the straight line method, the reducing balance method gives a higher depreciation charge in the early years of an asset's life (hence lower profits) and lower charges (higher profits) in the later years. Thus we can see that care is needed in interpreting the results of enterprises that have charged depreciation. Examine which method has been used, what assumptions have been made? What is the estimated UEL of the assets in question?

## *Estimating the UEL*

3.7 Normally this is as suggested—an estimate. However, the UEL may be determined by the firm's policy. For example, it may be company policy that all motor cars are kept for three years and then replaced. In other instances the UEL may be *predetermined* e.g. a lease.

3.8 All tangible fixed assets have a finite UEL with one exception—freehold land. Normally this asset has an infinite UEL. Apart from this one category of asset, all fixed assets, even buildings, have a finite useful life and therefore should be depreciated.

# FINANCIAL REPORTING, ANALYSIS AND PLANNING

### Adjustments to depreciation

3.9 When a company purchases a fixed asset its UEL and any residual value are estimated, using information available at the time of purchase. However, some of the assumptions made at that time can be altered in later periods and in that instance the depreciation rate/policy may need to be amended. For example, it may be found that the asset is wearing out more quickly than anticipated, or it may be that technological advances have made the fixed asset obsolete. In these instances the UEL may need to be reduced, possibly even to zero in the second instance. Thus the whole remaining NBV of the (now obsolete) fixed asset could be written off.

3.10 The Companies Act also distinguishes between 'temporary' diminutions in value and 'permanent' diminutions. Only those diminutions in value which are judged to be permanent should be incorporated in the accounts. What constitutes permanent as opposed to temporary is a matter of conjecture. However, the effect on the profit and loss account could be significant.

### Other adjustments to carrying value

3.11 The most common instance when the carrying value of a fixed asset is amended is the *revaluation of land and buildings*. Land and buildings that were purchased 10, 20, 30 years ago are likely to be worth more currently than their NBV. The Companies Act 1985 allows for the revaluation of such fixed assets. The revaluation amount is calculated as the difference between the *carrying value* (NBV) and the *current value* (usually open market valuation). The revaluation amount is credited to a special reserve – the revaluation reserve. This reserve is an example of an *unrealised* profit. It is a profit that has been recognised but not yet realised in cash or cash equivalent terms. Thus it cannot be paid out as a dividend.

**Example 4.2**

On 1 January 19X0 Hancock Ltd. purchased freehold land and buildings for £140,000. The land element was valued at £20,000, the buildings at £120,000. At the time of purchase the estimated UEL of the buildings was 40 years.

Sixteen years later on 1 January 19Y6 Hancock decided to show the asset at its current market value of £1,000,000 including £280,000 for the land. Show the revaluation in the accounts of Hancock.

## VALUATION OF ASSETS

**Solution**

The first step is to calculate the current NBV of the asset.

|  | £000 |
|---|---:|
| Cost | 140,000 |
| *Accumulated depreciation* | |
| At 1/1/Y6 | |
| Depreciable amount = £120,000 | |
| Annual charge = 120,000/40 = £3,000 | |
| Years expired £3,000 × 16 | 48,000 |
| *Net book value* | 92,000 |

3.12 Current valuation is £1,000,000. Therefore revalue by £908,000 (£1m less £92,000). The revaluation is effected by crediting the revaluation reserve and debiting the asset value in the balance sheet. The revaluation should also be shown in the Statement of Total Recognised Gains and Losses (see Unit 6).

The normal practice is to write off any accumulated depreciation and to uplift the cost to the valuation:

Position immediately after revaluation

|  | £000 |
|---|---:|
| *Valuation* | |
| Cost at 1/1/Y6 | 140,000 |
| Revaluation | 860,000 |
| Adjusted at 1/1/Y6 | 1,000,000 |
| *Accumulated depreciation* | |
| At 1/1/Y6 | 48,000 |
| Revaluation | (48,000) |
| Adjusted at 1/1/Y6 | 0 |
| *Net book value* | 1,000,000 |

Thus a net £908,000 (£860,000 plus £48,000) is credited to revaluation reserve.

3.13 In subsequent years depreciation must be charged on the revalued amount, not on the original cost. This is on the grounds of consistency. The balance sheet is reflecting the higher asset value, therefore the profit and loss account should reflect the higher write off.

3.14 Consider the situation, one year later, at the end of 19Y6. (Assume that the original UEL of 40 years still applies.)

# FINANCIAL REPORTING, ANALYSIS AND PLANNING

|  | £000 |
|---|---:|
| *Valuation* | |
| At 1/12/Y6 and 31/12/Y6 | 1,000,000 |
| *Accumulated depreciation* | |
| At 1/1/Y6 | 0 |
| Charge for year | |
| Depreciable amount £1,000,000 – 280,000 = 720,000 | 30,000 |
| Annual charge £720,000/24 years remaining UEL | |
| At 31/12/Y6 | 30,000 |
| *Net book value* | |
| At 1/1/Y6 | 1,000,000 |
| At 31/12/Y6 | 970,000 |

We can see that the implications of revaluing upwards are *higher* assets values and *lower* profits.

## Bases of valuation

3.15 So far we have assumed that there is an easily obtainable current valuation available for any fixed asset we care to revalue. This assumption is, in the case of the majority of assets, not necessarily true. There are different bases of valuation and indeed different methods of valuation. As a starting point the Companies Act 1985 Schedule 4 states that:

(a) tangible fixed assets may be included at market value or current cost;

(b) intangible fixed assets, excluding goodwill, may be included at current cost;

(c) investments may be included at market value or at the directors' valuation.

Of course, all such assets may be valued at historic cost i.e. original purchase price plus related expenditure (see above).

3.16 Thus we can already see three different valuation bases- 'market value', 'current cost' and 'director's valuation'. Unfortunately the Act did not define the three bases—if indeed they are valuation bases at all. For instance, 'director's valuation' is neither a valuation base nor a valuation method.

To simplify if the problem we can look at the three valuation 'bases' in turn.

## *Market Value (often called Open Market value)*

3.17 Generally this can be defined as the best price which might be obtained on a sale assuming a willing buyer and seller. In addition other factors, such as that sufficient time has been allowed for the marketing of the assets or that no rival bidders have upped the valuation, need to be taken into consideration.

3.18 Another assumption which is made when valuing a fixed asset is that the *existing use of the asset be maintained*. For example, a surveyor may be asked to value an adjoining pair of semi-detached houses. If the potential purchaser is

# VALUATION OF ASSETS

a property developer intent on demolishing the houses to make way for an access road to a new development, the change in existing use is likely to greatly inflate their value.

3.19 A valuation on an existing use basis may well take into account the trading potential of the asset, together with associated (possibly off balance sheet) assets. For instance, a public house's value will partly reflect the value and position of the bricks and mortar; but of probably greater importance will be the trading record of the establishment together with the appropriate licence to carry on such a business there.

## Current cost

3.20 Current cost is a valuation concept rather than a method of valuation. It is generally defined by the following diagram.

**Table 4.1**

Current cost is the lower of:

| Net current replacement cost | and | Recoverable amount |

which in turn is the higher of

| Net realisable value | and | Value in use |

*Source: 'Accounting for the effects of changing prices' ASC Handbook*

3.21 There may be problems in obtaining all the individual figures within this valuation base. For instance, obtaining the current replacement cost may be difficult if the asset is unique or if that particular asset is no longer made because of technological advances or consumer preference.

3.22 The net realisable value is at best an estimate. There may be no ready market for the particular asset.

3.23 The value in use involves estimating the future cash flows that the asset will generate—which is likely to be a subjective and inconclusive exercise.

## Director's valuation

3.24 This is not really a valuation base as such. The Companies Act allows the directors to use their judgement and discretion in selecting an appropriate base to value the fixed asset.

3.25 A further option was explored in Exposure Draft 52 'Accounting for Intangible assets'. ED 52 introduced the idea of valuing assets on the basis of depreciated replacement cost – if this represented the current cost of the asset.

FINANCIAL REPORTING, ANALYSIS AND PLANNING

### *Depreciated replacement cost*

3.26 This method can be used where it is difficult/impossible to obtain a market value for an asset. The asset may be unique or rarely traded. The depreciated replacement cost (DRC) of a property is based on the open market value of the land (in its existing use) together with an estimated replacement cost of the building. This figure is then 'depreciated', taking into account the building's age, condition and other factors affecting its useful economic life.

3.27 DRC usually gives a higher valuation than using an open market basis. Hence it will lead to higher deprecation charges. Further the valuation is predicated on an existing use basis, which means that the likelihood of the continuation of the use of the specialised asset must be assessed.

### *Valuers*

3.28 Surprisingly it is not a requirement of the Companies Act for the valuers to be professionally qualified. The Act states that the name or the qualification of the valuer should be disclosed in the financial statements. Also, if the valuer is an employee this should be noted. However, the over-riding requirement that the accounts should show a 'true and fair' view implies that the valuer should have some degree of competence. In particular, if we are using the DRC for specialised assets it is likely that specialised advice be sought in making a valuation.

## 4 Investment properties

4.1 SSAP19 'Accounting for investment properties' introduced another concept of fixed assets. Such property assets are held for their investment potential rather than for consumption within the business. As such these assets *should not be depreciated* but rather be valued in the accounts at 'market value' with annual revaluations. Any differences in valuation should be accounted for in a non-distributable reserve: the 'Investment Revaluation Reserve' (IRR) and movements in this reserve should be shown in the statement of total realised gains and losses (see Unit 6). Only upon final disposal of the assets should any gains or losses be recognised in the profit and loss account (see exception below).

4.2 The criteria to classify a fixed asset as an investment property are quite straightforward: an interest in land and/or buildings where the following apply.

(i) The asset should be held for its investment potential—any rental agreement for the asset should have been arranged at arms length.

(ii) The property should not be occupied by the company or its subsidiaries.

(iii) The building must be complete.

4.3 The only exception to the rule of non-depreciation is leasehold properties with less than 20 years to run.

4.4 The standard principles apply regarding the valuation of the asset. If there is a permanent diminution in value of the investment property the deficit should be charged to the Profit and Loss account. Temporary diminutions in

# VALUATION OF ASSETS

value should be reflected in the IRR. The distinction between 'temporary' and 'permanent' deficits is a difficult area and subject to differing interpretations.

**Example 4.3**

Simpson plc purchases Building X on 1 January 19X1 for £3.5m. Simpson is intending to hold the asset for its investment potential. Over the next few years, its value fluctuates as follows.

| 31 December | Value £m |
|---|---|
| 19X1 | 4.0 |
| 19X2 | 3.6 |
| 19X3 | 3.3 |
| 19X4 | 3.7 |

On 1 July 19X5 the building is sold for £3.9m. Show the asset in the books of Simpson plc.

**Solution**

*Year ended 31 December 19X1*
In fixed assets show as a separate category – investment properties.

| | £m |
|---|---|
| *Investment properties* | |
| Addition in year | 3.5 |
| Revaluation | 0.5 |
| Value at 31 December 19X1 | 4.0 |
| *Investment revaluation reserve* | |
| Revaluation in year | 0.5 |
| Balance at 31 December 19X1 | 0.5 |

No charge in the profit and loss account

Show the £0.5m revaluation in the statement of total recognised gains and losses (see Unit 6).

*Year ended 31 December 19X2*

| | £m |
|---|---|
| *Investment properties* | |
| Value at 1 January 19X2 | 4.0 |
| Revaluation | (0.4) |
| Value at 31 December 19X2 | 3.6 |
| *Investment revaluation reserve* | |
| Balance at 1 January 19X2 | 0.5 |
| Revaluation in year | (0.4) |
| Balance at 31 December 19X2 | 0.1 |

No charge in the profit and loss account

Show the £0.4m devaluation in the statement of total recognised gains and losses (see Unit 6).

# FINANCIAL REPORTING, ANALYSIS AND PLANNING

*Year ended 31 December 19X3*

|  | £m |
|---|---:|
| *Investment properties* | |
| Value at 1 January 19X3 | 3.6 |
| Revaluation | (0.3) |
| Value at 31 December 19X3 | 3.3 |
| *Investment revaluation reserve* | |
| Balance at 1 January 19X3 | 0.1 |
| Revaluation in year | (0.4) |
|  | (0.3) |
| Transfer from profit and loss account | 0.3 |
| Balance at 31 December 19X3 | 0.0 |

Charge to the profit and loss account the negative balance on the IRR £0.3m.

*(This assumption is made on the basis that the deficit is expected to be permanent; if the deficit is expected to be temporary then the £0.3m negative balance on the IRR can remain).*

Show the net £0.1m reduction in the IRR in the statement of total recognised gains and losses (see Unit 6).

*Year ended 31 December 19X4*

|  | £m |
|---|---:|
| *Investment properties* | |
| Value at 1 January 19X4 | 3.3 |
| Revaluation | 0.4 |
| Value at 31 December 19X4 | 3.7 |
| *Investment revaluation reserve* | |
| Balance at 1 January 19X4 | 0.0 |
| Revaluation in year | 0.4 |
| Balance at 31 December 19X4 | 0.4 |

No charge in the profit and loss account

Show the £0.4m revaluation in the statement of total recognised gains and losses (see Unit 6).

*Year ended 31 December 19X5*

|  | £m |
|---|---:|
| *Investment properties* | |
| Value at 1 January 19X5 | 3.7 |
| Disposal | (3.7) |
| Value at 31 December 19X5 | 0.0 |
| *Investment revaluation reserve* | |
| Balance at 1 January 19X5 | 0.4 |
| Disposal | (0.4) |
| Balance at 31 December 19X5 | 0.0 |

# VALUATION OF ASSETS

The gain on disposal in the profit and loss account should be shown as £0.2m (the difference between the proceeds of £3.9m and the carrying value of £3.7m).

The release of the £0.4m in the IRR should be shown as a movement on reserves in the statement of total recognised gains and losses (see Unit 6).

4.5 The area of valuing fixed assets is of importance chiefly because of the significant value of these assets in most company's accounts. However, the degree of flexibility in judging an asset's useful life, estimating of residual values, distinguishing between permanent and temporary deficits, choosing the depreciation method and computing the asset's 'cost' can lead to a great variation in the overall value of similar fixed assets between different enterprises and consequently the amount of reported profits.

## Student Activity 1

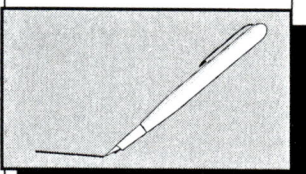

Before reading the next section of text, answer the following questions and then check your answers against the paragraph(s) indicated.

1. Define a fixed asset. *(Paragraph 2.2)*
2. What further items may be included in the cost of a fixed asset in addition to purchase price? *(Paragraphs 2.4 & 2.6)*
3. Discuss the merits of capitalising interest and illustrate the effect on the accounts. *(Paragraphs 2.8 & 2.9)*
4. Explain the purpose of calculating depreciation. *(Paragraphs 3.1 & 3.2)*
5. Which depreciation methods are permitted by SSAP12 and what is their effect on reported profits? *(Paragraphs 3.3 – 3.6)*
6. What are the implications of revaluing fixed assets? *(See Example 4.2 & Paragraphs 3.12 – 3.14)*
7. Explain current cost. *(Paragraph 3.20)*
8. Outline the criteria to qualify as an investment property. *(Paragraphs 4.2)*

If your answers are basically correct, then proceed to the next section. If significant parts of your answers are wrong, then study the whole of the relevant sections again in detail. Note your areas of weakness and be prepared for further questions on these areas at the end of this unit.

## 5 Stock

5.1 Stock is another major asset in the balance sheet of most companies. Its valuation directly affects the balance sheet and reported profits. Thus in a similar way to the valuation of fixed assets, stock valuation is an area where judgment needs to be exercised and care taken in interpreting the results of companies holding stock. Different stock valuations will give different profits.

**General rule**

5.2 SSAP9 'Stocks and long term contracts' introduces the broad rule that stock should be valued at cost. 'Cost' comprises the costs incurred in bringing the

FINANCIAL REPORTING, ANALYSIS AND PLANNING

stock to its present condition and location. This you will remember is similar to the definition of 'cost' used for fixed assets above. Thus 'cost' can incorporate:

- purchase price
- conversion costs
- overheads
- carriage inwards
- import duties etc.

5.3 At this point it is well to consider which type of organisation is involved. A *trader* is likely only to buy and sell items of stock. Thus he will likely only have one sort of stock – *finished goods*. On the other hand a *manufacturer* will purchase *raw materials*, work on them and convert them into *finished goods*. Stock part way through conversion is referred to as *work in progress*.

5.4 Initially we will consider the stock valuation of a trader. SSAP9 states that stock should be valued at the lower of cost and net realisable value (NRV). NRV is the estimated selling price of the stock less estimated future costs to enable the stock to be sold. (This could include, for example, packing or distribution costs.)

5.5 The comparison between cost and NRV is made on the grounds of prudence, i.e. it would be imprudent to value stock at more than what it could be sold for.

5.6 The comparison should be made for each item of stock—not globally. Consider the following example.

**Example 4.4**

James Limited holds three types of stock, and their cost and NRVs are as follows.

| Stock | Cost £ | NRV £ |
|-------|--------|-------|
| A | 2,000 | 2,900 |
| B | 1,400 | 1,200 |
| C | 3,800 | 5,000 |
| Total | 7,200 | 9,100 |

**Solution**

In total the estimated selling proceeds are more than the cost. However, examining each stock line individually, we should value the stock:

| Stock | £ |
|-------|---|
| A | 2,000 (Cost) |
| B | 1,200 (NRV) |
| C | 3,800 (Cost) |
| Total | 7,000 |

5.7 Why might NRV be less than cost—surely we are in business to make a profit?

Some of the reasons might be:

# VALUATION OF ASSETS

- loss leaders e.g. tins of baked beans sold for 3p to attract custom into the shop
- old/obsolete/damaged stock
- collapse in the market—this might apply to commodities where the market price is volatile and fluctuating.

5.8 Defining cost can be problematic where the purchase price of stock bought is fluctuating. Consider the following example.

**Example 4.5**

During the week Kerr Ltd. purchased the following identical stock items.

|  |  | £ per kg | Total |
|---|---|---|---|
| Monday a.m. | 4 kg | 2.00 | 8.00 |
| Tuesday a.m. | 8 kg | 2.10 | 16.80 |
| Wednesday a.m. | 3 kg | 2.15 | 6.45 |
| Thursday a.m. | 10 kg | 2.16 | 21.60 |
| Friday a.m. | 6 kg | 2.20 | 13.20 |
| TOTAL |  |  | 66.05 |

On Wednesday afternoon Kerr sold 6 kg and on Thursday afternoon 12 kg. Calculate Kerr's cost of sales.

**Solution**

There are three methods we can adopt. One method is First In First Out (FIFO). We assume that the oldest stock is sold first, we are left with the newest stock.

(i) FIFO

*Position*

|  |  |  | £/kg | Cost of sales £ |
|---|---|---|---|---|
| Monday a.m. | Purchase | 4 kg | 2.00 |  |
| Tuesday a.m. | Purchase | 8 kg | 2.10 |  |
| Wednesday a.m. | Purchase | 3 kg | 2.15 |  |
| Wednesday p.m. | Sale | 4 kg | 2.00 | 8.00 |
|  |  | 2 kg | 2.10 | 4.20 |
| *Left remaining* |  | 6 kg | 2.10 |  |
|  |  | 3 kg | 2.15 |  |
| Thursday a.m. | Purchase | 10 kg | 2.16 |  |
| Thursday p.m. | Sale | 6 kg | 2.10 | 12.60 |
|  |  | 3 kg | 2.15 | 6.45 |
|  |  | 3 kg | 2.16 | 6.48 |
| *Left remaining* |  | 7 kg | 2.16 |  |
| Friday a.m. | Purchase | 6 kg | 2.20 |  |
| TOTAL |  |  |  | 37.73 |

# FINANCIAL REPORTING, ANALYSIS AND PLANNING

Thus we will be left with:

|  | £/kg | £ |
|---|---|---|
| 7 kg | 2.16 | 15.12 |
| 6 kg | 2.20 | 13.20 |
| 13 kg | TOTAL | 28.32 |

(ii) Consider the position using Last In First Out (LIFO) i.e. assuming that we sell the newest stock and keep the oldest.

*Position*

|  |  |  | £/kg | Cost of sales £ |
|---|---|---|---|---|
| Monday a.m. | Purchase | 4 kg | 2.00 | |
| Tuesday a.m. | Purchase | 8 kg | 2.10 | |
| Wednesday a.m. | Purchase | 3 kg | 2.15 | |
| Wednesday p.m. | Sale | 3 kg | 2.15 | 6.45 |
|  |  | 3 kg | 2.10 | 6.30 |
| *Left remaining* |  | *4 kg* | *2.00* | |
|  |  | *5 kg* | *2.10* | |
| Thursday a.m. | Purchase | 10 kg | 2.16 | |
| Thursday p.m. | Sale | 10 kg | 2.16 | 21.60 |
|  |  | 2 kg | 2.10 | 4.20 |
| *Left remaining* |  | *4 kg* | *2.00* | |
|  |  | *3 kg* | *2.10* | |
| Friday a.m. | Purchase | 6 kg | 2.20 | |
| TOTAL |  |  |  | 38.55 |

Thus we will be left with:

|  | £/kg | £ |
|---|---|---|
| 6 kg | 2.20 | 13.20 |
| 3 kg | 2.10 | 6.30 |
| 4 kg | 2.00 | 8.00 |
| 13 kg | TOTAL | 27.50 |

(iii) Finally consider using AVerage COst (AVCO). With this method we re-calculate the average cost of stock at every purchase or sale.

*Position*

|  |  |  | £/kg | Total | Cost of sales £ |
|---|---|---|---|---|---|
| Monday a.m. | Purchase | 4 kg | 2.00 | 8.00 | |
| Tuesday a.m. | Purchase | 8 kg | 2.10 | 16.80 | |
| *Stock at av. cost* |  | *12 kg* | *2.067* | *24.80* | |
| Wednesday a.m. | Purchase | 3 kg | 2.15 | 6.45 | |
| *Stock at av. cost* |  | *15 kg* | *2.083* | *31.25* | |
| Wednesday p.m. | Sale | (6 kg) | 2.083 | (12.50) | 12.50 |
| Thursday a.m. | Purchase | 10 kg | 2.16 | 21.60 | |
| *Stock at av. cost* |  | *19 kg* | *2.124* | *40.35* | |

## VALUATION OF ASSETS

| | | | | | |
|---|---|---|---|---|---|
| Thursday p.m. | Sale | (12 kg) | 2.124 | (25.48) | 25.48 |
| Friday a.m. | Purchase | 6 kg | 2.20 | 13.20 | |
| *Stock at av. cost* | | *13 kg* | *2.159* | *28.07* | |
| **TOTAL** | | | | | 37.98 |

Thus we will be left with:

| | £/kg | £ |
|---|---|---|
| 13 kg | 2.159 | 28.07 |

To compare the effect of the three methods, assume that all stock was sold for £3.00 per kg.

| | FIFO £ | LIFO £ | AVCO £ |
|---|---|---|---|
| *Sales* (18 kg @ £3.00) | 54.00 | 54.00 | 54.00 |
| *Cost of sales* | | | |
| Opening stock | 0 | 0 | 0 |
| Purchases | 66.05 | 66.05 | 66.05 |
| Closing stock | (28.32) | (27.50) | (28.07) |
| Cost of sales | 37.73 | 38.55 | 37.98 |
| Gross Profit | 16.27 | 15.45 | 16.02 |

5.9 In summary in times of inflation, FIFO will give the highest stock values and consequently the highest profit, LIFO will give the lowest stock value and consequently the lowest profit; whilst AVCO will give figures in between the other two methods.

5.10 SSAP9 recommends that LIFO is an inappropriate method, due to its inherent *under* statement of stock values. In addition the Inland Revenue will not accept LIFO as a method of stock valuation for use in stock valuation, mainly because it understates stock values and consequently taxable profits.

5.11 One final point to note is that although manipulating the stock value does affect profit, the following year's results are affected as well but with the opposite result. This is because last year's closing stock becomes this year's opening stock.

## Manufacturing accounts

5.12 As stated earlier different types of enterprise will prepare accounts. One such is a manufacturing organisation. These companies generally buy one type of stock, raw materials, and convert them into finished goods. Part completed units are called work-in-progress.

5.13 However at this stage you should be aware that the SSAP9 rules still apply, that is, stock is valued at the lower of cost and NRV and that the stock valuation method adopted should be applied consistently.

# 6 Long Term Work in Progress (LT WIP)

6.1 Certain companies are engaged in long-term contracts that straddle more than one accounting period. For example, a major construction company may build a power station that takes three years to complete. Under the realisation principle, we cannot recognise the profit on the project until it is complete (i.e. it turns from work in progress to finished goods). This can lead to a distortion of the company's results. Consider the following example.

**Example 4.6**

Jacques plc is a construction company building a dam. It is the only project the company is currently engaged in. Apart from the project, the company incurs general overheads and interest of £0.5m per year. The contract price is £10m. Total costs of the project are £8m, spread £4m in Year 1, £3m in Year 2 and £1m in Year 3. The contract specifies that the client will pay Jacques half of the contract price at the end of Year 2, with the remainder upon satisfactory completion of the project.

**Solution**

Assuming we account for this project in the normal way the results will be as follows:

*Profit and loss account*

| Year | 1 £m | 2 £m | 3 £m |
|---|---|---|---|
| Sales | – | – | 10 |
| Cost of sales | – | – | (8) |
| Gross Profit | – | – | 2 |
| Overheads | (0.5) | (0.5) | (0.5) |
| Net profit/(loss) | (0.5) | (0.5) | 1.5 |

*Balance sheet*

| Year | 1 £m | 2 £m | 3 £m |
|---|---|---|---|
| Stock – LT WIP | 4 | 7 | 0 |
| Creditors – payments in advance | 0 | 5 | 0 |

6.2 Without knowing the story behind this company we might have difficulty in interpreting its performance. A loss for two years is converted into a profit in Year 3. One might get the impression its performance is improving from a poor start. In reality the company has performed similarly for all three years.

6.3 The provisions of SSAP9 regarding LT WIP cater for this. They allow the company to recognise part of the overall profit *before it has been realised* (i.e. before the end of the contract). This is called *attributable profit*. Thus the project profit is spread over the three years not all taken in Year 3.

# VALUATION OF ASSETS

6.4 Concurrently, the project's *costs* are also spread over the three years—and taken to profit and loss account—using the same method used to allocate the project profit.

**How to determine attributable profit**

6.5 This can be done in several ways:

(a) The *cost* basis.

The profit through the contract is determined with reference to the proportion of total costs incurred to total contract costs. In the case above, at the end of Years 1, 2 and 3 we will be respectively 4/8ths, 7/8ths and 8/8ths through the contract. Thus we will take those proportions of sales, cost of sales and consequently gross profit to the profit and loss accounts for the three years. To illustrate see Example 4.7.

**Example 4.7**

*Profit and loss account*

| Year | 1 £m | 2 £m | 3 £m |
|---|---|---|---|
| Sales | 5.00 (4/8ths × £10m) | 3.75 (7/8ths × £10m less £5m taken in Yr. 1) | 1.25 (8/8ths × £10m less £8.75m taken in Yrs. 1 & 2) |
| Cost of sales | 4.00 (4/8ths × £8m) | 3.0 (7/8ths × £8m less £4m taken in Yr. 1) | 1.00 (8/8ths × £8m less £7m taken in Yrs. 1 & 2) |
| Gross Profit | 1.00 | 0.75 | 0.25 |
| Overheads | (0.5) | (0.5) | (0.5) |
| Net profit/(loss) | 0.25 | 0.25 | (0.25) |

These results may reflect the truer nature of the company's results—declining profitability over the three years as the project activity decreases.

*Balance sheet*

| Year | 1 £m | 2 £m | 3 £m |
|---|---|---|---|
| **Stock** | | | |
| Costs incurred | 4 | 7 | 8 |
| less taken to P/L a/c | (4) | (7) | (8) |
| LT WIP/(Creditors) | (0) | 0 | 0 |
| **Debtors** | | | |
| Sales less | 5.00 | 8.75 | 10.00 |
| progress payments received | (0) | (5.00) | (10.00) |
| Debtors | 5.00 | 3.75 | 0 |

6.6 **(b) The *sales* basis**

An architect/quantity surveyor's opinion is used to ascertain the current value of the contract in selling terms. For example, in this case an architect may value the contract at £2m, £7m and £10m for Years 1, 2, 3 respectively. To illustrate see example 4.8.

**Example 4.8**

*Profit and loss account*

| Year | 1 | 2 | 3 |
|---|---|---|---|
| | £m | £m | £m |
| Sales | 2 | 5 | 3 |
| | | (£7m less £2m taken in Yr. 1) | (£10m less £7m taken in Yrs. 1 & 2) |
| Cost of sales | 1.60 | 4.0 | 2.40 |
| | (2/10ths × £8m) | (7/10ths × £8m less £1.6m taken in Yr. 1) | (10/10ths × £8m less £5.6m taken in Yrs. 1 & 2) |
| Gross Profit | 0.40 | 1.00 | 0.60 |
| Overheads | (0.5) | (0.5) | (0.5) |
| Net profit/(loss) | (0.10) | 0.50 | 0.10 |

These results may reflect in truer terms the nature of the company's activity —reflecting the increased value of the project in sales terms earned in Year 2.

*Balance sheet*

| Year | 1 | 2 | 3 |
|---|---|---|---|
| | £m | £m | £m |
| *Stock* | | | |
| Costs incurred | 4 | 7 | 8 |
| less taken to P/L a/c | (1.6) | (5.6) | (8) |
| LT WIP/ (Creditors) | 2.4 | 1.4 | 0 |
| *Debtors* | | | |
| Sales less | 2.00 | 7.00 | 10.00 |
| progress payments received | (0) | (5.00) | (10.00) |
| *Debtors* | 2.00 | 2.00 | 0 |

6.7 **(c) Other bases**

Finally you may be told what proportion you are through the contract e.g. 15%, 65% etc.

In that way you would take 15% of the contract price as sales in Year 1, 50% (65% less 15% taken in Year 1) in Year 2 and 35% (100% less 65% taken in Years 1 & 2) in Year 3. Similarly, you would take 15% of total contract costs in Year 1, 50% in Year 2 and 35% in Year 3.

6.8 Note however, that under all methods, even the original method of not taking attributable profit, the *total* contract profit over the three years will be the same. The difference in the methods is in the *allocation* of that profit to the

# VALUATION OF ASSETS

various accounting periods. Once again different methods of allocation will lead to different asset valuations and different profits.

6.9 What constitutes a long-term contract? No hard and fast rules are given. Indeed a long term contract need not exceed one year. It must, however, straddle more than one accounting period. If we are accounting for attributable profit the outcome of the project must be foreseeable with 'reasonable certainty', an example of the application of the prudence concept again.

**Losses on long-term contracts**

6.10 Another application of the prudence concept occurs if the project is estimated to show a loss. It would be imprudent to only account for the *attributable* loss—therefore the *whole* of the loss is anticipated.

**Example 4.9**

Using our example above, and assuming we have used the sales basis, consider the situation at the end of Year 2 if the cost profile were as follows.

|  | 1 | 2 | 3 |
|---|---|---|---|
|  | £m | £m | £m |
| Costs | 4 (actual) | 3 (actual) | 4 (estimated) |

At the end of Year 2, Year 3 costs are now estimated at £4m instead of the original estimate of £1m. We would have accounted to date as follows.

*Profit and loss account*

| Year | 1 | 2 |
|---|---|---|
|  | £m | £m |
| Sales | 2 | 5 (£7m less £2m taken in Yr. 1) |
| Cost of sales | 1.60 (2/10ths × £8m) | 4.0 (7/10ths × £8m less £1.6m taken in Yr. 1) |
| Gross Profit | 0.40 | 1.00 |
| Overheads | (0.5) | (0.5) |
| Net profit/(loss) | (0.10) | 0.50 |

However we will now need to rework Year 2's figures in line with the new estimate.

*Profit and loss account*

| Year | 2 |
|---|---|
|  | £m |
| Sales | 5 (as before) |
| Cost of sales | (6.40)† |
| Gross Profit/(Loss) | (1.40)* |
| Overheads | (0.5) |
| Net profit/(loss) | (1.90) |

# FINANCIAL REPORTING, ANALYSIS AND PLANNING

\* We need to account for the whole of the anticipated loss as well as writing back any profit we have recognised in earlier periods. Thus:

| Year 2 loss | £m |
|---|---|
| Contract price | 10 |
| less costs to date | (7) |
| costs to complete | (4) |
| Anticipated total project loss | (1) |
| Plus attributable profit taken in Year 1 | (0.4) |
| Loss for Year 2 | (1.4) |

† Another way of calculating this is to look at the cost of sales figure required.

| | £m |
|---|---|
| On the sales basis | |
| 7/10ths × total costs £11m | 7.7 |
| plus 3/10ths of loss not accounted for | 0.3 |
| Total cost of sales to end Year 2 | 8.0 |
| less taken in Year 1 | (1.6) |
| Charge in year 2 | 6.4 |

As always the balance sheet entries follow on from the profit and loss calculations

*Balance sheet*

| Year | 2 |
|---|---|
| | £m |
| *Stock* | |
| Costs incurred | 7 |
| less taken to P/L a/c | (8.0) |
| LT WIP/ *(Provisions for losses on long term contracts)* | (1.0) |
| *Debtors* | |
| Sales less | 7.00 |
| progress payments received | (5.00) |
| *Debtors* | 2.00 |

## Student Activity 2

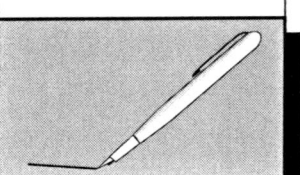

Before reading the next section of text, answer the following questions and then check your answers against the paragraph(s) indicated.

1. When accounting for stock what items can be included in 'cost'? *(Paragraph 5.2)*
2. Why might net realisable value be less than cost? *(Paragraph 5.7)*
3. Which valuation methods does SSAP9 approve of? *(Paragraph 5.10)*
4. Why should a company account for a long term contract taking attributable profit? *(Paragraphs 6.1 – 6.3)*

# VALUATION OF ASSETS

If your answers are basically correct, then proceed to the next section. If significant parts of your answers are wrong, then study the whole of the relevant sections again in detail. Note your areas of weakness and be prepared for further questions on these areas at the end of this unit.

## 7 Intangible assets

7.1 By their very nature intangible assets are of less interest to a banker. Their intangibility means that they are less suitable for use as loan collateral and intangible assets tend to be more difficult to identify and value than tangible assets. This, however, does not mean that such assets are insignificant. In some businesses, their major assets may be intangible. Consider the most valuable assets of an advertising agency. They are likely to be its reputation, its creative staff and its client base. None of those assets is 'easy' to identify and value. None of those assets is traditionally recorded on the balance sheet, but they are major assets of the business.

7.2 The prudence concept raises its head again here. Because of their inherent intangibility—normally we do not account for the majority of intangibles—including the three assets mentioned above. By tradition, we generally only account for two classes of intangible asset—research and development expenditure and goodwill. However, as expected our inclusion of these intangibles in our balance sheet is subject to the over-riding prudence concept. For example, expenditure on pure research is prohibited under, SSAP13 'Accounting for research and development' from being included in the accounts as an asset. Similarly, internally generated goodwill arising from a company's reputation, advertising campaigns, positive employee relations etc., is not permitted to be capitalised by FRS10.

## 8 Research and development expenditure

8.1 SSAP 13 divides expenditure into three categories which are defined as follows.

**Pure research**

8.2 This is defined as experimental or theoretical work undertaken primarily to acquire new scientific or technical knowledge for its own sake rather than directed towards any specific aim or application.

**Applied research**

8.3 SSAP 13 defines this as original or critical investigation undertaken in order to gain new scientific or technical knowledge that is directed towards a specific practical aim or objective.

**Development expenditure**

8.4 This is the use of scientific or technical knowledge in order to produce new or substantially improved materials, devices, products or services, to install new processes or systems prior to the commencement of commercial production or commercial applications, or to improve substantially those already produced or installed.

# FINANCIAL REPORTING, ANALYSIS AND PLANNING

8.5 According to SSAP13, development expenditure *may* be capitalised if certain criteria are met. Note that this is an option, not a requirement. The criteria allowing the capitalisation of development expenditure are as follows.

   (i) There must be a clearly defined project.

   (ii) The expenditure must be clearly distinguishable and measurable.

   (iii) The project must be overall commercially viable.

   (iv) The project must be assessed as to its technical feasibility.

   (v) Expected future revenue from the project should exceed expected future costs and the cost, being capitalised.

   (vi) The enterprise must have the resources to complete the project. Resources include not just financial means but also competent management, technical resources over the useful economic life of the project, know how, human resources etc.

8.6 The expenditure must meet *all* the criteria for the capitalisation option to be exercised. If the expenditure is capitalised it does not remain a permanent item in the company's balance sheet. It should be capitalised as an intangible fixed asset and then amortised (depreciated) over of the commercial life of the underlying product or service. Amortisation should begin on commercial production.

8.7 The rules on permanent/temporary diminution of this asset are the same as for other fixed assets (see above).

8.8 The issue of research and development expenditure is an example of the frequent clashes between the fundamental accounting principles. In this case, the clash is between the matching concept and the prudence concept. Matching would suggest that research expenditure should be deferred until it can be matched to future benefits arising from the research. Prudence, on the other hand, would suggest that such future benefits are tenuous and unpredictable and therefore such expenditure should not be capitalised, rather prudently written off. Consider Example 4.10.

**Example 4.10**

A company incurs considerable advertising expenditure in December, promoting the forthcoming January sales. History suggests that such a campaign has always proved successful, in increased turnover and profits in the New Year. The company's year end is the 31st December.

Following the matching concept would imply that the advertising expenditure should be capitalised and deferred until the following year. The prudence concept on the other would compel the company to write off the expenditure in December on the grounds that the future benefits cannot be guaranteed and are difficult to quantify.

**Expenditure on fixed assets used for research and development**

8.9 Fixed assets used for research and development activity should be treated as any normal fixed asset (see above). The only distinction is that any depreciation on such fixed assets may qualify as research and development 'expenditure' in its own right and may be capitalised if it meets the appropriate criteria (see later).

# 9 Goodwill

9.1 A business is normally worth more than the combined sum of its net assets. The reason for this is known as goodwill and is created by such diverse factors as a good reputation, full order book, loyal/talented employees, successful management team, good location, profitable product lines etc.

9.2 Goodwill, by its very nature, is the difference between two variables. The overall worth of the business will be dependent on internal and external factors ranging from the state of the economy to consumer fashion. The values of individual assets and liabilities are subject to variation because of many factors; an asset's value may be inherently unstable; market sentiment may affect asset valuations; variations may be caused by choice of accounting policy, exercise of professional judgement, the performance of the firm, the state of the company's market or the influence of competition, among other factors.

9.3 Thus goodwill is a constantly fluctuating value. It can even have a negative value. In this case a company would be worth more when broken up into its constituent assets and liabilities than as a whole entity.

9.4 Because of these uncertainties (the prudence concept again) the capitalisation of internally generated goodwill is not allowed under either the Companies Act 1985 or FRS 10 'Goodwill and Intangible Assets'.

9.5 Purchased goodwill, on the other hand, can be established at a point in time. It represents the difference between the total purchase price of a business and the total fair value of its separable net assets.

**Example 4.11**

Williams Ltd purchases 100% of Cheam Ltd's share capital for £3m. At the time of purchase Cheam's balance sheet is as follows:

|  | £m |
|---|---|
| Fixed assets: | |
| Intangible | 0.5 |
| Tangible | 1.6 |
|  | 2.1 |
| Net current assets | 1.1 |
|  | 3.2 |
| Creditors: due after one year | (0.5) |
|  | 2.7 |
| Share capital | 1.0 |
| Reserves | 1.7 |
|  | 2.7 |

We can see that Williams has paid £3m for separable net assets valued at £2.7m. Therefore the difference of £0.3m represents the premium Williams has paid over the book value of the net assets purchased – this is purchased positive goodwill, assuming the book values represent the fair values of Cheam's assets and liabilities. If the book values did not represent the fair values then they would have to be revalued so that they did in order to comply with FRS 7 Fair Values in Acquisition Accounting.

In incorporating the purchase of Cheam into Williams' accounts we would:

- deduct the consideration of £3m from Williams' asset of cash, or add £3m to Williams' capital and share premium if the purchase consideration comprised a share issue by Williams.
- add £0.8m to Williams' intangible assets – £0.5m of Cheam's intangible assets plus the £0.3m positive goodwill.
- add £1.6m to Williams' tangible fixed assets
- add £1.1m to Williams' net current assets
- add £0.5m to Williams' creditors due after more than one year.

9.6 Where the useful economic life of goodwill is believed to be 20 years or less, the carrying value should be amortised in the profit and loss account on a systematic basis over the useful life. However, if the useful economic life is believed to exceed 20 years *and* the value of the goodwill is significant and is also expected to be capable of continued measurement in the future, either of the following approaches may be adopted.

- The carrying value may be amortised over the useful economic life (providing it can be estimated).
- Alternatively, if the useful economic life is deemed to be indefinite, the goodwill need not be amortised.

Whichever approach is adopted, an annual impairment review will be required.

9.7 An impairment review is a formal test performed at specified points in time (or after the occurrence of certain specified events) to ensure that the asset's carrying value has not fallen below its recoverable amount. A recoverable amount is taken to be the market value for an intangible asset but because this is not ascertainable for goodwill a value has to be calculated for this. An impairment review would compare the carrying value with the recoverable amount. A change in value could be attributable to various aspects of the business, for example, the loss of key employees, an adverse change in the legal or other regulatory environment in which the business operates or the development of new technology making the business' products obsolete. Goodwill is deemed to be impaired to the extent that the carrying value exceeds the recoverable amount and this must be written off to the profit and loss account.

9.8 FRS 10 specifies that goodwill which is being amortised over a period of 20 years or less from the date of acquisition needs to be reviewed for impairment at the end of the first full financial year following acquisition but only in any subsequent period if unforeseen events or changes in circumstances indicate that carrying values may not be recoverable.

**Negative goodwill**

9.9 Negative goodwill arises when the amount paid is less than the fair value of the separable net assets. For example, if Williams had paid £2m for its interest in Cheam, there would be negative goodwill of £0.7m. Any negative goodwill should be included in the balance sheet as an intangible asset after positive goodwill.

# VALUATION OF ASSETS

9.10 Negative goodwill up to the fair values of the non-monetary assets acquired should be recognised in the profit and loss account in the periods in which the non-monetary assets are recovered, whether through depreciation or sale.

9.11 Any negative goodwill in excess of the fair values of the non-monetary assets acquired should be recognised in the profit and loss account in the periods expected to be benefited.

## 10 Brands and other intangible assets

10.1 In considering whether brands are actually assets it is well to consider commercial reality. Why would a company pay more than the book value for another company? Why did Williams pay £3m for Cheam when its book value was only £2.7 m? The answer is partly the existence of unspecified intangible assets. Normally these are all rolled up together and subsumed within 'goodwill'. It can be argued that goodwill is not one asset, it is an amalgam of numerous different intangible assets some of which have been mentioned earlier. These unspecified intangibles have varying values and characteristics. Some are more easily identifiable and easier to prescribe a value to. Others, such as 'employee morale' are too intangible, too ethereal to be reliably identifiable and measured.

10.2 In the late 1980s a consensus emerged that brands were such an identifiable, measurable intangible asset—part of but also separate from 'goodwill'. The argument was that brands had characteristics common to other assets—they could be identified, expenditure relating to their upkeep could be identified, a market existed for the assets i.e. they could be bought and sold—without necessarily affecting the running of the whole company. This last point is important, one of the characteristics of goodwill is that the asset goodwill cannot be disposed of without disposing of the company as a whole. Brands however were different, it would be possible for Bloggs Limited to sell the brand name 'Bloggs Cornflakes' and still carry on in business manufacturing other products, not necessarily under the Bloggs brand name.

10.3 The amounts involved can be significant. Rank Hovis McDougal's 1991 accounts included brands in its balance sheet at a value of £608m; representing a significant proportion of the company's net assets.

10.4 Incidentally the brands, both home-grown and acquired, were valued by outside experts Interbrand Group plc, brand consultants, and according to the accounts had increased in value by £20m over the previous year.

10.5 The following year the company was taken over by Tomkins plc who decided in their accounts not to account for brands in the balance sheet.

10.6 FRS 10 'Goodwill and Intangible Assets' requires that intangible assets be capitalised at their cost. Where such assets have been purchased separately this is straightforward. When acquired as part of a business acquisition, however, such assets must be capable of being separated from goodwill and being measured reliably. Also, internally developed intangible assets other than goodwill may be recognised providing they have an ascertainable market value.

10.7 The same FRS 10 rules apply to intangible assets as to goodwill. This means they should be amortised or reviewed for impairment as described in paragraphs 9.6 to 9.8 above.

## Student Activity 3

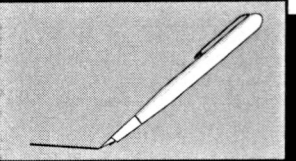

Before reading the next section of text, answer the following questions and then check your answers against the paragraph(s) indicated.

1. Why are intangible assets of less interest to a banker than tangible assets?
*(Paragraph 7.1)*

2. Define the four categories of research and development expenditure as explained by SSAP13. *(Paragraphs 8.1 – 8.4)*

3. What are the criteria allowing the capitalisation of development costs?
*(Paragraph 8.7)*

4. Define purchased goodwill. *(Paragraph 9.5)*

If your answers are basically correct, then proceed to the next section. If significant parts of your answers are wrong, then study the whole of the relevant sections again in detail. Note your areas of weakness and be prepared for further questions on these areas at the end of this unit.

VALUATION OF ASSETS

## Summary

Now that you have completed this Unit you should be able to:

- define a fixed asset and identify the components of its cost
- discuss the merits for capitalising interest and enhancement costs
- apply the principles of SSAP12
- examine various bases of valuation for fixed assets
- understand the factors affecting the carrying value of fixed assets
- explain the methods and accounting for revaluations of fixed assets
- identify and account for investment properties in accordance with SSAP19
- calculate the valuation of stock in the financial statements in accordance with SSAP9
- account for long term contracts in accordance with SSAP9
- account for research and development expenditure in accordance with SSAP13
- understand the characteristics of goodwill and apply FRS 10 in accounting for the asset
- consider the attributes of other intangible assets and discuss the merits for balance sheet inclusion.

## Self-assessment questions

### Short answer questions

1. What effect does the company's choice of depreciation method have on its reported profits?
2. Discuss the merits of revaluing fixed assets and illustrate the effect on a company's financial statements.
3. Define and explain the following: market value, current cost, depreciated replacement cost.
4. How should a company account for a deficit on investment revaluation reserve?
5. Illustrate the effect of a company's choice for valuing purchased stock.
6. Should brands be capitalised?

*(Answers are given in the Appendix)*

### Multiple choice questions

1. SSAP12 requires that fixed assets should be depreciated using:
    (a) the straight line method
    (b) the reducing balance method

(c) a method charging a fair proportion of cost or valuation to each period when the asset is in use

(d) a method charging a fair proportion of the depreciable amount to each period when the asset is in use.

2. Investment properties should be:

   (a) valued annually by a qualified valuer

   (b) valued on a regular basis by a qualified valuer

   (c) valued annually by a company employee

   (d) none of the above.

3. The Companies Act 1985 allows:

   (a) LIFO, FIFO or AVCO only

   (b) LIFO or FIFO only

   (c) FIFO or AVCO only

   (d) any reasonable method.

*Data for questions 4 to 6*

Arthur Ltd. Has the following projects in hand at 31 December 19X1.

|  | Hound £000 | Racquet £000 |
|---|---|---|
| Contract price | 2,000 | 1,000 |
| Costs to date | 1,200 | 750 |
| Estimated costs to completion | 600 | 450 |
| Progress payments received | 500 | 500 |

Using the cost basis answer the following.

4. What is the amount to be shown in cost of sales in respect of the two contracts?

   (a) £1,950

   (b) £1,875

   (c) £2,025

   (d) £2,000

5. What is the amount to be shown in debtors in respect of the two contracts?

   Debtors
   £000

   (a) 850

   (b) 700

   (c) 2,000

   (d) 958

## VALUATION OF ASSETS

6. What is the amount to be shown in work in progress in respect of the two contracts?

   Work in progress
   £000

   (a)   (75)

   (b)   45

   (c)   120

   (d)   nil

   *(Answers are given in the Appendix)*

**Exam-style questions**

1  Vilitar Ltd was incorporated some years ago and trades in a range of goods sold principally on the UK market. The following trial balance has been prepared at the end of the year to 30 September 1995:

|  | £000 | £000 |
|---|---|---|
| Sales |  | 11,470 |
| Opening stock | 1,850 |  |
| Cost of goods produced | 6,260 |  |
| Administration and selling expenses | 2,850 |  |
| Share capital (ordinary shares of £1 each) |  | 3,000 |
| Retained profit |  | 3,470 |
| Trade creditors |  | 1,070 |
| Plant and machinery at cost | 5,000 |  |
| Goodwill at cost | 1,600 |  |
| Trade debtors | 1,500 |  |
| Bank overdraft |  | 50 |
|  | 19,060 | 19,060 |

The following additional information is made available.

1. The company replaced its entire plant and machinery on 1 October 1994, with the old plant disposed of at book value. It is estimated that the new fixed assets have a useful working life of four years and can be reduced to their expected residual value of approximately £1,200,000, using either the straight line method or applying a rate of 30% on the reducing balance basis. No charge for depreciation is included in the above trial balance.

2. The goodwill arose on the acquisition of the business assets of a local competitor on 1 October 1994. The goodwill is estimated to have a useful economic life of five years from the date of acquisition.

3. The value of Vilitar's stock at the beginning and end of the current year is:

|  | 1 October 1994 £000 | 30 September 1995 £000 |
|---|---|---|
| First in first out (FIFO) basis | 2,050 | 3,010 |
| Average cost basis | 1,850 | 2,770 |

The company has used the average cost basis in the past.

FINANCIAL REPORTING, ANALYSIS AND PLANNING

**Required**

(a) Identify the accounting policies which Vilitar should use to account for plant and machinery, goodwill, and stock, assuming that the directors wish to report:

   (i) the lowest possible profit figure for the year to 30 September 1995

   (ii) the highest possible profit figure for the year to 30 September 1995.

   The methods selected should comply with acceptable accounting practice.
   [6]

(b) Prepare separate profit and loss accounts for the year ended 30 September 1995 and the balance sheets at that date:

   (i) applying the procedures identified under (a)(i); and

   (ii) applying the procedures identified under (a)(ii). [16]

(c) (i) Calculate the rates of return on shareholders' equity using the alternative accounting policies identified under (a). [2]

   (ii) Discuss the effect of the alternative accounting policies on the rates of return for shareholders. [6]

   [Total 30]

2  French Ltd makes up its accounts to 30 September. The accounts for the year to 30 September 1994 are being prepared at present.

   1. The following information is provided in respect of three entirely diferent items of stock belonging to French Ltd as at 30 September 1994.

   | Stock Item | Cost | Net realisable value |
   |---|---|---|
   | | £ | £ |
   | A | 3,600 | 3,900 |
   | B | 2,500 | 2,800 |
   | C | 7,100 | 5,000 |
   | | 13,200 | 11,700 |

   2. French Ltd has a stock of Product D which has been assembled at a total cost of £50,000. The cost of each unit of Product D is £50 and the selling price at 30 September 1994 was £60. The company pays a distribution firm £2 for each unit delivered to a customer.

   3. Assume the same costs as given under item 2 above. On 10 October 1994 the market for Product D collapsed. It is expected that the company will be able to sell each unit in stock to cutomers for £40.

   4. French Ltd manufactures 'cambers' and incurred the following costs during the year to 30 September 1994.

   | | £ |
   |---|---|
   | Materials costs | 10,000 |
   | Direct labour costs | 8,000 |
   | Factory overheads | 20,000 |
   | Administrative overheads | 8,500 |

# VALUATION OF ASSETS

The company planned to manufacture 800 cambers during the year to 30 September 1994 – the normal level of production. Due to unexpected stoppages, only 500 units were produced, of which 400 were sold and 100 remained in stock at the end of the year. There was no opening stock on 1 October 1993.

**Required**

(a) Outline the basic rules governing the valuation of stock. [6]

(b) Taking each of the above items of information (1-4) separately:

  (i) calculate the amount of the stock value to be included in the accounts

  (ii) outline the accounting principles underlying each of the calculations, and explain bow they affect your answers. [14]

[Total 20]

(CIB exam question, October 1994, question 5)

# Further reading

SSAP12 'Accounting for depreciation'

SSAP19 'Accounting for investment properties'

SSAP9 'Stocks and long term contracts'

SSAP13 'Accounting for research and development'

FRS 10 'Goodwill and Intangible Assets'

# Unit 5

## Accounting for Liabilities

### Objectives

After studying this chapter you should be able to:

- define a liability and distinguish between liabilities and shareholders' funds

- explain the treatment for dealing with various types of capital instruments as outlined by FRS4 'Capital instruments'

- identify and account for post balance sheet events in accordance with SSAP17 'Accounting for post balance sheet events'

- account for contingent gains and losses in accordance with the provisions of SSAP18 'Accounting for contingencies'

- identify different types of pension scheme and explain their importance in the preparation of financial statements

- apply the provisions of SSAP24 'Accounting for pension costs'.

## 1  Introduction

1.1   This Unit concerns accounting for various company liabilities. Considerable effort has been expended in accounting for assets (See Unit 4). Accounting for liabilities has been, until recently, a neglected area. In this Unit we are going to consider accounting for capital instruments, such as shares and loans; accounting for post balance sheet events; identifying and accounting for contingencies; and finally accounting for a major potential balance sheet liability—pension obligations.

**Capital instruments**

1.2   With the development of new and innovative methods of financing in the 1980s, it became clear that there was a lack of direction in accounting for many general forms of debt and share capital. This neglected area was addressed by the ASB in December 1993 when they issued FRS4 'Capital Instruments'—covering the accounting for certain liabilities and capital items.

*Overview*

1.3   The standard lays down a framework for distinguishing between debt and shares. Effectively by drawing on the *Statement of Principles* definition of a

# FINANCIAL REPORTING, ANALYSIS AND PLANNING

liability i.e. 'an obligation to transfer economic benefits as a result of past transactions or events.'

1.4 Capital instruments are simply instruments used to raise finance and include shares, loans, warrants etc.

1.5 The key distinction made in the standard is between *shareholders' funds* and *liabilities*. All capital instruments (in non-consolidated accounts) fall into one of these two categories. These are further subdivided as follows.

| Shareholders' funds | Liabilities |
|---|---|
| Equity | Convertible |
| Non-equity | Non-convertible |

1.6 Some instruments have features of both debt and equity. Consider for example convertible debt, i.e. debt which at some point in the future could be converted into shares. Applying the principle of substance over form (see Unit 6) this can be likened to normal debt with a warrant attached enabling shares to be acquired in the future. If possible the 'debt' element and the 'warrant' element should be accounted for separately as liabilities and shareholders' funds respectively.

1.7 The distinction between shareholders' funds and liabilities is made by applying the definition of liabilities above. If the instrument does not carry an obligation to transfer future economic benefits, then it is not a liability and must be classified as shareholders' funds. The obligation to transfer economic benefits applies whether the obligation is unconditional or merely contingent. For example, convertible debt must be shown as a liability rather than classifying it as shares, on the basis that it might be converted to shares in the future.

1.8 Distinguishing between equity and non-equity is in theory equally straightforward. Equity shares are said to have an unencumbered right to participation—participation either in the company's income or in the company's capital. Thus preference shares, which have a restricted right to participate in the company's profits, are *non-equity* shares. Some shares of a hybrid nature, which for example have a guaranteed fixed dividend with a right to participate in any remaining profits, are also non-equity shares because of the limited element in their participation.

1.9 The distinction between convertible and non-convertible liabilities is also relatively straightforward in theory. Convertible liabilities, as the name suggests, carry the right (not necessarily an obligation) to convert to shareholders funds at some point in the future.

1.10 Consider for a moment the reason behind these classifications. Why should accounts users wish to know the distinction between, for example, convertible and non-convertible debt? The reason is to provide the account users with relevant information. In this case the accounts users may be existing shareholders, who are interested in ascertaining whether their control of the company could be diluted at some point in the future.

ACCOUNTING FOR LIABILITIES

## 2 Accounting for liabilities: the principles

2.1 Accounting for capital instruments can get extremely complicated due to the nature of the instruments involved. For the purpose of this examination, only the main principles need to be understood, together with the application of the principles to a number of situations. There are three broad principles.

- Debt should be recorded at its *fair value*. The carrying amount of the debt will be *reduced* by any repayments of the principal and *increased* by any finance charges.

- The finance cost of the debt is broadly speaking the difference between the *proceeds of the debt and the aggregation of the total repayments*.

- The finance cost is allocated to accounting periods so as to produce *a constant rate of interest on the carrying amount*.

**Example 5.1**

On 1 January 19X1 Winston Smith Limited raised £100m (net of issue expenses) by issuing a five year bond, carrying interest at 5% payable annually in arrears. The bond is redeemable at £130.50 per £100 at the end of five years.

*(The rate of interest inherent in the bond is 10% per annum.)*

**Solution**

The loan schedule would be as follows.

| Year ending 31 December | Opening balance £m | Finance charge (10%) £m | Cash flow £m | Closing balance £m |
|---|---|---|---|---|
| 19X1 | 100 | 10 | (5) interest | 105 |
| 19X2 | 105 | 10.5 | (5) interest | 110.5 |
| 19X3 | 110.5 | 11 | (5) interest | 116.5 |
| 19X4 | 116.5 | 11.7 | (5) interest | 123.2 |
| 19X5 | 123.2 | 12.3 | (5) interest (130.5) redemption | 0 |

As can be seen from the loan schedule we have applied the principle of substance over form. The interest on the bond is recorded at the effective rate of 10%, not the coupon rate of 5%. Using 10% *gives a constant rate on the carrying amount of the loan*. Using the effective rate recognises that the premium on redemption is part of the total finance cost in addition to the coupon interest of 5%.

In the accounts, the finance charge would be debited to the profit and loss account and the closing balance shown within creditors in the balance sheet. The closing balance would be split between creditors: amounts falling due within one year and amounts falling due after more than one year. In the example above, *all* the balance is due after more than one year.

FINANCIAL REPORTING, ANALYSIS AND PLANNING

## 3 Other types of capital instrument

3.1 We will now look at six examples of different types of capital instrument.

*(a) Zero coupon bonds*

This is a modification of the example above, where in fact the capital instrument carries no interest.

**Example 5.2**

On 1 January 19X1 Bernard Marx plc issues a zero coupon bond for consideration of £100m. The bond is redeemable at £161 per £100 in five years time.

*(The rate of interest inherent in the bond is 10% per annum.)*

**Solution**

The loan schedule would be as follows.

| Year ending 31 December | Opening balance £m | Finance charge (10%) £m | Cash flow £m | Closing balance £m |
|---|---|---|---|---|
| 19X1 | 100 | 10 | | 110 |
| 19X2 | 110 | 11 | | 121 |
| 19X3 | 121 | 12.1 | | 133.1 |
| 19X4 | 133.1 | 13.3 | | 146.4 |
| 19X5 | 146.4 | 14.6 | (161) redemption | 0 |

Although technically no interest is payable on the loan, the accounts should recognise that the premium on redemption is part of the finance costs and therefore should be allocated to accounting periods over the term of the loan.

3.2 *(b) Convertible debt with varying interest*

**Example 5.3**

Savage plc issues convertible debt on 1 January 19X1 for £100m. The debt carries a coupon rate of 5.9% for the first five years and a coupon rate of 14.1% for the next ten years; after which it is redeemable at par.

*(The rate of interest inherent in the debt is 10% per annum.)*

# ACCOUNTING FOR LIABILITIES

## Solution

The loan schedule would be as follows:

| Year ending 31 December | Opening balance £m | Finance charge (10%) £m | Cash flow £m | Closing balance £m |
|---|---|---|---|---|
| 19X1 | 100 | 10 | (5.9) | 104.1 |
| 19X2 | 104.1 | 10.4 | (5.9) | 108.6 |
| 19X3 | 108.6 | 10.9 | (5.9) | 113.6 |
| 19X4 | 113.6 | 11.4 | (5.9) | 119.1 |
| 19X5 | 119.1 | 11.9 | (5.9) | 125.1 |
| 19X6 | 125.1 | 12.5 | (14.1) | 123.5 |
| 19X7 | 123.5 | 12.4 | (14.1) | 121.8 |
| 19X8 | 121.8 | 12.2 | (14.1) | 119.9 |
| 19X9 | 119.9 | 12 | (14.1) | 117.8 |
| 19Y0 | 117.8 | 11.8 | (14.1) | 115.5 |
| 19Y1 | 115.5 | 11.6 | (14.1) | 113 |
| 19Y2 | 113 | 11.3 | (14.1) | 110.2 |
| 19Y3 | 110.2 | 11 | (14.1) | 107.1 |
| 19Y4 | 107.1 | 10.7 | (14.1) | 103.7 |
| 19Y5 | 103.7 | 10.4 | (14.1) interest (100) redemption | 0 |

As can be seen, although the debt carries variable interest, the profit and loss account should bear a *constant* rate on the carrying value of the loan; in this case 10% per annum.

3.3 **(c) Deep discounted bonds**

These are a variation on the zero-coupon bonds above. The bonds (usually) carry no interest, rather they are issued at a substantial discount and redeemed at par.

**Example 5.4**

On 1 January 19X1 Eurasia plc issues a £100m bond at a discount of 37.91%. The bond carries no interest and is redeemable at par in five years.

*(The rate of interest inherent in the bond is 10% per annum.)*

## Solution

The loan schedule would be as follows.

| Year ending 31 December | Opening balance £m | Finance charge (10%) £m | Cash flow £m | Closing balance £m |
|---|---|---|---|---|
| 19X1 | (£100m less discount of 37.91%) 62.1 | 6.2 | | 68.3 |
| 19X2 | 68.3 | 6.8 | | 75.1 |
| 19X3 | 75.1 | 7.5 | | 82.6 |
| 19X4 | 82.6 | 8.3 | | 90.9 |
| 19X5 | 90.9 | 9.1 | (100) redemption | 0 |

# FINANCIAL REPORTING, ANALYSIS AND PLANNING

Once again, although the debt carries no interest, the profit and loss account reflects the fact that the deep discount on issue is part of the finance cost of the loan. The loan is initially recorded at its *fair value* of £62.1m.

3.4 *(d) Debt issued with warrants*

This is an example of a hybrid type of capital instrument mentioned earlier. The instrument has characteristics of both a liability and shareholders' funds.

**Example 5.5**

On 1 January 19X1 Ingsoc plc issues debt and warrants together for a total consideration of £125m. The debt is redeemable at £125m in five years and carries interest of 4.7% per annum (£5.9 million on £125m).

The initial question is how to divide the proceeds between the debt (liability) and warrant (shareholders funds) elements. Considering the market values of the debt and the warrants after the issue shows that the fair value of the debt and warrants is, say, £100m and £25m respectively.

*(The rate of interest inherent in the debt/warrant issue is 10% per annum.)*

**Solution**

Initially the debt should be recognised in the books at its fair value of £100m and the warrants in shareholders' funds at £25m.

*1 January 19X1*
Dr. Cash £125m
Cr. Liabilities—Creditors £100m
Cr. Shareholders' funds—Warrants £25m

The loan schedule will be as follows.

| Year ending 31 December | Opening balance £m | Finance charge (10%) £m | Cash flow £m | Closing balance £m |
|---|---|---|---|---|
| 19X1 | 100 | 10 | (5.9) | 104.1 |
| 19X2 | 104.1 | 10.4 | (5.9) | 108.6 |
| 19X3 | 108.6 | 10.9 | (5.9) | 113.6 |
| 19X4 | 113.6 | 11.3 | (5.9) | 119 |
| 19X5 | 119 | 11.9 | (5.9) interest | |
| | | | (125) redemption | 0 |

The profit and loss account should reflect the finance cost of the loan. That is, recognising in effect that £100m was borrowed for five years with a premium on redemption of £25m together with annual interest of £5.9m.

Depending on their terms, the warrants may be exercised at any time during the currency of the debt or after. Assume, for example, that all the warrant holders exercise their right to subscribe, for say 30m £1 ordinary shares in Ingsoc on consideration of one warrant and £1.50 per share.

*Accounting treatment*
Dr. Cash (30m × £1.50) £45m
Dr. Shareholders funds—Warrants £25m
Cr. Share capital £30m
Cr. Share premium account £40m

*\* Share issue @ £1.50 plus one warrant per share \**

# ACCOUNTING FOR LIABILITIES

The premium on the share issue can be proved as follows:

|  | £m |
|---|---|
| Proceeds from original debt/warrant issue | 125 |
| Less debt element | (100) |
| Net proceeds from warrant issue | 25 |
| Warrant exercise proceeds | 45 |
| Total proceeds | 70 |
| Less nominal value of shares issued | (30) |
| Premium | 40 |

3.5 *(e) Repackaged perpetual debt*

Occasionally debt is issued carrying a relatively high interest rate for a period, followed by a period of nominal/zero interest. The debt may be irredeemable.

The high interest early period is usually referred to as the primary period and the later period the secondary period.

**Example 5.6**

On 1 January 19X1 Soma plc issued an irredeemable bond for proceeds of £125m. The bond carries interest of 16.275% per annum (£20.3m) for a primary period of ten years, with no further interest payments after that.

*(The rate of interest inherent in the bond is 10% per annum.)*

**Solution**

In substance, we can see that Soma is borrowing £125m over *a ten year period* – not indefinitely. The value of the bond at the end of the primary period will be *zero* as henceforth it will carry no interest. Therefore, to Soma, the finance cost of the bond incorporates the high interest payments in the primary period, mitigated by the fact that the principal of £125m never needs to be repaid.

*(The rate of interest inherent in the bond is 10%.)*

The loan schedule would be as follows.

| Year ending 31 December | Opening balance £m | Finance charge (10%) £m | Cash flow £m | Closing balance £m |
|---|---|---|---|---|
| 19X1 | 125 | 12.5 | (20.3) | 117.2 |
| 19X2 | 117.2 | 11.7 | (20.3) | 108.6 |
| 19X3 | 108.6 | 10.8 | (20.3) | 99.1 |
| 19X4 | 99.1 | 9.9 | (20.3) | 88.7 |
| 19X5 | 88.7 | 8.8 | (20.3) | 77.2 |
| 19X6 | 77.2 | 7.7 | (20.3) | 64.6 |
| 19X7 | 64.6 | 6.4 | (20.3) | 50.7 |
| 19X8 | 50.7 | 5 | (20.3) | 35.4 |
| 19X9 | 35.4 | 3.5 | (20.3) | 18.6 |
| 19Y0 | 18.6 | 1.7 * | (20.3) | 0 |

\* *rounding*

Note that at the end of ten years the bond has been written down to zero, even though it is technically irredeemable. Note also, that although the bond carries a high coupon rate of 16.275%, the effect of the non-redemption brings the effective rate down to 10% per annum.

# FINANCIAL REPORTING, ANALYSIS AND PLANNING

3.6    *(f) Variable rate/Index linked loans*

*Variable rates*

Sometimes debt is issued that does not carry a specific interest/repayment rate. Instead the terms of the debt include a formula to base future repayments and interest. A simple example is a floating rate loan at say 4% over Base Rate. To calculate the rate to be used in the financial statements, we would have to use the variable rate currently in force as well as adjusting for any premium on redemption or non-redemption variation seen above.

*Index linked loans*

These type of loans carry the feature that the repayable value of the loan is uprated at each year end with reference to an index—for example the Retail Price Index. The loan will usually also carry a nominal rate of interest as well.

**Example 5.7**

On 1 January 19X1 Proles plc issues a loan for £125m, carrying 6% (£7.5m) interest. The loan is uprated at the end of every year with reference to an index. The loan is redeemable in five years time.

| Index at end of year | Index |
|---|---|
| 19X0 | 100 |
| 19X1 | 106 |
| 19X2 | 108 |
| 19X3 | 116 |
| 19X4 | 122 |
| 19X5 | 132 |

**Solution**

The loan schedule would be as follows.

| Year ending 31 December | Opening balance | Finance charge (balancing figure) | Cash flow | Closing balance | |
|---|---|---|---|---|---|
| | £m | £m | £m | £m | |
| 19X1 | 125 | 15 | (7.5) | 132.5 | 125 × 106/100 |
| 19X2 | 132.5 | 10 | (7.5) | 135 | 132.5 × 108/106 |
| 19X3 | 135 | 17.5 | (7.5) | 145 | 135 × 116/108 |
| 19X4 | 145 | 15 | (7.5) | 152.5 | 145 × 122/116 |
| 19X5 | 152.5 | 20 | (165) redemption | | 152.5 × 132/122 |
| | | | (7.5) interest | 0 | |

The financing charge comprises two elements (i) the uplift in relation to the index and (ii) the 6% nominal interest rate. Thus, for example, in 19X2 the index rises from 106 to 108. Therefore the index element finance charge is (108 − 106)/106 × carrying value £132.5m = £2.5m. Added to the 6% nominal interest of £7.5m (6% × £125m) gives the total finance charge of £10m.

ACCOUNTING FOR LIABILITIES

## Student Activity 1

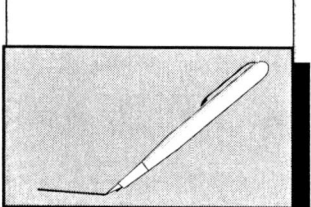

Before reading the next section of text, answer the following questions and then check your answers against the paragraph(s) indicated.

1. Define a liability. *(Paragraph 1.3)*
2. Distinguish between equity and non-equity shareholders funds *(Paragraph 1.8)*
3. Distinguish between convertible and non-convertible liabilities. *(Paragraph 1.9)*
4. List and explain the three main principles in accounting for capital instruments. *(Paragraph 2.1)*

If your answers are basically correct, then proceed to the next section. If significant parts of your answers are wrong, then study the whole of the relevant sections again in detail. Note your areas of weakness and be prepared for further questions on these areas at the end of this Unit.

## 4 Post balance sheet events

4.1 Post balance sheet events (PBSE) are incidents that occur between the company's year end and the publication of the company's accounts. SSAP 17 'Accounting for Post Balance Sheet Events' indicates that the financial statements need to take account of circumstances after the reporting year end. The standard distinguishes between the following:

(a) adjusting events

(b) non-adjusting events.

4.2 The distinction between the two is that adjusting events are those which provide additional evidence about *conditions existing at the balance sheet date* thus indicating that the balance sheet, if unadjusted, could give a misleading impression of how things stood at the time.

4.3 Non-adjusting events are those that have occurred since the year end but which *do not relate to a condition existing at the year end.*

4.4 Examples of adjusting events:

- debtor insolvency
- evidence concerning the net realisable value of stock
- evidence concerning the profitability of a long term contract
- a change in the valuation of property
- an amendment to a dividend payable or receivable.

4.5 Examples of non-adjusting events:

- disasters such as fires or floods
- shares or loan stock issues
- take-overs/mergers
- strikes
- major purchases or disposals of fixed assets
- closure or opening of areas of operation.

# FINANCIAL REPORTING, ANALYSIS AND PLANNING

**Accounting treatment**

4.6  As the name suggests, SSAP17 requires that adjusting events be adjusted in the financial statements for the year. If necessary the requirements of FRS3 'Reporting financial performance' can be followed with appropriate disclosure if the PBSE is an 'exceptional' or 'extraordinary' item (see Unit 6).

### Example 5.8

Doublespeak Limited's year end is 31 December 19X1. At the year end debtors stood at £1,400,000, including £300,000 owed by Truth Limited. On 1 March 19X2, Doublespeak discovers that Truth has gone into administrative receivership and that creditors are likely to get only 10p in the £. At 1 March 19X2, Truth owed Doublespeak £360,000.

### Solution

In the year end accounts Doublespeak should write off 90% of the year end debts owed by Truth i.e. £300,000 × 90% = £270,000. The £270,000 should be charged to Doublespeak's Profit and loss account—possibly as an exceptional item if appropriate.

4.7  Non-adjusting events, again as the name suggests, do not need to be incorporated in the year end accounts. However the PBSE may need to be *disclosed*, in a note to the accounts, in order that readers can get a fuller picture of the company's activities.

4.8  Finally a non-adjusting event could turn into an adjusting event. This would be under the unusual circumstances where the non-adjusting PBSE was so serious that it called into question the going concern concept.

### Example 5.9

Julia Limited's year end is 31 December 19X1. On 13 February 19X2 a catastrophic fire destroyed the company's main centre of operations. The loss was insured only for the physical damage and not the resulting loss of turnover and profits. How should we account for the fire in the accounts for the year ended 31 December 19X1?

### Solution

Normally such a post year end fire would be a non-adjusting event, with appropriate disclosure in the accounts if necessary. However, because of the catastrophic nature of the fire the appropriateness of the going concern concept has been called into account. Thus the company should account for the effects of the loss; the actual losses (if any are uninsured); any penalty clauses arising from cancelled contracts; if the whole business is in jeopardy, reclassification of fixed assets into current assets; revaluation of assets to realisable values; provisions for redundancy, insolvency costs, etc.

**Window dressing**

4.9  This is an attempt by accounts preparers to deliberately alter the impression of a business by changing certain features just before the balance sheet date. The reversing transaction occurs after the year end. A fairly innocuous

# ACCOUNTING FOR LIABILITIES

example would be issuing cheques to creditors before the year end thereby reducing year end creditors, but not actually sending out the cheques. After the year end the cheques would be eventually not issued or even cancelled.

4.10 Other more sophisticated schemes could involve the sale of an asset, at a large profit, prior to the year end, with a repurchase shortly after the year end. Such schemes have been addressed under FRS5 'Reporting the substance of transactions' (see Unit 6)

## 5 Contingencies

5.1 A contingency is described as 'a condition which exists at the balance sheet date, where the outcome will be confirmed only on the occurrence or non-occurrence of one or more uncertain future events'. A contingent gain or loss is a gain or loss dependent on a contingency.

5.2 As can be seen from the definition, contingencies arise from *uncertainties*. Therefore there is no prescribed way of accounting for all contingencies. Under SSAP18 'Accounting for contingencies', exercise of judgment is required. The standard gives a rule of thumb table for dealing with contingencies.

| *Likelihood* | *Contingent gain* | *Contingent loss* |
|---|---|---|
| Remote | No action required | No action required |
| Possible | No action required | Disclose |
| Probable | Disclose | Make a provision |
| (Reasonably) certain | Treat as accrued income | Make a provision |

5.3 The Companies Act 1985 does not recognise contingent gains, but contains similar principles to SSAP18 regarding contingent losses.

### Disclosure

5.4 The nature of the event, an estimate of the likely financial effects and an indication of the activating events should all be disclosed.

### Accounting treatment

5.5 The treatment for contingencies is a prime example of the application of the prudence concept. The concept requires recognition of potential losses and non-recognition of potential gains.

5.6 In practice the distinction between the categories of probability above are not easy to make. In the examination it is well to consider the surrounding circumstances in making a judgment as to the likelihood of the contingency crystallising. However, also be aware of the need to accrue for associated expenses. Example 5.10 illustrates this.

### Example 5.10

Epsilon Limited is being sued by a customer for breach of contract. The plaintiff is claiming damages of £100,000 from Epsilon.

# FINANCIAL REPORTING, ANALYSIS AND PLANNING

*Evaluation*

The key judgment to make is how likely is it that the customer's claim will succeed? In an exam situation the question will usually indicate the degree of probability of success. If, for instance, the question states that the plaintiff has a 50% chance of success, that could be interpreted as 'Probable' and hence an accrual should be made. In any event the company will need to accrue for the expected legal costs in defending the claim.

If the plaintiff has a reasonably certain chance of success, say 85%, then in fact this is not a contingency, and the company should make provision for the loss (and any anticipated legal expenses). Be careful to state what assumptions you are making and if in doubt apply the overriding prudence concept.

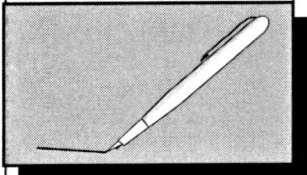

## Student Activity 2

Before reading the next section of text, answer the following questions and then check your answers against the paragraph(s) indicated.

1. Define a post balance sheet event *(Paragraph 4.1)*

2. Give four examples of adjusting and non-adjusting post balance sheet events. *(Paragraphs 4.4 & 4.5)*

3. Under what circumstances might a non-adjusting event become an adjusting event? *(Example 5.9)*

4. Define a contingency. *(Paragraph 5.1)*

5. How should a probable contingency be accounted for? *(Paragraph 5.2)*

If your answers are basically correct, then proceed to the next section. If significant parts of your answers are wrong, then study the whole of the relevant sections again in detail. Note your areas of weakness and be prepared for further questions on these areas at the end of this Unit.

## 6 Pension costs

6.1 Accounting for pension costs is important because of the large sums usually involved. For some companies the value of the company's pension fund can exceed that of its own assets. Companies with valuable pension funds can be vulnerable to take-over, not because of the value of the business, but due to the hidden value within the companies' pension funds. Also, the potential liabilities can be significant as has been seen recently in certain notorious fraud cases.

6.2 Prior to the introduction of SSAP24 'Accounting for pension costs', accounting for pensions was very simple. In essence, the P/L account charge equalled the cash paid. SSAP24 introduced an accruals basis in accounting for pension costs. Before considering the details of the standard, first let us look at the different types of pension schemes that a company may have.

6.3 Pension funds can either be funded or unfunded. With unfunded schemes the assets and obligations of the company to its current and future pensioners are *not* separately accounted for; they are incorporated within the company's

# ACCOUNTING FOR LIABILITIES

own balance sheet. Much more common is a funded scheme, where the company sets up a pension fund, administered by trustees, to look after pension funds assets and discharge pension liabilities.

6.4 The company makes contributions to the scheme and the scheme pays out pensions to the company's pensioners. There are two types of pension scheme: *defined benefit schemes* and *defined contribution schemes.*

## Defined benefit scheme

6.5 Under such a scheme the eventual benefits paid to the employee are determined by a pre-set formula, usually linked to the employee's salary immediately prior to retirement. For example, the scheme may entitle the pensioner to 50% of his/her salary on retirement. Or with a scheme common in many governmental organisations, the pensioner is entitled to one-eightieth of his/her salary as a pension, for every year of pensionable employment. So if an employee joined the company in 1960 and retired in 1995, he will be entitled to 35/80ths of his final salary as a pension. In addition the schemes usually allow for a lump sum payable on retirement; the amount usually again linked to the level of final salary.

6.6 The defined benefit scheme obligates the company. The company has a contractual commitment to pay its employee a pension, at an unknown amount, from retirement (which may be an unknown future date) until the employee's death—which is an unknown future date. As can be appreciated there are a significant number of uncertainties; the *exact* value of the company's liability cannot be assessed.

6.7 Under such a scheme the *benefits define the contributions*. The company, on the advice of an actuary, will make contributions to the scheme (and usually take contributions from the employee) sufficient to fund the estimated likely future obligation.

## Defined contribution scheme

6.8 Under such a scheme the opposite applies; *the contributions define the benefits*. In simple terms the pensioner receives what is in the fund at the time of his/her retirement. The company does not have an obligation to pay out a set percentage of salary nor a set lump sum. The company and the employee may make contributions towards a goal of funding a set level of pension but there is no obligation for the company to pay that sum.

6.9 As can be seen this type of scheme is potentially less onerous for the company. The burden of risk lies with the future pensioner not the company.

## The pension fund

6.10 The fund is usually administered by trustees who may or may not be separate from the company. One of the ramifications of the Maxwell pension scandal was a move to divorce the management of the company from the administration of the pension fund. The pension fund will hold assets, long term and short term and will settle the liabilities of the scheme.

6.11 The income of the fund is normally from three sources (i) investment income (ii) contributions from the employer (iii) contributions from the employee

# FINANCIAL REPORTING, ANALYSIS AND PLANNING

(this does not occur in all schemes—certain employers run *non-contributory* pension schemes).

6.12 The expenses of the fund fall into two categories (i) administration expenses (ii) pension obligations.

6.13 The pension fund is required to prepare its own audited accounts.

**Role of the actuary**

6.14 The actuary is an expert whose role is assess the level of contributions the company (and its employees if appropriate) need to make in order for the fund to discharge its current and future liabilities. The actuary will also take into account the investment income the fund will generate. Some of the variables that the actuary has to consider are:

- the age profile of the employees
- the likely length of service of the employees
- future salary increases
- economic factors; future taxation, inflation, interest rates, etc.
- the likely future performance of the pension fund investments.

6.15 The scheme will be bound by its own rules and relevant tax legislation. For example, there may be a maximum level of contributions, a minimum period of service before eligibility for joining the scheme, a maximum final pension entitlement.

6.16 The actuary has to take all these factors into account when assessing the level of contributions that the company (and the employee) has to make. Usually the employer contributes a percentage of current salary. For example, under the Local Authority Superannuation Scheme (mentioned above) the employee contributes 6% of salary.

6.17 As can be imagined with all the variables outlined above, the actual performance of the fund will invariably differ from the forecast performance. The investments may perform more favourably, final salaries may rise by more than was anticipated, the employees may even live longer than expected after retirement. When such differences arise, unless the differences are compensating, the scheme will be in deficit or surplus.

**Scheme surpluses or deficits**

6.18 The remedy is usually quite simple—in the event of a deficit the company contributes more; in the event of a surplus the company contributes less (or even has a 'contributions holiday). Note that the obligation is on the *company* to remedy the deficit, or it is the company that benefits from the surplus.

ACCOUNTING FOR LIABILITIES

## 7 Accounting for pension costs (SSAP24)

### Defined benefit scheme

7.1 The company has to account for the annual payments it makes to the pension scheme and any extra payments it has to make in the event of a scheme deficit. Equally it has to account for any periods when reduced or zero contributions are payable due to a scheme surplus.

7.2 As mentioned earlier, prior to SSAP24, the actual cash paid to the scheme represented the P/L charge for the period. Thus, for instance, in the event of a contributions holiday, there would have been no profit and loss charge that year. Or in the event of a fund deficit, any shortfall made up by the company through increased contributions would be directly charged to the profit and loss account in the period of the extra payment.

7.3 This policy clashed with the fundamental matching concept. By only accounting on a cash basis the company, for example, took advantage and full account of the pension fund surplus *immediately and only over one accounting period*. More appropriate would have been to match the benefit with the periods expected to benefit, i.e. the remaining service lives of the employees.

7.4 SSAP24 introduced the principle of spreading fund surpluses or deficits *over the expected remaining service lives of the current employees*. The rationale is the matching concept together with the recognition that the current employees are (i) contributing to future and current pension obligations and (ii) are providing the company with *benefits* (in terms of their contribution to the company's operations) which are *matched* against *costs* (i.e. pension obligations, current and future).

7.5 The profit and loss charge is calculated by adding the 'regular ongoing cost' to any fund surplus/deficit spread over the remaining service life of the employees.

$$\text{Regular cost} \quad \text{less} \quad \frac{\text{Surplus}}{\text{Remaining service lives}}$$

or

$$\text{Regular cost} \quad \text{plus} \quad \frac{\text{Deficit}}{\text{Remaining service lives}}$$

7.6 The balance sheet figure is the residual after deducting the actual cash paid and is classified either as a prepayment or an accrual.

### Example 5.11

Telescreen Limited's pension fund shows a £24m surplus. The company's regular contribution to the scheme is £5m per annum. An actuary recommends that the company reduce its contributions by £3m for the next few years to eliminate the surplus. The average remaining service life of the company's employees is 12 years.

# FINANCIAL REPORTING, ANALYSIS AND PLANNING

**Solution**

*Profit and loss account*

Apply the formula:

$$\text{Regular cost} - \frac{\text{Surplus}}{\text{Remaining service lives}}$$

$$£5m - \frac{£24m}{12} = £3m$$

| *Balance sheet* | £m |
|---|---|
| Profit and loss charge | 3 |
| less cash paid (£5m less £3m reduction in contribution) | (2) |
| Accrual | 1 |

### Exceptions to the spreading surpluses/deficits rule

7.7 There are two main instances when the general rule that any surpluses or deficits should be spread over the remaining service lives of employees does not apply:

(a) significant reduction in the number of employees

(b) material deficits recognised over a shorter period.

### (a) Significant reduction in the number of employees

7.8 For example, a company may undertake a significant downsizing operation. As a result it may shed large numbers of employees. The departing employees, as part of their leaving package will normally receive redundancy pay (usually linked to length of service and final salary—in a similar manner to a defined benefit pension scheme). The departees may also lose their entitlements to future pensions as part of the package or they may keep their pension rights. In any event it is not logical to still account for their interest in the pension scheme. The cost of providing for the pensions of the departed employees should be accounted for as part of the reorganisation costs. In addition, when considering the position of the pension fund it is inconsistent to use the service lives of the *remaining employees* to spread a surplus or deficit *partly caused by the departing employees.*

### Example 5.12

Hatcheries plc's pension fund valuation shows a surplus of £20m. According to the actuary, half of the surplus is due to the recent significant reduction in the company's staff. The remaining service life of the company's employees is 10 years. The ongoing regular cost will be £6m per annum. The company didn't make any contributions to the scheme in the year because of the existing surplus.

# ACCOUNTING FOR LIABILITIES

**Solution**

*Profit and loss account*

Apply the formula:

Regular cost    less    $\dfrac{\text{Surplus attributable to } \textit{remaining} \text{ employees}}{\text{Remaining service lives}}$

£6m    less    $\dfrac{£20m \times 1/2 = £10m}{10}$    =    £5m

*Balance sheet*                                                                £m

Profit and loss charge                                                           5
less cash paid                                                                 (0)
Accrual                                                                          5

7.9 Incidentally, the £10m pension fund surplus arising from the significant reduction in the number of employees can, in certain circumstances, be used to offset the redundancy costs. Under an amendment brought in by FRS3, where the cost/credit results from a significant number of employees related to the *sale or termination of an operation*, then the credit/charge should be recognised immediately.

7.10 Thus, assuming that Hatcheries plc did sell or terminate an operation, the pension fund surplus of £10m could be offset in the profit and loss account against the cost of the termination.

## (b) Material deficits recognised over a shorter period

7.11 This arises from an application of the prudence concept. It may be felt that in the case of a material deficit it is imprudent to spread the deficit over the remaining service lives of the existing employees. The standard allows the deficit to be spread over a *shorter period* (not charged in full immediately) on the grounds of prudence. This is only allowed where (i) additional contributions are necessary and (ii) the deficit is as a result of external factors, outside the normal scope of actuarial assumptions.

### Example 5.13

Victory plc's pension fund, wholly due to a major fraud by the trustees, shows a deficit of £50m. The company has been advised to increase its contributions from the usual £3m per annum, to £10m. The average remaining service lives of the employees is 10 years; however because of the nature of the fund deficit the company has decided to write the deficit off over four years.

**Solution**

*Profit and loss account*

Apply the formula:

Regular cost    add    $\dfrac{\text{Deficit}}{\text{Write off period}}$

# FINANCIAL REPORTING, ANALYSIS AND PLANNING

£3m  add  $\dfrac{£50m}{4}$ = £15.5m

*Balance sheet* £m

Profit and loss charge 15.5
less cash paid (10)
Accrual 5.5

## Defined contribution scheme

7.12 Accounting for defined contribution schemes is much simpler than that for defined benefit schemes. The profit and loss charge is simply the accrued contribution for that period. The balance sheet entry is for any prepaid or accrued contributions.

### Student Activity 3

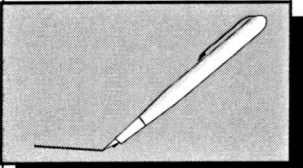

Before reading the next section of text, answer the following questions and then check your answers against the paragraph(s) indicated.

1. Explain how a defined benefit pension scheme operates.  *(Paragraph 6.5 - 6.7)*

2. What is the likely income and expenditure of a pension fund?
   *(Paragraphs 6.11 - 6.12)*

3. Describe the role of a pension fund actuary.  *(Paragraphs 6.14 - 6.16)*

4. Under SSAP24, how is the pension charge in the profit and loss account calculated?  *(Paragraph 7.5)*

5. What are the two exceptions to the general rule of spreading fund surpluses and deficits over the remaining service lives of employees?  *(Paragraph 7.7)*

If your answers are basically correct, then proceed to the next section. If significant parts of your answers are wrong, then study the whole of the relevant sections again in detail. Note your areas of weakness and be prepared for further questions on these areas at the end of this Unit.

# ACCOUNTING FOR LIABILITIES

> **Summary**
>
> Now that you have completed this Unit you should be able to:
>
> ☐ define a liability and distinguish between liabilities and shareholders funds
>
> ☐ outline the differences between convertible and non-convertible liabilities
>
> ☐ distinguish between equity and non-equity shareholders funds
>
> ☐ explain the treatment for dealing with various types of capital instruments as outlined by FRS4
>
> ☐ identify and account for post balance sheet events in accordance with SSAP17
>
> ☐ account for contingent gains and losses in accordance with the provisions of SSAP18
>
> ☐ identify different types of pension scheme and explain their importance in the preparation of financial statements
>
> ☐ outline the role of the pension fund actuary and explain why fund deficits or surpluses may arise
>
> ☐ apply the provisions of SSAP24 in general situations and in exceptional circumstances.

## Self-assessment questions

### Short answer questions

1. Explain the principles in accounting for capital instruments.

2. Why should a user of company accounts be interested in events after the balance sheet date?

3. Discuss how the application of the prudence concept affects the company's treatment of contingencies.

4. Why is accounting for pension costs a difficult area in accounting?

5. How should a fund surplus or deficit be accounted for?

*(Answers are given in the Appendix)*

### Multiple choice questions

1. According to the ASB's *Statement of Principles*, liabilities result from past transactions or events and are:

   (a) amounts owed by an enterprise

   (b) debts owed by an enterprise

   (c) obligations to transfer funds

   (d) obligations to transfer economic benefits.

2. Redsash plc issued a £2m bond at a deep discount, for £1,241,800 on 1 January 19X1. The bond carries no interest and is redeemable at par in five years time.

   Assuming the bond carries an inherent interest rate of 10%, what is the carrying value of the bond in one year's time and the finance charge for 19X1?

   |     | Carrying value £000 | Interest charge £000 |
   | --- | --- | --- |
   | (a) | 2,000 | 200 |
   | (b) | 2,000 | 124 |
   | (c) | 1,366 | 200 |
   | (d) | 1,366 | 124 |

3. Which of the following statements is correct?

   (a) The debt should be initially recorded at fair value with the finance cost allocated to periods so as to produce a constant rate of interest on the carrying amount.

   (b) The debt should be initially recorded at nominal value with the finance cost allocated to periods so as to produce a constant rate of interest on the carrying amount.

   (c) The debt should be initially recorded at fair value with the finance cost allocated to periods so as to produce a constant rate of interest on the nominal amount.

   (d) The debt should be initially recorded at nominal value with the finance cost allocated to periods so as to produce a constant rate of interest on the nominal amount.

4. Which of the following is *not* an adjusting post balance event:

   (a) discovery that a year end debtor is now insolvent

   (b) collapse in the market price of company year end stock

   (c) discovery that the attributable profit taken on a long term contract is inappropriate

   (d) payment of the year end corporation tax at a different amount to that anticipated in the year end accounts.

5. According to SSAP18 how should probable contingent gains and losses be accounted for?

   |     | Gains | Losses |
   | --- | --- | --- |
   | (a) | Accrue | Provide |
   | (b) | Disclose only | Provide |
   | (c) | Disclose only | Disclose only |
   | (d) | Ignore | Disclose only |

6. Gamma Limited's pension fund shows a £12m surplus. The remaining service life of the company's employees is eight years. The company's actuary recommends that the company's regular contribution of £3m be reduced by

## ACCOUNTING FOR LIABILITIES

£2m over the next few years to eliminate the surplus. What is the pension fund charge and the balance sheet figure?

|     | P/L charge £m | B/S figure £m |
| --- | --- | --- |
| (a) | 1.5 | 0.5 accrual |
| (b) | 1.5 | 0.5 prepayment |
| (c) | 3.0 | 1.0 prepayment |
| (d) | 4.5 | 3.5 accrual |

*(Answers are given in the Appendix)*

### Exam style questions

Note: to assist in dealing with the information given in points 7 and 8 of this question relating to taxation and dividends see Unit 7.

1. The following trial balance has been prepared for Moonitz plc as at 31 March 1995.

| Trial Balance at 31 March 1995 | £000 | £000 |
| --- | --- | --- |
| Ordinary share capital (£1 shares) | | 2,000 |
| Retained profit at 1 April 1994 | | 2,726 |
| Revaluation reserve at 1 April 1994 | | 2,200 |
| 12% debentures redeemable 2001 | | 5,000 |
| Debenture redemption reserve at 1 April 1994 | | 3,250 |
| Trade creditors and accruals | | 2,602 |
| Turnover | | 49,100 |
| Cash in hand | 5 | |
| Bank balance | | 216 |
| Freehold properties at valuation | 8,200 | |
| Proceeds from sale of freehold property | | 3,150 |
| Plant and machinery at cost | 12,240 | |
| Accumulated depreciation on plant and machinery at 1 April 1994 | | 2,150 |
| Stocks at 31 March 1995 | 3,685 | |
| Trade debtors and prepayments | 5,194 | |
| Cost of goods sold | 37,000 | |
| Administration, selling and distribution costs | 4,375 | |
| Debenture interest paid 30 September 1994 | 300 | |
| Interim dividend paid | 400 | |
| Goodwill arising on acquisition of Stamp & Co. | 1,400 | |
| Provision for deferred taxation | | 405 |
| | 72,799 | 72,799 |

You are given the following additional information.

1. It is the directors' policy to make an annual transfer of £250,000 to the debenture redemption reserve in anticipation of the redemption to take place in the year 2001.

2. The company sold a freehold property, surplus to requirements, for £3,150,000 on 1 April 1994. The property had initially cost £2,000,000 and is included in the above trial balance at £2,750,000. The proceeds were

used to acquire the business assets of Stamp & Co on 1 April 1994. The goodwill arising on this acquisition is estimated to have a useful economic life of seven years.

3. The remaining freehold properties were revalued at £9,650,000 on 1 April 1994. It is the company's policy not to depreciate freehold properties, on the grounds that their lives are so long and residual values so high that depreciation is insignificant.

4. In April 1995 the company's entire stock of widgets, which had been damaged by a flood in March, were sold off for £63,000. The widgets, which were uninsured, are included in the above trial balance at £150,000.

5. The figure for administration, selling and distribution costs includes repairs required as the result of storm damage amounting to £75,000. It has become apparent that the company is under-insured and it has been offered £40,000 by the insurance company. There is a possibility that the insurers can be persuaded to increase the offer to £52,000.

6. The company issued 100,000 ordinary shares of £1 each for £3 per share in April 1995.

7. A provision should be made for corporation tax of £2,120,000. In addition, a transfer of £124,000 should be made from the deferred taxation account.

8. The directors plan to propose a final dividend of 30 pence per share. The rate of ACT is 20/80.

9. Due to a fundamental error made by the team responsible for counting the stock at 31 March 1994, stock was included in last year's accounts at £3,816,000 instead of £3,310,000.

10. A depreciation charge of £1,750,000 is required in respect of plant and machinery.

**Required**

(a) The following financial statements for Moonitz plc for the year to 31 March 1995:

(i) the profit and loss account and appropriation account; [9]

(ii) the statement of movements on reserves; [6]

(iii) the balance sheet. [9]

*Notes:*

1. The accounts need not comply with the detailed requirements of the Companies Act concerning layout, but should be presented in 'good form' and comply with standard accounting practice so far as the information permits.

2. Notes to the accounts are not required.

(b) Explain the significance of the information, given in notes 4-6, for the final accounts of Moonitz plc for the year to 31 March 1995. [6]

[Total 30]

## ACCOUNTING FOR LIABILITIES

2. The following balances relate to the affairs of Willett plc as at 3 April 1995.

|  | £ |
|---|---|
| Value added tax payable | 37,500 |
| Advance corporation tax payable | 20,000 |
| Mainstream corporation tax payable | 153,700 |
| Provision for deferred taxation | 75,100 |
| Proposed dividends | 80,000 |
| Stocks | 375,400 |
| Tangible fixed assets at cost or revalued amount | 3,850,000 |
| Cash at bank and in hand | 12,600 |
| Issued share capital | 1,000,000 |
| Share premium account | 220,000 |
| Investment in Armstrong Ltd | 750,000 |
| Trade creditors and accruals | 262,100 |
| Revaluation reserve | 950,000 |

**Required**

(a) (i) Prepare the balance sheet of Willett plc as at 30 April 1995. Retained profit should be inserted as the balancing item. The balance sheet should be prepared in good form, but need not comply with the requirements of the Companies Act concerning layout. [8]

  (ii) Identify *two* categories of business assets which might belong to Willet plc but are not normally reported in the balance sheet. Why are they excluded? [4]

(b) Explain briefly the purpose of FRS5 entitled 'Reporting the Substance of Transactions'. Give one example of a 'special purpose transaction' and indicate the way in which FRS5 requires it to be treated in the accounts. [8]

[Total 20]

## Further reading

FRS4 'Capital instruments'

SSAP17 'Accounting for post balance sheet events

SSAP18 'Accounting for contingencies'

SSAP24 'Accounting for pension costs'

# Unit 6

## Financial Statements

### Objectives

After studying this Unit you should be able to:

- understand the rationale for the introduction of FRS3 'Reporting financial performance'

- apply the principles of FRS3 and compile a layered profit and loss account, statement of total recognised gains and losses, reconciliation of shareholders' funds and note of historical profits

- account for leases in accordance with SSAP21 'Accounting for leases and hire purchase contracts'

- identify and account for situations where the economic substance of a transaction differs from its legal form

- understand the principles of FRS5 'Reporting the substance of transactions' and apply the standard to various situations

- calculate earnings per share in accordance with FRS14 'Earnings per share'

- apply the conventions of SSAP25 'Segmental reporting' in reporting the segmented operations of enterprises

- consider alternative reports to stakeholders such as employee reports

- account for grants in accordance with SSAP4 'Accounting for government grants'.

## 1 Introduction

1.1 This Unit covers four broad areas; two of major import and two of secondary concern. First we will consider the landmark standard FRS3 'Reporting financial performance'; its rationale, its content and its effect. Secondly, we will consider the equally important area concerning the need for accounts to reflect commercial substance rather than strict legal form. The third part of the Unit looks at alternative reports to stakeholders. Finally the relatively minor area of accounting for government grants is addressed.

## 2 Reporting financial performance

**Purpose of financial statements**

2.1 The purpose of financial statements is to convey information to the users of those statements about the enterprise's financial position, financial performance and financial adaptability. The users' needs are varied. However, for bankers the primary need is information to assess the enterprise's ability to remain profitable, to repay outstanding or future borrowings; in short its ability to survive.

2.2 Previously, we have seen the standard formats required by the Companies Act 1985. The formats prescribing a profit and loss account and balance sheet together with associated notes set a minimum level of disclosure and style of presentation—all designed to furnish users with the information they require.

2.3 The Accounting Standards Board have set out their objectives for financial reporting: providing information on the three 'Financials' (position, performance and adaptability) to a wide range of users, to assist them in decision making and assessing stewardship.

2.4 As part of this ongoing programme to improve financial reporting, the ASB have introduced new standards, for example the Cashflow Statement (see Units 12 and 13). However their main thrust to facilitate improvements in corporate reporting has been through FRS3 'Reporting Financial performance, introduced in 1993. FRS3 is a wide ranging standard. Its chief components are:

- replacement of SSAP6 'Extraordinary items'
- a new 'layered' profit and loss account
- the introduction of a new primary financial statement—the 'statement of total recognised gains and losses' (SORG)
- amendments to the now obsolete SSAP 3 'Earnings per share'.

2.5 FRS3 is an attempt to prevent some of the abuses that companies used to present financial information in a more than justified favourable light. For example, reform of SSAP6 has virtually 'abolished' extraordinary items. Previously, companies could classify bad news items such as restructuring costs as extraordinary items, presented 'below the line'; and leaving earnings per share and profit on ordinary activities before taxation unaffected.

2.6 The chief reform within FRS3 is the new presentation of information in the profit and loss account. Bankers use the profit and loss account to:

- analysis and comprehend past performance
- predict future performance
- assess and forecast resulting cash flows.

2.7 In order to assess the above the user has to have sufficient information to answer such questions as:

- where is the company generating its profits from?
- how will closure of a business segment affect next year's profit and cash flow?

FINANCIAL STATEMENTS

- what affect has that new acquisition had on profit and cash flow?

2.8 FRS3 requires company results to be presented in three segments: Continuing, ongoing operations, Discontinued operations and new Acquired operations; together with previous period comparatives. Thus the underlying performance of the company can be more easily assessed. The impact of the new business acquired during the year can be appraised, the effect of the closure of a segment of operations can be analysed. Note that FRS3 only presents this information in *profit* terms. The effect in cash flow terms is not analysed. This is an additional factor the banker has to account for.

## 3 Replacement of SSAP6

3.1 FRS3 replaced the old SSAP6 'Extraordinary items and prior year adjustments'. The definition of an extraordinary item has been changed, the criteria tightened. The effect has been to make extraordinary items extremely rare. In the year following the release of FRS3, the accounts of the top 100 companies were surveyed by Coopers & Lybrand, the chartered accountants. None of the companies surveyed showed an extraordinary item. In a previous survey, prior to FRS3, over half the companies surveyed showed an extraordinary item.

**Definition**

3.2 *Extraordinary items* are items which are:

- material
- derive from outside the ordinary course of business
- not expected to recur
- highly abnormal in nature.

3.3 It is this last criteria which distinguished the requirements of FRS3 from that of SSAP6. Previously, certain profit and loss items, even if they occurred on a regular basis, could have been classified as extraordinary. The prime instance was provisions for re-organisations; which were invariably classified as extraordinary items, even though they recurred fairly regularly. In essence such expenses were the result of the normal ongoing reviews of operations that companies undertook. Frequently companies only classified items as extraordinary if they were debits. Beneficial items were not classified as extraordinary; instead they were left to boost profit on ordinary activities.

3.4 The importance of protecting the profit on ordinary activities derived from the key Earnings per Share (EPS) ratio. If a debit item could be classified as extraordinary, then often it was. The auditors were invariably in compliance because of the liberal way in which the old SSAP could be interpreted. The EPS figure was left unaffected.

**Effect of 'abolition' of extraordinary items**

3.5 The main effect has been that earnings (profit after tax) have become much more volatile. Previous one-off items which would have counted as extraordinary are now shown 'above the line', i.e. as part of profit on ordinary activities. Thus arguably it is now harder to interpret the results and trend of companies over a period of time. In fact, some analysts attempt to get behind the published figures and search for a measure of maintainable earnings, eliminating items which previously would have qualified as extraordinary. However, in addition to tightening the rules on extraordinary items the ASB reformatted the profit and loss account to give more information as to the sources of income and expenses.

**Exceptional items and prior period adjustments**

3.6 Definitions

*Exceptional items* are items which are:

- material
- derive from the company's ordinary course of business
- exceptional due to size or incidence.

3.7 Exceptional items need to be disclosed because failure to disclose would not enable users to obtain a full picture of the company's results.

3.8 In the survey quoted above, 30% of the companies surveyed showed an exceptional item in their accounts. These included reorganisation costs (e.g. redundancy provisions), provisions for environmental liabilities, current asset write downs and provisions for losses on contracts.

*Prior period adjustments*

3.9 These result from either a change in accounting policy or correction of a fundamental error. A fundamental error is not merely the adjustment of previous periods accounting estimates, e.g. the accrual for corporation tax.

**Example 6.1**

**CHANGE IN ACCOUNTING POLICY**

Lawton Limited's previous policy was to capitalise qualifying development expenditure and to amortise it over five years. The company has decided to change its policy and now writes off such expenditure as incurred. In the balance sheet as at 31 December 19X1, development expenditure was shown as a fixed asset of £2,200,000. Expenditure in 19X2 totalled £300,000.

**Accounting treatment**

This should be treated as a prior period adjustment because it results from a change in accounting policy. It should be accounted for by restating the comparative figures for 19X1 in the profit and loss account and balance sheet and by adjusting the opening balance of reserves by deducting the previously capitalised £2.2m. The effect of the prior period adjustment should be disclosed in a note to the accounts. The charge in the 19X2 profit and loss account would be £300,000.

# FINANCIAL STATEMENTS

**Example 6.2**

**FUNDAMENTAL ERROR**

Turtle Limited purchased a leased building on 1 January 19X0 for £10,000. On 1 January 19X6 the company discovered that the building was in fact on a 50-year lease, not 99 years as had been previously thought. The remaining lease is currently worth £40,000.

*(Assume that the amounts involved are material.)*

**Accounting treatment**

This is an example of a fundamental error—even though it was made 36 years previously. The treatment is to present the asset in the books now as if it had been accounted correctly throughout its ownership. The building would be in Turtle's books:

|  | £000 |
|---|---|
| *Cost* | |
| At 1 January 19X6 | 10,000 |
| | |
| *Accumulated depreciation* | |
| At 1 January 19X6 (£10,000/99 × 36) | 3,636 |
| | |
| *Net book value* | |
| At 1 January 19X6 | 6,364 |

If the company did not wish to incorporate the revaluation into its accounts, it would deal with the prior period adjustment as follows.

|  | £ |
|---|---|
| *Cost* | |
| At 1 January 19X6 and 31 December 19X6 | 10,000 |
| | |
| *Accumulated depreciation* | |
| At 1 January 19X6 | 3,636 |
| Prior period adjustment (see working) | 3,564 |
| Adjusted at 1 January 19X6 | 7,200 |
| Charge for the year (£10,000/50) | 200 |
| At 31 December 19X6 | 7,400 |
| | |
| *Net book value* | |
| At 1 January 19X6 | 6,364 |
| Prior period adjustment (working 1) | (3,564) |
| Adjusted at 1 January 19X6 | 2,800 |
| At 31 December 19X6 | 2,600 |

*Working*

The prior period adjustment is calculated as follows.

|  | £ |
|---|---|
| Correct depreciation | |
| £10,000/50 = £200 per annum × 36 years = | 7,200 |
| Actual depreciation | (3,636) |
| Prior period adjustment | 3,564 |

FINANCIAL REPORTING, ANALYSIS AND PLANNING

The prior period adjustment of £3,564 would be deducted from opening reserves of the company and shown in the statement of total recognised gains and losses (see below). The comparative figures for 19X5 would need to altered. Also a note to the accounts explaining the error and its effect should be made.

Assuming that the company wishes to incorporate the revaluation in the accounts:

|  | £ |
|---|---|
| *Cost* | |
| At 1 January 19X6 | 10,000 |
| Revaluation | 30,000 |
| Adjusted 1 January 19X6 and 31 December 19X6 | 40,000 |
| *Accumulated depreciation* | |
| At 1 January 19X6 | 3,636 |
| Prior period adjustment (see working) | 3,564 |
| Adjusted at 1 January 19X6 | 7,200 |
| Revaluation | (7,200) |
|  | 0 |
| Charge for the year (£40,000/14) | 2,857 |
| At 31 December 19X6 | 2,857 |
| *Net book value* | |
| At 1 January 19X6 | 6,364 |
| Prior period adjustment (working 1) | (3,564) |
| Adjusted at 1 January 19X6 | 2,800 |
| Revaluation | 37,200 |
| Adjusted and revalued at 1 January 19X6 | 40,000 |
| At 31 December 19X6 | 37,143 |

The prior period adjustment was dealt with first then the revaluation in the 'normal' way. Note that the revalued amount of £40,000 is depreciated over its remaining useful life, i.e. 14 years.

The revaluation of £37,200 would be credited to revaluation reserve and also shown in the statement of total recognised gains and losses (see later).

## 4 Layered profit and loss account

4.1 The layered format is used to highlight the individual components of financial performance:

(a) results of continuing operations

(b) results of discontinued operations

(c) results of acquired operations

(d) profits or losses on the sale or termination of an operation, costs of a fundamental restructuring or re-organisation, profits and losses on the sale of fixed assets and extraordinary items.

# FINANCIAL STATEMENTS

4.2 The analysis between continuing, acquired and discontinued operations is made to the level of operating profit.

4.3 Exceptional items (except those below) should be included under the appropriate heading to which they belong e.g. cost of sales item under a continuing operation. Appropriate narrative explanation should be given in a note to the accounts.

4.4 The following item should be shown separately on the face of the profit and loss account after operating profit but before interest payable:

(a) costs of a fundamental restructuring/re-organisation

(b) profits/losses on the sale or termination of an operation

(c) profits/losses on the disposal of fixed assets.

4.5 These three are sometimes referred to as 'super-exceptional' items. By their very incidence, they should be disclosed on the face of the (layered) profit and loss account. In the survey previously mentioned, 71% of the companies surveyed included one or more of the super-exceptionals.

4.6 The style of presentation can be outlined using the following illustration.

|  | Continuing operations | | Discontinued operations | Total 19X5 | Total 19X4 |
|---|---|---|---|---|---|
|  | Continuing | Acquisitions |  |  |  |
| Turnover | X | X | X | X | X |
| Cost of sales | (X) | (X) | (X) | (X) | (X) |
| Gross profit | X | X | X | X | X |
| Administration expenses | (X) | (X) | (X) | (X) | (X) |
| Distribution costs | (X) | (X) | (X) | (X) | (X) |
| Operating profit | X | X | X | X | X |
| Profit on sale on termination of operation |  |  | X | X | X |
| Fundamental restructuring | (X) |  |  | (X) | (X) |
| Loss on sale of fixed assets | (X) |  | (X) | (X) | (X) |
| Profit on ordinary activities before interest | X | X | X | X | X |
| Interest payable |  |  |  | (X) | (X) |
| Profit on ordinary activities before tax |  |  |  | X | X |
| Tax on profit on ordinary activities |  |  |  | (X) | (X) |
| Profit on ordinary activities after tax |  |  |  | X | X |
| Extraordinary items |  |  |  | X/(X) | X/(X) |
| Profit for the financial year |  |  |  | X | X |
| Dividends |  |  |  | (X) | (X) |
| Retained profits for the financial year |  |  |  | X | X |

## Discontinued operations

4.7 This term means exactly what is says. Operations must actually have been discontinued. Thus it is distinguished from so-called 'discontinuing' operations; where a company is winding down a business segment over a period of time. FRS3 gives the following definition of a discontinued operation:

(a) the sale or termination of the operation is either in the period or before the earlier of three months after the commencement of the subsequent period and the date on which the financial statements are approved;

(b) if a termination, the former activities have ceased permanently;

(c) the sale or termination has a material effect on the nature and focus of the company's operations and represents a material reduction in its operating facilities resulting either from its withdrawal from a particular market (whether class of business or geographical) or from a material reduction in turnover in the company's continuing markets; and

(d) the assets, liabilities, results of operations and activities are clearly distinguishable, physically, operationally and for financial reporting purposes.

Operations must satisfy *all* these conditions to be classified as discontinuing.

4.8 In explanation, parts (c) and (d) above concern ascertaining whether a business segment can be classified as an operation and whether the operation has actually discontinued. For example, a hotel company may withdraw from the luxury hotel market but keep in the budget hotel market. Or the hotel group may withdraw from the North American market. Or the company could significantly 'downsize', it could sell three-quarters of its hotel chain. These instances give *prima facie* evidence of a discontinued operation (provided the other criteria are met).

## 5 Statement of total recognised gains and losses

5.1 FRS3 introduced a new primary financial statement, the statement of total recognised gains and losses (SORG). By being a primary statement, it is ostensibly as important as the other primary statements: the profit and loss account, the balance sheet, the cash flow statement and notes.

5.2 The SORG is designed to show the profit for the period together with other movements on reserves which reflect recognised gains and losses attributable to shareholders. For example, if a revaluation of fixed assets has taken place during the year, then this is a recognised (not realised) gain and will be shown in the SORG. Another item which is taken to the SORG are exchange gains and losses taken directly to reserves. Under SSAP20 'Foreign currency transactions', under certain circumstances exchange gains or losses are taken directly to reserves, effectively bypassing the profit and loss account. However, the net assets of the business are affected. Therefore it was felt that this gain/loss in the net assets of the business should be brought to the attention of the accounts' users by its inclusion in the SORG.

FINANCIAL STATEMENTS

### 5.3 *Illustration of the SORG*

|  | 19X5 £ | 19X4 £ |
|---|---|---|
| Profit for the financial year | X | X |
| Unrealised surplus on the revaluation of properties | X | X |
| Currency translation differences on foreign currency investments | X | (X) |
| Total recognised gains and losses relating to the year | X | X |
| Prior year adjustments (explained in note to the accounts) | (X) | |
| Total gains and losses recognised since last annual report | X | X |

5.4 Since its inception, the SORG has attracted some criticism, the chief one questioning its overall usefulness. As mentioned earlier it is a primary statement—on a par with the balance sheet, cash flow statement and the profit and loss account. The ASB's *Statement of Principles* promotes the SORG as a key indicator used in assessing a company's financial performance, in tandem with the P & L account.

5.5 However, recent experiences suggest that the SORG has not been used as an indicator of company performance and is relegated to a misunderstood and largely irrelevant note to the accounts. The explanation why it is not felt to be overly useful concerns the additivity of the Statement. Using the illustration above, we are adding a profit earned over the current financial year to a property revaluation which may have been earned over 40 years but only recognised in the current year. We then add to that an adjustment for exchange gains/losses, usually relating to external exchange rate factors unrelated to the trading performance of the business. It is arguable of what use is the overall total—'Total recognised gains and losses relating to the year.'

## 6 Reconciliation of movements in shareholders' funds

6.1 An additional requirement per FRS3 is to show a reconciliation of movements in shareholders' funds.

6.2 This statement incorporates all items in the SORG together with any items directly affecting shareholders' funds; for example, new share issues.

### 6.3 *Illustration of the reconciliation of movements in shareholders funds*

|  | 19X5 £ | 19X4 £ |
|---|---|---|
| Profit for the financial year | X | X |
| Dividends | (X) | (X) |

FINANCIAL REPORTING, ANALYSIS AND PLANNING

| | | |
|---|---|---|
| Other recognised gains and losses relating to the year (from SORG) | X | X |
| New share capital subscribed | X | X |
| Net addition to shareholders' funds | X | X |
| Opening shareholders' funds (originally £X before prior year adjustment of £X) | X | X |
| Closing shareholders' funds | X | X |

## 7 Note of historical profits and losses

7.1 A further requirement of FRS3 was to report on the difference between the *actual* reported profit and the *historical* profit (i.e. the profit which would have been reported had the company followed strict historical cost accounting).

7.2 In essence the reconciling items are likely to result from any revaluation of fixed assets from historic cost to current cost. Remember that under SSAP12 depreciation must be charged on the *revalued* amount of a fixed assets—not the original historic cost. Thus the depreciation charge is higher and the profits lower. Also any profit on disposal of a fixed asset is likely to be lower (or the loss greater), if the asset has been revalued. This is because the gain/loss on sale is calculated by comparing the proceeds with the *carrying value*. Thus a revalued asset is likely to show a lower profit or higher loss on disposal.

7.3 *Illustration of historic cost reconciliation*

| | 19X5 £ | 19X4 £ |
|---|---|---|
| Reported profit on ordinary activities before taxation | X | X |
| Realisation of property revaluation gains of previous year | X | X |
| Difference between historical cost depreciation charge and the actual depreciation charge | X | X |
| Historical cost profit on ordinary activities before taxation | X | X |
| Historical cost profit for the year retained after taxation, minority interest, extraordinary items and dividends | X | X |

## 8 Amendment to 'Earnings per share'

8.1 A final amendment made by FRS3 to the now obsolete SSAP3 'Earnings per share' (EPS) was in the calculation of Earnings Per Share (EPS). Prior to FRS3, EPS was calculated using the company's profit *before* extraordinary items. FRS3 changed this so that earnings now include extraordinary items. Remember that extraordinary items were virtually disallowed anyway by FRS3. So, even in the event of a company actually having an extraordinary item, it should still be included when calculating the EPS. This amendment to SSAP3 is reflected in FRS14 Earnings per share, which replaced SSAP3 in 1998.

8.2 For a discussion on the importance of EPS and an outline of the methods of calculating EPS (see below and Unit 11). The effect of including

# FINANCIAL STATEMENTS

extraordinary items within Earnings has been to make those earnings more volatile and arguably more difficult to interpret (see below).

## Student Activity 1

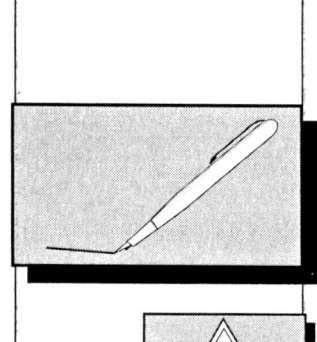

Before reading the next section of text, answer the following questions and then check your answers against the paragraph(s) indicated.

1. What has the ASB identified as the purpose of financial reporting?

    *(Paragraph 2.1)*

2. What would bankers use a profit and loss account for?   *(Paragraphs 2.6 & 2.7)*

3. Define an extraordinary item.   *(Paragraph 3.2)*

4. What are the required disclosures to be made on the face of the layered profit and loss account?   *(Paragraph 4.1)*

5. What items are included in the SORG and why might the statement not be overly useful?   *(Paragraphs 5.2, 5.4 & 5.5)*

6. What amendment to SSAP3 did FRS3 make?   *(Paragraphs 8.1)*

If your answers are basically correct, then proceed to the next section. If significant parts of your answers are wrong, then study the whole of the relevant sections again in detail. Note your areas of weakness and be prepared for further questions on these areas at the end of this Unit.

## 9 Substance over form

9.1 The concept of substance over form is the idea that a transaction should be treated in the accounts in accordance with its underlying *commercial substance*—rather than its technical legal form. In most transactions, the economic substance and the *legal form* are the same, but FRS5 'Reporting the substance of transactions' requires, where the two differ, that the economic substance should govern the accounting rather than its legal form.

9.2 FRS5 was introduced to cater for situations, where matters had been arranged usually by connivance, to artificially affect the presentation of items in the financial statements. This area is sometimes referred to as 'off-balance sheet' financing. The following is a simple example.

### Example 6.3

Richardson Limited wishes to purchase a new fixed asset for £10m. However the company does not have any spare funds and has to borrow the money. Richardson currently has a level of gearing (the relationship between debt and equity, see Unit 11) which it considers high enough. In fact, Richardson's bankers are already concerned at the level of borrowing. A further increase in borrowing would not be tolerated. Richardson's balance sheet is currently:

# FINANCIAL REPORTING, ANALYSIS AND PLANNING

|  | £m |
|---|---|
| Fixed assets | 13 |
| Net current assets | 2 |
| Long term loans | (5) |
|  | 10 |
| Capital and reserves | 10 |

Currently, using the ratio long term loans/ capital and reserves, gearing is 50% (£5m/£10m × 100). Assuming that Richardson borrows £10m long term and buys the fixed asset, its balance sheet will be:

|  | £m |
|---|---|
| Fixed assets (£13m + £10m) | 23 |
| Net current assets | 2 |
| Long-term loans (£5m + £10m) | (15) |
|  | 10 |
| Capital and reserves | 10 |

Gearing is now 150% (£15m/£10m × 100). This would obviously be unacceptable to the company and the bank and indeed would also probably be unacceptable to the company's investors. High gearing is perceived as being risky and the company's share price could fall as a result.

As a way around this dilemma, the company could set up an enterprise to loan the money and buy the asset on its behalf. Assume that Mortimer Enterprises is set up to do this. Richardson would control Mortimer; however, under the doctrine of separate legal entity, Mortimer would prepare its own accounts. The accounts of the two enterprises would be as follows.

|  | Richardson £m | Mortimer £m |
|---|---|---|
| Fixed assets | 13 | 10 |
| Net current assets | 2 | 0 |
| Long term loans | (5) | (10) |
|  | 10 | 0 |
| Capital and reserves | 10 | 0 |

In effect Richardson's gearing and balance sheet would be unaffected by the acquisition of the asset. Richardson, through its control of Mortimer, would benefit from the use of the asset.

Can you see where the application of the doctrine of substance over form would affect this situation? In *substance* Richardson controls Mortimer (and its only asset). Legally Mortimer owns the asset *not* Richardson. Applying the doctrine of substance over form, Richardson would have to bring the asset and the loan back on the balance sheet; and would end up with a balance sheet showing gearing at 150%.

# FINANCIAL STATEMENTS

9.3 The ASB and its predecessor the Accounting Standards Committee (ASC) have embarked on a continuing programme to eliminate such perceived abuses, examples of misleading creative accounting. One of the first actions was to compel companies to incorporate controlled enterprises, such as Mortimer above, into the accounts of Richardson. This was implemented through FRS2 'Accounting for Subsidiary Undertakings'(see Unit 11). Controlled enterprises, such as Mortimer above, would have to be consolidated with the accounts of Richardson.

9.4 Previously the ASC had sought to bring *leased assets* on the balance sheet. This was partially effected through SSAP21 'Accounting for Leases and Hire Purchase contracts' (see below).

9.5 However, as quickly as the ASC and ASB introduced standards, so the accounts' preparers and their advisers devised new ways of circumventing the standards, so as to mask the true situation. Usually the aim was to present an overly favourable impression of the balance sheet—chiefly to reduce gearing. To reiterate, high gearing implied high risk which in turn led to a number of unwelcome consequences for the company: higher borrowing costs, pressure on loan covenants, investor reluctance, depressed share price, etc.

9.6 To deal with this situation, the ASB introduced the wide ranging FRS5. The standard was designed to cover *all* transactions and to be *principle* rather than *rule* based. The overriding doctrine is that the accounts should report the *economic substance* rather than the strict *legal form*. The standard drew heavily on the *Statement of Principles*, by utilising its definitions of 'Assets and Liabilities'. The definitions should be employed to determine whether a transaction resulted in the creation of an asset or liability.

9.7 Assets are defined as 'rights or other access to future economic benefits controlled by an entity as a result of past transactions or events'. Legal title is not a criterion, economic rights and control over those rights are the important criteria.

A key determinant is to ascertain where the risks and rewards lie. Consider another example.

**Example 6.4**

The McFee Distillery Limited sells £20m worth of whisky to a finance house. The agreement specifies that the distillery can repurchase the stock in three years for £22m.

*Evaluation*

The strict legal interpretation is that there has been a sale of stock with an equivalent receipt of cash. Depending on the terms of the agreement, the substance of the transaction may well be that McFee has entered into a three year secured loan, with £2m (£22m – £20m) of interest payable.

The terms of the agreement would have to be considered. For example, how likely is it that the Finance House will exercise its option to sell the stock back to the distillery? Is it an option or is it compelled to re-sell the stock?

If in our judgment the whisky was going to be sold back to the distillery, McFee would have to bring the whisky back on the balance sheet. Thus

McFee would still record the whisky as stock of £20m, the £20m cash received would be recorded along with a three year secured loan of £20m. Over the three years the £2m of interest payable would be charged to the profit and loss account, and added to the carrying value of the loan in McFee's accounts. No sale would be recorded. Legally there has been a sale and the stock is owned by the finance house. In substance, McFee has borrowed £20m over three years, using the whisky as security.

To make a judgment we need to ascertain where the risks and rewards lie. This is a good indicator of what the economic substance of the transaction is. For instance, in the above example if the market value of whisky doubles in the three year period, who would reap the benefits? McFee or the Finance House? Who is responsible for insuring the whisky?

9.8 The terms of any agreement need to be carefully examined. Consider for instance another sale and repurchase situation.

**Example 6.5**

Hawkins sells Asset X to Booth for £20m. Both Hawkins and Booth have a put and call option at the same price; say £23m, exercisable between 12 and 36 months.

*Evaluation*

Thus Hawkins has the right, at any time between 12 and 36 months, to exercise its call option and repurchase Asset X. If say the market value of X rises to £30m, Hawkins will exercise its option and repurchase.

Booth also has the right to exercise its put option between 12 and 36 months. So if, for example, the market price falls to £15m, then Booth will exercise its option. Thus it is *certain* that Asset X will return to Hawkins, hence there has been no genuine sale, therefore it should not be recognised as a sale and X should remain on Hawkins' balance sheet.

9.9 Some of the other instances where the doctrine can be applied include the following.

*(a) Discounting bills of exchange*

When a business holds a bill of exchange it represents an asset which will be converted into cash in the future, when the debtor pays at the due date. If the bill is discounted the debt is turned into cash straight away, but there is a risk that the bill will not be paid at maturity. If there is a default on the bill the business which arranged for it to be discounted at the bank will be liable for the amount received, so there is a contingent liability. The contingency should be disclosed as a note to the accounts. In effect the bank provides a loan with the bill of exchange as security, but the loan does nor appear in the balance sheet. Instead the balance sheet reflects a reduction in the debt owed by the drawee of the bill (since the business can no longer claim the proceeds having sold the bill to the bank).

*(b) Factoring*

If a business sells its debts to a factor as a way of getting cash more quickly, the effect is similar to discounting bills of exchange. The finance provided by the factor does not appear as a loan in the balance sheet, rather the amount

FINANCIAL STATEMENTS

for debtors is reduced instead. A note to the accounts should show any contingent liability—this would arise where the debts are sold with recourse. That is if the debtor does not ultimately pay the factor in full, the factor can go back to the company and reclaim some of the cash already paid up front.

Again the terms of the factoring agreement should be examined. FRS5 allows for 'linked presentation', where the proceeds of an asset (in this case the debtors) are directly linked to an advance. Consider the following example.

**Example 6.6**

Harvey Limited sells £100,000 of its book debts to a factor, Baines Finance. The terms are 90% payable up front, with the remainder (up to a maximum of 98%) payable, dependent on the success Baines has in collecting the debts.

*Evaluation*

This is a situation where we can utilise linked presentation. Legally, Harvey has sold all the debts. In substance though, Harvey has retained an interest in the performance of the debts. Baines Finance is bearing the catastrophic risk that none of the debtors will pay. However, we can see that Harvey is still carrying some of the risks of these debts. In fact, it is the risk most likely to have a commercial effect, i.e. that the likelihood is that not all the debtors are going to pay and not all on time, and that therefore Harvey will not receive the full 98%.

The recommended presentation of such a situation is:

| Debtors: | £000 |
|---|---|
| Amounts subject to financing arrangement (98% × £100,000 less say £1,000 provision) | 97 |
| less non-refundable finance proceeds | (90) |
| | 7 |

*(c) Consignment stock*

This occurs frequently in the motor industry where a dealer obtains stock from a manufacturer on a sale or return basis. The stock is held on the dealer's premises where he can later (i) adopt it, e.g. by using the car as a demonstration model, (ii) transfer it to another dealer, (iii) sell it to a customer or (iv) return it to the manufacturer.

Again the terms of the agreement would need to be examined to ascertain if, in substance, the stock is an asset of the dealer or the manufacturer. For example, judging which party bears the risk of obsolescence. Can the dealer return the stock to the manufacturer at the original value, if say a new model is brought out and the value of the old model falls? Is a finance charge payable by the dealer contingent upon the length of time the stock is held?

# 10 Leasing

10.1 As indicated above, the issue of accounting for leases was tackled before the introduction of FRS5. In 1984 the ASC released SSAP21 'Accounting for

# FINANCIAL REPORTING, ANALYSIS AND PLANNING

leases and hire purchase contracts' in an attempt to bring certain leased assets (and of course the associated liability) onto the balance sheet. Again the motive for excluding such leased assets was to improve the appearance of the balance sheet—mainly the gearing ratio. Leased assets are legally owned by the lessor therefore, applying the strict legal form, they should not appear on the lessee's balance sheet. However in certain circumstances leased assets are, *in substance*, assets of the lessee; the risks and rewards of holding the asset fall on the lessee not the lessor.

10.2 The standard, as did the succeeding FRS5, outlined the *principles* on which a situation should be judged. In the case of leases, the criterion was to examine whether the significant risks and rewards of holding the asset had been transferred from the lessor (legal owner) to the lessee (the user).

10.3 Contrast, for example, the difference between leasing a car for five years from a manufacturer, with hiring a car for the weekend. In the former, the holder is likely to be responsible for the insurance and maintenance of the car. He is likely to be able to benefit from any gain in value or suffer if the value falls; he is likely to be able (legally) to buy the car at the end of the five years. Conversely, the hire company rather than the hirer is likely to be responsible for the maintenance of the hire car. The hirer is unlikely to have any exposure to the risks in hiring that car over the weekend. The hirer would certainly not be responsible for any fall in the market value of that model over the weekend.

10.4 The standard gave a rule of thumb to ascertain whether in substance the risks and rewards of holding the asset had been transferred to the lessee: whether at the inception of the lease, the terms were such that the *present value of the minimum lease payments amounts to substantially all (normally 90% or more) of the assets' fair value*. If so, then such a lease would be classified as a Finance Lease. The implications are that the asset should be recorded as an asset in the books of the *lessee* and the obligation (to pay the rentals to the lessor) should be likewise be recorded as a liability.

10.5 A lease which does not meet the criteria of an finance lease is an *operating lease*.

**Example 6.7**

Tatum plc uses three identical pieces of machinery. The machines were all delivered on the same day on the following terms.

(i) Machine A was rented from Meg Limited at £200 per month payable in advance. The agreement could be terminated at any time, with one week's notice, by either party.

(ii) Machine B was rented from Sandy Limited at £2,000 per annum, payable in advance, over four years.

(iii) Machine C was rented from Jill Limited at £500 per quarter, payable in advance, over three years.

The cash price of this type of machine is £7,500; and it has an estimated useful life of five years.

FINANCIAL STATEMENTS

**Assessment**

(i) Machine A is an operating lease as there is no transfer of the risks and rewards of ownership. The only charge to the profit and loss account will be the accrued amount of the lease rentals.

(ii) The total payment for Machine B is £8,000 (£2,000 × 4). It is likely, in present value terms, that this represents more than 90% of the fair value of the machine (90% × £7,500 = £6,750). Therefore this is a finance lease. Machine B should be capitalised in Tatum's books at its fair value, with a corresponding amount recorded as a lease liability. The profit and loss account charge will comprise depreciation on the leased asset (written off over its useful life or the lease term if shorter) and the interest inherent in the lease.

(iii) The total payment for Machine C is £6,000 (£500 × 6). Thus in present value terms, this does not represent more than 90% of the fair value of the machine (90% × £7,500 = £6,750). Therefore this is an operating lease. Machine C should not be capitalised in Tatum's books nor should any lease liability be recognised. The only charge to the profit and loss account will be the accrued amount of the lease rentals.

**Accounting for finance leases**

10.6 Having seen how to identify finance leases, let us look at an example showing how we account for such transactions.

**Example 6.8**

Downend Limited leases a machine, on a finance lease, on 1 January 19X1. The terms are for eight payments of £1,000, half-yearly, in advance. The fair value of the machine is £5,868. The useful economic life of the machine is five years.

*(The interest rate inherent in the lease is 10% per half year)*

**Solution**

Initially the machine needs to be capitalised in the balance sheet at its fair value, with a corresponding amount recorded in creditors, as a lease liability.

*Fixed assets*

| | £ |
|---|---|
| Cost | |
| At 1 January 19X1 | – |
| Addition | 5,868 |
| At 31 December 19X1 | 5,868 |
| *Accumulated depreciation* | |
| At 1 January 19X1 | |
| Charge (£5,868/4 years *) | 1,467 |
| At 31 December 19X1 | 1,467 |
| *Net book value* | |
| At 31 December 19X1 | 4,401 |

# FINANCIAL REPORTING, ANALYSIS AND PLANNING

*\* Note the leased asset is written off over the shorter of the estimated useful life and the lease period.*

The lease liability is calculated by setting up a lease schedule.

*Lease schedule*

| Period | Opening balance £ | Cashflow £ | Sub-total £ | Interest 10% £ | Closing balance £ |
|---|---|---|---|---|---|
| 19X1 – I | 5,868 | (1,000) | 4,868 | 487 | 5,355 |
| 19X1 – II | 5,335 | (1,000) | 4,355 | 436 | 4,790 |
| 19X2 – I | 4,790 | (1,000) | 3,790 | 379 | 4,169 |
| 19X2 – II | 4,169 | (1,000) | 3,169 | 317 | 3,486 |
| 19X3 – I | 3,486 | (1,000) | 2,486 | 249 | 2,735 |
| 19X3 – II | 2,735 | (1,000) | 1,735 | 174 | 1,909 |
| 19X4 – I | 1,909 | (1,000) | 909 | 91 | 1,000 |
| 19X4 – II | 1,000 | (1,000) | 0 | | |

Thus in 19X1, there will be a profit and loss account charge of £923 (£487 plus £436) representing the finance cost of the lease. In addition depreciation on the leased asset of £1,467 will be shown.

In the balance sheet, at the end of 19X1, under Creditors 'Obligations under finance leases' will be the year end balance—£4,790; split between Creditors: due within one year and Creditors: due after more than one year.

As can been seen the finance charge falls over the term of the lease, reflecting the decreasing lease liability.

Note that in 19X4, the lease liability is in fact paid off half way through the year—thus there is only one finance charge of £91.

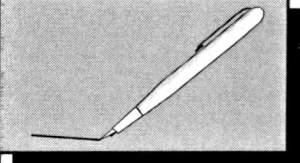

## Student Activity 2

Before reading the next section of text, answer the following questions and then check your answers against the paragraph(s) indicated.

1. What are the motives for off balance sheet financing? *(Paragraph 9.5)*

2. How can you assess the substance of a transaction? *(Paragraphs 9.7 & Example 6.4)*

3. In a consignment stock situation, what are some of the indicators you would use to establish, in substance, whose stock it is? *(Paragraph 9.10(b))*

4. What is the rule of thumb outlined by SSAP21, for defining a finance lease? *(Paragraph 10.4)*

5. Define an operating lease. *(Paragraph 10.5)*

If your answers are basically correct, then proceed to the next section. If significant parts of your answers are wrong, then study the whole of the relevant sections again in detail. Note your areas of weakness and be prepared for further questions on these areas at the end of this Unit.

FINANCIAL STATEMENTS

## 11 Earnings per share (EPS)

11.1 Earnings per share is a key indicator of the financial performance of the company. It expresses, in an amount per share, how much profit the company has earned in the last financial year. It is not necessarily the amount of dividend that is paid, nor is it the maximum dividend that could be paid, because the company can pay out a dividend from previous years' profits. However, the EPS is a good indicator of the performance of the company in profit terms. The key price-earnings (PE) ratio is derived from dividing the share price by the EPS. The PE ratio is an indication of the value the market places on a company's shares relative to its profitability.

**Calculation of EPS**

11.2 FRS14 'Earnings per share', outlines the method for calculating EPS. The following formula should be applied.

$$\text{Earnigs share} = \frac{\text{Earnings}}{\text{Ordinary shares}}$$

11.3 *'Earnings'* being defined as profits after:

- tax
- preference dividends and
- extraordinary items (this last item was an amendment introduced by FRS3—see above).

11.4 *'Ordinary shares'* being equity shares in issue ranking for dividend—where the dividend is not limited, e.g. a preference share (with preference to dividends or capital) is not an equity share.

**Example 6.9**

Grimshaw plc has ordinary share capital of £1.5 million (50p shares) and £500,000 preference shares (5% cumulative £1 shares) in issue. For the year ended 31 December 19X4 the company has the following results.

|  | £ | £ |
|---|---:|---:|
| Profit before tax |  | 1,510,000 |
| Tax |  | (585,000) |
| Profit after tax |  | 925,000 |
| Extraordinary loss | (300,000) |  |
| Tax on extraordinary loss | 120,000 |  |
|  |  | (180,000) |
| Profit for financial year |  | 745,000 |
| Dividends: |  |  |
| Ordinary – interim paid | 50,000 |  |
| Ordinary – final proposed | 50,000 |  |
| Preference – interim paid | 12,500 |  |
| Preference – final proposed | 12,500 |  |
|  |  | (125,000) |
| Retained profit |  | 620,000 |

*Note: it is extremely unlikely that a company will have an extraordinary loss. It has only been included for illustrative purposes.*

# FINANCIAL REPORTING, ANALYSIS AND PLANNING

Calculate the EPS for 19X4.

**Solution**

First calculate earnings.

| *Earnings* | £ | £ |
|---|---|---|
| Profit after tax | | 925,000 |
| Extraordinary loss | (300,000) | |
| Tax on extraordinary loss | 120,000 | |
| | | (180,000) |
| Preference—interim paid | 12,500 | |
| Preference—final proposed | 12,500 | |
| | | (25,000) |
| Earnings | | 720,000 |
| *Shares* | | |
| Ordinary | | 3,000,000 |
| EPS | | 24p |

Thus if its share price were £2.40, Grimshaw would have a PE ratio of 10 (£2.40/24p).

**Taxation**

11.5 As will be seen in Unit 7, a company's corporation tax charge in the profit and loss account incorporates a number of items:

- corporation tax for the current year
- over/(under) provisions for previous years
- tax on franked investment income
- movements in the deferred tax provision.

11.6 Exceptionally, the charge will also include irrecoverable Advance Corporation Tax (ACT) which has been written off, rather than set-off or carried back or forward. This represents ACT that the company has paid and is not able to reclaim; for example if the company has considerable overseas income.

11.7 The standard method of calculating EPS is the 'net basis'—calculating EPS by incorporating earnings after deducting *all* components of the tax charge—including any irrecoverable ACT. However FRS14 recommends that if there is any material irrecoverable ACT charged in the accounts, then the EPS should also be calculated ignoring this 'unusual' charge. The rationale is so that the EPS will reflect the ongoing activities of the business, not a one-off, unlikely to be repeated, tax charge.

# FINANCIAL STATEMENTS

**Example 6.10**

Assume, in Example 6.9 above, that the tax charge comprises the following items.

|  | £ |
|---|---:|
| Corporation tax at 33% | 573,000 |
| Under provision of tax in 19X3 | 12,000 |
| Tax on franked investment income | 40,000 |
| Transfer (from) deferred tax provision | (100,000) |
| Irrecoverable ACT written off | 60,000 |
|  | 585,000 |

The EPS on the nil basis (i.e. ignoring the ACT write off) will be:

|  | £ | £ |
|---|---:|---:|
| Profit after tax |  | 925,000 |
| *Add back irrecoverable ACT* |  | 60,000 |
| Extraordinary loss | (300,000) |  |
| Tax on extraordinary loss | 120,000 |  |
|  |  | (180,000) |
| Preference—interim paid | 12,500 |  |
| Preference—final proposed | 12,500 |  |
|  |  | (25,000) |
| Earnings |  | 780,000 |
| *Shares* |  |  |
| Ordinary |  | 3,000,000 |
| EPS (nil basis) |  | 26p |

According to FRS14, EPS on both bases should be disclosed if the difference is 'Material'.

### Changes in capital structure

11.8 If there are any changes in the capital structure during an accounting period the earnings per share figure will have to be amended to account for the change. We are going to consider three types of share issue: a share issue at full market price, a bonus issue and a rights issue.

*Issue at full market price*

11.9 The accounting treatment here is quite straightforward—simply divide company earnings by the weighted average number of shares in issue over the year.

**Example 6.11**

On 1 January 19X1, Scott plc had in issue 2m 50p ordinary shares. On 1 April 19X1, the company issued, at full market price, 400,000 ordinary shares. Scott's earnings for the year were £280,000 (19X0 £140,000). Calculate the EPS for the company for 19X1 including comparatives.

**Solution**

$$EPS = \frac{Earnings}{Weighted\ average\ number\ of\ shares}$$

Earnings = £280,000

Weighted average number of shares:
2m × 3/12ths + 2.4m × 9/12ths = 2,300,000

$$EPS = \frac{£280,000}{2,300,000} = 12.17p$$

*Comparative 19X0*

$$EPS = \frac{£140,000}{2,000,000} = 7.0p$$

*Evaluation*

We can see that although the profits have doubled from 19X0 to 19X1, the EPS has not increased by the same amount. This is because Scott has had extra shares in issue (and correspondingly extra cash available), therefore earnings per share are correspondingly less.

### Bonus issue

11.10 A bonus issue is an issue of shares 'for free'. It is sometimes called a capitalisation of reserves. The company issues shares, with no cash received, using balances in reserve accounts to 'finance' the issue. As no cash has been raised there is no corresponding effect on earnings.

To calculate the EPS use the new number of shares in issue as the denominator for both the current year and the previous year's comparative—regardless of when during the year the bonus issue took place.

### Example 6.12

On 1 January 19X1, Doyle plc had in issue 2m 50p ordinary shares. On 1 October 19X1, the company decided to issue bonus shares on a one for two basis. Doyle's earnings for the year were £600,000 (19X0 £400,000). Calculate the EPS for 19X1 with comparatives.

**Solution**

$$EPS = \frac{Earnings}{New\ number\ of\ shares}$$

$$EPS = \frac{£600,000}{3,000,000} = 20.0p$$

*Comparative 19X0*

# FINANCIAL STATEMENTS

$$\text{EPS} = \frac{\text{Earnings}}{\text{New number of shares}}$$

$$\text{EPS} = \frac{£400,000}{3,000,000} = 13.33\text{p}$$

*Evaluation*

The bonus issue has had no effect on the earning capacity of the company as no funds were raised. Therefore there is no need to pro rata the EPS before and after the issue. We can see that EPS has increased from 13.33p to 20p, an increase of 50%. This is exactly in line with earnings which rose from £400,000 to £600,000.

Note the likely effect on a company's share price of a bonus issue. Doyle has issued an extra 1m shares with no consideration in return. Thus the company's intrinsic worth is identical before and after the issue. Hence the company's share price should fall by the inverse of the bonus, i.e. by 2/3rds.

Assume that Doyle's share price before the bonus issue was £3.00. The company's market capitalisation (share price × number of shares in issue) would have been 2m × £3.00 = £6m. After the bonus issue the company's market value should be the same. However there are now 3m shares in issue. Thus the new share price must be £6m/3m = £2.00.

## Rights issue

**11.11** The final share issue we need to consider is a rights issue. This merges the effects of a bonus (free) issue and an issue at the full market price. Think of a rights issue as a normal issue at market price with some bonus shares allocated as well.

A rights issue is made to existing shareholders in proportion to their existing shareholdings. The shares are issued for cash—but at a discount to the current market price (hence the bonus element in the share issue). The shares are sold for less than market value because the existing shareholders have to be given some incentive to buy extra shares.

To calculate the EPS we need to go through four stages.

**Stage 1** *Calculate the theoretical ex-rights price*

This is the predicted share price after the rights issue. Remember that the rights issue incorporates a bonus issue, after which we would anticipate a fall in the share price (see Doyle above).

**Stage 2** *Calculate the weighted average number of shares for use in the EPS denominator.*

Use the formula:

# FINANCIAL REPORTING, ANALYSIS AND PLANNING

Proportion of year × Number of shares in × $\dfrac{\text{Market price at issue}}{\text{Theoretical ex-rights price}}$
*before* issue     issue before rights

plus

Proportion of year × Number of shares in
*after* issue     issue after rights

**Stage 3** *Calculate EPS using the formula:*

$$\dfrac{\text{Earnings}}{\text{Adjusted weighted average number of shares}}$$

**Stage 4** *Adjust comparative by:*

EPS as originally × $\dfrac{\text{Theoretical ex-rights price}}{\text{Market price at issue}}$
calculated

## Example 6.13

On 1 January 19X1 Wilcox plc had in issue 2m 50p shares. On 1 October 19X1, the company had a rights issue on a two for five basis at £2.95 per share. The share price at the time of the rights issue was £4.00. Wilcox's earnings in 19X1 were £200,000 (19X0 £100,000). Calculate EPS for 19X1 including comparative.

## Solution

*Stage 1 Calculate the theoretical ex-rights price.*

We can anticipate that the share price should have fallen. However we can also anticipate that the share price would have been more than the rights issue price.

Assume a holder of 10 shares:

| | | | |
|---|---|---|---|
| Before rights issue | 10 | @ £4.00 | £40.00 |
| Rights issue | 4 | @ £2.95 | £11.80 |
| After rights issue | 14 | | £51.80 |

The holder now has 14 shares and has 'contributed' £51.80. Thus each share is now theoretically worth £3.70 (£51.80/14)

*Stage 2 Calculate a weighted average number of shares for use in the EPS denominator.*

# FINANCIAL STATEMENTS

Use the formula:

Proportion of year × Number of shares in × Market price at issue / Theoretical ex-rights price
*before* issue    issue before rights

plus

Proportion of year × Number of shares in
*after* issue    issue after rights

$$9/12\text{ths} \times 2\text{m} \times \frac{£4.00}{£3.70} = 1{,}621{,}622$$

plus

$$3/12\text{ths} \times 2{,}800{,}000 = 700{,}000$$

Total      2,321,622

*Stage 3 Calculate EPS using formula:*

$$\frac{\text{Earnings}}{\text{Adjusted weighted average number of shares}}$$

$$\frac{£200{,}000}{2{,}321{,}622} = 8.61\text{p}$$

*Stage 4 Adjust comparative by:*

EPS as originally calculated × Theoretical ex-rights price / Market price at issue

$$\frac{£100{,}000}{2{,}000{,}000} = 5\text{p} \times \frac{£3.70}{£4.00} = 4.63\text{p}$$

*Evaluation*

Again comparing 19X0 and 19X1, we can see that although earnings have doubled EPS has not. This is because of the effect of the rights issue in 19X1.

Note the effect of recalculating the 19X0 EPS. This has fallen from 5p as originally reported to 4.63p. This reflects the bonus element in the 19X1 rights issue. The same effect (i.e. a fall in the comparative EPS) was noted above when we looked at bonus issues.

## 12 Segmental reporting

12.1 One of the last acts of the ASC was to release SSAP25 'Segmental Reporting'. The standard only applies to large companies.

12.2 In essence, the standard requires that account information should be analysed into segments. Segments being a Class of business and Geographical. The information to be segmentalised is Turnover, Profit before taxation and Net assets. Thus, key ratios of Turnover/Assets and Profit/Assets can be calculated for each segment of the business.

**Segments**

12.3 A class of business is a distinguishable part of a business that provides a separate service/product or group of services/products.

12.4 A geographical segment is a geographical area comprising a country or group of countries in which the business operates.

12.5 The overall purpose of the standard is similar in many ways to the requirements for a layered profit and loss account under FRS3 (see above). In short, it is to assist the provision of useful information to accounts users to assess the performance of the business. As can be seen by the information required, the user will be able to compare the performance of the various segments of the business and to ascertain their relative performance in profit and profit/asset terms.

## 13 Historical summaries

13.1 One of the purposes of interpreting financial information is to identify and analyse trends. For instance, over the course of the last few years, a company's gross margins may have been declining, its current ratio may have been improving, its effective tax rate may have been increasing.

13.2 The Companies Act requires companies to present accounts with one year's comparative figures. This is often insufficient to identify such trends. Thus, it has become increasingly common for large companies to present a five-year summary of results in an appendix to the main accounts. This is not a requirement of the Companies Act, however it has become best practice for corporate reporting purposes.

13.3 However, preparing a five-year summary may not be as simple as it sounds. For example, there may have been some prior year adjustments. Logically the summary should be adjusted to show the accounts as they should have been presented rather than how they were actually presented. Consider if a new accounting standard has been introduced in the five year period. Should the old results be adjusted in line with the new accounting treatment?

## 14 Reports to employees

14.1 One of the main direct account user groups identified by the ASB are the company's employees. The purpose of corporate reporting is to furnish useful information to assist decision making. The *Statement of Principles* recognises that such information must be relevant and understandable to be useful.

14.2 It is arguable whether the company's full statutory financial statements are either relevant or understandable to the majority of the company's employees. Therefore some companies have produced employee reports. The main features of these reports are usually:

- a summary of the full accounts
- employee information e.g. analyses of average numbers of employees, pay levels, total pay/pension data

FINANCIAL STATEMENTS

- narrative description of the company's results, operations and prospects especially in relation to employment issues
- comparative pay information, information relative to any pay claims, health and safety, promotion/grading issues etc.

## 15 Government grants

15.1 SSAP4 'Accounting for government grants' covers the situation when an enterprise is in receipt of a government grant. A grant normally encompasses one of two forms: Capital grants and Revenue grants.

**Capital grants**

15.2 These are basically grants against the cost of purchasing fixed assets. For example, a government grant to assist a company in the construction of a factory.

**Revenue grants**

15.3 These are, as the name implies, grants against revenue, profit and loss account items. For example, a local authority may give a company a grant against the cost of employing apprentices over a stated period.

15.4 The principle of SSAP4 is to apply the matching concept. Matching the grant with the associated profit and loss expense (revenue grant) or fixed asset cost (capital grant). The general application of the standard is relatively straightforward.

**Example 6.14**

**REVENUE GRANT**

On 1 January 19X1 Luke Limited receives a grant of £200,000 from the Northshire Development Corporation; on condition of it continuing to employ 30 staff for the next two years at one of its rural workshops. The company's year end is 30 June.

**Accounting treatment**

1 January 19X1

Dr. Cash £200,000
Cr. Deferred credit £200,000

*The grant receipt is not taken to the profit and loss account in full—instead it is credited to a deferred income account.*

30 June 19X1 (the company year end)

Dr. Deferred credit £50,000
Cr. Profit and loss account—wages £50,000

*Representing the netting off of the grant against the wages cost for the six months to 30 June 19X1 (6/24 × £200,000).*

30 June 19X2

Dr. Deferred credit £100,000
Cr. Profit and loss account—wages £100,000

*Representing the netting off the grant against the wages cost for the year to 30 June 19X12 (12/24 × £200,000)*

30 June 19X3

Dr. Deferred credit £50,000
Cr. Profit and loss account—wages £50,000

*Representing the netting off of the grant against the wages cost for the six months to 31 December 19X2 (6/24 × £200,000).*

**Capital grant**

15.5 The standard allows for two treatments. Either credit a deferred credit (as above) or net-off against the cost of the fixed asset. The net effect on the profit and loss account is identical whichever treatment is adopted.

**Example 6.15**

**CAPITAL GRANT**

On 1 January 19X1 Scott Limited received a government grant of £300,000 against the purchase price of £1.5m for a new machine. The machine has a useful economic life of six years. The company's year end is 31 December.

**Accounting treatment**

*(i) Deferred credit method*

1 January 19X1

Dr. Fixed asset—Machine £1,500,000
Cr. Cash £1,500,000

*Purchase of new machine*

Dr. Cash £300,000
Cr. Deferred credit £300,000

*The grant receipt is not taken to the profit and loss account nor set-off against the cost of the asset; instead it is credited to a deferred income account.*

31 December 19X1/X2/X3/X4/X5/X6

Dr. Profit and loss account—Depreciation of machine £250,000 (£1.5m/6)
Cr. Provision for depreciation £250,000
*Writing off cost of machine over 6 years straight line basis.*

31 December 19X1/X2/X3/X4/X5/X6

Dr. Deferred credit £50,000 (£300,000/6)
Cr. Profit and loss account—grant receivable £50,000

*Crediting grant to profit and loss account over life of associated asset.*

FINANCIAL STATEMENTS

*(ii) Netting off method*

1 January 19X1

Dr. Fixed asset—Machine £1,500,000
Cr. Cash £1,500,000

*Purchase of new machine.*

Dr. Cash £300,000
Cr. Fixed asset—Machine £300,000

*Netting off grant against cost of machine.*

31 December 19X1/X2/X3/X4/X5/X6

Dr. Profit and loss account—Depreciation of machine £200,000 (£1.2m/ 6)
Cr. Provision for depreciation £200,000

*Writing off net cost of machine over 6 years straight line basis.*

As can be seen the net effect on the profit and loss account is the same under either method.

15.6 An argument against the second method is that it falls foul of the Companies Act rule disallowing netting off of account items. For example, it is not permitted to show 'net sales income' instead of 'Turnover' and 'Cost of Sales' separately. However, netting off of the grant against the cost of the fixed asset *is* allowed, on the justification of the true and fair override. That is, the accounts must show a true and fair view applying accounting standards (in this case SSAP4) is necessary for the accounts to show a true and fair view, thus the standard not the letter of the law should be applied in this instance.

**Further consideration**

15.7 In accord with the prudence concept the company should consider what to do if the grant is potentially repayable. This could be if the grant conditions have been, or are likely to be breached. If for example, Luke Limited (above) is no longer able to employ 30 people at its rural workshop and the grant is then repayable, then it would be prudent to provide in the accounts for the likely repayment of the grant. If there is a possibility that the grant could be repaid in the event of uncertain future events, the appropriate treatment would be to disclose the potential repayment as a contingent loss (see Unit 5)

## Student Activity 3

Before reading the next section of text, answer the following questions and then check your answers against the paragraph(s) indicated.

1. What is the basic formula for calculating earnings per share? *(Paragraph 11.2)*
2. Define earnings. *(Paragraph 11.3)*
3. What is the difference between the 'net' and the 'nil' bases of calculating EPS? *(Paragraphs 11.5—11.7 Example 6.10)*
4. Define a segment as per SSAP25. *(Paragraphs 12.3 & 12.4)*
5. What features might an employee report contain? *(Paragraph 14.2)*

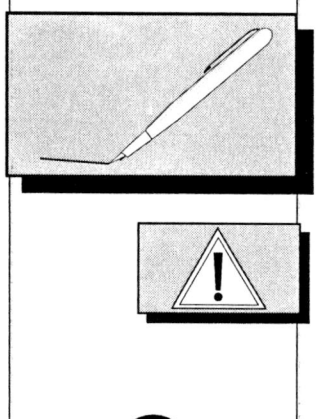

# FINANCIAL REPORTING, ANALYSIS AND PLANNING

6. Explain the difference between and the accounting for Revenue and Capital grants. *(Paragraphs 15.2 & 15.3)*

If your answers are basically correct, then proceed to the next section. If significant parts of your answers are wrong, then study the whole of the relevant sections again in detail. Note your areas of weakness and be prepared for further questions on these areas at the end of this Unit.

## Summary

**Now that you have completed this Unit you should be able to:**

- [ ] **understand the rationale for the introduction of FRS3 and apply its principles in various scenarios**
- [ ] **compile a layered profit and loss account, primary statement of total recognised gains and losses, reconciliation of shareholders funds and note of historical profits**
- [ ] **account for leases in accordance with SSAP21**
- [ ] **identify and account for situations where the economic substance of a transaction differs from its legal form**
- [ ] **understand the principles of FRS5 and apply the standard to various situations**
- [ ] **calculate earnings per share in accordance with FRS14**
- [ ] **apply the conventions of SSAP25 in reporting the segmented operations of enterprises**
- [ ] **consider alternative reports to stakeholders such as employee reports**
- [ ] **discuss the merits of historical summaries**
- [ ] **account for government and other grants in accordance with SSAP4.**

## Self-assessment questions

**Short answer questions**

1. What is the rationale for the introduction of FRS3?

2. Do you think that FRS3 has improved corporate reporting?

3. Explain when a prior period adjustment may be necessary and how it may be accounted for.

4. Why should the accounts reflect the economic substance of a transaction rather than its legal form?

5. Define 'asset'; explain its significance in applying FRS5.

6. Why are a company's earnings per share of interest to accounts users?

# FINANCIAL STATEMENTS

7. In what ways might the provision of historical summaries improve corporate reporting?

8. When might the prudence concept effect the accounting treatment of a government grant?

*(Answers are given in the Appendix)*

## Multiple choice questions

1. The SORG incorporates:

    1   profit for the financial year

    2   accumulated profit for the previous years

    3   movements in the revaluation reserve

    4   prior period adjustments

    (a) all the above

    (b) 1, 2 and 3

    (c) 1, 2 and 4

    (d) 1, 3 and 4

2. Earnings are calculated as:

    (a) profit after tax

    (b) profit after tax after extraordinary items

    (c) profit after tax, extraordinary items and preference dividends.

    (d) profit after tax, extraordinary items, preference dividends and transfers to reserves.

3. The FRS3 amendment to SSAP3 resulted, on average, in:

    (a) more volatile EPS

    (b) less volatile EPS

    (c) higher EPS

    (d) lower EPS.

4. Which of the following statements is correct?

    (a) if the accounts are prepared correctly economic substance always equates with the legal form;

    (b) if the accounts are prepared correctly economic substance rarely equates with the legal form;

    (c) if the accounts are prepared correctly economic substance never equates with the legal form;

    (d) none of the above.

5. Parker Limited leases a machine on a finance lease. The terms are:

    ● fair value of the asset £40,000

    ● lease term four years

# FINANCIAL REPORTING, ANALYSIS AND PLANNING

- interest rate inherent in the lease 10% p.a.
- useful economic life of the asset five years
- annual repayments in arrears
- 10% deposit in advance.

For the first year of the assets use, which of the following charges to the profit and loss account are correct?

|     | Lease finance charges £000 | Depreciation £000 |
| --- | --- | --- |
| (a) | 4 | 10 |
| (b) | 3.6 | 10 |
| (c) | 4 | 8 |
| (d) | 3.6 | 8 |

6. The primary financial statements are:

   1. profit and loss account
   2. the statement of total recognised gains and losses
   3. cash flow statement
   4. balance sheet
   5. directors' report
   6. the five year historic summary.

   (a) all the above

   (b) all except 6

   (c) all except 5 and 6

   (d) 1 and 4 only.

*(Answers are given in the Appendix)*

**Exam-style question**

Taken from the CIB exam paper, October 1995.

The following information is provided for Brownlee plc:

### Profit and loss account extracts, 1994

|  | £000 |
| --- | ---: |
| Profit before taxation | 5,600 |
| Corporation tax | 1,680 |
|  | 3,920 |
| Dividends: Ordinary shares | (2,000) |
| Preference shares | (800) |
| Retained profit for the year | 1,120 |

# FINANCIAL STATEMENTS

## Balance sheet extracts at 31 December 1994

|  | £000 |
|---|---:|
| Issued share capital (£1 shares) | 5,000 |
| Retained profit | 26,100 |
|  | 31,100 |
| 8% Preference shares | 10,000 |
| Shareholders' funds | 41,100 |

**Required**

(a) Define 'earnings per share' and explain the purpose of this calculation. [3]

(b) Calculate the earnings per share of Brownlee plc for 1994 based on the above information. [4]

(c) (i) Explain the nature and purpose of a bonus (capitalisation) issue of ordinary shares. [4]

    (ii) Produce revised balance sheet extracts as at 31 December 1994 for Brownlee plc, assuming that a bonus issue of five fully paid ordinary shares was made at that date for every ordinary share previously held. [2]

(d) Recalculate the earnings per share of Brownlee plc for 1994, assuming that the bonus issue referred to under (c) had been made. Indicate the adjustment required to the corresponding figure for 1993 which was reported in the previous year's accounts at 54p per share, and explain the reason for the adjustment. [7]

*Note:* The directors have no plans to increase the total dividend payable should the bonus issue be made.

[Total 20]

## Further reading

FRS3 'Reporting financial performance'

SSAP21 'Accounting for leases and hire purchase contracts'

SSAP25 'Segmental reporting'

SSAP4 'Accounting for government grants'

# FINANCIAL REPORTING, ANALYSIS AND PLANNING

# Unit 7

# Taxation

> **Objectives**
>
> After studying this Unit you should be able to:
>
> - account for mainstream corporation tax
>
> - prepare a basic corporation tax computation
>
> - prepare a basic capital allowances computation
>
> - apply the principles of SSAP8 'The treatment of taxation under the imputation system in the accounts of companies' in accounting for advance corporation tax (ACT)
>
> - understand the need for and apply the concept of deferred taxation
>
> - apply the principles of SSAP15 'Accounting for deferred tax'

Note: This unit is primarily concerned with the principles of taxation and you should be aware that the rates of taxation are continually changing.

## 1 Introduction

1.1 Businesses are concerned mainly with two types of tax, tax based on profits (corporation tax) and tax based on sales (VAT). Sales based taxation is not part of the syllabus. The main aspect of tax you need to be concerned with is the tax based on the profits of companies.

1.2 Because companies have a separate legal identity, they are taxed independently from the owners (shareholders) of that company. Companies pay tax at different rates and using different rules from individuals. The tax applicable to companies is called corporation tax (CT) and is payable at two different rates, currently 24% for 'small' profits and 33% for 'large' profits. CT is levied on a company's *taxable* profits. This is *not* the same as its *accounting* profit.

### Calculation of taxable profit

1.3 The starting point is the company's accounting profit, i.e. the profit before taxation. This profit is adjusted for the following items.

- Expenses charged in the profit and loss account not allowed for tax purposes, e.g. depreciation; personal expenses (strictly these should not be put through the company's accounts under the proprietorship concept

FINANCIAL REPORTING, ANALYSIS AND PLANNING

either); certain non-specific provisions, for instance a general provision for doubtful debts.

- Income credited to the profit and loss account which is not taxable, e.g. certain government grants.
- Capital allowances for the purchase of qualifying fixed assets (see below).

## 2 Capital allowances

2.1 Capital allowances are amounts allowed by the Inland Revenue against the cost of purchasing certain qualifying fixed assets. In the financial statements we write off the cost of fixed assets by depreciating them over their useful economic life (see Unit 4). As you may remember, the method of depreciation used, the rate used or depreciation period are all estimates made at the start of the asset's useful life. Different companies may make different estimates, use different methods or different rates. The Inland Revenue allows no such latitude in calculating capital allowances. Strict rules exist regarding which assets qualify for capital allowances and the rates allowed.

2.2 Generally qualifying assets fall into two categories:

- industrial buildings
- plant and machinery (including motor vehicles).

2.3 Capital allowances are currently 4% and 25% p.a. reducing balance respectively. Rules also restrict the maximum capital allowances that can be claimed in certain circumstances. For example, the maximum capital allowance on a motor car is £2,000 per annum.

2.4 The carrying value of fixed assets in capital allowance terms is called the Tax Written Down Value (WDV).

## 3 Corporation tax computation

### Example 7.1

Sibrey plc, for the year ended 31/12/X4 has made an accounting profit of £6m. Entertaining expenditure charged in the accounts amounts to £500,000. In addition, a non-taxable receipt of £300,000 has been included in the accounts.

Extracts from the company's fixed assets note:

|  | Land & buildings £000 | Motor vehicles £000 | Plant & machinery £000 | Total £000 |
|---|---|---|---|---|
| *Cost* | | | | |
| At 1/1/X4 | 2,400 | 600 | 5,400 | 8,400 |
| Additions (all 30/9/X4) | – | 200 | 600 | 800 |
| At 31/12/X4 | 2,400 | 800 | 6,000 | 9,200 |

# TAXATION

*Accumulated depreciation*

| | | | | |
|---|---|---|---|---|
| At 1/1/X4 | 300 | 200 | 2,800 | 3,300 |
| Charge for year | 50 | 200 | 320 | 570 |
| At 31/12/X4 | 350 | 400 | 3,120 | 3,870 |

*Net book value*

| | | | | |
|---|---|---|---|---|
| At 31/12/X4 | 2,050 | 400 | 2,880 | 5,330 |
| At 1/1/X4 | 2,100 | 400 | 2,600 | 5,100 |

The tax written down value at 1/1/X4 is £1,400,000 for the buildings and £2,300,000 for plant and machinery (including motor vehicles).

Calculate the tax liability assuming the company pays tax at the 33% rate.

**Solution**

**Corporation tax computation**

| | £000 |
|---|---|
| Profit per accounts | 6,000 |
| add back non-allowables: | |
| Depreciation | 570 |
| Entertaining | 500 |
| less non-chargeable income | (300) |
| less capital allowances (see below) | (681) |
| Taxable profit – called *Profits chargeable to corporation tax* | 6,089 |
| Tax at 33% | 2,009 (payable nine months after the year end) |

**Capital allowance computation**

| | Industrial buildings | Plant & machinery pool | Capital allowances |
|---|---|---|---|
| | £000 | £000 | £000 |
| Tax WDV at 1/1/X4 | 1,400 | 2,300 | |
| Writing down allowance at 4% (Ind.bldgs.) and 25% (Plant) | (56) | (575) | 631 |
| | 1,344 | 1,725 | |
| Additions | 0 | 800 | |
| Writing down allowance at 25% on additions £800 × 3/12ths | | (50) | 50 |
| Tax WDV at 31/12/X4 | 1,344 | 2,475 | |
| Total capital allowances | | | 681 |

# FINANCIAL REPORTING, ANALYSIS AND PLANNING

### Asset disposals and non-pool assets

3.1 General assets are pooled together, as can be seen above. Certain unusual non-pool assets or cars costing more than £8,000 will not be pooled but must be accounted for separately. Remember that the maximum CA for a motor vehicle is £2,000, therefore if a car costing £20,000 were included in the pool above, £5,000 (25% × £20,000) may be calculated, in error, as the capital allowance. Thus such assets are not pooled, but are accounted for individually.

3.2 On the sale or ultimate disposal of a non-pool asset, a balancing charge or allowance is made. The proceeds are credited to the assets tax WDV, any positive remainder (where the proceeds are less than the WDV) is given as a balancing allowance, a negative remainder (where the proceeds are more than the WDV) is a balancing charge – a kind of negative capital allowance.

3.3 On the sale or disposal of a pool asset, the proceeds are simply taken away from the pool, and the pool continues as before – assuming that the company still has qualifying assets. If all its pool assets have been sold (for instance if the business has been liquidated) then a balancing charge or balancing allowance on the whole pool will arise.

### Example 7.2

Because of a cash crisis, Sibrey plc (above) sells and leases back all its land and buildings on 1 January 19X5 for a consideration of £2,000,000 (including £400,000 for the land). On 1 January 19X5 Sibrey sells some plant and machinery for proceeds of £200,000. On 1 July 19X5, Sibrey buys a car for £10,000.

Calculate Sibrey's capital allowances for 19X5.

Solution

### *Capital allowance computation*

|  | *Industrial buildings* | *Plant & machinery pool* | *Car regn. No. XXXX XXX* | *Capital allowances* |
|---|---|---|---|---|
|  | £000 | £000 | £000 | £000 |
| Tax WDV at 1/1/X5 | 1,344 | 2,475 |  |  |
| Disposal proceeds | (1,600) | (200) |  |  |
|  | (256) | 2,275 |  |  |
| Balancing charge | 256 |  |  | (256) |
| Writing down allowance at 25% |  | (569) |  | 569 |
|  |  | 1,706 |  |  |
| Additions |  |  | 10 |  |
| Writing down allowance Maximum £2,000 × 6/12ths |  |  | (1) | 1 |
| Tax WDV at 31/12/X5 | 0 | 1,706 | 9 |  |
| Total capital allowances |  |  |  | 314 |

# TAXATION

## 4 Advance corporation tax (ACT)

4.1 If a company makes a qualifying distribution (usually a dividend), it is required to pay some of its corporation tax *earlier than normal* – in advance. This advance tax is called, not surprisingly, advance corporation tax (ACT). Accounting for ACT is covered by SSAP8 'The treatment of taxation under the imputation system in the accounts of companies.' The title is off-putting enough and applying this standard can be problematic. However, for the purposes of this examination, only the basic principles need to be understood. You are training to be a banker with accounting knowledge; not a tax expert.

4.2 As mentioned above, ACT is linked to dividend payments. In principle, the amount of ACT to be paid is equivalent to the basic rate of income tax on the gross amount which the company pays. The shareholders receive the net amount, as though basic rate income tax had already been deducted. This has been complicated in recent years by the introduction of different lower rate tax bands. In the examination you will be given the appropriate rate.

4.3 At present the rate for ACT purposes is 20%. Thus if a company pays a gross dividend of £100,000, it will pay £80,000 (80%) to the shareholder and £20,000 (20%) to the Inland Revenue as ACT. The shareholder receives a certificate of tax deducted showing that the £20,000 (20%) tax has been paid on his behalf. If, for example, the taxpayer was liable at the higher 40% rate he/she would have to account for the extra £20,000 at a later date.

4.4 ACT is not an *extra* tax – it is corporation tax in *advance*. Thus when the company comes to settle its year end liability it can deduct any ACT already paid.

4.5 ACT is payable 14 days after the end of 'return periods'. These are the four quarters of the year and also the year end, if it does not end on one of the quarter ends.

### Example 7.3

Algar Limited wishes to pay an interim dividend of 10% on its issued share capital of £1m. Assume the company pays the dividend on 1/9/X6. For the year ended 31 December 19X6, the company's profits chargeable to corporation tax are £5m. Using a corporation tax rate of 33% and an ACT rate of 1/4 (20/80ths), calculate the actual tax payable and the due dates.

### Solution

Tax computation:

|  | £000 |  |
|---|---|---|
| Profits chargeable to corporation tax | 5,000 |  |
| Tax thereon at 33% | 1,650 |  |
| *less ACT paid* |  |  |
| Dividend 10% × £10m = £1m × 1/4 | (250) | paid 14/10/X6 |
| Tax liability | 1,400 | payable 1/10/X7 |

# FINANCIAL REPORTING, ANALYSIS AND PLANNING

## ACT set-off

4.6 The basic rule is that only ACT *actually paid* can be set off against that year's liability. Thus for example, if our dividend above had been paid in October, the ACT on it would not have been due until 14 January in the following year - 19X7; therefore it would not have been available for offset against the profits for the year ended 30/12/X6. Instead ACT on that dividend could be offset against corporation tax on the profits of the year ending 31/12/X7, payable 1/10/X8.

4.7 In exceptional circumstances ACT can be set-off against corporation tax paid in the *previous* six years. For example, a company may make a loss in its current year – but could still pay a dividend and hence ACT. It will have no tax liability for the current year due to the loss. However it has still paid some advance corporation tax. This ACT paid can be used to offset corporation tax paid in earlier (profitable) years. It would actually result in a tax refund – as the previous years' corporation tax will have been paid.

4.8 If the company does not have any previous tax paid to reclaim, perhaps in the case of a new company, it can carry forward ACT and set it off against future tax liabilities.

Try and think of ACT paid as an asset – a kind of prepayment of tax.

## Proposed dividends

4.9 Another consideration arises in the common situation when, at a company's year end, a company's directors *propose* a dividend.

### Example 7.4

On 2/2/X7 Gillham Limited declares a first and final dividend of £300,000 for the year ended 31/12/X6. No dividends have been paid during the year and the corporation tax liability, before any deduction of ACT, is estimated at £250,000. Gillham customarily pays its final dividend five months after the year end. Show the entries for taxation in Gillham's books. *Assume an income tax rate of 25%, i.e. ACT at 1/4 (20/80ths).*

### Solution

#### At the year end

Debit    Profit and loss account – corporation tax £250,000
Credit   Creditors due within one year – corporation tax £250,000.

*\* Recognising the tax liability due next year \**

Also the company will have to account for the proposed dividend.

Debit    Profit and loss account – dividends £300,000
Credit   Creditors due within one year – proposed dividends £300,000.

However the company will also have to recognise that, when it pays the dividend next year, it will also have to account for ACT (of £300,000 × 1/4 = £75,000) on that dividend.

# TAXATION

Therefore, assuming that the dividend will be paid in May as normal, the company will have to pay ACT of £75,000 on 14 July 19X7 (14 days after the quarter end in which the dividend is paid).

Credit     Creditors due within one year – ACT payable £75,000.

What is the other side of that entry?

Remember that ACT is not an extra tax – it is tax paid in advance, a kind of prepayment. Therefore the company should set up an corresponding *debtor* for £75,000, to account for the ACT it will eventually be able to recover:

Debit debtors – ACT recoverable £75,000.

### *In 19X7*

In May the company will pay the final dividend.

Debit      Creditors due within one year – proposed dividend £300,000.
Credit     Cash £300,000.

On 14 July it will pay the ACT on the dividend.

Debit      Creditors due within one year – ACT payable £75,000.
Credit     Cash £75,000.

On 1 October it will pay the MCT liability.

Debit      Creditors due within one year – corporation tax £250,000.
Credit     Cash £250,000.

(Note that there is no ACT set off here as no ACT was paid in 19X6)

### *In 19X8*

The company will be able to offset the ACT paid in the previous year – by deducting £75,000 from the tax liability. Assume for example that 19X7's liability is £500,000 (19X6 £250,000):

1 October 19X8

Debit      Creditors due within one year – corporation tax £500,000
Credit     Cash £425,000
Credit     Debtors ACT recoverable £75,000.

4.10    One final point to bear in mind regarding the ACT recoverable. Remember we have said that when a company proposes a dividend, it should account for the ACT payable (in the next year) and the ACT recoverable (in the following year). The debtor will be 'receivable' in all likelihood in 21 months time – nine months after the end of next year. Thus, it should be shown within current assets – but disclosed as an item receivable after more than one year (this is a requirement for all such long term receivables).

4.11    Finally, if the company has set up a provision for deferred taxation (a kind of long term tax liability – see below) then any ACT recoverable should not be shown as a separate asset. Instead it should be shown as a deduction from the deferred tax provision. The logic here is netting off a long term tax receivable (ACT recoverable) against a long term tax 'liability' (deferred tax).

### Investment income from other companies

4.12 When a company holds shares in another company – any dividends it receives will be received *net*, i.e. the paying company will have deducted tax on its behalf. This tax that they have paid on its behalf can be deducted from any ACT that it needs to pay.

### Example 7.5

In February, Irons Limited pays last year's final dividend of £600,000. In March it also receives a dividend of £80,000 from its investment in Bowers Limited. What is the ACT position?

### Solution

Irons needs to account for ACT, on the dividend paid of $1/4 \times £600,000 = £150,000$, to the Inland Revenue. However, Bowers Limited has, in effect, paid £20,000 ACT on its behalf – Irons has received £80,000 (net, 80%), Bowers has paid 20% – £20,000 on Irons' behalf.

Thus only the *net* £130,000 (£150,000 less £20,000) needs to be paid to the Inland Revenue, on 14 April.

4.13 Finally, how do we present these dividends in and out in our accounts? There is a simple rule:

> Dividends in – show *gross*
>
> Dividends out – show *net*

Thus Irons will show:

- dividend income – called 'income from fixed asset investments' or 'franked investment income' – of £100,000 (£80,000 received grossed up by £20,000)
- dividends payable of £600,000 (actually this would have been shown in last year's accounts).

4.14 To complete the double entry we need to account for the £20,000 tax that we have used to gross up the dividend receivable. This is added to the tax charge for the year.

|  | £ |
|---|---|
| Mainstream corporation tax at $x$% | X |
| Tax on franked investment income | 20,000 |

Finally, of course, the net ACT paid in the year, including the £130,000 paid on 14 April will be available to set off against this year's tax liability.

TAXATION

## Student Activity 1

Before reading the next section of text, answer the following questions and then check your answers against the paragraph(s) indicated.

1. Why is accounting profit different from taxable profit? *(Paragraph 1.2)*
2. Explain the principles for dealing with asset disposals. *(Paragraphs 3.1 – 3.3)*
3. How do we calculate the rate of ACT? *(Paragraphs 4.3)*
4. When is ACT payable? *(Paragraphs 4.5)*
5. What are the tax effects of proposing a dividend? *(Paragraph 4.9 and Example 7.4*

If your answers are basically correct, then proceed to the next section. If significant parts of your answers are wrong, then study the whole of the relevant sections again in detail. Note your areas of weakness and be prepared for further questions on these areas at the end of this unit.

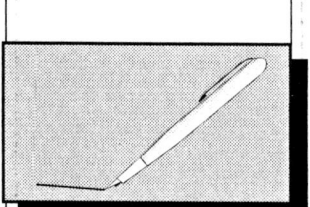

## 5 Deferred taxation

5.1 Strangely, this is a tax that is never payable to the Inland Revenue! The Inland Revenue is concerned with corporation tax and ACT as explained above. However, once again we must exercise the prudence concept and account for tax that is hypothetically payable in the future.

**Example 7.5**

On 1 January 19X4, in order to finance a project, Glass Limited takes out a two year loan of £1m with interest of 10% payable six monthly in arrears, starting 1 July 19X4. Thus Glass makes interest payments of £50,000 (£1m × 10% × 6/12ths) on 1 July 19X4, 1 January 19X5, 1 July 19X5 and 1 January 19X6. The project is not particularly profitable – in fact it only breaks even – therefore it results in increased revenue of £100,000 a year, balanced by the interest charge of £100,000 per year.

In respect of the interest on the loan, the accounts for the year ended 31 December 19X4 will show:

|  | £ |
|---|---|
| *in the profit and loss account:* | |
| Interest payable and similar charges | 100,000 |
| | |
| *in the balance sheet:* | |
| Creditors due <1 year – accrued interest | 50,000 |

Glass has, before interest, ongoing profits of £300,000 (all taxable) for 19X4 – 19X6 and the company pays tax at the 24% rate.

Show the extracts from the profit and loss account for the three years.

### Solution

**Profit and loss extracts**

|  | 19X4<br>£000 | 19X5<br>£000 | 19X6<br>£000 |
|---|---|---|---|
| Profit before interest and tax | 400 | 400 | 300 |
| Interest payable | (100) | (100) | 0 |
| Profit before taxation | 300 | 300 | 300 |
| Taxation (workings below) | (84) | (72) | (60) |
| Profit after taxation | 216 | 228 | 240 |
| *Tax computation* | | | |
| Taxable income | 400 | 400 | 300 |
| Tax relief on interest *paid* | (50) | (100) | (50) |
| Profits chargeable to corporation tax | 350 | 300 | 250 |
| Tax thereon at 24% | 84 | 72 | 60 |

5.2  We will have some difficulty in attempting to interpret this set of accounts. We would have expected profits to be the same in all three years – the two years of the break-even project and the following year. However, we can see that post-tax profits start off at a low level and increase for the three years, implying that Glass' performance is improving. The reason for this inconsistency, between our expectations and the actual results, is the tax treatment of the interest. Interest is tax deductible *only when paid*. However, we account for it in the profit and loss account on an *accruals basis* – regardless of whether it is has been paid or not.

5.3  The tax charge decreases from £84,000 to £72,000 down to £60,000; when profits before tax are static at £300,000 each year.

**Differences**

5.4  The cause of this situation is the different tax treatment of the interest with the accounts treatment. Accrued interest is only one example of such a *difference.* Other examples of differing treatments in the tax computation to that in the accounts include the following:

| *Item* | *Tax Computation* | *Accounts* |
|---|---|---|
| Fixed assets | Capital allowances | Depreciation |
| Interest/Royalties | Receipts and payments basis | Accruals basis |
| Provisions, e.g. bad debts | General provisions not allowable | General provisions made |
| Revaluation of fixed assets | No tax effects | Revaluations incorporated |

5.5  These differences are normally only relevant for a period of time. For example, over the course of the life of a fixed asset eventually the tax computation will write off all its cost. In the accounts, depreciation will write off all the cost. It will just be at *different times*. Thus these type of differences are called *timing differences*. They are said to *originate* and then *reverse*.

5.6  There are differences in the tax treatment of items and the accounts treatment which are *permanent*. Entertaining expenditure is one such permanent difference. It will never be allowed in the tax computation,

# TAXATION

although it is charged in the accounts. We do not need to account for these permanent differences.

5.7 SSAP15 'Accounting for deferred tax' was introduced to adjust the accounts for the effects of such timing differences. Let us continue our example to see how the provisions of SSAP15 are implemented.

**Example 7.5 continued**

### ACCOUNTING FOR DEFERRED TAX

We can see that a timing difference has arisen. At the end of 19X4, Glass has accrued for £50,000 of interest *payable but not yet paid*. The solution is to provide for tax on the difference arising in the year.

Only £50,000 is allowed in the tax computation, but Glass has charged £100,000 in the accounts. Thus a timing difference of £50,000 has originated. Glass needs to make a provision at 24% = £12,000

Dr. Provision for deferred taxation £12,000
Cr. Profit and loss account £12,000.

In 19X5 no timing difference arises because the tax allowance of £100,000 equates with the charge in the accounts of £100,000.

In 19X6 the timing difference reverses. There is no charge in the accounts but £50,000 tax paid is allowed in the tax computation. Thus Glass needs to reverse the provision by £50,000 × 24% = £12,000

Dr. Profit and loss account £12,000
Cr. Provision for deferred taxation £12,000

*Adjusted profit and loss accounts*

|  | 19X4 £000 | 19X5 £000 | 19X6 £000 |
|---|---|---|---|
| Profit before interest and tax | 400 | 400 | 300 |
| Interest payable | (100) | (100) |  |
| Profit before taxation | 300 | 300 | 300 |
| Taxation: |  |  |  |
| Corporation tax | (84) | (72) | (60) |
| *Deferred tax* | 12 | – | (12) |
| Profit after taxation | 228 | 228 | 228 |

As you can see, the level of profits after taxation has now been equalised for all three years – in line with the underlying performance of the company.

In the balance sheet we will have:

|  | 19X4 £000 | 19X5 £000 | 19X6 £000 |
|---|---|---|---|
| Deferred tax asset/(provision) | 12 | 12 | 0 |

The deferred tax balance can be either an asset or a provision. In the above example, because the originating difference was *unfavourable* (Glass had the full £100,000 charge in the accounts – but tax relief of only £50,000), the company needed to set up a deferred tax asset (or a negative provision). The asset is there for the future *favourable* reversal (in 19X6 when there is no profit and loss charge but tax relief of £50,000). Let us look at an example which results in a deferred tax provision.

**Example 7.6**

Nevard Limited purchases a fixed asset for £120,000 on 1 January 19X0. The asset has a useful life of 10 years, when it will be disposed with a nil residual value. The company has profits before tax and depreciation (all taxable) of £20,000 per annum. Tax is payable at 33%.

Accounts before taking account of deferred tax are shown below.

|  | X0 £000 | X1 £000 | X2 £000 | X3 £000 | X4 £000 | X5 £000 | X6 £000 | X7 £000 | X8 £000 | X9 £000 |
|---|---|---|---|---|---|---|---|---|---|---|
| Profit before depreciation | 20 | 20 | 20 | 20 | 20 | 20 | 20 | 20 | 20 | 20 |
| Depreciation | (12) | (12) | (12) | (12) | (12) | (12) | (12) | (12) | (12) | (12) |
| Profit before tax | 8 | 8 | 8 | 8 | 8 | 8 | 8 | 8 | 8 | 8 |
| Tax credit/(charge) | 3.3 | 0.82 | (1.02) | (2.44) | (3.47) | (4.26) | (4.85) | (5.28) | (5.61) | (3.60) |
| Profit after tax | 11.3 | 8.82 | 6.98 | 5.56 | 4.53 | 3.74 | 3.15 | 2.72 | 2.39 | 5.4 |
| *Tax computation* |  |  |  |  |  |  |  |  |  |  |
| Taxable profit | 20 | 20 | 20 | 20 | 20 | 20 | 20 | 20 | 20 | 20 |
| Capital allowances (25% reducing balance basis) | (30) | (22.5) | (16.9) | (12.6) | (9.5) | (7.1) | (5.3) | (4) | (3.0) | (9.1) balancing allowance |
| Profits liable to tax | (10) | (2.5) | 3.1 | 7.4 | 10.5 | 12.9 | 14.7 | 16 | 17 | 10.9 |
| Tax at 33% | (3.3) | (0.82) | 1.02 | 2.44 | 3.47 | 4.26 | 4.85 | 5.28 | 5.61 | 3.60 |

Again the underlying performance of the business is identical in all ten years – but the profit and loss account does not reflect that. Post-tax profits peak at £11,300 in 19X0 falling to £2,390 in 19X8.

We need to account for deferred tax on the timing differences arising – to smooth out the level of post-tax profits. The distortion is caused by a timing difference; this time accelerated capital allowances (ACAs).

To calculate the differences arising we can compare the year end tax values of the asset with the accounts value of the asset. That is, we compare the tax written down value (WDV) with the net book value (NBV) of the asset. Deferred tax at 33% should be provided on the resulting difference.

# TAXATION

|  | X0 £000 | X1 £000 | X2 £000 | X3 £000 | X4 £000 | X5 £000 | X6 £000 | X7 £000 | X8 £000 | X9 £000 |
|---|---|---|---|---|---|---|---|---|---|---|
| *Tax value* | | | | | | | | | | |
| Cost/WDV | 120 | 90 | 67.5 | 50.6 | 38 | 28.5 | 21.4 | 16.1 | 12.1 | 9.1 |
| Less capital allowances | (30) | (22.5) | (16.9) | (12.6) | (9.5) | (7.1) | (5.3) | (4) | (3.0) | (9.1) |
| WDV | 90 | 67.5 | 50.6 | 38 | 28.5 | 21.4 | 16.1 | 12.1 | 9.1 | 0 |
| *Accounts value* | | | | | | | | | | |
| Cost/NBV | 120 | 108 | 96 | 84 | 72 | 60 | 48 | 36 | 24 | 12 |
| Depreciation | (12) | (12) | (12) | (12) | (12) | (12) | (12) | (12) | (12) | (12) |
| NBV | 108 | 96 | 84 | 72 | 60 | 48 | 36 | 24 | 12 | 0 |
| | | | | | | | | | | |
| *Difference* | 18 | 28.5 | 33.4 | 34 | 31.5 | 26.6 | 19.9 | 11.9 | 2.9 | 0 |
| Provision at 33% | 5.94 | 9.41 | 11.02 | 11.22 | 10.4 | 8.78 | 6.57 | 3.93 | 0.96 | 0 |
| P/L charge/ (credit) | 5.94 | 3.47 | 1.61 | 0.20 | (0.82) | (1.62) | (2.21) | (2.64) | (2.97) | (0.96) |

Incorporating this into the accounts:

|  | X0 £000 | X1 £000 | X2 £000 | X3 £000 | X4 £000 | X5 £000 | X6 £000 | X7 £000 | X8 £000 | X9 £000 |
|---|---|---|---|---|---|---|---|---|---|---|
| Profit before depreciation | 20 | 20 | 20 | 20 | 20 | 20 | 20 | 20 | 20 | 20 |
| Depreciation | (12) | (12) | (12) | (12) | (12) | (12) | (12) | (12) | (12) | (12) |
| Profit before tax | 8 | 8 | 8 | 8 | 8 | 8 | 8 | 8 | 8 | 8 |
| *Tax* | | | | | | | | | | |
| Corporation tax | 3.3 | 0.82 | (1.02) | (2.44) | (3.47) | (4.26) | (4.85) | (5.28) | (5.61) | (3.60) |
| Deferred tax | (5.94) | (3.47) | (1.61) | (0.20) | 0.82 | 1.62 | 2.21 | 2.64 | 2.97 | 0.96 |
| *Profit after tax* | 5.36 | 5.35 | 5.37 | 5.36 | 5.35 | 5.36 | 5.36 | 5.36 | 5.36 | 5.36 |

Accounting for deferred tax has effectively smoothed the profits over the 10 year period, at £5,360 per year. This incidentally, is the profit before taxation of £8,000 less tax at 33%.

## Alternative methods of accounting for deferred taxation

5.8 SSAP15 recognises three methods of accounting for deferred tax. The first method – the 'flow through approach' – basically ignores deferred tax entirely. The argument is that the accounts should reflect the actual tax payable, not an hypothetical amount not actually due to the Inland Revenue. However, the counter argument to this is the prudence concept. It is imprudent not to account for tax which is, in theory, payable in albeit long distant future accounting periods.

5.9 On the other extreme is the 'full provision approach' – illustrated in the examples above, which argues that provision should be made for all timing differences.

5.10 Finally, the preferred approach is encompassed in the 'partial provision approach' which argues that provision should only be made for *timing differences that are likely to reverse*.

### Example 7.7

Schroeder Limited holds an investment in $3^{1}/_{2}\%$ Government War loan stock. Under the accruals convention the company would accrue for interest receivable, regardless of whether by the year end the interest has actually been received. Thus a timing difference would arise representing the difference between the interest *received* and the interest *receivable*.

However, this Government stock is irredeemable and, assuming that Schroeder has no plans to sell the stock, then the timing difference would have no prospect of reversing or crystallising. Thus the argument is that no provision should be made for this difference. However the *unprovided* difference should be disclosed in the accounts.

A final point regarding a deferred tax provision. Remember that any deferred tax provision can be set off by an ACT asset; which usually arises from an accrual for a proposed dividend.

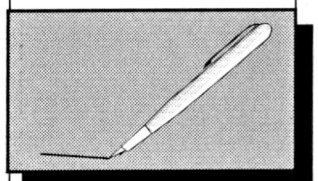

## Student Activity 2

Answer the following questions and then check your answers against the paragraphs indicated.

1. Give some examples where the tax treatment of an item is different from the accounts treatment. *(Paragraph 5.4)*

2. Explain the distinction between a permanent difference and a timing difference. How do we account for each? *(Paragraphs 5.5 & 5.6)*

3. What are the arguments for and against the flow through approach? *(Paragraph 5.8)*

If your answers are basically correct, then proceed to the Summary and questions. If significant parts of your answers are wrong, then study the whole of the relevant sections again in detail. Note your areas of weakness and be prepared for further questions on these areas at the end of this Unit.

# TAXATION

> **Summary**
>
> Now that you have completed this unit you should be able to:
> - [ ] prepare a basic corporation tax computation with capital allowances
> - [ ] account for advanced corporation tax in line with SSAP8
> - [ ] present dividends received and paid in the financial statements
> - [ ] understand the need for and apply the concept of deferred taxation, applying the principles of SSAP15
> - [ ] outline the alternative methods of accounting for deferred taxation.

## Self-assessment questions

**Short answer questions**

1. Explain why in the case of fixed assets, timing differences arise. In addition, explain why the Inland Revenue sets rules for calculating capital allowances and does not rely on the figures in the financial statements.

2. What is advance corporation tax?

3. How do we show dividend income and dividend payments in the financial statements?

4. Is a deferred tax provision a liability?

5. When might a company disclose but not provide for deferred taxation?

*(Answers are given in the Appendix)*

**Multiple choice questions**

The following data should be used for questions 1, 2 and 3.

Rutherford plc's financial statements for the year ended 31 December 19X1 include the following items:

|  | £000 |
|---|---:|
| Corporation tax at 33% | 1,000 |
| Dividend income (received 1 May 19X1) | 72 |
| Interim dividend (paid 1 June 19X1) | 228 |
| Final proposed dividend | 344 |

There was no ACT balance brought forward at the start of the year. ACT rate is 20/80ths.

1. What is the total balance for corporation tax payable to be included within creditors as at 31 December 19X1?

    (a) £1,000,000

    (b) £961,000

# FINANCIAL REPORTING, ANALYSIS AND PLANNING

(c) £1,047,000

(d) £875,000

2. In the profit and loss account for the year ended 31 December 19X1 which of the following is correct?

|     | Income from fixed asset investments £000 | Dividends payable £000 |
|-----|---:|---:|
| (a) | 72 | 228 |
| (b) | 72 | 572 |
| (c) | 90 | 228 |
| (d) | 90 | 572 |

3. If in 19X2, the company agreed with the Inland Revenue that the corporation tax payable for 19X1 is not £1m but £990,000, how should the difference be accounted for?

   (a) As a prior year adjustment in the 19X2 accounts.

   (b) By deducting £10,000 from the 19X2 tax charge.

   (c) By deducting £10,000 from the 19X2 tax charge, and disclosing as an exceptional item.

   (d) No special accounting treatment needed.

4. According to SSAP15, deferred tax should be calculated:

   (a) using the full provision basis on timing differences originating in the year

   (b) using the partial provision basis on timing differences reversing in the year

   (c) using the full provision basis on timing differences reversing in the year

   (d) using the partial provision basis on timing differences originating during the year.

5. An extract from Russell Limited's profit and loss account for the year ended 31 December 19X1 shows the following items:

   **Taxation on ordinary activities**

   |  | £000 |
   |---|---:|
   | Corporation tax at 33% | 500 |
   | Underprovision in 19X0 | 30 |
   | Deferred tax | 60 |
   |  | 590 |

   The company paid a dividend of £100,000 in the year and proposes a final dividend of £200,000. The company had no dividend income during the year and there were no opening ACT balances. The deferred tax provision as at 1 January 19X1 was £300,000.

   The ACT rate is 20/80ths.

   What is the deferred tax provision in the balance sheet at 31 December 19X1?

TAXATION

| | £000 |
|---|---|
| (a) | 310 |
| (b) | 290 |
| (c) | 300 |
| (d) | 285 |

*(Answers are given in the Appendix)*

**Exam-style question**

Taken from the CIB exam paper, May 1996.

The final accounts of Pavin Ltd are in the process of being prepared. The following information is provided.

### *Profit and loss account for the year ended 31 December 1995*

| | £000 |
|---|---|
| Turnover | 3,620 |
| Franked investment income (amount received) | 88 |
| | 3,708 |
| Cost of goods sold | 2,105 |
| Administrative expensess | 526 |
| Distribution costs | 317 |
| Profit | 760 |

### *Statement of Movement on Reserves*

| | |
|---|---|
| Retained profit brought forward | 560 |
| Retained profit for 1995 | 760 |
| Retained profit carried forward | 1,320 |

### *Balance sheet as at 31 December 1995*

| | | |
|---|---|---|
| Plant and machinery at cost | | 2,108 |
| Less Accumulated depreciation to 31 December 1994 | | 1,000 |
| | | 1,108 |
| Development expenditure | | 190 |
| Stocks | | 351 |
| Debtors and prepayments | | 410 |
| Cash at bank and in hand | | 7 |
| | | 2,066 |

### *Capital, reserves and liabilities*

| | |
|---|---|
| Called up share capital (£0.50 shares) | 500 |
| Profit and loss account | 1,320 |
| | 1,820 |
| 10% debentures | 120 |
| Trade creditors | 126 |
| | 2,066 |

# FINANCIAL REPORTING, ANALYSIS AND PLANNING

1. The development expenditure ledger account showed the following movements during 1995.

   |  | £000 |
   |---|---|
   | Balance 1 January 1995 | 88 |
   | Expenditure during 1995 | 102 |
   | Balance 31 December 1995 | 190 |

   The directors have now decided that it would give a fairer view of the company's performance and financial position if development expenditure was written off immediately it was incurred.

2. The directors have previously valued stock on the first in first out (FIFO) basis. The directors have now decided that the average cost (AVCO) basis should be used. The following valuations are provided:

   |  | 31 December 1994 £000 | 31 December 1995 £000 |
   |---|---|---|
   | FIFO | 316 | 351 |
   | AVCO | 292 | 321 |

3. The company's manufacturing plant was purchased on 1 January 1990 and has been depreciated to 31 December 1994 on the straight line basis at 10% per annum assuming a residual value of £108,000. The remaining useful life was re-assessed at three years on 1 January 1995 and the residual value at the end of that period was estimated to be £148,000.

4. The figure for debtors and prepayments includes £90,000 due from one of Pavin's customers which went into receivership on 5 January 1996. It is not thought that any of the debt will be recovered.

5. The debentures were raised on 1 January 1995. The directors have decided to make an annual transfer of £12,000 to debenture redemption reserve in anticipation of repayment on 31 December 2004. Provision is to be made in the accounts for the interest due.

6. The corporation tax charge for the year (excluding tax credits) is estimated at £40,000.

7. The directors propose to pay a final dividend of 8 pence per share. The rate of advance corporation tax is 20/80ths.

**Required**

(a) Define the following terms and, where possible, provide an example:

   (i) exceptional item;

   (ii) extraordinary item:

   (iii) prior year adjustment [6]

(b) Prepare for Pavin Ltd:

   (i) a profit and loss account for 1995; [7]

   (ii) a statement of movement on reserves for 1995; [7]

(iii) a balance sheet as at 31 December 1995. [10]

The accounts should give effect, as appropriate, to the information provided in 1-7 above. The accounts need not be presented in accordance with the precise provisions of the Companies Acts but should be presented in good form and comply with relevant standard accounting practice so far as the information permits.

*Note:* all items are to be considered material for disclosure purposes. Notes to the accounts are not required.

[Total 30]

## Further reading

SSAP8 'The treatment of taxation under the imputation system in the accounts of companies'

SSAP15 'Accounting for deferred tax'

# Unit 8

## Accounting for Investments

### Objectives

After studying this Unit you should be able to:

- identify various forms of investment: less than 20% holding, associated companies, subsidiary undertakings

- apply the principles of FRS 9 'Associates and Joint Ventures' in using the equity method of accounting to account for such investments

- prepare consolidated accounts where a parent-subsidiary relationship exists

- account for dividends in parent-subsidiary relationships

- deal with inter company items, including unrealised profits on stock

- account for goodwill on acquisition

- apply FRS7 'Fair values in acquisition accounting' in the fair valuation of assets and liabilities

- apply the criteria of FRS6 'Acquisitions and mergers' in identifying situations where merger accounting may be used

- distinguish between merger accounting and acquisition accounting

- identify situations where control exists under the principles of FRS2 'Accounting for subsidiary undertakings'.

## 1 Introduction

1.1 If a company wishes to expand its range of operations, it can do so by acquiring additional assets and liabilities, for example by buying new equipment with borrowed money or by buying the net assets of another company. In either case, the new assets are incorporated in the company's balance sheet and should help to generate future profit.

1.2 An alternative policy is to take a shareholding in another company, and through controlling that company, expand its level of operations.

FINANCIAL REPORTING, ANALYSIS AND PLANNING

1.3 However, a company may make an investment in another company not to expand its operations but purely as an investment. The company may hope that the investment will increase in value and or will pay dividends.

1.4 Sometimes an investment is both an investment for income and a degree of operational control. We are going to look at three types of investment a company may hold – depending of the level of investment made:

- trade investment
- associated company
- subsidiary.

## 2 Trade investment

2.1 Generally a company will hold such an investment for its growth potential and dividend income. As a rule of thumb, when a company acquires less than 20% of another company's share capital, it is treated as a trade investment.

**Accounting treatment**

2.2 Treat the investment as an asset – either fixed or current, depending on how long the company intends to keep the shares. The usual rules for valuing fixed and current assets apply. For example, the fixed asset may be revalued to current value. If there is a permanent diminution in value, the fixed asset should be correspondingly written down. If the investment is held as a current asset, it should be valued at the lower of cost and net realisable value (as for all current assets – see Unit 4).

2.3 Income from such investments should be recorded in the profit and loss account as 'Income from fixed asset investments' or 'Income from other investments' as appropriate. Remember from Unit 7 that such dividend income, will likely be received net (with tax deducted at the basic rate) but should be shown in the accounts gross, with the corresponding tax element added to the tax charge for the period.

## 3 Associated companies

3.1 As a rule of thumb, an investment of between 20% and 50% of another company's share capital should be treated as an associated company. FRS 9 'Associates and Joint Ventures' covers accounting for such investments. The Companies Act 1985 refers to such companies as related companies. At this level of shareholding the investor has *influence on* but not *control of* the company.

**Accounting treatment**

3.2 The equity method of accounting should be used. This method requires the holding company to value the investment on an equity basis, i.e. reflecting the holding company's interest in its share of the associate's assets.

# ACCOUNTING FOR INVESTMENTS

**Example 8.1**

On 31 December 19X1 Henry Limited purchased 25% of the share capital of Katherine Limited for £10m. Katherine Limited's balance sheet at that date shows:

|  | £m |
|---|---|
| Fixed assets – tangible | 30 |
| Net current assets | 8 |
|  | 38 |
| Creditors due >1 year | (6) |
|  | 32 |
| Share capital (£1 shares) | 10 |
| Reserves | 22 |
|  | 32 |

Thus Henry has spent £10m securing influence over Katherine's net assets of £32m. Henry's influence could be equated to its shareholding of 25%. However, Henry's exact degree of influence depends mainly on the other shareholdings in Katherine. If there is only one other shareholder with 75%, then Henry may have *no* influence. If the other 75% were spread between a disparate number of very small shareholders, however, Henry's influence may well be more than 25%. For the purposes of this illustration we will use 25%.

So the situation is:

|  |  | £m |
|---|---|---|
| Consideration paid |  | 10 |
| Katherine's assets | £32m |  |
| × Henry's shareholding | × 25% |  |
|  |  | (8) |
| Goodwill |  | 2 |

Henry has paid £2m over the book value of Katherine's net assets for goodwill. Why? This may have been because the assets were undervalued in Katherine's books, or that certain assets were excluded from Katherine's accounts.

Henry's balance sheet at the year end is as follows.

|  | £m |
|---|---|
| Fixed assets – tangible | 50 |
| Investment in Katherine | 10 |
| Net current assets | 16 |
|  | 76 |
| Creditors due >1 year | (12) |
|  | 64 |
| Share capital (£1 shares) | 20 |
| Reserves | 44 |
|  | 64 |

As can be seen, the investment in Katherine is shown (i) as a fixed asset and (ii) at cost. The former implies that Henry intends to keep the shares in Katherine for the foreseeable future. However, we can now see that showing the investment at cost is *incorrect*. We are going to show the investment using the equity method of accounting, i.e. reflecting Henry's share in the net assets of Katherine.

**Balance sheet**
*Valuation of Katherine*

Katherine should be valued using the following formula:

Investing company's share × Net assets of associated company at balance sheet date

$$25\% \times £32m = £8m$$

Another way of calculating this figure is to use the formula:

| | |
|---|---|
| cost | X |
| less goodwill | (X) |
| plus | |
| investing company's share × | |
| increase in net assets of associate from date of | |
| purchase to balance sheet date | X |

Thus:

| | | £m |
|---|---|---|
| cost | | 10 |
| less goodwill | | (2) |
| | | 8 |
| plus | | |
| investing company's share × | 25% | |
| increase in net assets of Associate from date of purchase to balance sheet date | zero | 0 |
| value of associate | | 8 |

Look at the situation in one year's time: at the end of 19X2 Katherine's balance sheet is as follows.

| | 19X2 £m | 19X1 £m |
|---|---|---|
| Fixed assets – tangible | 36 | 30 |
| Net current assets | 12 | 8 |
| | 48 | 38 |
| Creditors due >1 year | (4) | (6) |
| | 44 | 32 |

# ACCOUNTING FOR INVESTMENTS

| | | |
|---|---:|---:|
| Share capital (£1 shares) | 10 | 10 |
| Reserves | 34 | 22 |
| | 44 | 32 |

As can be seen, the balance sheet of Katherine has risen in value by £12m. We would expect Henry's share in that increase to be £3m (25% × £12m).

## Valuation of Katherine

Using the formula:

Investing company's share × Net assets of associated company at balance sheet date

25% × £44m = £11m.

Or using the alternative formula:

| | | £m |
|---|---|---:|
| Cost | | 10 |
| less goodwill | | (2) |
| plus | | 8 |
| investing company's share × increase in net assets of Associate from date of purchase to balance sheet date | 25% × £44m – £32m | 3 |
| value of associate | | 11 |

As can be seen, using the equity method of accounting, Henry's investment reflects its interest in the *whole* performance of Katherine. The increase/decrease in the carrying value of the Investment is in direct relation to the value of the associate's balance sheet.

## Profit and loss account

In a similar way the investing company (Henry) should account for its share of the Associate's (Katherine's) profits; by using the following formula.

Include

> Investing company's share × Associate's profit before tax

and

> Investing company's share × Associate's tax charge

In 19X1, Henry did not purchase its investment in Katherine until the year end, therefore Henry should not record any share of Katherine's profit or tax for that year.

In 19X2 Katherine's profit and loss account (extract) was as follows.

|  | £m |
|---|---|
| Profit before tax | 32 |
| Tax | (12) |
| Profit after tax | 20 |
| Dividends | (8) |
| Retained profit for financial year | 12 |
| Profit and loss reserve brought forward | 22 |
| Profit and loss reserve carried forward | 34 |

**Solution**

Include the following in Henry's profit and loss account.

Investing company's share × Associate's profit before tax

25%  ×  £32m =  £8m

and

Investing company's share × Associate's tax charge

25%  ×  £12m =  £3m

In addition, Henry, of course, would have been a recipient of 25% of Katherine's dividends. However, by utilising the equity method of accounting, Henry should not show this dividend income in the profit and loss account.

***Overall effect***

|  | £m |
|---|---|
| Investing company's share of associate's profit before tax | 8 |
| less |  |
| Investing company's share of associate's tax charge | (3) |
| less |  |
| Dividends received but not shown in P & L account (25% × £8m) | (2) |
| *Increase in balance sheet valuation of Associate* | 3 |

Where there has been an impairment in any goodwill attributable to an associate or joint venture, the goodwill should be written down. The amount written off in the accounting period should be separately disclosed.

In the consolidated statement of total recognised gains and losses the investor's share of the total recognised gains and losses of its associates should be included, shown separately under each heading where material.

## Student Activity 1

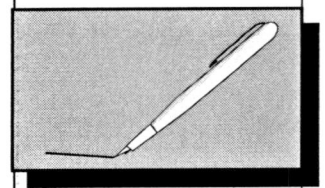

Before reading the next section of text, answer the following questions and then check your answers against the paragraphs indicated.

1. Which three types of investment are you likely to encounter in an exam situation?  *(Paragraph 1.4)*

2. How should trade investments be accounted for?  *(Paragraphs 2.2 & 2.3)*

## ACCOUNTING FOR INVESTMENTS

3. How should associate companies be valued in the balance sheet? *(Example 8.1)*
4. What entries will there be in the profit and loss account relating to associated companies? *(Example 8.1)*

If your answers are basically correct, then proceed to the next section. If significant parts of your answers are wrong, then study the whole of the relevant sections again in detail. Note your areas of weakness and be prepared for further questions on these areas at the end of this Unit.

## 4 Subsidiary

4.1 The implication when a company has a subsidiary is that it has control over that company. Thus it can control the other company's operations and consequently its net assets and profits.

4.2 The rule of thumb is that if an investing company holds more than 50% of the (voting) shares in another company it has a subsidiary. There are other circumstances in which a holding company – subsidiary company situation can arise (see FRS2 below). However, initially for the purposes of this explanation we shall assume that a holding >50% represents a subsidiary.

4.3 If an investor owns, say, 60% of the shares of a company, what degree of control does the investor have? Not 60%. In fact the investor has total control of the company, he can outvote any other shareholders, and as long as he does not infringe their limited statutory rights as a minority, the investor can exercise that control unreservedly.

**Accounting treatment**

4.4 The correct procedure is to prepare *consolidated accounts* – accounts consolidating or aggregating the individual assets and liabilities of the Subsidiary with the individual assets and liabilities of the Investing company. Instead of a one-line entry as with associated companies, add in the subsidiary's fixed assets, current assets, current liabilities, etc.

4.5 However, if the parent company does not own 100% of the subsidiary, the accounts should also reflect that another party – called 'minority interest' – has an interest in the net assets of the subsidiary.

**Example 8.2**

On 31 December 19X1, Pistol plc purchased 80% of the share capital in Fluellen Limited for consideration of £80m. At the time of purchase Fluellen's accounts were as follows:

|  | £m |
|---|---|
| Fixed assets – tangible | 40 |
| Net current assets | 20 |
|  | 60 |
| Creditors due >1 year | (10) |
|  | 50 |

# FINANCIAL REPORTING, ANALYSIS AND PLANNING

| | |
|---|---:|
| Share capital (£1 shares) | 30 |
| Reserves | 20 |
| | 50 |

We can see that the investing company (Pistol) has paid a premium to invest in Fluellen. Pistol has paid £80m for an 80% share in Fluellen's assets of £50m. Thus a premium (called *goodwill on acquisition*) of £40m has arisen (£80m − [80% × £50m]). We will deal with the accounting treatment of the goodwill later, but first let us consider how to incorporate the assets and liabilities of Fluellen in Pistol's accounts.

Pistol's balance sheet at 31 December 19X1 is as follows.

| | £m |
|---|---:|
| Fixed assets – tangible | 100 |
| Investment in Fluellen Limited | 80 |
| | 180 |
| Net current assets | 40 |
| | 220 |
| Creditors due > 1 year | (30) |
| | 190 |
| Share capital (£1 shares) | 100 |
| Reserves | 90 |
| | 190 |

We need to aggregate the assets and liabilities of Pistol and Fluellen. Pistol owns 80% of the equity of Fluellen; however it has control over *all* the assets and liabilities, not just 80% of the assets and liabilities. Therefore we should firstly aggregate all Fluellen's assets and liabilities with those of Pistol.

Simply consolidating the accounts of Pistol and Fluellen we get the following.

| | Pistol £m | Fluellen £m | Group £m |
|---|---:|---:|---:|
| Fixed assets – tangible | 100 | 40 | 140 |
| Investment in Fluellen Ltd. | 80 | – | 80 |
| | 180 | 40 | 220 |
| Net current assets | 40 | 20 | 60 |
| | 220 | 60 | 280 |
| Creditors due >1 year | (30) | (10) | (40) |
| | 190 | 50 | 240 |
| Share capital (£1 shares) | 100 | 30 | 130 |
| Reserves | 90 | 20 | 110 |
| | 190 | 50 | 240 |

However, we have failed to recognise a number of issues.

# ACCOUNTING FOR INVESTMENTS

- We should eliminate the 'investment in Fluellen' in the consolidated accounts. Pistol's investment represents two elements: (i) Pistol's share of Fluellen's net assets and (ii) goodwill on acquisition. Thus it is illogical to include the investment as well. We can represent this by using a 'T' account.

**Cost of Control account**

|  | £m |  | £m |
|---|---|---|---|
| Cost of investment | 80 | Share capital (80% × £30m) | 24 |
|  |  | Reserves (80% × £20m) | 16 |
|  |  | Positive goodwill (balancing figure) | 40 |
|  | 80 |  | 80 |

The cost of control account is fixed at the moment of acquisition. The account reflects the purchase price paid by the parent, less the parent company's share of the subsidiary's net assets, at the date of acquisition. Once calculated this goodwill figure will not change. However, we need alternative accounting treatments to present the goodwill in our accounts (see Unit 4 and below).

- We have failed to recognise that although Pistol has control of all the assets of Fluellen, there is a minority interest in Fluellen's assets at the balance sheet date. Again we can use a 'T' account to show this.

**Minority Interest account**

|  | £m |  | £m |
|---|---|---|---|
| Balance carried down | 10 | Share capital (20% × £30m) | 6 |
|  |  | Reserves (20% × £20m) | 4 |
|  | 10 |  | 10 |

This is a snapshot of the minority's interest in the balance sheet of the subsidiary at one moment in time – in this case 31 December 19X1. The minority's interest will fluctuate in line with the performance of the subsidiary. If the subsidiary's net assets increase, so the minority's share will increase, and vice versa.

- Finally we need to look at the capital and reserves of the consolidated entity. Remember that Pistol controls its own assets and the assets of Fluellen. Thus in the consolidated accounts we should only show the share capital of Pistol plus the reserves *which Pistol controls* – its own *plus its share of the subsidiary's reserves since acquisition:* – the 'group reserves'.

How do we calculate group reserves? These incorporate the reserves of the holding company plus the holding company's share of the subsidiary's reserves since acquisition. If you think about it, the reserves pre-acquisition are part of the cost of control (see above). Also we only incorporate the holding company's share – the minority's share of the subsidiary's capital and reserves (its net assets) is included in the minority interest.

Again we can use a 'T' account.

# FINANCIAL REPORTING, ANALYSIS AND PLANNING

## Consolidated/Group reserves

|  | £m |  | £m |
|---|---|---|---|
|  |  | Holding company | 90 |
| Cost of control | 16 | Subsidiary | 20 |
| Minority interest | 4 |  |  |
| Balance carried down | 90 |  |  |
|  | 110 |  | 110 |

Effectively, in a group context, we are only including the holding company's reserves plus our share of the subsidiary's reserves since acquisition – in this case zero.

These adjustments can be summarised as follows.

|  | Pistol £m | Fluellen £m | Adjustments £m | Group £m |
|---|---|---|---|---|
| Intangible assets – positive goodwill |  |  | 40 (v) | 40 |
| Fixed assets – tangible | 100 | 40 |  | 140 |
| Investment in Fluellen Ltd. | 80 | – | (80) (i) | 0 |
|  | 180 | 40 |  | 180 |
| Net current assets | 40 | 20 |  | 60 |
|  | 220 | 60 |  | 240 |
| Creditors due >1 year | (30) | (10) |  | (40) |
|  | 190 | 50 |  | 200 |
| Share capital (£1 shares) | 100 | 30 | (30) (ii) | 100 |
| Reserves | 90 | 20 | (20) (iii) | 90 |
| Minority interest |  |  | 10 (iv) | 10 |
|  | 190 | 50 |  | 200 |

## Adjustments

Thus we have excluded the £80m (i) we have paid for Fluellen. The consideration was to acquire Pistol's share of the net assets in Fluellen. Hence representing Fluellen's net assets we have excluded the £30m (ii) share capital and the £20m (iii) reserves.

In addition we recognise that Pistol only has an interest of 80% in Fluellen. Thus a minority interest of £10m (iv) is included.

Finally we have paid £80m for control of assets worth £40m. Hence positive goodwill of £40m(v) arises.

## One year later

Consider the situation in one year's time. Let's look at our two balance sheets then.

## ACCOUNTING FOR INVESTMENTS

Balance sheets as at 31 December 19X2

|  | Pistol £m | Fluellen £m |
|---|---|---|
| Fixed assets – tangible | 120 | 50 |
| Investment in Fluellen Ltd. | 80 | – |
|  | 200 | 50 |
| Net current assets | 50 | 30 |
|  | 250 | 80 |
| Creditors due > 1 year | (40) | (20) |
|  | 210 | 60 |
|  |  |  |
| Share capital (£1 shares) | 100 | 30 |
| Reserves | 110 | 30 |
|  | 210 | 60 |

Prepare consolidated accounts for the Pistol Group as at 31 December 19X2.

**Solution**

Initially aggregating the accounts of Pistol and Fluellen we get the following.

|  | Pistol £m | Fluellen £m | Group £m |
|---|---|---|---|
| Fixed assets – tangible | 120 | 50 | 170 |
| Investment in Fluellen Ltd. | 80 | – | 80 |
|  | 200 | 50 | 250 |
| Net current assets | 50 | 30 | 80 |
|  | 250 | 80 | 330 |
| Creditors due >1 year | (40) | (20) | (60) |
|  | 210 | 60 | 270 |
|  |  |  |  |
| Share capital (£1 shares) | 100 | 30 | 130 |
| Reserves | 110 | 30 | 140 |
|  | 210 | 60 | 270 |

- As previously the cost of control account is unchanged. Thus the goodwill figure is fixed permanently.

### Cost of control account

| Cost of investment | 80 | Share capital (80% × £30m) | 24 |
|---|---|---|---|
|  |  | Reserves (80% × £20m) | 16 |
|  |  | Goodwill (balancing figure) | 40 |
|  | 80 |  | 80 |

We again need to account for the minority share. Unlike the goodwill figure, the minority interest will fluctuate each year, in line with the subsidiary's balance sheet. Again we can use a 'T' account to show this.

### Minority interest account

| Balance carried down | 12 | Share capital (20% × £30m) | 6 |
|---|---|---|---|
|  |  | Reserves (20% × £30m) | 6 |
|  | 12 |  | 12 |

We can see that the minority interest has increased from £10m to £12m. This reflects the minority's 20% share in Fluellen's increased net assets of £10m over the year.

Again we need to look at the capital and reserves of the consolidated entity. Remember we should only show the share capital of Pistol plus the reserves of the group. The group reserves incorporate the holding company's reserves plus the holding company's share of the subsidiary's reserves since acquisition.

### Consolidated reserves

|  |  | Holding company | 110 |
|---|---|---|---|
| Cost of control | 16 | Subsidiary | 30 |
| Minority interest | 6 |  |  |
| Balance carried down | 118 |  |  |
|  | 140 |  | 140 |

This can be proved as follows.

|  | £m | £m |
|---|---|---|
| *Holding company reserves* |  | 110 |
| *Subsidiary's post-acquisition reserves* |  |  |
| Reserves now | 30 |  |
| less Reserves on Acquisition | (20) |  |
|  | 10 |  |
| Holding company's share | × 80% |  |
|  |  | 8 |
| *Group reserves* |  | 118 |

Effectively, since Pistol purchased Fluellen, the latter's net assets have increased by £10m. Pistol's share of that increase is 80%, therefore group reserves include the £8m of Fluellen's post-acquisition reserves as well as Pistol's own reserves.

We can now prepare the consolidated accounts as follows.

## ACCOUNTING FOR INVESTMENTS

|  | Pistol £m | Fluellen £m | Adjustments | | Group £m |
|---|---|---|---|---|---|
| Intangible assets – goodwill |  |  | 40 | (vi) | 40 |
| Fixed assets – tangible | 120 | 50 |  |  | 170 |
| Investment in Fluellen Ltd. | 80 |  | (80) | (i) | 0 |
|  | 200 | 50 |  |  | 210 |
| Net current assets | 50 | 30 |  |  | 80 |
|  | 250 | 80 |  |  | 290 |
| Creditors due > 1 year | (40) | (20) |  |  | (60) |
|  | 210 | 60 |  |  | 230 |
| Share capital (£1 shares) | 100 | 30 | (30) | (ii) | 100 |
| Reserves | 110 | 30 | (20) | (iii) | 118 |
|  |  |  | (2) | (v) |  |
| Minority interest |  |  | 10 | (iv) | 12 |
|  |  |  | 2 | (v) |  |
|  | 210 | 60 |  |  | 230 |

### Adjustments

Thus again we have excluded the £80m (i) we have paid for Fluellen. We have also excluded Fluellen's £30m (ii) share capital and £20m (iii) pre-acquisition reserves.

On acquisition we recognised that Pistol only has an interest of 80% in Fluellen. Thus an opening minority interest of £10m (iv) is included. Since Pistol purchased Fluellen, the subsidiary has generated £10m of reserves; 20% of these, £2m (v), should be allocated to the minority.

Finally, the goodwill on acquisition is incorporated of £40m (vi).

According to FRS 10, the goodwill should be amortised over its useful economic life; where it is felt that the useful economic life exceeds 20 years or is indefinite it should be subject to impairment reviews (described earlier in this book).

## 5 Subsidiary accounts: some complications

**Inter-company balances**

5.1 We are preparing the accounts of the group to be presented to the outside world. Thus any inter-company balances should be excluded from the group accounts.

### Example 8.3

During 19X1 Gower Limited purchased 51% of the shares in one of its suppliers Orleans Limited. At the year end Gower owed £20,000 to Orleans.

### Solution

In the group balance sheet we need to exclude:

- £20,000 from group trade debtors (representing the balance in Orleans' books due from Gower) and

# FINANCIAL REPORTING, ANALYSIS AND PLANNING

- £20,000 from group trade creditors (representing the balance in Gower's books due to Orleans).

*Note we exclude all the intercompany balances, not just 51%.*

### Inter-company stock

5.2 When group companies trade with each other, they may do so at a profit. Any stock left in the balance sheet of the purchasing company will reflect the profit element charged by the selling company. However, this profit has not yet been realised *outside the group*. The scope for profit manipulation would be great if the 'profit' element were not eliminated on consolidation.

5.3 The group could easily boost profits by selling stock to a fellow group company at an inflated value. The gross profit would show in the accounts and the inflated closing stock value in the balance sheet.

### Example 8.4

Williams plc sold £100,000 worth of stock to its 80% subsidiary Ely Limited at a mark-up of 60%. At the year end a quarter of the stock had not been sold. Ely still owed Williams £30,000 for purchases at the year end.

### Solution

Initially eliminate the inter-company balances.

Exclude:

- £30,000 from group trade debtors (representing the balance in Williams' books due from Ely) and

- £30,000 from group trade creditors (representing the balance in Ely's books due to Williams).

*Note again we exclude all the intercompany balances, not just 80%.*

Secondly, we need to exclude the profit element in the year end stock.

The stock was sold at a mark-up of 60%, therefore the profit element was £60,000 (60% × £100,000). However three-quarters of this has been realised, i.e. sold outside the group. Therefore only a quarter needs to be excluded.

Thus we deduct £15,000 (£60,000 × 1/4) from the balance sheet value of closing stock.

In addition we need to exclude the £15,000 unrealised profit from group reserves. This is charged to consolidated reserves and (if appropriate) minority interest.

Reduce group reserves by £12,000 (80% group share × £15,000)
Reduce minority interest by £3,000 (20% minority × £15,000)

### Dividends

5.4 When a subsidiary pays a dividend, it will be income for the holding company. If it is a proposed dividend, it will be a liability of the subsidiary and an asset of the holding company. Such balances would need to be eliminated

# ACCOUNTING FOR INVESTMENTS

on consolidation (as for other inter-company balances – see above). However, there are a number of other complications when a dividend is made from subsidiary to parent.

## (i) Dividends shortly after acquisition

### Example 8.5

On 31 December 19X1, Isabel plc purchased 100% of the share capital in Nym plc for consideration of £40m. Nym's year end is 31 December 19X1 and the company proposed a dividend of £1m for the year just ended. Nym's share capital was £20m with reserves of £10m at 31 December 19X1.

### Solution

Initially when compiling the group balance sheet we will need to eliminate the inter-company balance.

Exclude:

- £1m from group debtors (representing the dividend debtor in Isabel's books due from Nym) and
- £1m from group creditors (representing the dividend creditor in Nym's books due to Isabel).

Next consider the treatment of the dividend. Isabel has just paid out £40m to control the net assets of Nym. Immediately Nym 'repays' part of that consideration by declaring a £1m dividend. Effectively, Isabel has paid only £39m for the shares in Nym. Thus our cost of control account will appear as follows.

### Cost of Control account

|  | £m |  | £m |
|---|---|---|---|
| Cost of Investment | 40 | Share capital (100% × £20m) | 20 |
|  |  | Reserves (100% × £10m) | 10 |
|  |  | *Pre-acquisition dividend* | 1 |
|  |  | Positive goodwill (balancing figure) | 9 |
|  | 40 |  | 40 |

## (ii) Dividend straddling year end

### Example 8.6

On 30 June 19X1 MacMorris plc purchased 100% of the share capital in Bates Ltd. for consideration of £40m. Bates' year end is 31 December 19X1 and the company proposed a dividend of £1m for the year just ended. Bates' share capital was £20m with reserves of £10m at 31 December 19X1. Bates' retained profit for the year is £2m.

### Solution

This raises two separate problems. First we have a mid-year acquisition. Secondly, how to deal with the dividend.

# FINANCIAL REPORTING, ANALYSIS AND PLANNING

- Mid-year acquisition

In order to prepare the cost of control account and hence find the goodwill figure we need to know the position of the subsidiary at the date of acquisition. In this instance, mid-way through the 19X0/X1 year. In the absence on any other information, we can assume that the company accrues profits at an even rate throughout the year. Thus we can look at the balance sheet at the start of the year and work forward, or look at the year end balance sheet and calculate back.

Remember the basic equation:

Net assets = Capital and reserves

*Share capital*
Position at year end 31/12/X1 – £20m.
Position at acquisition 30/6/X1 – assume unchanged – £20m

*Reserves*
Position at year end 31/12/X1 – £10m.

Position at acquisition 30/6/X1:

Retained profits for the year have been £2m. Therefore six months of retained earnings are £1m (6/12ths × £2m). Thus reserves at 30/6/X1 must have been £10m less £1m = £9m.

**Cost of Control account**

|  | £m |  | £m |
|---|---|---|---|
| Cost of investment | 40 | Share capital (100% × £20m) | 20 |
|  |  | Reserves (100% × £9m) | 9 |
|  |  | Pre-acquisition dividend | ? |
|  |  | Positive goodwill (balancing figure) | ? |

- Dividend

At the year end Bates proposed a dividend of £1m. In the absence of any further information, we can assume that the dividend accrues throughout the year. Thus the dividend covers six months pre-acquisition and six months post-acquisition. Effectively therefore, MacMorris paid £39.5m for Bates (£40m less £0.5m pre-acquisition dividend).

To complete the cost of control account:

**Cost of control account**

|  | £m |  | £m |
|---|---|---|---|
| Cost of investment | 40 | Share capital (100% × £20m) | 20 |
|  |  | Reserves (100% × £9m) | 9 |
|  |  | Pre-acquisition dividend | 0.5 |
|  |  | Positive goodwill (balancing figure) | 10.5 |
|  | 40 |  | 40 |

Finally let us calculate the group reserves in this context. Let us say that MacMorris has reserves of £100m, before accounting for any dividends from Bates.

# ACCOUNTING FOR INVESTMENTS

## Consolidated Reserves

|  | £m |  | £m |
|---|---|---|---|
|  |  | Holding company | 100 |
| Cost of control | 9 | Subsidiary | 10 |
| Minority interest | 0 |  |  |
|  |  | Post-acquisition dividend | 0.5 |
| Balance carried down | 101.5 |  |  |
|  | 110.5 |  | 110.5 |

To prove this figure we can add the following.

|  | £m |
|---|---|
| *Holding company reserves* | 100 |
| plus *dividend not yet accounted for* |  |
| (£1m × 6/12ths post-acquisition) | 0.5 |
|  | 100.5 |
| plus *holding company's share of subsidiary's post-acquisition reserves* |  |
| 100% (Reserves now £10m less reserves on acquisition £9m) | 1 |
| *Group reserves* | 101.5 |

Finally if applicable we would need to eliminate any inter-company balances, e.g. dividends payable in Bates' books and dividends receivable in MacMorris' books.

### (iii) Dividends after acquisition

5.5 These are normally quite straightforward. You need to watch out if the dividend has been put through in the books of the subsidiary and the holding company. Also note any minority share in the dividend.

**Comprehensive example 8.7**

On 1 January 19X1 Charles Limited purchased 60% of the share capital in Suffolk Limited for £22m. At the time of purchase Suffolk had net assets of £30m with share capital of £20m and reserves of £10m. At the year ended 31 December 19X4 the two companies' balance sheets are as follows.

|  | Charles £m | Suffolk £m |
|---|---|---|
| Fixed assets – tangible | 110 | 60 |
| Investment in Suffolk Ltd. | 22 | – |
|  | 132 | 60 |
| Current assets | 80 | 65 |
| Current liabilities | (20) | (35) |
|  | 192 | 90 |
| Creditors due >1 year | (32) | (20) |
|  | 160 | 70 |
|  |  |  |
| Share capital (£1 shares) | 100 | 20 |
| Reserves | 60 | 50 |
|  | 160 | 70 |

# FINANCIAL REPORTING, ANALYSIS AND PLANNING

Suffolk declared a dividend for the year ended 31 December 19X4 of £5m. This has not yet been incorporated into the accounts above. Prepare the consolidated balance sheet of the Charles Group as at 31 December 19X4.

**Solution**

The first stage is to account for the proposed dividend.

None of the dividend is pre-acquisition. Therefore all the dividend can be included when calculating the holding company's share. Note that the holding company is only accountable for 60% – £3m of the dividend. If we were to represent the two balance sheets after accounting for the dividend they would look like this.

|  |  | Charles £m |  | Suffolk £m |
|---|---|---|---|---|
| Fixed assets – tangible |  | 110 |  | 60 |
| Investment in Suffolk Ltd. |  | 22 |  | - |
|  |  | 132 |  | 60 |
| Current assets (£80m plus divi. receivable of £3m) |  | 83 |  | 65 |
| Current liabilities |  | (20) | (£35m plus divi. payable of £5m) | (40) |
|  |  | 195 |  | 85 |
| Creditors due >1 year |  | (32) |  | (20) |
|  |  | 163 |  | 65 |
| Share capital (£1 shares) |  | 100 |  | 20 |
| Reserves (£60m plus divi. receivable of £3m) |  | 63 | (£50m less divi. payable of £5m) | 45 |
|  |  | 163 |  | 65 |

We can now proceed with our usual workings.

**Cost of control account**

|  | £m |  | £m |
|---|---|---|---|
| Cost of investment | 22 | Share capital (60% × £20m) | 12 |
|  |  | Reserves (60% × £10m) | 6 |
|  |  | Pre-acquisition dividend | 0 |
|  |  | Positive goodwill (balancing figure) | 4 |
|  | 22 |  | 22 |

**Minority interest account**

|  | £m |  | £m |
|---|---|---|---|
| Balance carried down | 26 | Share capital (40% × £20m) | 8 |
|  |  | Reserves (40% × £45m) | 18 |
|  | 26 |  | 26 |

## ACCOUNTING FOR INVESTMENTS

### Consolidated reserves

|  | £m |  | £m |
|---|---|---|---|
|  |  | Holding company | 63 |
| Cost of control | 6 | Subsidiary | 45 |
| Minority interest | 18 |  |  |
|  |  |  |  |
| Balance carried down | 84 |  |  |
|  | 108 |  | 108 |

To prove this figure we can add the following.

|  | £m |
|---|---|
| *Holding company reserves* | 63 |
| plus *holding company's share of subsidiary's post-acquisition reserves* |  |
|    60% (Reserves now £45m less reserves on acquisition £10m) | 21 |
| *Group reserves* | 84 |

### Consolidated balance sheet as at 31 December 19X4

|  | Charles £m | Suffolk £m | Adjustments £m | Group £m |
|---|---|---|---|---|
| *Fixed assets* |  |  |  |  |
| Intangible – positive goodwill |  |  | 4 | 4 |
| Fixed assets – tangible | 110 | 60 |  | 170 |
| Investment in Suffolk Ltd. | 22 | – | (22) | 0 |
|  | 132 | 60 |  | 174 |
| Current assets | 83 | 65 | (3) | 145 |
| Current liabilities | (20) | (40) | 3 | (57) |
|  | 195 | 85 |  | 262 |
| Creditors due > 1 year | (32) | (20) |  | (52) |
|  | 163 | 65 |  | 210 |
|  |  |  |  |  |
| Share capital (£1 shares) | 100 | 20 | (20) | 100 |
| Reserves | 63 | 45 | (6) | 84 |
|  |  |  | (18) |  |
| Minority interest |  |  | 8 |  |
|  |  |  | 18 | 26 |
|  | 163 | 65 |  | 210 |

Note that the inter-company dividend balances have been netted off.

## 6 Fair value accounting

6.1 FRS 7 'Fair Value accounting' is concerned with the valuation of the subsidiary company at the date of acquisition. Using acquisition accounting, the requirement is that the balance sheet of the subsidiary should be stated at *fair value* – immediately prior to consolidation. Thus a number of adjustments will probably have to be made to the subsidiary's balance sheet. For example, land and buildings will probably need to be revalued upwards, whilst certain stocks or debtors may need to be revalued downwards.

FINANCIAL REPORTING, ANALYSIS AND PLANNING

**Procedure**

6.2   The method for restating the subsidiary's balance sheet is as it would be implemented in normal circumstances. Revaluations of fixed assets would be shown in a revaluation reserve; other changes in valuations of current assets would be charged to or credited to the profit and loss account.

**Example 8.8**

On 31 December 19X1 Talbot plc purchased 90% of the share capital in Gloucester Limited for consideration of £100m. The two companies' balance sheets at that date were as follows.

|  | Talbot £m | Gloucester £m |
|---|---|---|
| Fixed assets – tangible | 400 | 20 |
| Investment in Gloucester Ltd. | 100 |  |
|  | 500 | 20 |
| Current assets | 210 | 30 |
| Current liabilities | (120) | (10) |
|  | 590 | 40 |
| Creditors due > 1 year | (100) | (10) |
|  | 490 | 30 |
| Share capital (£1 shares) | 400 | 10 |
| Profit and loss account | 70 | 20 |
| Revaluation reserve | 20 |  |
|  | 490 | 30 |

At first glance Talbot has paid £100m for £27m worth of assets (90% × £30m), generating positive goodwill of £73m. However, we need to state the balance sheet of the subsidiary at fair value. Let's say, for example, that the fair value of the fixed assets should be £50m; that stock has been overvalued by £5m; and that there are missing provisions of £2m. Incorporating this into Gloucester's balance sheet we get:

|  | Before £m | Adjustments £m |  | After £m |
|---|---|---|---|---|
| Fixed assets – tangible | 20 | 30 | [i] | 50 |
| Current assets | 30 | (5) | [ii] | 25 |
| Current liabilities | (10) | (2) | [iii] | (12) |
|  | 40 |  |  | 63 |
| Creditors due >1 year | (10) |  |  | (10) |
|  | 30 |  |  | 53 |
| Share capital (£1 shares) | 10 |  |  | 10 |
| Profit and loss account | 20 | (5) | [ii] | 13 |
|  |  | (2) | [iii] |  |
| Revaluation reserve | — | 30 | [i] | 30 |
|  | 30 |  |  | 53 |

## Adjustments

[i] The uplift in the fixed asset valuation has been credited to a revaluation reserve.

[ii] and [iii] The stock write-down and the provision inclusion have been charged to the profit and loss account.

Having made the fair value adjustments we can now prepare our schedules and the consolidated balance sheet.

## Cost of control account

|  | £m |  | £m |
|---|---|---|---|
| Cost of investment | 100 | Share capital (90% × £10m) | 9 |
|  |  | P&L Reserve (90% × £13m) | 11.7 |
|  |  | Revaluation reserve (90% × £30m) | 27 |
|  |  | Positive goodwill (balancing figure) | 52.3 |
|  | 100 |  | 100 |

*Note:* we have included the revaluation reserve in the cost of control account. This is because the cost of control account reflects the parent company's investment in all the subsidiary's net assets at fair value. The subsidiary's net assets are of course represented by all the subsidiary's reserves.

## Minority interest account

|  | £m |  | £m |
|---|---|---|---|
| Balance carried down | 5.3 | Share capital (10% × £10m) | 1 |
|  |  | P&L reserve (10% × £13m) | 1.3 |
|  |  | Revaluation reserve (10% × £30m) | 3 |
|  | 5.3 |  | 5.3 |

*Note:* the minority benefits/suffers from any fair value adjustments made.

We need a 'T' account for each of the reserves.

## Consolidated profit and loss account reserve

|  | £m |  | £m |
|---|---|---|---|
|  |  | Holding company | 70 |
| Cost of control | 11.7 | Subsidiary | 13 |
| Minority interest | 1.3 |  |  |
| Balance carried down | 70 |  |  |
|  | 83 |  | 83 |

# FINANCIAL REPORTING, ANALYSIS AND PLANNING

### Consolidated revaluation reserve

|  | £m |  | £m |
|---|---|---|---|
|  |  | Holding company | 20 |
| Cost of control | 27 | Subsidiary | 30 |
| Minority interest | 3 |  |  |
| Balance carried down | 20 |  |  |
|  | 50 |  | 50 |

The balance on both of these reserves reflect the fact that Talbot has only just acquired Gloucester and that there are no post-acquisition reserves.

### Consolidated balance sheet as at 31 December 19X1

|  | Talbot £m | Gloucester £m | Adjustments £m | Group £m |
|---|---|---|---|---|
| Fixed assets – intangible |  |  |  |  |
| Positive goodwill |  |  | 52.3 | 52.3 |
| Fixed assets – tangible | 400 | 50 |  | 450 |
| Investment in Gloucester | 100 |  | (100) | 0 |
|  | 500 |  |  | 502.3 |
| Current assets | 210 | 25 |  | 235 |
| Current liabilities | (120) | (12) |  | (132) |
|  | 590 | 63 |  | 605.3 |
| Creditors due > 1 year | (100) | (10) |  | (110) |
|  | 490 | 53 |  | 495.3 |
| Share capital (£1 shares) | 400 | 10 | (10) | 400 |
| Profit and loss account | 70 | 13 | (11.7) | 70 |
|  |  |  | (1.3) |  |
| Revaluation reserve | 20 | 30 | (27) | 20 |
|  |  |  | (3) |  |
| Minority interest |  |  | 1 |  |
|  |  |  | 1.3 |  |
|  |  |  | 3 | 5.3 |
|  | 490 | 53 |  | 495.3 |

6.3 As can be seen the fair value adjustments have two effects (i) on the level of goodwill on acquisition, (ii) in the post acquisition balance sheet. FRS7 was introduced to prevent companies from using creative accounting either to manipulate the amount of goodwill that arises or to effect the post acquisition balance sheet.

6.4 Consider the example above. Gloucester wrote off £5m from stocks and made a provision of £2m. The effect of these two adjustments would be to *increase* the profits of the group post acquisition by £7m higher than they would have been had the adjustments not been made.

## ACCOUNTING FOR INVESTMENTS

6.5 The reason for this is that the opening stock will be £5m lower in 19X2, therefore cost of sales will be £5m lower. Also the £2m provision can be used to offset some of 19X2's expenses.

6.6 The ASB were well aware of the temptation to make provisions on acquisition to boost profits *post* acquisition.

6.7 Thus FRS7 introduced strict criteria regarding provisions that can be made on acquisition and also detailed guidance on the valuation of assets and liabilities. We will deal with provisions first.

**Provisions**

6.8 The basic principle is that the company should adopt the *acquired company's perspective*. This means that when looking at the balance sheet of the subsidiary, the assets and liabilities should be valued *from that company's point of view* – taking the hypothetical position that the take-over had not, nor was ever going to take place. This is very much an attitude of mind and can be difficult to conceptualise. For example, the acquirer may be intending to merge product lines and to streamline the companies product base. Thus the intention may be to delete some of the subsidiary's product lines. The effect of this policy could well be to depress the net realisable values of such stock. However under FRS7, we have to adopt the *acquired* company's perspective – thus the plans of the acquirer are irrelevant. We must value the stock on the basis that the take-over is *not* going to take place.

6.9 FRS7 specifies that the valuation of assets and liabilities should be on the following basis.

(a) Tangible fixed assets.

The fair value of a tangible fixed asset should be based on the following.

(i) Market value, if assets similar in type and condition are bought and sold on an open market; or

(ii) depreciated replacement cost, reflecting the acquired business' normal buying process and the sources of supply, and prices available to it. The fair value should not exceed the recoverable amount of the asset.

(b) Intangible assets.

Where an intangible asset is recognised, its fair value should be based on its replacement cost, which is normally its estimated market value.

(c) Stocks and work in progress.

Value at the lower of cost and net realisable value.

(d) Quoted investments.

Value at market price.

(e) Monetary assets and liabilities.

The fair value of monetary assets and liabilities, including accruals and provisions, should take into account the amounts expected to be received or paid and their timing. Fair value should be determined by reference to market prices, where available, by reference to the current price at which

# FINANCIAL REPORTING, ANALYSIS AND PLANNING

the business could acquire similar assets or enter into similar obligations or any discounting to present value.

(f) Contingencies

Contingent assets and liabilities should be measured at fair values where these can be determined. For this purpose reasonable estimates of the expected outcome may be used.

## Effect of FRS7

6.10 The main effect of FRS7 has been to prevent acquiring companies from setting up re-organisation provisions. These provisions are used to mop up expenses of the combined entities *after* the acquisition. This has the effect of distorting the profit trends and giving a false impression of the performance of the combined entity post-acquisition. Consider the effect on the return on capital employed ratio.

Simply put the ratio can be expressed as:

$$\frac{\text{Profits}}{\text{Net assets}}$$

6.11 The effect of making provisions on acquisition is (a) to boost post-acquisition profits (see above) and (b) to depress assets values on acquisition. The effect of (a) and (b) is to increase the return on capital employed post-acquisition unfairly.

## Effect in future years

6.12 It should be noted that the fair value adjustments actually need to be put through only in the consolidated accounts. The situation can occur where the adjustments are not actually put through in the subsidiary's own accounts. Let us continue our example above and see the situation one year later, assuming that the subsidiary has not incorporated the fair value adjustments in its own accounts.

### Example 8.8 (continued)

Remember that on 31 December 19X1 Talbot plc purchased 90% of the share capital in Gloucester Limited for consideration of £100m. The two company's balance sheets at that date were as follows.

### *Balance sheets as 31 December 19X1*

|  | Talbot £m | Gloucester £m |
|---|---:|---:|
| Fixed assets – tangible | 400 | 20 |
| Investment in Gloucester Ltd. | 100 |  |
|  | 500 | 20 |
| Current assets | 210 | 30 |
| Current liabilities | (120) | (10) |
|  | 590 | 40 |
| Creditors due > 1 year | (100) | (10) |
|  | 490 | 30 |

## ACCOUNTING FOR INVESTMENTS

|  |  |  |
|---|---:|---:|
| Share capital (£1 shares) | 400 | 10 |
| Profit and loss account | 70 | 20 |
| Revaluation reserve | 20 |  |
|  | 490 | 30 |

On 31 December 19X1 the fair value of the fixed assets should have been £50m; stock was overvalued by £5m and there were missing provisions of £2m.

The balance sheets on 31 December 19X2 are as follows:

|  | Talbot £m | Gloucester £m |
|---|---:|---:|
| Fixed assets – tangible | 500 | 39 |
| Investment in Gloucester Ltd. | 100 |  |
|  | 600 | 39 |
| Current assets | 240 | 50 |
| Current liabilities | (140) | (20) |
|  | 700 | 69 |
| Creditors due > 1 year | (120) | (10) |
|  | 580 | 59 |
|  |  |  |
| Share capital (£1 shares) | 400 | 10 |
| Profit and loss account | 110 | 49 |
| Revaluation reserve | 70 |  |
|  | 580 | 59 |

During the year, Gloucester has purchased £20m of new fixed assets (not yet depreciated) and depreciated the old fixed assets by £1m.

Assuming that the fair value adjustments have not been incorporated, we now need to adjust Gloucester's accounts at the end of 19X2. Consider the fair value adjustments one at a time.

### (i) *Revaluation of fixed assets*

On 31 December 19X1, the fair value of the assets were £50m as opposed to book value of £20m. Thus we needed to revalue by £30m. However remember that if an asset is revalued depreciation needs to be charged on the *revalued* amount (see Unit 4). Thus, as well as incorporating the £30m revaluation, we need to take off the extra depreciation on the revalued amount. The depreciation in Gloucester's books is £1m. Thus we can assume that the useful life of the asset is 20 years (£20m/£1m). Therefore we need to ensure that one twentieth of the *fair value* is written off in 19X2. That is, depreciation of £2.5m (£50m/20) needs to be charged, instead of the original £1m.

## Fair value of fixed assets

|  | £m |
|---|---|
| Book value | 39 |
| Revaluation to fair value (£50m – £20m) | 30 |
| Extra depreciation on revalued amount | (1.5) |
| Fair value at 31 December 19X2 | 67.5 |

This can be proved as follows.

|  | £m |
|---|---|
| Original assets at 31 December 19X1 | 20 |
| Revaluation | 30 |
| Fair value at 31 December 19X1 | 50 |
| Depreciation (over 20 years) | (2.5) |
| Adjusted fair value at 31 December 19X2 | 47.5 |
| New assets purchased in 19X2 (assume at fair value) | 20 |
| Fair value at 31 December 19X2 | 67.5 |

### (ii) Stock valuation and provisions

At the end of 19X1 we needed to write down stock by £5m and make a provision of £2m. Assume that that situation still exists. But now we need to write down stock by £6m and make a provision of £3m. Thus we need to adjust Gloucester's balance sheet.

|  | Before £m | Adjustments £m | After £m |
|---|---|---|---|
| Fixed assets – tangible | 39 | 30 | |
|  |  | (1.5) | 67.5 |
| Current assets | 50 | (6) | 44 |
| Current liabilities | (20) | (3) | (23) |
|  | 69 |  | 88.5 |
| Creditors due >1 year | (10) |  | (10) |
|  | 59 |  | 78.5 |
| Share capital (£1 shares) | 10 |  | 10 |
| Profit and loss account | 49 | (6) | |
|  |  | (3) | 40 |
| Revaluation reserve |  | 30 | |
|  |  | (1.5) | 28.5 |
|  | 59 |  | 78.5 |

Having made the fair value adjustments we can now prepare our schedules and the consolidated balance sheet.

The cost of control account will remain unchanged because it is fixed at that moment in time of the acquisition.

# ACCOUNTING FOR INVESTMENTS

### Cost of control account

|  | £m |  | £m |
|---|---|---|---|
| Cost of investment | 100 | Share capital (90% × £10m) | 9 |
|  |  | P&L Reserve (90% × £13m) | 11.7 |
|  |  | Revaluation reserve (90% × £30m) | 27 |
|  |  | Positive goodwill (balancing figure) | 52.3 |
|  | 100 |  | 100 |

However the minority interest account will change every year; it will reflect the underlying value of the subsidiary's balance sheet:

### Minority Interest account

|  | £m |  | £m |
|---|---|---|---|
| Balance carried down | 7.85 | Share capital (10% × £10m) | 1 |
|  |  | P&L reserve (10% × £40m) | 4 |
|  |  | Revaluation reserve (10% × £28.5m) | 2.85 |
|  | 7.85 |  | 7.85 |

We need a 'T' account for each of the reserves.

### Consolidated profit and loss account reserve

|  | £m |  | £m |
|---|---|---|---|
| Cost of control | 11.7 | Holding company | 110 |
| Minority interest | 4 | Subsidiary | 40 |
| Balance carried down | 134.3 |  |  |
|  | 150 |  | 150 |

*Proof*

We can calculate the group reserves figure by using a formula.

|  | £m | £m |
|---|---|---|
| Holding company |  | 110 |
| *plus Holding company's share of subsidiary's post-acquisition reserves* |  |  |
| Reserves now | 40 |  |
| Reserves on acquisition | (13) |  |
| Increase | 27 |  |
| × Holding company's share | × 90% = | 24.3 |
| Group reserves |  | 134.3 |

This will also hold true for the revaluation reserve. But first we will construct the 'T' account.

# FINANCIAL REPORTING, ANALYSIS AND PLANNING

## Consolidated revaluation reserve

|  | £m |  | £m |
|---|---|---|---|
|  |  | Holding company | 70 |
| Cost of control | 27 | Subsidiary | 28.5 |
| Minority interest | 2.85 |  |  |
|  |  |  |  |
| Balance carried down | 68.65 |  |  |
|  | 98.5 |  | 98.5 |

This can be proved by using the above formula.

|  | £m | £m |
|---|---|---|
| Holding company |  | 70 |
| plus Holding company's share of subsidiary's post-acquisition reserves |  |  |
| Reserves now | 28.5 |  |
| Reserves on acquisition | (30) |  |
| Decrease | (1.5) |  |
| × Holding company's share | × 90% = | (1.35) |
| Group reserves |  | 68.65 |

## Consolidated balance sheet as at 31 December 19X2

|  | Talbot £m | Gloucester £m | Adjustments £m | Group £m |
|---|---|---|---|---|
| Fixed assets – Intangible |  |  |  |  |
| Goodwill |  |  | 52.3 | 52.3 |
| Fixed assets – tangible | 500 | 67.5 |  | 567.5 |
| Investment in Gloucester | 100 |  | (100) | 0 |
|  | 600 |  |  | 619.8 |
| Current assets | 240 | 44 |  | 284 |
| Current liabilities | (140) | (23) |  | (163) |
|  | 700 | 88.5 |  | 740.8 |
| Creditors due >1 year | (120) | (10) |  | (130) |
|  | 580 | 78.5 |  | 610.8 |
|  |  |  |  |  |
| Share capital (£1 shares) | 400 | 10 | (10) | 400 |
| Profit and loss account | 110 | 40 | (11.7) | 134.3 |
|  |  |  | (4) |  |
| Revaluation reserve | 70 | 28.5 | (27) | 68.65 |
|  |  |  | (2.85) |  |
| Minority interest |  |  | 1 | 7.85 |
|  |  |  | 4 |  |
|  |  |  | 2.85 |  |
|  | 580 | 78.5 |  | 610.8 |

ACCOUNTING FOR INVESTMENTS

### Student Activity 2

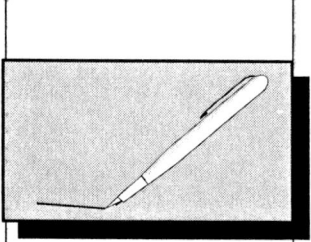

Before reading the next section of text, answer the following questions and then check your answers against the paragraphs indicated.

1. What is the principle in deciding whether a parent-subsidiary relationship exists? *(Paragraph 4.1)*
2. How is minority interest calculated? *(Example 8.2)*
3. Which items make up the cost of control account? *(Example 8.2)*
4. How are the consolidated reserves calculated? *(Example 8.2)*
5. What are the potential adjustments to be made when group companies trade with one another? *(Paragraphs 5.2, 5.3 & Example 8.4)*
6. What is the correct treatment for a pre-acquisition dividend? *(Example 8.5)*
7. Why was FRS7 introduced? *(Paragraphs 6.6 & 6.10 – 6.12)*
8. What is the overall view to be adopted when valuing the subsidiary's assets on acquisition? *(Paragraph 6.8)*

If your answers are basically correct, then proceed to the next section. If significant parts of your answers are wrong, then study the whole of the relevant sections again in detail. Note your areas of weakness and be prepared for further questions on these areas at the end of this unit.

## 7 Merger accounting

7.1 So far we have referred to combinations of businesses as acquisitions. You might be familiar with the term 'merger'. In business parlance this has a general application relating to two business combining their operations or assets in some formal or informal arrangement. In accounting terms it has a strict interpretation. Businesses that combine can either be accounted for under 'acquisition accounting' or 'merger accounting'. The principles of acquisition accounting have been explained above. There are strict criteria when merger accounting can be used, which we will see later.

7.2 Initially though let us look at the differences in accounting under the two bases.

|  | *Acquisition accounting* | *Merger accounting* |
|---|---|---|
| Valuation of assets/liabilities | Use fair values | Use book values |
| Value of consideration | Use fair values | Use nominal values |
| Criteria | None | Very strict criteria |
| Reserves | Distinct split between pre-acquisition and post-acquisition | No split between pre- and post-merger |
| Goodwill calculation | Difference between fair value of consideration and fair value of separable net assets acquired | Difference between nominal value of consideration and nominal value of shares acquired |

# FINANCIAL REPORTING, ANALYSIS AND PLANNING

**Example 8.9**

On 31 December 19X1 York plc purchases 90% of the share capital in Lewis plc. The consideration is 10 million York £1 ordinary shares. At the time of the takeover the shares of York are valued at £10 each. The balance sheets of the two companies at 31 December 19X1 are as follows.

|  | York £m | Lewis £m |
|---|---|---|
| Fixed assets – tangible | 100 | 50 |
| Current assets | 60 | 30 |
| Current liabilities | (40) | (20) |
|  | 120 | 60 |
| Creditors due >1 year | (40) | (20) |
|  | 80 | 40 |
|  |  |  |
| Share capital (£1 shares) | 20 | 8 |
| Profit and loss account | 60 | 32 |
|  | 80 | 40 |

The share issue to account for the purchase of Lewis has not been entered into the books. The fair values of Lewis' assets are as follows.

|  | £m |
|---|---|
| Fixed assets – tangible | 90 |
| Current assets | 28 |
| Current liabilities | 23 |
| Creditors due >1 year | 20 |

Prepare the consolidated balance sheets, first using (i) acquisition accounting and then (ii) merger accounting.

**Solutions**

*(i) Acquisition accounting*

The first stage is to recalculate the balance sheets of the two companies incorporating the share issue and the fair value adjustments.

|  | York £m | Lewis £m |
|---|---|---|
| Fixed assets – tangible | 100 | 90 |
| Investment in Lewis plc (10m × £10) | 100 |  |
| Current assets | 60 | 28 |
| Current liabilities | (40) | (23) |
|  | 220 | 95 |
| Creditors due > 1 year | (40) | (20) |
|  | 180 | 75 |

## ACCOUNTING FOR INVESTMENTS

| | | | |
|---|---|---|---|
| Share capital (£1 shares) | (20m + 10m) 30 | | 8 |
| Share premium account | (10m × £9 premium) 90 | | |
| Profit and loss account | 60 | (£32m – 2m – 3m) | 27 |
| Revaluation reserve | | (£90m – 50m) | 40 |
| | 180 | | 75 |

We can now prepare our consolidation schedules.

### Cost of control account

| | £m | | £m |
|---|---|---|---|
| Cost of Investment | 100 | Share capital (90% × £8m) | 7.2 |
| | | P&L reserve (90% × £27m) | 24.3 |
| | | Revaluation reserve | |
| | | (90% × £40m) | 36 |
| | | Positive goodwill (balancing figure) | 32.5 |
| | 100 | | 100 |

### Minority interest account

| | £m | | £m |
|---|---|---|---|
| Balance carried down | 7.5 | Share capital (10% × £8m) | 0.8 |
| | | P&L reserve (10% × £27m) | 2.7 |
| | | Revaluation reserve | |
| | | (10% × £40m) | 4 |
| | 7.5 | | 7.5 |

We need a 'T' account for each of the reserves.

### Consolidated profit and loss account reserve

| | £m | | £m |
|---|---|---|---|
| | | Holding company | 60 |
| Cost of control | 24.3 | Subsidiary | 27 |
| Minority interest | 2.7 | | |
| Balance carried down | 60 | | |
| | 87 | | 87 |

### Consolidated revaluation reserve

| | £m | | £m |
|---|---|---|---|
| | | Holding company | 0 |
| Cost of control | 36 | Subsidiary | 40 |
| Minority interest | 4 | | |
| Balance carried down | 0 | | |
| | 40 | | 40 |

# FINANCIAL REPORTING, ANALYSIS AND PLANNING

**Consolidated balance sheet as at 31 December 19X4**

|  | York £m | Lewis £m | Adjustments £m | Group £m |
|---|---|---|---|---|
| Fixed assets- Intangible |  |  |  |  |
| Positive goodwill |  |  | 32.5 | 32.5 |
| Fixed assets – tangible | 100 | 90 |  | 190 |
| Investment in Lewis | 100 |  | (100) |  |
|  | 200 | 90 |  | 222.5 |
| Current assets | 60 | 28 |  | 88 |
| Current liabilities | (40) | (23) |  | (63) |
|  | 220 | 95 |  | 247.5 |
| Creditors due >1 year | (40) | (20) |  | (60) |
|  | 180 | 75 |  | 187.5 |
| Share capital (£1 shares) | 30 | 8 | (8) | 30 |
| Share premium account | 90 |  |  | 90 |
| Profit and loss account | 60 | 27 | (24.3) | 60 |
|  |  |  | (2.7) |  |
| Revaluation reserve |  | 40 | (36) | 0 |
|  |  |  | (4) |  |
| Minority interest |  |  | 0.8 | 7.5 |
|  |  |  | 2.7 |  |
|  |  |  | 4 |  |
|  | 180 | 75 |  | 187.5 |

### (ii) Merger method

Using the merger method we do not have to account for the fair value of the consideration nor the fair value of the net assets acquired. Thus we start with the original balance sheets; the only adjustment is to include the investment in the subsidiary at nominal value.

|  | York £m | Lewis £m |
|---|---|---|
| Fixed assets – tangible | 100 | 50 |
| Investment in Lewis plc | 10 |  |
| Current assets | 60 | 30 |
| Current liabilities | (40) | (20) |
|  | 130 | 60 |
| Creditors due > 1 year | (40) | (20) |
|  | 90 | 40 |
| Share capital (£1 shares) | (£20m + 10m) 30 | 8 |
| Profit and loss account | 60 | 32 |
|  | 90 | 40 |

Instead of a cost of control account in a merger situation we recognise that it is not a parent-subsidiary control type scenario. Rather it is a merger, a pooling of interests. Thus we set up a merger account.

## ACCOUNTING FOR INVESTMENTS

### Merger account

|  | £m |  | £m |
|---|---|---|---|
| Cost of investment *(NB Nominal terms)* | 10 | Share capital (90% × £8m) | 7.2 |
|  |  | Premium on merger | 2.8 |
|  | 10 |  | 10 |

The merger account simply reflects the difference between the nominal value of the consideration and the nominal value of the subsidiary's shares which have been purchased by the holding company. Any difference between these two amounts should be treated as a movement on reserves.

### Minority interest account

|  | £m |  | £m |
|---|---|---|---|
| Balance carried down | 4 | Share capital (10% × £8m) | 0.8 |
|  |  | P&L reserve (10% × £32m) | 3.2 |
|  | 4 |  | 4 |

### Consolidated profit and loss account reserve

|  | £m |  | £m |
|---|---|---|---|
| Minority interest | 3.2 | Holding company | 60 |
| Premium on merger | 2.8 | Subsidiary | 32 |
| Balance carried down | 86 |  |  |
|  | 92 |  | 92 |

Note that we have not taken any of the subsidiary's reserves to a cost of control account. We have in fact merged the reserves of both companies, since incorporation.

### Consolidated balance sheet as at 31 December 19X4

|  | York £m | Lewis £m | Adjustments £m | Group £m |
|---|---|---|---|---|
| Fixed assets – tangible | 100 | 50 |  | 150 |
| Investment in Lewis Ltd. | 10 |  | (10) |  |
|  | 110 | 50 |  | 150 |
| Current assets | 60 | 30 |  | 90 |
| Current liabilities | (40) | (20) |  | (60) |
|  | 130 | 60 |  | 180 |
| Creditors due >1 year | (40) | (20) |  | (60) |
|  | 90 | 40 |  | 120 |

# FINANCIAL REPORTING, ANALYSIS AND PLANNING

| | | | | |
|---|---|---|---|---|
| Share capital (£1 shares) | 30 | 8 | (8) | 30 |
| Profit and loss account | 60 | 32 | (3.2) | 86 |
| Minority interest | | | 0.8 | 4 |
| | | | 3.2 | |
| | 90 | 40 | | 120 |

**Comparison of merger accounting and acquisition accounting**

7.3 We can see that the balance sheets under the two methods are different. The asset base is higher under the acquisition method, mainly due to the revaluation of fixed assets. We also end up with a significantly higher goodwill figure of £32.5m, in comparison to the premium on merger of £2.8m. This results from using the fair value for the consideration as opposed to the nominal value. It is partly mitigated though by using the fair value of assets not the book value.

7.4 Group reserves are different. The profit and loss reserve is higher under the merger method: £86m versus £60m. This is because we have pooled the reserves since incorporation not since the combination of the entities.

**Criteria for applying merger accounting**

7.5 FRS6 'Acquisitions and mergers' issued in 1994 set strict criteria for which business combinations should use merger accounting. The objectives of the standard were to ensure that only genuine mergers should use merger accounting. Situations where one party gained control over another, or where the acquirer is significantly larger than the acquired, or where the acquired company's directors/management/shareholders had reduced influence in the combined entity were not genuine mergers and therefore should not be accounted as such.

7.6 The criteria are as follows.

*(a) Role of the parties*

No party to the combination should be portrayed as either acquirer or acquired.

If one party has paid over the market price for the shares in another company, for example, it is an *indication* that a control premium has been paid. The onus is on the 'acquirer' to rebut this insinuation.

Other indicators may be, for example, the corporate name after the combination, the closure of any operational sites post combination, etc.

*(b) Dominance of management*

All parties to the combination should participate in establishing the management structure and personnel for the combined entity. The decisions should be based upon consensus rather than an exercise of voting rights.

*(c) Relative size of the parties*

Where one party to the combination is substantially larger than the other parties it is presumed that the larger party can or will dominate the combined undertaking.

## ACCOUNTING FOR INVESTMENTS

The presumption is that if one party is more than 50% larger than each of the others, judged by reference to the ownership interest, then the combination is an acquisition not a merger.

Again the onus is on the parties, if they are substantially different in size, to rebut the notion that this is an acquisition not a merger.

### (d) Non-equity consideration

All but an immaterial amount of the consideration received by the acquirer must be in the form of equity shares in the acquired company. Immaterial is not defined – although previously a 10% benchmark has been applied.

Thus the consideration must be (virtually wholly) financed by shares in the acquirer. In effect what happens is that the shareholders in the old parties now become shareholders in the new combined enterprise – a 'pooling of interests'.

### (e) Interests in the performance of the combined entity

No equity shareholders after the combination should have an interest in the post combination performance of a *part* of the enterprise.

The requirements are that *all five* criteria must be met for merger accounting to be used. If the combination meets the criteria, merger accounting *must* be used.

## 8 Definition of a subsidiary

8.1 So far we have used the term subsidiary for all companies where one company holds more than 50% of the shares in another company. Initially we discussed situations where the investing company's shareholding was less than 20%, situations where the investment was between 20% and 50%; and situations where the investment was over 50%. In the last situation a parent-subsidiary relationship was assumed to exist.

8.2 Normally that is the case; however the Companies Act 1989 and FRS2 'Accounting for subsidiary undertakings' put the weight of evidence not just on the level of shareholding. The degree of control is the important factor. Usually owning 51% of the shares will give the investor control. This might not always be the case. If, for example, an investing company owned 51% of the non-voting 'A' shares, but did not own any of the voting 'B' shares, the investing company might have little or no control over the investee.

8.3 The Companies Act 1989 introduced the term 'subsidiary undertaking', indicating that a relationship can exist between unincorporated enterprises as well. Under the Act, a subsidiary undertaking is one in which the parent:

(a) has a majority of the voting rights; or

(b) is a member and can appoint or remove a majority of the board; or

(c) is a member and controls alone a majority of the voting rights by agreement with other members; or

(d) has the right to exercise a dominant influence through the memorandum and articles or a control contract; or

# FINANCIAL REPORTING, ANALYSIS AND PLANNING

(e) has a participating interest and either

   (i) actually exercises a dominant influence over it, or

   (ii) manages both on a unified basis.

8.4 In addition, it recognised the situation where a subsidiary undertaking is itself the parent undertaking of another undertaking. Then a parent – subsidiary – sub-subsidiary relationship would exist.

8.5 FRS2 was drawn up in accordance with the Companies Act 1989, but it also amplified and explained some of the Act's terms.

*'Dominant influence'*

This was defined as influence that can be exercised to achieve the operating and financial policies desired by the holder of the influence.

*'Managed on a unified basis'*

This situation would occur where the whole of the operations of the undertakings are integrated and they are managed as a single unit.

*'Participating interest'*

This is defined as an interest held by an undertaking in the shares of another undertaking, which it holds for the long term, for the purpose of securing a contribution to its activities by the exercise of control or influence arising from or related to that interest.

- A holding of 20% or more of the shares of an undertaking shall be presumed to be a participating interest unless the contrary is shown.

- An interest in shares includes an interest which is convertible into shares or an option to convert.

**Exemptions from consolidation**

8.6 FRS2 requires that under the following circumstances a subsidiary undertaking should not be consolidated:

- where there are severe long-term restrictions over the parent's rights of control (for example, a subsidiary undertaking operating in a war-torn area)

- where an undertaking is held exclusively for subsequent resale and had not previously been consolidated in group accounts prepared by the parent undertaking

- where the activities of the parent and the subsidiary undertaking are dissimilar. This would be in the exceptional situation where consolidating the enterprises' results would give a misleading view. FRS2 gives strict criteria as to when this exemption may apply. It stresses this should only be in very exceptional circumstances. For example, a bank and a manufacturing company would not, in themselves, be sufficiently dissimilar. Nor would the combination of a profit making and a non-profit making enterprise, in itself, be sufficient grounds for non-consolidation.

8.7 The Companies Act permits exclusion from consolidation in all the circumstances mentioned above, except for dissimilar activities where exclusion is a *requirement*. CA also permits exclusion for two other reasons:

ACCOUNTING FOR INVESTMENTS

- where the subsidiary undertaking's inclusion would be immaterial
- where the information needed to prepare consolidated accounts cannot be obtained without disproportionate expense or delay.

The latter two criteria are *not* grounds for exclusion under FRS2.

8.8 In summary, we can see that the emphasis is on *control* not ownership. The principle of substance over form applies again. In assessing whether a control situation exists many factors need to be considered:

- the ownership interest
- the degree of influence potentially liable to be exercised
- the degree of influence actually exercised
- the influence of other participating interests.

For example, a company might own only 30% of another company. But, if the other shareholders are a disparate collection of 70 passive individuals owning 1% each, then it is likely a control situation exists.

## Student Activity 3

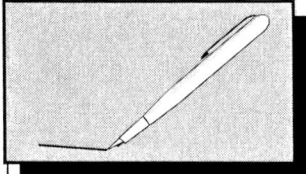

Now answer the following questions and then check your answers against the paragraph(s) indicated.

1. What are the principal differences between merger accounting and acquisition accounting? *(Paragraph 7.2)*

2. Which method will give the higher group reserves – merger accounting or acquisition accounting? *(Paragraph 7.4)*

3. What are the five criteria for merger accounting to be used? *(Paragraphs 7.5 & 7.6)*

4. Give some examples of situations where a parent-subsidiary undertaking relationship might exist apart from control of >50% of the voting shares. *(Paragraphs 8.1 – 8.3)*

5. Define 'dominant influence'. *(Paragraph 8.5)*

6. Define 'managed on a unified basis'. *(Paragraph 8.5)*

If your answers are basically correct, then proceed to the Summary and questions. If significant parts of your answers are wrong, then study the whole of the relevant sections again in detail. Note your areas of weakness and be prepared for further questions on these areas at the end of this Unit.

FINANCIAL REPORTING, ANALYSIS AND PLANNING

> **Summary**
>
> Now that you have completed this Unit you should be able to:
>
> - identify and account for various forms of investment: less than 20% holding, associated companies, subsidiary undertakings
> - use the equity method of accounting to account for associated undertakings
> - prepare consolidated accounts, including adjustments for dividends, inter-company balances/profits stock
> - account for goodwill on acquisition and explain the effect on group reserves and profits
> - apply FRS7 in the fair valuation of assets and liabilities
> - apply the criteria of FRS6 in identifying situations where merger accounting may be used
> - distinguish between merger accounting and acquisition accounting
> - explain the principles of FRS2 and identify control situations.

## Self-assessment questions

### Short answer questions

1. How might a company expand its level of operations?

2. Why should we prepare consolidated accounts?

3. Explain why, when in the situation of a parent owing 75% of the equity of a subsidiary, in the consolidated accounts we do not add the holding company's assets and liabilities to 75% of the subsidiary's assets and liabilities.

4. Why are inter-company balances excluded in the consolidated accounts?

5. How do we treat dividends that straddle the acquisition date?

6. How should monetary assets and liabilities be accounted on a fair value basis?

7. What is the likely effect of FRS7 on the return on capital employed (ROCE) ratio?

8. Why should a group of companies wish to use merger accounting instead of acquisition accounting?

9. Explain the different calculation of goodwill on acquisition and premium on merger.

10. Why was FRS2 introduced?

*(Answers are given in the Appendix)*

# ACCOUNTING FOR INVESTMENTS

**Multiple choice questions**

1. On 1 July 19X1, Southampton Limited purchased 25% of the shares in Crispin Limited for consideration of £100m. Extracts from Crispin's profit and loss account for the year ended 31 December 19X1 are as follows.

   |  | £m |
   |---|---|
   | Profit before tax | 100 |
   | Tax | (40) |
   | Profit after tax | 60 |

   In the consolidated profit and loss accounts for the year ended 31 December 19X1, before accounting for minority interest, what is the net effect of the purchase of the shares in Crispin?

   (a) Increase in net income of £60m

   (b) Increase in net income of £30m

   (c) Increase in net income of £15m

   (d) Increase in net income of £7.5m

2. At the year end, Crispin's capital and reserves are £280m. What value will the associate be in the consolidated accounts?

   |  | £m |
   |---|---|
   | (a) | 70 |
   | (b) | 32.5 |
   | (c) | 107.5 |
   | (d) | 115 |

3. London plc acquired 90% of the shares in France plc on 1 June 19X1. Both companies have a December year end.

   How many months' profit of France plc will be included in London's consolidated profit and loss account for the year ended 31 December 19X1 under each of the following methods:

   |  | Merger method | Acquisition method |
   |---|---|---|
   | (a) | 7 months | 7 months |
   | (b) | 12 months | 7 months |
   | (c) | 7 months | 12 months |
   | (d) | 12 months | 12 months |

4. Bourbon Limited acquired 60% of the equity share capital of Salisbury Limited many years ago, when the latter's net assets were £60m. The consideration was £100m. On 31 December 19X1, Bourbon's and Salisbury's reserves were as follows.

   |  | £m | £m |
   |---|---|---|
   | Share capital | 100 | 50 |
   | Profit and loss account | 130 | 80 |
   | Revaluation reserve | 40 | 10 |

FINANCIAL REPORTING, ANALYSIS AND PLANNING

What are the group consolidated reserves as at 31 December 19X1?

|     | £m  |
| --- | --- |
| (a) | 218 |
| (b) | 172 |
| (c) | 146 |
| (d) | 154 |

5. FRS2 and the Companies Act 1989 state that a subsidiary engaging in dissimilar activities:

|     | FRS2 | Companies Act 1989 |
| --- | --- | --- |
| (a) | must not be consolidated | must not be consolidated |
| (b) | must not be consolidated | may not be consolidated |
| (c) | may not be consolidated | must not be consolidated |
| (d) | may not be consolidated | may not be consolidated |

*(Answers are given in the Appendix)*

### Exam-style questions

Taken (amended) from the CIB exam papers, May 1996 and October 1994.

1. The following are the summarised balance sheets of Lyle Ltd, Toye Ltd and Brown Ltd as at 31 December 1995.

|     | Lyle Ltd £000 | Toye Ltd £000 | Brown Ltd £000 |
| --- | --- | --- | --- |
| Sundry assets less current liabilities | 917 | 2,500 | 800 |
| Investments |     |     |     |
| 480,000 shares in Toye Ltd | 800 | – | – |
| 225,000 shares in Brown Ltd | 503 | – | – |
| Total assets less current liabilities | 2,220 | 2,500 | 800 |
| 13% debenture stock | 500 | 600 | 200 |
|     | 1,720 | 1,900 | 600 |
| Financed by: |     |     |     |
| Share capital (£1 shares) | 500 | 800 | 300 |
| Profit and loss account: |     |     |     |
| Balance at 1 January 1993 | 220 | 300 | 200 |
| Profit (loss) for: 1993 | 300 | 160 | 109 |
| 1994 | 610 | 510 | (45) |
| 1995 | 90 | 130 | 36 |
|     | 1,720 | 1,900 | 600 |

Lyle Ltd acquired the shares in Toye Ltd on 31 December 1993 and in Brown Ltd on 31 December 1994.

No dividends were paid or proposed by any of the companies in the relevant years.

# ACCOUNTING FOR INVESTMENTS

Goodwill is estimated to have an indefinite life and will therefore not be amortised (it will be subject to impairment reviews in the future).

**Required**

(a) The consolidated balance sheet of Lyle Ltd and its subsidiaries as at 31 December 1995 based on the acquisition method as specified by FRS2.

(b) Examine the gearing position of each of the companies separately and the group as a whole as at 31 December 1995 using the debt:equity ratio. Comment briefly on the debt:equity ratios calculated.

*Note:* ignore taxation.

2. The following information is provided for Rowland plc and its subsidiary Coase Ltd.

   *Balance sheet as at 30 September 1994*

   |  | Rowland plc £000 | Coase Ltd £000 |
   |---|---|---|
   | *Debit balances* | | |
   | Fixed assets at book value | 12,000 | 3,700 |
   | Stocks | 1,250 | 1,360 |
   | Debtors | 920 | 217 |
   | Cash | 50 | 10 |
   |  | 14,220 | 5,287 |
   | *Credit balances* | | |
   | Issued share capital (£1 shares) | 8,000 | 1,000 |
   | Retained profit at 30 September 1993 | 4,466 | 2,640 |
   | Profit, year to 30 September 1994 | 196 | 296 |
   | Trade creditors | 558 | 551 |
   | 12% debenture | 1,000 | 800 |
   |  | 14,220 | 5,287 |

   On 1 October 1993, Rowland plc issued 1,200,000 of its own shares in exchange for the entire share capital of Coase Ltd. The market price of shares in Rowland plc on 1 October 1993 was £3.50 per share. The financial effects of this transaction have not been entered in the books of Rowland plc.

   There were no material differences between the book value and fair value of any of the assets of either Rowland plc or Coase Ltd on 1 October 1993.

   Any goodwill arising from the acquisition of Coase Ltd is estimated to have a useful economic life of four years.

   **Required**

   (a) The consolidated balance sheet of Rowland plc and its subsidiary Coase Ltd as at 30 September 1994 prepared in accordance with:

   (i) the acquisition method as specified by FRS2;

   (ii) the merger method as specified by FRS6.

The accounts should be prepared in good form but do not necessarily have to be presented in a form suitable for publication. [14]

(b) Advise the directors of Rowland plc as to how the financial information contained in present and future published accounts of the group would differ depending on which method given in (a) is adopted. [6]

[Total 20]

## Further reading

FRS2 'Accounting for subsidiary undertakings'

FRS6 'Acquisitions and mergers'

FRS7 'Fair values in acquisition accounting'

# Unit 9

## Capital Reorganisation

### Objectives

After studying this Unit you should be able to:

- describe the Companies Act provisions for the redemption or purchase of own shares, and calculate the effect on the company's balance sheet

- describe the Companies Act provisions for schemes of capital reduction and reorganisation, and amend a company's balance sheet accordingly

- rank liquidation claims

- evaluate capital reconstruction schemes.

## 1  Introduction

1.1 Companies finance their businesses by raising money from their shareholders, by retaining their profits and by borrowing. As time passes the need for capital changes. If they are growing, fresh finance needs to be raised. However, in mature industries it may be that the company now has more cash than it needs. In these circumstances the company may wish to return the excess cash to its shareholders.

1.2 A company's share capital constitutes a 'creditors' buffer' which helps protect its creditors who may suffer due to the company's limited liability. Company law therefore seeks to ensure that share capital cannot be repaid to the shareholders if the creditors are placed at risk.

1.3 The opposite scenario occurs when a company has made losses in recent years and has a debit balance on its profit and loss reserve and is therefore unable to pay dividends. The company may be more optimistic about its future but be unable to raise fresh capital due to its inability to pay dividends.

1.4 Under these circumstances it is necessary to write off sufficient share capital to eliminate the negative profit and loss reserve balance. Once again company law requires that certain conditions must be met before this takes place to protect the company's creditors.

FINANCIAL REPORTING, ANALYSIS AND PLANNING

## 2 Redemption or purchase of a company's own shares – the Companies Act requirements

2.1 The Companies Act 1985 allows companies to issue both redeemable preference shares and redeemable ordinary shares. One of the objectives of the legislation was to encourage equity investment in small businesses. The issuing of redeemable shares allows the proprietors to buy back the shares, at an appropriate time, without permanently losing control of the business.

2.2 A company may issue redeemable shares if this is authorised by its articles of association. However they may only be issued if other shares are in issue which cannot be redeemed.

2.3 The Companies Act contains the following provisions concerning the redemption of redeemable shares:

*Section 159(3)* – redeemable shares may not be redeemed unless they are fully paid and the company must pay for the shares on redemption and not at a later date.

*Section 160(1)* – redeemable shares may only be redeemed out of distributable profits or out of the proceeds of a fresh issue of shares made for that purpose. Any premium payable on redemption must be paid out of the distributable profits of the company, unless the shares being redeemed were issued at a premium.

*Section 170(1)* – where shares are redeemed out of profits, a sum equal to the nominal value of the shares redeemed must be transferred from the company's profit and loss account to a non-distributable reserve called the 'capital redemption reserve'. (This maintains the creditors' buffer.)

*Section 160(4)* – redeemed shares are treated as cancelled and the issued share capital of the company will be reduced by the nominal value of the shares redeemed. The authorised share capital is not reduced.

*Section 160(2)* – if the shares being redeemed were themselves issued at a premium, any premium on their redemption may be paid out of the proceeds of a fresh issue of shares made for the purposes of redemption up to an amount equal to:

(a) the aggregate of the premiums received by the company on the issue of the shares redeemed, or

(b) the current amount of the company's share premium account (including any sum transferred to that account in respect of premiums on the new shares) whichever is less, and in that case the amount of the company's share premium account shall be reduced by a sum corresponding (or by sums in the aggregate corresponding) to the amount of any payments made by virtue of section 160(2) out of the proceeds of the issue of the new shares.

2.4 The Companies Act allows private companies to purchase or redeem shares partly from capital when the company concerned has neither sufficient distributable profits nor the ability to raise all the money required by an issue of shares.

# CAPITAL REORGANISATION

2.5 Before a private company can make such a payment out of capital the following conditions must be met under sections 171–177 of the Companies Act.

(a) It must be authorised by the company's articles.

(b) The payment must not exceed the 'permissible capital payment'. (The permissible capital payment is the amount required to purchase the shares, less the company's available profits and any proceeds from a new issue of shares.)

(c) The directors must make a statutory declaration specifying the amount of the permissible capital payment and also that they are of the opinion that the company will be able to pay its debts:

(i) immediately following the purchase or redemption; and

(ii) also for one year immediately following.

(d) A report by the company's auditors must be annexed to the statutory declaration stating that:

- they have enquired into the company's affairs;

- the permissible capital payment has been properly determined; and

- they are not aware of anything to indicate that the opinion expressed by the directors is unreasonable.

(e) The payment must be approved by a special resolution. The special resolution is invalid if it is passed only because the shares being purchased were voted.

(f) The payments out of capital must not be made earlier than five weeks nor later than seven weeks after the date of the resolution.

2.6 In addition to redeeming shares which were issued for that purpose a company can also purchase its own shares. This may be a 'market purchase' or an 'off-market purchase'.

2.7 A market purchase is the purchase of listed shares, while the purchases of other types of shares are off-market purchases. Both types must be authorised by the company's articles to be legal.

2.8 Before a company can make a market purchase it must be authorised by an ordinary resolution which:

(a) specifies the maximum number of shares which the company may acquire;

(b) states the maximum and minimum prices which the company may pay for those shares;

(c) specifies a date when the authority given by the resolution will expire. This must not be later than 18 months after the passing of the resolution.

The authority may be varied, revoked or renewed by a later ordinary resolution.

2.9 A company may make an off-market purchase under a specific contract which has been authorised by a special resolution. If the resolution is passed

FINANCIAL REPORTING, ANALYSIS AND PLANNING

by a public company, it must give a date on which the authority will expire which is not later than 18 months after the resolution is passed.

## 3 Redemption or purchase of a company's own shares – the effect on the company's balance sheet

3.1 In this section we will illustrate the accounting treatment for each of the following scenarios:

- the purchase or redemption out of distributable profits
- the purchase or redemption financed by a new issue
- the purchase or redemption at a premium
- a premium paid on redemption and a new issue at a premium.

3.2 The purchase or redemption out of distributable profits.

**Example 9.1**

ABC Ltd's balance sheet as at 31 December 19X5 is as follows:

|  | £000 |
|---|---|
| Net assets | 130 |
| £1 Ordinary shares – redeemable | 40 |
| – non-redeemable | 40 |
| Profit and loss account | 50 |
|  | 130 |

Assuming the company redeems the redeemable ordinary shares on this day the entries will be:

|  | £000 | £000 |
|---|---|---|
| Debit – £1 Ordinary shares | 40 |  |
| Credit – Bank |  | 40 |

being the payment to the shareholders and the cancelling of the shares.

|  | £000 | £000 |
|---|---|---|
| Debit – Profit and loss account (reserve) | 40 |  |
| Credit – Capital redemption reserve |  | 40 |

being the transfer from distributable to non-distributable reserves to maintain the creditors' buffer.

The revised balance sheet is as follows:

|  | £000 |
|---|---|
| Net assets | 90 |
| £1 Ordinary shares | 40 |
| Capital redemption reserve | 40 |
| Profit and loss account | 10 |
|  | 90 |

# CAPITAL REORGANISATION

**3.3** The purchase or redemption financed by a new issue.

### Example 9.1 continued

Continuing the previous example, assume that ABC Ltd issued 20,000 £1 ordinary shares at par to help finance the redemption.

The entries would be:

|  | £000 | £000 |
|---|---|---|
| Debit – £1 Ordinary shares | 40 | |
| Credit – Bank | | 40 |

being the payment to the shareholders and the cancelling of the shares.

|  | £000 | £000 |
|---|---|---|
| Debit – Bank | 20 | |
| Credit – £1 Ordinary shares | | 20 |

being the issue of the new shares.

|  | £000 | £000 |
|---|---|---|
| Debit – Profit and loss account (reserve) | 20 | |
| Credit – Capital redemption reserve | | 20 |

being the transfer from distributable to non-distributable reserves to maintain the creditors' buffer at £80,000.

The revised balance sheet is as follows:

|  | £000 |
|---|---|
| Net assets | 110 |
| | |
| £1 Ordinary shares | 60 |
| Capital redemption reserve | 20 |
| Profit and loss account | 30 |
| | 110 |

**3.4** The purchase or redemption at a premium.

### Example 9.1 continued

Still using the same example assume that there was an issue of 20,000 £1 ordinary shares and that the 40,000 £1 ordinary shares were redeemed for £1.50 each, i.e. at a 50p premium.

The entries would be:

|  | £000 | £000 |
|---|---|---|
| Debit – £1 Ordinary shares | 40 | |
| Debit – Profit and loss account (reserve) | 20 | |
| Credit – Bank | | 60 |

being the payment to the shareholders and the cancelling of the shares. The premium must be written off to the profit and loss account.

|  | £000 | £000 |
|---|---|---|
| Debit – Bank | 20 | |
| Credit – £1 Ordinary shares | | 20 |

being the issue of the new shares.

|  | £000 | £000 |
|---|---|---|
| Debit – Profit and loss account (reserve) | 20 | |
| Credit – Capital redemption reserve | | 20 |

being the transfer from distributable to non-distributable reserves to maintain the creditors' buffer at £80,000.

The revised balance sheet is as follows:

|  | £000 |
|---|---|
| Net assets | 90 |
| £1 Ordinary shares | 60 |
| Capital redemption reserve | 20 |
| Profit and loss account | 10 |
|  | 90 |

3.5 A premium paid on redemption and a new issue at a premium.

In the previous example the premium on redemption was written off against the profit and loss account. However if a new issue is used to finance the redemption, part or all of the premium on redemption may be written off to the share premium account. This is allowed under section 160(2) of the Companies Act and was covered in paragraph 2.3. This stipulates that the write off to the share premium account is the lowest of:

- the premium on any new shares issued
- the premium paid on redemption
- the balance on the share premium account after the new issue
- any premium created on the original issue of the shares to be redeemed.

**Example 9.2**

Assume ABC Ltd's balance sheet as at 31 December 19X7 is as follows:

|  | £000 |
|---|---|
| Net assets | 155 |
| £1 Ordinary shares – redeemable | 40 |
|                 – non-redeemable | 40 |
| Share premium account | 25 |
| Profit and loss account | 50 |
|  | 155 |

The redeemable shares were redeemed for £1.50 per share. A fresh issue of 20,000 £1 ordinary shares at £1.60 each was made to finance the redemption. The redeemable shares were originally issued for £1.25 each.

Before making the journal entries it is necessary to establish the write off to the share premium account.

| | |
|---|---|
| The premium on the new issue is | £12,000 |
| The premium paid on redemption is | £20,000 |
| The balance on the share premium account after the new issue is | £37,000 |
| The premium on the original issue was | £10,000 |

Thus £10,000, being the lowest amount, can be written off to the share premium account.

# CAPITAL REORGANISATION

The entries are therefore:

|  | £000 | £000 |
|---|---|---|
| Debit – £1 Ordinary shares | 40 |  |
| Debit – Profit and loss account (reserve) | 10 |  |
| Debit – Share premium account | 10 |  |
| Credit – Bank |  | 60 |

being the payment to the shareholders, the cancelling of the shares and the write off of the premium on redemption against the share premium and profit and loss accounts.

|  | £000 | £000 |
|---|---|---|
| Debit – Bank | 32 |  |
| Credit – £1 Ordinary shares |  | 20 |
| Credit – Share premium account |  | 12 |

being the issue of the new shares.

|  | £000 | £000 |
|---|---|---|
| Debit – Profit and loss account (reserve) | 20 |  |
| Credit – Capital redemption reserve |  | 20 |

being the transfer from distributable to non-distributable reserves.

The revised balance sheet is as follows:

|  | £000 |
|---|---|
| Net assets | 127 |
|  |  |
| £1 Ordinary shares | 60 |
| Share premium account | 27 |
| Capital redemption reserve | 20 |
| Profit and loss account | 20 |
|  | 127 |

3.6  In paragraph 2.5 you learnt that in certain circumstances a private company is permitted to make payments out of capital when redeeming their shares. When this occurs it is still necessary to create a capital redemption reserve. However this will fall short of the shares redeemed by the permissible capital repayment. See example 9.3.

**Example 9.3**

Assume ABC Ltd's balance sheet as at 31 December 19X8 is as follows:

|  | £000 |
|---|---|
| Net assets | 145 |
|  |  |
| £1 Ordinary shares – redeemable | 40 |
|                 – non-redeemable | 60 |
| Share premium account | 25 |
| Profit and loss account | 20 |
|  | 145 |

The company issues 10,000 £1 ordinary shares at £1.30 to provide part of the purchase consideration for the redemption of the redeemable shares at £1.10 each.

The permissible capital payment is:

|  | £000 | £000 |
|---|---|---|
| Cost of redemption |  | 44 |
| less: Proceeds from new issue | 13 |  |
| and Distributable reserves | 20 |  |
|  |  | 33 |
| Permissible capital payment |  | 11 |

The capital redemption reserve needed is:

|  | £000 | £000 |
|---|---|---|
| Nominal value of shares redeemed |  | 40 |
| less: Permissible capital payment | 11 |  |
| Proceeds of the new issue | 13 |  |
|  |  | 24 |
|  |  | 16 |

The revised balance sheet will be as follows:

|  | £000 |
|---|---|
| Net assets | 114 |
|  |  |
| £1 Ordinary shares | 70 |
| Share premium account | 28 |
| Capital redemption reserve | 16 |
|  | 114 |

The non-distributable reserves have been reduced by £11,000, the permissible capital payment.

## Student Activity 1

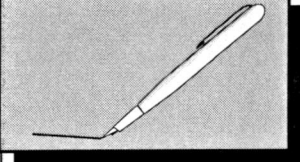

Ace Ltd has the following balance sheet:

|  | £000 |
|---|---|
| Net assets | 500 |
|  |  |
| £1 Ordinary shares | 300 |
| Share premium account | 120 |
| Profit and loss account | 80 |
|  | 500 |

Prepare a revised balance sheet, making the following assumptions.

(a) The ordinary shares were originally issued at £1.40. The company purchases 100,000 £1 ordinary shares for £1.50.

The purchase was partially financed by the issue of 50,000 £1 ordinary shares at £1.60.

(b) The company purchases 100,000 £1 shares at par.

*The answer follows; do this Activity before reading on.*

## CAPITAL REORGANISATION

3.7 You should have obtained the following answer:

(a) The premium on the new issue is £30,000
The premium paid on redemption is £50,000
The balance on the share premium account
after the new issue is £150,000
The premium on the original issue was £40,000

Thus £30,000, being the lowest amount, can be written off to the share premium account.

This results in the following balance sheet:

|  | £000 |
|---|---|
| Net assets | 430 |
|  |  |
| £1 Ordinary shares | 250 |
| Share premium account | 120 |
| Capital redemption reserve | 50 |
| Profit and loss account | 10 |
|  | 430 |

(b) The shares redeemed have a nominal value in excess of the available distributable profits. However as Ace Ltd is a private company it is allowed the 'permissible capital payment'. The revised balance sheet is therefore as follows.

|  | £000 |
|---|---|
| Net assets | 400 |
|  |  |
| £1 Ordinary shares | 200 |
| Share premium account | 120 |
| Capital redemption reserve | 80 |
|  | 400 |

## 4 Schemes of capital reduction and reorganisation – the legal background

4.1 Under section 135 of the Companies Act 1985 a company may:

- write off unpaid share capital;
- write off any share capital which is lost or not represented by available assets;
- write off any paid up share capital which is in excess of requirements.

Before the company's capital can be reduced in this way court approval must be obtained. The reduction must also be allowed by the company's articles of association and a special resolution must be passed.

4.2 Section 425 of the Companies Act 1985 is often used in conjunction with section 135. Under section 425 a company may:

- write off debenture interest arrears
- replace existing debentures with a lower interest debenture

FINANCIAL REPORTING, ANALYSIS AND PLANNING

- write off preference dividend arrears
- write off amounts owing to trade creditors.

4.3 The following procedure must be followed if section 425 is to be used.

  (i) The court has to be consulted and must be asked to direct the holding of meetings of members, creditors and debenture holders to discuss the proposed scheme. The court may decline to do this if the meetings would serve no purpose due to opposition from parties holding a majority of the votes, or due to certain groups within each class having different interests. For example, some creditors may also be shareholders.

  (ii) The scheme must be approved by a majority in number and three-quarters in value of the members, creditors and debenture holders.

  (iii) After the scheme has been voted through by the various parties it must be placed before the court for final approval.

4.4 An alternative to the internal reorganisation, given above, is to liquidate the existing company and transfer the business to a new company specially created to carry out the scheme arrangements. This is known as an external reconstruction or reorganisation.

4.5 The Companies Act contains two sections allowing different forms of external scheme, section 427 of the Companies Act 1985 and section 110 of the Insolvency Act 1986.

4.6 Under section 427 a court-enforced liquidation involves the assets and liabilities being transferred to a new company. The old stakeholders are offered shares or debentures in the new company.

4.7 A voluntary liquidation under section 110 of the Insolvency Act 1986 has to be approved by a special resolution, but does not require court approval. However, if it is a creditors' voluntary liquidation the scheme must be approved by the court and by the liquidation committee.

4.8 Individual stakeholders have the right to dissent and can apply to receive the cash equivalent of their holding or to insist that the sale to the new company is abandoned.

# 5 Accounting for an internal scheme of capital reduction and reorganisation

5.1 When a company needs to raise fresh finance but is unable to do so because of a negative balance on its profit and loss reserve, it may seek to eliminate this balance by a scheme of capital reduction. We will first examine the accounting entries of a scheme of internal reconstruction.

5.2 Once the legal requirements are met and court approval is obtained, the negative balance can be eliminated against the company's share capital and non-distributable reserves. The company will usually take this opportunity to adjust the book value of its assets to more realistic levels.

5.3 The bookkeeping entries are made through a capital reduction and reorganisation account. The following example illustrates what is required.

# CAPITAL REORGANISATION

**Example 9.4**

*XYZ Plc balance sheet as at 31 March 19X5*

| | £000 |
|---|---:|
| Intangible fixed assets | |
| Patents | 10,000 |
| Tangible fixed assets | 30,000 |
| Net current assets | (3,000) |
| | 37,000 |
| | |
| Represented by: | |
| £1 Ordinary shares | 100,000 |
| 8% Preference shares | 8,000 |
| Profit and loss account | (71,000) |
| | 37,000 |

The following scheme of reorganisation has been approved by the court.

(1) Patents to be written off.

(2) The tangible fixed assets are to be revalued to £41,000,000.

(3) The debit balance on the profit and loss reserve is to be eliminated.

(4) The £1 ordinary shares are to be reduced to 30 pence fully paid shares.

The journal entries will be as follows:

| | £000 | £000 |
|---|---:|---:|
| (1) Debit CRR account | 10,000 | |
|     Credit Patents | | 10,000 |
| (2) Debit Fixed assets | 11,000 | |
|     Credit CRR account | | 11,000 |
| (3) Debit CRR account | 71,000 | |
|     Credit Profit and loss account | | 71,000 |
| (4) Debit Ordinary shares | 70,000 | |
|     Credit CRR account | | 70,000 |
| | 162,000 | 162,000 |

The revised balance sheet is as follows.

*XYZ Plc balance sheet as at 31 March 19X5*

| | £000 |
|---|---:|
| Tangible fixed assets | 41,000 |
| Net current assets | (3,000) |
| | 38,000 |
| | |
| Represented by: | |
| £1 Ordinary shares | 30,000 |
| 8% £1 Preference shares | 8,000 |
| | 38,000 |

5.4 The capital reduction must always match or exceed the losses written off. In this example, the capital reduction is £70,000 (reduction to ordinary share

FINANCIAL REPORTING, ANALYSIS AND PLANNING

capital) and the balance sheet 'losses' written off are: net £70,000 (£71,000 P & L account + £10,000 Patents - £11,000 fixed assets).

5.5 If they exceed the losses written off then the difference is transferred to a non-distributable capital reserve. For example, if in the above reorganisation the Preference shares were also reduced to 80p fully paid the balance sheet would be:

|  | £000 |
|---|---|
| Tangible fixed assets | 41,000 |
| Net current assets | (3,000) |
|  | 38,000 |
|  |  |
| Represented by: |  |
| £1 Ordinary shares | 30,000 |
| 8% £1 Preference shares | 6,000 |
| Capital reserve | 2,000 |
|  | 38,000 |

5.6 The purpose of these schemes is usually to allow the company to raise fresh capital. The bookkeeping entries for the capital raised are the same as usual, i.e. debit bank and credit share capital.

## Student Activity 2

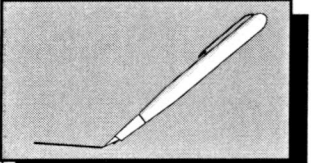

PQR Ltd has the following balance sheet as at 31 March 19X5.

|  | £000 |
|---|---|
| Fixed assets | 3,600 |
| Net current assets | 3,775 |
|  | 7,375 |
|  |  |
| Ordinary shares of £1 each fully paid | 10,000 |
| 7% Preference shares of £1 each fully paid | 2,500 |
| Profit and loss balance | (8,625) |
| 10% Debentures | 3,500 |
|  | 7,375 |

The following scheme of capital reduction and reconstruction has been approved by the court.

(a) The existing ordinary shares are to be cancelled.

(b) The 10% debentures are to be retired and the debenture holders issued in exchange with:

  (i) £3,000,000 14% redeemable debentures 2010, and

  (ii) 2,000,000 ordinary shares of 25p each, fully paid up.

(c) The 7% cumulative preference shareholders to be issued with 2,000,000 ordinary shares of 25p each, fully paid up, in payment of three years' arrears of preference dividend.

(d) The existing ordinary shareholders will be issued with 3,500,000 ordinary shares of 25p each fully paid up.

CAPITAL REORGANISATION

You are required to:

(a) Post the entries to the capital reduction reorganisation account; and

(b) prepare the balance sheet after the scheme has been put into effect.

*The answer follows, do this Activity before reading on.*

5.6 You should have obtained the following answer.

(a) *Capital reduction and reorganisation account*

|  | £000 |  | £000 |
|---|---|---|---|
| 14% debentures | 3,000 | £1 Ordinary shares | 10,000 |
| 25p ordinary shares | 1,875 | 11% Debentures | 3,500 |
| Profit & loss balance | 8,625 |  |  |
|  | 13,500 |  | 13,500 |

(b) *Balance sheet as at 31 March 19X5*

|  | £000 |
|---|---|
| Fixed assets | 3,600 |
| Net current assets | 3,775 |
|  | 7,375 |
|  |  |
| Ordinary shares of 25p each fully paid | 1,875 |
| 7% Cumulative preference shares | 2,500 |
| 14% Redeemable debentures | 3,000 |
|  | 7,375 |

# 6 Accounting for an external scheme of capital reduction and reorganisation

6.1 The main idea is the same as for an internal reconstruction, i.e. the elimination of a negative profit and loss account balance against the company's non-distributable capital. This is achieved by closing the books of the old company and opening the new company's books with the new asset values.

6.2 The books of the old company are closed through a realisation account. The other accounts needed are for the new company, sundry members and the bank account. The entries are then as follows.

1. Debit the realisation account with the assets at their book value.

2. Transfer the reserves, profit and loss account, share capital and intangible assets written off to the sundry members account.

3. Transfer the debts to be settled by the new company to the new company account.

4. The old company's debts, which are not transferred but paid, should be cleared against the bank account. The sale proceeds from the sale of the assets not transferred should be debited to the bank account and credited to the realisation account.

# FINANCIAL REPORTING, ANALYSIS AND PLANNING

5. Credit the realisation account with the purchase consideration and debit the new company account.

6. Debit the sundry members' account with the purchase consideration and credit the new company account.

7. The sundry members' account should now be closed by a transfer from the bank account, which also closes the bank account.

6.3 The books of the new company are now opened using the revised asset values.

**Example 9.5**

Aye Ltd has the following balance sheet as at 31 March 19X5:

|  | £000 |
|---|---|
| Land and buildings | 2,000 |
| Other fixed assets | 1,600 |
| Stock and debtors | 3,900 |
| Creditors | (1,200) |
| Bank | 1,000 |
|  | 7,300 |
|  |  |
| Represented by: |  |
| Ordinary shares of £1 each fully paid | 15,000 |
| 7% Preference shares of £1 each fully paid | 2,500 |
| Profit and loss account | (12,700) |
| 10% Debentures | 2,500 |
|  | 7,300 |

Preference dividends are two years in arrears, but trading conditions have recently improved. A team of consultants has proposed the following scheme of reconstruction.

- Aye Ltd is to go into voluntary liquidation and a new company, Bee Ltd, is to be formed to take over Aye Ltd's business.

- The land and buildings are to be sold and new premises leased. The lease will be classified as an operating lease and the sale proceeds from the land and buildings, expected to be £2.8m, will be used to repay the 10% debentures.

- Bee Ltd will take over the other fixed assets for £1.5m. Stock and debtors are to be taken over at book value.

- Aye Ltd will pay the creditors in full.

- The ordinary shareholders are to receive one fully paid £1 share in Bee Ltd for every five shares they hold in Aye Ltd.

- The preference shareholders are to receive one fully paid 9% £1 preference share in Bee Ltd for every share held in Aye Ltd. The increased dividend is compensation for the dividend arrears.

# CAPITAL REORGANISATION

Aye Ltd's books will be closed as follows.

*Realisation account*

|  | £000 |  | £000 |
|---|---|---|---|
| Land and buildings | 2,000 | New company | 5,500 |
| Other fixed assets | 1,600 | Bank (sale of land | |
| Stock and debtors | 3,900 | and buildings) | 2,800 |
| Gain on realisation | 800 | | |
| | 8,300 | | 8,300 |

*Sundry members*

|  | £000 |  | £000 |
|---|---|---|---|
| Profit & loss Account | 12,700 | Ordinary shares | 15,000 |
| New company | 5,500 | Preference shares | 2,500 |
| Bank | 100 | Gain on realisation | 800 |
| | 18,300 | | 18,300 |

*New company*

|  | £000 |  | £000 |
|---|---|---|---|
| Realisation account (Purchase consideration) | 5,500 | Sundry members | 5,500 |

*Bank*

|  | £000 |  | £000 |
|---|---|---|---|
| Balance brought forward | 1,000 | Creditors | 1,200 |
| Realisation account | 2,800 | 10% Debentures | 2,500 |
| | | Sundry members | 100 |
| | 3,800 | | 3,800 |

The new company's opening balance sheet will be as follows.

|  | £000 |
|---|---|
| Positive goodwill | 100 |
| Fixed assets | 1,500 |
| Stock and debtors | 3,900 |
| | 5,500 |
| | |
| Represented by: | |
| £1 Ordinary shares | 3,000 |
| 9% Preference shares | 2,500 |
| | 5,500 |

FINANCIAL REPORTING, ANALYSIS AND PLANNING

## 7 The ranking of liquidation claims

7.1 After a company goes into liquidation certain creditors take priority when the proceeds of the liquidation are distributed. The order is as follows.

1. Loans secured by fixed charges; to the extent that they can be met from the net proceeds of the assets to which they are secured, any outstanding balances will rank as unsecured creditors. When more than one loan is secured on an asset the loans are paid in order of priority, i.e. the first charge must be repaid before any monies are available for the second charge, and so on.

2. The liquidation costs.

3. Preferential debts. These rank equally amongst themselves and include PAYE, wages, etc.

4. Debts secured by a floating charge.

5. Unsecured creditors.

6. The remainder is distributed between the shareholders.

7.2 Contrary to popular belief, preference shareholders do not automatically receive priority in the repayment of capital and outstanding dividends to the ordinary shareholders in a liquidation. The rights of the preference shares will be contained in the terms of their issue and they should be treated accordingly.

### Student Activity 3

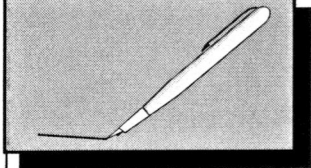

ST Plc was placed in receivership and liquidated. The company's assets raised the following amounts.

|  | £000 |
|---|---|
| Land and buildings | 2,600 |
| Plant and machinery | 3,400 |
| Stock | 960 |

The liquidation expenses amounted to £20,000.

The company had the following debts:

|  | £000 |
|---|---|
| Bank mortgage on the land and buildings | 3,000 |
| Bank overdraft (floating charge on stock) | 800 |
| Preferential creditors | 1,400 |
| Unsecured creditors | 1,920 |

Calculate the amount received by each party.

*The answer follows: do this Activity before reading on.*

CAPITAL REORGANISATION

7.3 You should have obtained the following answer.

|  | £000 | £000 |
|---|---|---|
| Land and buildings | | 2,600 |
| less Mortgage | | (2,600) |
| | | — |
| Plant and machinery | | 3,400 |
| Stock | | 960 |
| | | 4,360 |
| Liquidation expenses | | (20) |
| Preferential creditors | | (1,400) |
| Floating charge | | (800) |
| Available (for abatement) to unsecured creditors | | 2,140 |
| Unsecured creditors [1,920 + 400] | | (2,140) |
| Available to shareholders | | — |

The unsecured creditors will receive approximately 92.2 pence in the pound.

The bank will receive the following amounts relating to the mortgage.

|  | £000 |
|---|---|
| Land and buildings | 2,600 |
| Remainder as an unsecured creditor [400 × 0.922] | 369 |
| | 2,969 |

# 8 The evaluation of capital-reduction and reorganisation schemes

8.1 A scheme of capital reconstruction and reorganisation is only worthwhile if the company is going to be profitable in future. Typically a company may have traded at a loss for several years and is carrying large accumulated losses on its balance sheet. A thorough examination of its future prospects is therefore required before any further evaluation of the proposals takes place.

8.2 Once you are satisfied that the company has a reasonable future, the terms and conditions of the scheme can be examined. The scheme must be approved by all the parties involved, and care must be taken to ensure that none of them are worse off under the scheme than if the company had been liquidated.

8.3 In addition, no party must be perceived to have suffered more than their fair share of the loss.

8.4 In assessing the effects on the parties involved in the reconstruction, the following factors should be considered.

(a) Future income from the revised holdings should be at least equal to the income previously received from the company. It will hopefully be higher, owing to the company's improved prospects.

(b) The capital reduction should be proportional to the loss the parties could expect to suffer in a liquidation. It is possible to increase the rate of return on preference shares and debentures in exchange for a larger capital reduction. Alternatively, a conversion option could be included in the new securities allowing the parties to participate in the company's revival.

(c) Risks are borne by each party. It is unlikely that a debenture holder will be willing to exchange the debentures for ordinary shares or even preference shares without adequate compensation for the increased risk.

(d) Ordinary shareholders may be unwilling to relinquish control of the company, and it may be necessary to ensure that they retain at least 51% of the voting share capital.

8.5 The purpose of a scheme is usually to raise fresh capital. In evaluating the proposals it must be seen that adequate capital is being raised and that the source of that capital can be relied upon.

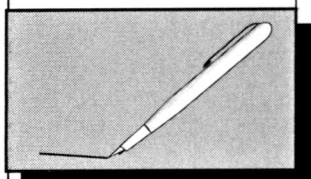

### Student Activity 4

Power PCs Ltd is a company that trades as a retailer selling computer equipment. For the past few years it has been making losses because of low price competition.

The company's balance sheet as at 30 June 19X6 was as follows:

|  | £000 |
|---|---:|
| Fixed assets | 7,200 |
| Net current assets | 7,550 |
|  | 14,750 |
| Represented by: |  |
| Ordinary shares of £1 each fully paid | 20,000 |
| 8% cumulative £1 preference shares | 5,000 |
| Profit and loss balance | (17,250) |
| 11% Debentures redeemable 19Y5 | 7,000 |
|  | 14,750 |

The company has changed its marketing strategy and is now expanding to sell mobile telephone technology. It is expected that the company will make a profit after tax of £3m for the next five years before accounting for any interest charge. Corporation tax is assumed to be at a rate of 35%.

The tax credit on dividends paid is assumed to be 20%.

The directors are proposing to reconstruct the company and have produced the following proposal for discussion.

(a) To cancel the existing ordinary shares.

(b) The 11% debentures are to be retired and the debenture holders issued in exchange with

(i) £6m 14% redeemable debentures 2010, and

(ii) 4,000,000 ordinary shares of 25p each, fully paid up.

(c) The 8% cumulative preference shareholders are to be issued with 4,000,000 ordinary shares of 25p each, fully paid up, in payment of four years' arrears of preference dividend.

# CAPITAL REORGANISATION

(d) The existing ordinary shareholders will be issued with 7,000,000 ordinary shares of 25p each fully paid up.

In the event of a liquidation, it is estimated that the net realisable values would be £6.2m for the fixed assets and £7m for the net current assets.

**Required**

(a) Prepare computations to show the effect of the proposed reconstruction scheme on each of the debenture holders, preference shareholders and ordinary shareholders.

(b) Write a brief report to advise a shareholder who owns 10% of the issued share capital on whether to agree to the reconstruction as proposed. The shareholder has informed you that he feels the proposals are unfair.

*The answer follows; do this Activity before reading on.*

8.6 Your answer should have been along the following lines.

(a) Gross income of the various parties

|  | Before the reconstruction £000 | After the reconstruction £000 |
|---|---|---|
| Debenture holders | 770 | 1,525 |
| Preference shareholders | – | 1,185 |
| Ordinary shareholders | – | 1,198.75 |

The nominal value of the securities involved is not important to the parties involved. They will be concerned with the market value of those securities, or in other words the future income from those securities.

Workings:

|  | £000 |
|---|---|
| Profit after tax and before interest | 3,000 |
| less interest [840 × 0.65] | (546) |
| Preference dividend |  |
| 5,000 × 8% | (400) |
| Available to ordinary shareholders | 2,054 |

15,000,000 shares in issue gives an e.p.s. of 13.7 pence.

| Debenture holders | £000 |
|---|---|
| – before £7,000,000 × 11% = | 770 |
|  |  |
| – after £6,000,000 × 14% = | 840 |
| + 4,000,000 × 13.7p × 100/80 = | 685 |
|  | 1,525 |

| Preference shareholders | £000 |
|---|---|
| £5,000,000 × 8% × 100/80 = | 500 |
| + 4,000,000 × 13.7p × 100/80 = | 685 |
|  | 1,185 |

Ordinary shareholders
− 7,000,000 × 13.7p × 100/80 =   1,198,750

(b) In assessing the fairness of the scheme it is necessary to establish what the parties would receive in the event of the company being wound up.

|  | £000 |
|---|---:|
| Fixed assets | 6,200 |
| Net current assets | 7,000 |
|  | 13,200 |
| less debentures | 7,000 |
|  | 6,200 |
| less preference dividend arrears | 1,600 |
|  | 4,600 |
| less preference shares | 5,000 |
| loss to preference shareholders | (400) |

The ordinary shareholders would not receive a capital repayment. This suggests that the ordinary shareholders should be grateful for any return whatsoever, particularly as they are not being asked to provide additional finance.

However the debenture holders are receiving a large increase in their income and the preference shareholders income has also increased. Both these parties would therefore benefit substantially from a reconstruction. It could be argued that the ordinary shareholders should also gain some benefit.

The scheme also involves a loss of control with the ordinary shareholders' stake falling to 47%. However this may be unimportant to a shareholder with only 10% of the shares.

## Summary

**Now that you have completed this Unit you should be able to:**

- [ ] **describe the Companies Act provisions for the redemption or purchase of own shares, and calculate the effect on the company's balance sheet**
- [ ] **describe the Companies Act provisions for schemes of capital reduction and reorganisation, and amend a company's balance sheet accordingly**
- [ ] **rank liquidation claims**
- [ ] **evaluate capital reconstruction schemes.**

# CAPITAL REORGANISATION

## Self-assessment questions

1. A court order is required before a company can purchase its own shares.
   True/False.

2. Zeta Plc redeems 50,000 £1 ordinary shares at £1.20, the same price at which they were issued. The company issues 20,000 £1 ordinary shares at £1.25 to finance the purchase. Before the redemption the balance on the share premium account was £20,000.

   Calculate the reduction in the company's distributable profits.

3. Using the example in question 2 calculate the capital redemption reserve.

4. What conditions must be met before a private company can make a payment out of capital to purchase its own shares?

5. A company can only purchase its own shares and cancel them if they have been issued as redeemable.
   True/False.

6. Sections 135 and 425 of 1985 Companies Act allow a company to undertake schemes of capital reconstruction. How do they do this?

7. What rights do individual stakeholders have if they disagree with an approved scheme of external reconstruction?

8. What action must be taken if under a proposed scheme of capital reduction and reorganisation:

   (a) the capital reduction is less than the accumulated losses; or

   (b) the capital reduction is greater than the accumulated losses?

9. Doomed Plc's assets have been liquidated and £200,000 has been raised.

   The company's creditors are owed £80,000 and the bank has a floating charge over the company's assets to secure the overdraft of £85,000.

   The company has 50,000 £1 ordinary shares and 30,000 £1 preference shares in issue.

   Calculate how much the preference shareholders would receive if:

   (a) they received repayment of capital in priority to the ordinary shareholders in a winding up; and

   (b) if the preference shareholders did not receive priority in the repayment of capital to the ordinary shareholders in a winding up.

10. Using the data in question 9, and assuming that the preference shareholders did receive a priority in the repayment of capital, give your opinion as to whether the preference shareholders would accept a scheme of reorganisation where the nominal value of their shares was reduced to £20,000.

    If you do not believe that they would accept this, what inducements could be offered?

    *(Answers are given in the Appendix)*

# Unit 10

## Business Valuations

> **OBJECTIVES**
>
> After studying this Unit you should be able to:
>
> - calculate a range of values for a business using the various methods available
> - understand which methods are appropriate for given circumstances, and
> - appreciate the practical aspects of negotiation and price fixing.

## 1 Introduction

1.1 A glance at the financial pages of any quality newspaper demonstrates how imprecise business valuations are. A typical share will have seen its price fluctuate over the past 12 months by 33% to 50%.

1.2 A share price rises when there are more buyers than sellers and falls when the opposite is true. This chapter will attempt to explain why different parties place a different value on a business and will examine the methods most commonly used to arrive at a valuation.

## 2 Valuation methods

### Balance sheet valuations

2.1 A business's balance sheet shows its assets and liabilities. The assets less the liabilities equal the owner's capital in the business. It is therefore tempting to state that this is what it is worth.

2.2 However, imagine that you have been offered £50,000 for the house that you live in which you bought 20 years ago for £10,000.

2.3 When you consider whether or not you should accept the offer the original cost of the house would be irrelevant. The original cost has no bearing on what the house is worth to you or the potential buyer. You would be more concerned with:

- where you would live once the house was sold;
- what it would cost to buy a similar property;
- whether you were likely to receive a better offer; and
- how desperately you needed the money.

# FINANCIAL REPORTING, ANALYSIS AND PLANNING

2.4 A business valuation based on the balance sheet can be based on the above considerations, namely:

- book value;
- replacement cost;
- net realisable value; and
- going concern values.

2.5 Book value depends upon the nature of the business's activities and its accounting policies. If its fixed assets were purchased several years ago it is highly likely that their book value no longer fairly represents their value to the business.

2.6 However, its current assets which are near to being turned into cash are usually stated close to their true value, assuming the business does not possess a large amount of obsolete stock or has not provided for all of its potential bad debts. Thus by deducting all of a business's liabilities from its current assets a minimum valuation can usually be obtained.

2.7 Given the tendency of modern economies continually to experience rising general prices it is usually more realistic to value assets using replacement costs. However problems can arise when it comes to obtaining the necessary values particularly where technological change means that the particular asset is no longer being produced.

2.8 The net realisable value of an enterprise is usually the same as the liquidation value given in the previous chapter. However, as the disposal of the business's assets in this instance is not forced it should be possible to obtain higher values for the assets sold.

2.9 A business that is profitable and earning a reasonable return on its capital employed is worth more to a potential buyer than the net realisable value of its individual assets. It is therefore not a reasonable method of valuing such a business, although once again it would provide a minimum value.

### *Disadvantage of balance sheet valuations*

2.10 The above valuation methods ignore the various advantages a business may have built up over the years in its particular market place. For example, any successful business will have an established customer base and its staff will have acquired expertise in the enterprise's areas of operation. This goodwill will earn a return in the same way that the company's other assets do.

### Methods of valuing goodwill

2.11 There are many different methods used to arrive at a value for goodwill. The various parties involved in the valuation of a business will often agree on a multiple of recent profits. Another commonly used method is the 'dual capitalisation method.'

2.12 The dual capitalisation method assumes that the excess profits earned over and above those expected from the tangible capital employed are earned by the goodwill. These excess profits can therefore be used to calculate the value of goodwill by dividing them by the rate of return expected on goodwill.

BUSINESS VALUATIONS

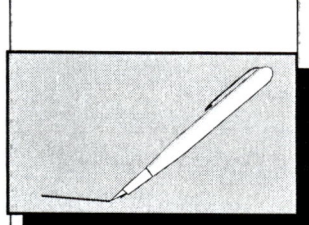

## Student Activity 1

Think about the following activity before looking at the answer which follows.

Z Ltd has been trading for many years and a summary of its balance sheet as at 31 December 19X5 was as follows:

|  | £000 |
|---|---:|
| Fixed Assets | 1,000 |
| Net Current Assets | 500 |
|  | 1,500 |

In each of the last years the company made a profit of £400,000 all of which was paid out in dividends.

Companies in Z Ltd's trade usually earn a return on capital employed of 12% per annum. However, Z plc earns a higher return due to its geographical location which is close to its customers, but where the market is too small for a competitor to become established. However, technological change means that it might be possible for a competitor to emerge at some time in the future.

For this reason the excess profits earned by the goodwill should in the opinion of industry experts be discounted at 20%.

What value would the industry experts place on Z Ltd?

A—£1,500,000

B—£2,000,000

C—£2,600,000

D—£3,333,333

The company would be valued as follows:

|  | £000 | £000 |
|---|---:|---:|
| Net tangible assets |  | 1,500 |
| Goodwill: |  |  |
| Total profit | 400 |  |
| Return on tangible assets 12% × £1,500,000 = | 180 |  |
| Excess profits | 220 |  |
| £220,000/0.2 = |  | 1,100 |
|  |  | 2,600 |

The correct answer is therefore C.

## 3 Earnings valuations

3.1 A business that is a going concern is worth to its owner the net present value of its future earnings. It is quite simple to arrive at a valuation using the most recent earnings and discounting them at the owner's adjusted cost of capital.

# FINANCIAL REPORTING, ANALYSIS AND PLANNING

For example, if the owner of Z Ltd in the previous activity had a 15% cost of capital the value of the business would be:

£400,000/0.15 = £2,666,667.

3.2 However, we are concerned not with the past but with the company's future earnings stream. Ideally we should forecast the company's earnings for each year for several years ahead and then calculate their net present value. Unfortunately the further ahead we look the more uncertain it becomes and such a forecast is arbitrary at best.

3.3 A simpler approach is to adjust the discount rate to reflect future growth and the risk that this growth might not be achieved. This can often be achieved by examining the price earnings (PE) ratio of similar quoted companies.

3.4 The price earnings ratio represents the number of years profits a company must earn to equal its current quoted value. For example a company whose shares are currently £1.60 each with earnings per share of 20p would have a PE ratio of 8 (160/20).

3.5 The PE ratio reflects all that is known about a company and its future profits. Once we have identified a quoted company (or group of companies) comparable to the company we wish to value, the only additional adjustment needed relates to the marketability of the company's shares. It is quite simple to sell shares in companies quoted on the Stock Exchange and a discount of at least 25% needs to be made to reflect the difficulties in selling unquoted securities.

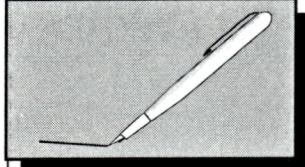

## Student Activity 2

Think about the following activity before looking at the answer which follows.

The Brown family has owned Straw Ltd for many years and have been approached by the company's management who wish to purchase the company from them. The company's profit after tax for each of the last three years was as follows:

|      | £000 |
|------|------|
| 19X2 | 460  |
| 19X3 | 520  |
| 19X4 | 600  |

There are two similar quoted companies:

|          | Share Price | Earnings per share |
|----------|-------------|--------------------|
| Barn plc | £2.70       | 18p                |
| Hay plc  | £5.20       | 40p                |

Calculate the highest price the family could reasonably expect to receive for the company.

The two quoted companies are selling on the following PE ratios:

|          |              |
|----------|--------------|
| Barn plc | 270/18 = 15  |
| Hay plc  | 520/40 = 13  |

Neither company would be exactly the same as Straw Ltd and in the absence of any further information an average of the two PE ratios should be used to value Straw Ltd, i.e. 14.

# BUSINESS VALUATIONS

The PE ratios are based on the companies' most recent earnings and recent profit growth or fluctuations in profits are adjusted for in the PE ratio. Straw Ltd's earnings for 19X4 should therefore be used.

The highest price that could be reasonably expected for the company is therefore:

|  | £000 |
|---|---:|
| 14 × £600,000 = | 8,400 |
| less 25% for lack of marketability | 2,100 |
|  | 6,300 |

3.6 Usually when an examination question provides three or more years' earnings you will be expected to calculate the average earnings to produce an earnings-based valuation, with greater weight being given to the profits of the more recent years. For example, in the previous activity, if you had been required to value Straw Ltd using a 10% average earnings yield, the calculation would have been as follows:

| Average profits |  | £000 |
|---|---|---:|
| 19X2 – £460,000 × 1 = |  | 460 |
| 19X3 – £520,000 × 2 = |  | 1,040 |
| 19X4 – £600,000 × 3 = |  | 1,800 |
|  | 6 | 3,300 |

The weighted average is £3,300,000/6 = £550,000.

The company valuation is therefore £550,000/.10 = £5,500,000.

## 4 Break-up valuation

4.1 In the 1960s one of the main motivations for hostile takeover bids was to acquire the target company in order to sell off its assets for a higher price than was paid for the company. This was possible at that time as many companies had large amounts of tangible assets which were under-utilised. These provided the 'asset strippers', as they became known, with ample opportunity.

4.2 This is an example of valuing companies at their net realisable value. In the 1980s the takeover boom included the operations of corporate raiders whose motivation was the same as in the 1960s – to sell off various parts of the acquired company at a profit.

4.3 However this did not usually involve the liquidation of the target company's assets. During that period, the target company would have grown by acquisitions and/or diversification. This variety of activities and apparent lack of direction lead to a low stock market rating.

4.4 The individual businesses owned by these diversified conglomerates would command a higher stock market rating separately. Therefore, they were demerged and had their own stock market quotations. The corporate raider sought to take over such a conglomerate and sell off the individual businesses it operated in the expectation that the parts would be worth more than the whole. Sir James Goldsmith described this as 'unbundling' during his abortive takeover bid for BAT Industries.

FINANCIAL REPORTING, ANALYSIS AND PLANNING

4.5 This illustrated in the following example.

**Example 10.1**

**LEGION PLC**

Legion plc has four subsidiaries as follows:

|  | Matt plc | Mark plc | Luke plc | John plc | Total |
|---|---|---|---|---|---|
|  | £m | £m | £m | £m | £m |
| Profit after tax | 25 | 10 | 35 | 30 | 100 |
| Net assets | 42 | 78 | 300 | 200 | 620 |

The subsidiaries operated the following businesses which are typically given the following PE ratios.

|  | PE ratio of similar quoted companies |
|---|---|
| Matt plc – Pharmaceuticals | 20 |
| Mark plc – Cigarette manufacturer | 8 |
| Luke plc – Computer software | 15 |
| John plc – Financial services | 12 |

At the time conglomerates were typically valued using a PE ratio of 10.

Legion plc would therefore have a stock market valuation of £100m × 10 = £1,000m.

However if the different businesses were sold off or demerged their combined value would amount to:

|  |  | £m |
|---|---|---|
| Matt plc | £25m × 20 = | 500 |
| Mark plc | £10m × 8 = | 80 |
| Luke plc | £35m × 15 = | 525 |
| John plc | £30m × 12 = | 360 |
|  |  | 1,465 |

## 5 Cashflow valuation

5.1 The above valuations are all based on accounting profits. At times these can be an arbitrary measure of a business's performance, with several accounting policies being highly subjective. Several commentators have argued that cashflow, as an objective figure, provides a better measure of how well a company has performed.

5.2 In order to calculate a business's cashflow it is necessary to adjust its net profit for non-cash items. The most important of these is depreciation. Not only does it not represent a cash outflow it is also one of the most subjective

# BUSINESS VALUATIONS

items in a set of accounts. Depreciation along with any other non-cash expenses needs to be added to the net profit.

5.3 Although depreciation is subjective it does represent the wearing out or consumption of a business's assets and it is a real cost to the business. These assets will have to eventually be replaced and this will result in a cash outflow.

5.4 The estimated annual expenditure to replace the business's worn out fixed assets therefore needs to be deducted from the net profit. This adjustment will often be roughly equivalent to the depreciation charge and the valuation can be based on the accounting profits.

5.5 Some industries possess fixed assets which they depreciate in line with accounting standards, but which have long lives and may never be replaced, for example, pipelines owned by oil and gas companies. In these instances a valuation based on cashflow is fully justified.

5.6 Having established the company's cashflow the net present value of the future cashflows must be calculated to arrive at a valuation.

5.7 An alternative approach to establishing a company's maintainable cashflow is to calculate its free cashflow from the cash flow statement.

**Example 10.2**

**BUTTONS PLC**

*Cashflow statement for the year ended 31 March 19X5*

|  | £000 |
|---|---:|
| Net cash flow from operating activities | 2,170 |
| Returns on investment and servicing of finance (Note 1) | (210) |
| Taxation | (580) |
| Capital expenditure (Note 1) | (1,950) |
| Equity dividends paid | (530) |
|  | (1,100) |
| Management of liquid resources | - |
| Financing | - |
| Decrease in cash | (1,100) |

*Reconciliation of operating profit to cash flow from operating activities*

|  | |
|---|---:|
| Profit before tax | 1,660 |
| Depreciation | 400 |
| Increase in stocks | (320) |
| Decrease in debtors | 350 |
| Increase in creditors | 80 |
| Net cash inflow from operating activities | 2,170 |

Note 1: Gross cash flows

Returns on investment and servicing of finance

|  | |
|---|---:|
| Interest paid | (270) |
| Dividends received | 60 |
|  | (210) |

FINANCIAL REPORTING, ANALYSIS AND PLANNING

Capital expenditure

| | |
|---|---:|
| Acquisition of subsidiary | (1,880) |
| Acquisition of other fixed assets | (750) |
| Disposal of shares in associate | 500 |
| Disposal of other fixed assets | 180 |
| | (1,950) |

5.8 We need to calculate the company's cashflow before it makes any discretionary payments or receipts. Thus adjustments are made for:

- dividends on ordinary shares;
- acquisitions and disposals; and
- purchases of fixed assets other than to replace old assets.

5.9 Therefore, assuming that Buttons plc's expenditure on fixed assets was only to replace worn out or obsolete assets, its free cash flow would be:

| | £000 |
|---|---:|
| *Net cash outflow before financing* | (1,100) |
| Plus: Dividends paid | 530 |
| Acquisition of subsidiary | 1,880 |
| | 1,310 |
| Less disposal of shares in associate | (500) |
| Free cashflow | 810 |

5.10 If the required rate of return was 10% the value of the company would be:

£810,000/0.10 = £8,100,000

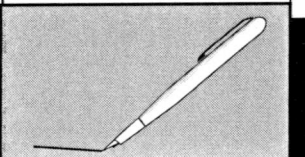

### Student Activity 3

Is the following statement true or false?

Cash flow is always a more objective measure of a company's performance than its accounting profits, which are highly subjective.

*(Paragraphs 5.1 and 5.2)*

## 6 Dividend valuation

6.1 Although a company many have high earnings per share and generate a large amount of cash the only return a shareholder receives, in the absence of the company being taken over or buying back its own shares, is the dividend that is paid. An investment is only worth the net present value of the future cashflows that will be returned to the purchaser of that investment.

6.2 The simplest approach is to divide the gross dividend by the purchaser's cost of capital. For example, if a company is paying 8 pence in dividends each year and the purchaser's cost of capital is 10% the value of a share to that purchaser would be:

# BUSINESS VALUATIONS

$$\frac{8p + 25\% \text{ ACT credit} = 10p}{0.10}$$
(the dividend must be grossed up for the 20% tax credit)

= £1.00.

6.3 However, it is probable that the dividend will increase over time and this needs to be built into the valuation model. For shares where the dividend is growing at a modest rate it is possible to use Gordon's Growth Model.

$$P = \frac{d \times (1 + g)}{(i - g)}$$

where:

P = the share price
d = the current dividend payment
i = the required rate of return
g = the dividend growth rate

Thus in the previous example if the dividend was expected to grow by 5% per annum the value of the shares would be:

$$\frac{10p \times 1.05}{(0.10 - 0.05)} = £2.10$$

6.4 The model does not work when the dividend growth rate exceeds the required rate of return. When this occurs it is necessary to discount each future estimated dividend payment to the current date.

## 7 The valuation of minority and majority interests

7.1 By now you will have discovered that there are numerous methods for valuing a business and that they can produce widely differing results. We will now discuss when each method may be appropriate.

7.2 You have already seen that an investment is worth the net present value of the cashflows that accrue to that investment. The only return a minority shareholder in a company will receive will be in the form of the dividends the company pays.

7.3 A minority shareholder has little or no influence over the company's dividend policy and the company's earnings and cashflow only provide assurance as to whether or not the company can afford the dividend each year. It is therefore appropriate to value a minority shareholding using the dividend valuation model.

7.4 A majority shareholder can control a company's dividend policy and in effect has access to the company's earnings. The majority shareholder also has control over the company's assets and is able to arrange for their sale if this is felt to be advantageous.

7.5 It is therefore usually appropriate to value a majority holding on an earnings basis. However if the liquidation value of the company exceeds the earnings valuation this would represent the value of the holding to the majority shareholder.

FINANCIAL REPORTING, ANALYSIS AND PLANNING

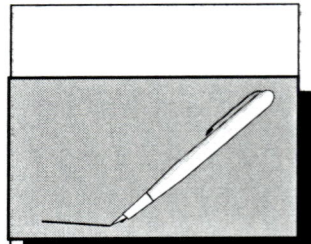

## Student Activity 4

Work out the answers to the questions that follow the profit and loss account below. Check your calculations against the answers which follow.

Beta Ltd produced the following profit and loss accounts for the five years ending 31 December 19X5:

*Profit and loss account for Beta Ltd*

|  | 19X1 £000 | 19X2 £000 | 19X3 £000 | 19X4 £000 | 19X5 £000 |
|---|---|---|---|---|---|
| Profit after tax | 220 | 240 | 180 | 290 | 320 |
| Dividends | 110 | 115 | 121 | 127 | 134 |
| Retained for year | 110 | 125 | 59 | 163 | 186 |

The company had 1,000,000 ordinary shares in issue throughout the five years. Its balance sheet as at 31 December 19X5 was as follows.

|  | £000 | £000 |
|---|---|---|
| *Fixed assets* | | |
| Land and buildings | | 1,250 |
| Plant and machinery | | 750 |
| | | 2,000 |
| *Current assets* | | |
| Stock | 300 | |
| Debtors | 480 | |
| Cash at bank | 500 | |
| | 1,280 | |
| Creditors due within 1 year | 730 | |
| Net current assets | | 550 |
| | | 2,550 |
| Creditors due in more than 1 year | | 400 |
| | | 2,150 |
| | | |
| *Represented by:* | | |
| £1 Ordinary shares | | 1,000 |
| Share premium account | | 200 |
| Profit & Loss Account | | 950 |
| | | 2,150 |

All the shares in the company are owned by the Cornwall family. Sidney Cornwall owns 15% of the shares and wishes to cash in his inheritance. He has made enquiries and the following parties have expressed some interest.

Highfield Estates plc, who are interested in purchasing the land and buildings for £1,800,000.

# BUSINESS VALUATIONS

Wellrusted Ltd, who buy and sell second-hand machinery and would pay £400,000 for the plant and machinery.

Bill Squires, an acquaintance of Sidney who would be interested in purchasing Sidney's shares from him. Bill currently has all his funds invested in government stock yielding 9% per annum. He feels that Beta Ltd's growth prospects outweigh the extra risk he would be taking.

Consolidated Conglomerates plc, who are prepared to make an offer for the company provided that they can achieve a return of 20% per annum on their investment.

Sidney has discussed this with the other members of the family. Their best alternative investment is in government stock yielding 9%. Sidney's uncle Cyril who owns 51% of the shares is prepared to sell his shares if he receives a 'reasonable offer'.

*Required*

(a) Calculate the amount Sidney can expect to receive under each of the alternatives available.

(b) Advise Sidney's uncle Cyril on whether liquidation or the sale to Consolidated Conglomerates plc is reasonable.

(c) Advise Sidney on what action he should take.

You should have obtained the following answer.

(a) Sidney would receive the following amounts from the available alternatives.

   (i) *Liquidation*

|  | £000 |
|---|---|
| Sale proceeds: |  |
| Land and buildings | 1,800 |
| Plant and machinery | 400 |
| Net current assets | 550 |
|  | 2,750 |
| Less creditors due in more than 1 year | 400 |
| Net proceeds | 2,350 |

   15% of which amounts to £352,500

   (ii) *Sale to Bill Squires*

   The dividend has grown by 5% per annum over the last four years. It is well covered by earnings and it can be assumed that this growth will continue in the future. Using the dividend growth model we obtain the following valuation:

   $$\frac{(134 + 25\% \text{ ACT credit}) \times 1.05}{0.09 - 0.05} = £4,396,875$$

   15% of which amounts to £659,531

   (iii) *Sale to Consolidated Conglomerates plc*

   The major difficulty here is in deciding which earnings to use. Any reasonable choice would probably be acceptable, but as several years' profits are given an average figure would be most appropriate.

   The three year weighted average profits are:

FINANCIAL REPORTING, ANALYSIS AND PLANNING

|  |  | £000 |
|---|---|---|
| 19X3 – £180,000 × 1 = | | 180 |
| 19X4 – £290,000 × 2 = | | 580 |
| 19X5 – £320,000 × 3 = | | 960 |
| | 6 | 1,720 |

£1,720,000/6 = £286,667

The required return is 20% per annum valuing the company at £286,667/0.20 = £1,433,333.

15% of which amounts to £215,000

(b) Sidney's uncle Cyril owns a majority holding and an earnings or break up valuation are relevant to him. However, his next best alternative investment is to invest in government stock yielding 9%. The dividend income from his shares will exceed the income from the government stock if he reinvests the sale proceeds from his shares.

The only 'reasonable' offer is from Bill Squires, but unless he is also prepared to buy Cyril's shares, Cyril should retain them.

(c) It is clear from the above calculations that Sidney will receive the highest offer from Bill Squires and should therefore sell his shares to him.

## 8 Negotiation and price fixing

8.1 When negotiating a valuation of a business the agreed valuation can vary widely depending upon the reason a valuation is needed. If a valuation is needed for the Inland Revenue or insurance purposes the rules laid down above will usually be followed.

8.2 Negotiations between a buyer and a seller are a different matter. Both parties will be attempting to achieve a price most favourable to themselves. They will both have a price that they realistically hope to achieve. In addition the buyer will have a maximum price after which the purchase would be uneconomic and seller will have a minimum below which the sale would not be worth while.

8.3 The seller would hope to achieve a price that fully reflects the business's earnings and the scope to improve those earnings in the future. However, the determination to wait until that price can be achieved may be undermined by the following.

- The business's borrowings. If loan covenants have been broken or the interest and capital repayments requirements are proving difficult to meet a quick sale would be the main priority.

- The interest expressed in the business. If several parties appear interested it would be logical to wait and see who is prepared to make the best offer.

- The general economic climate. If the economic outlook is poor the owners may feel that it is important to sell the business before the climate worsens. Alternatively if the outlook is expected to improve they may feel that it is better to wait in the hope that they will achieve a better price as business picks up.

# BUSINESS VALUATIONS

- The personal circumstances of the owner/s. This can vary from the need for money due to debt, divorce, etc; or a wish to retire or to move on to other things.

8.4 Buyers adjust their negotiating position to take into account the factors given above, if they are aware of them. The maximum price they would be prepared to offer would be where the additional profits earned would exceed the cost of the capital used to fund the purchase.

8.5 The buyer is therefore concerned with forecast profits and the net gain from the acquisition. If the buyer is already operating a similar business there may be some synergy and economies of scale that would enhance their profits which must be taken into account.

8.6 The buyer's initial offer will be based on current prospects, possibly taking into account future trading difficulties. This opening offer will be higher if the buyer is eager to purchase the business and there are other interested parties.

8.7 The final price will depend upon how desperate either party is to complete the sale. If the seller is under heavy pressure due to large amounts of debt he/she may be forced to accept the buyer's initial offer. Conversely, if the seller has no particular need to sell and there are several other interested parties the buyer will be forced to pay the maximum price.

## Summary

**Now that you have completed this Unit you should be able to:**

- calculate a range of values for a business using the various methods available;
- understand which methods are appropriate for given circumstances; and
- appreciate the practical aspects of negotiation and price fixing.

## Self-assessment questions

1. A business is always worth the replacement cost of its assets less its liabilities.
   TRUE/FALSE

2. Delta plc has £5m of capital employed and no debt. The company consistently earns a profit after tax of £1m. Assuming that a similar company would normally achieve a return of 12% on its capital employed, calculate the value of Delta plc using the dual capitalisation method assuming goodwill should earn a return of 18%.

3. Edge plc has 100,000 shares in issue and makes a profit after tax of £50,000. Its shares sell on a PE ratio of 12. What is the current share price?

4. What PE ratio does a company have if its shares are currently selling on an earnings yield of 12.5%?

5. Fox plc has retained profits of £12m per annum after charging £3.5m depreciation. The company purchases £5m of fixed assets each year £3m of which are used to expand existing capacity.

   Assuming the company is valued at ten times its non-discretionary cashflow and is worth £175m, how much is paid out in dividends?

6. Gorge plc paid dividend of 25p (including the tax credit) in the year ended 31 March 19X5. The company has a policy of increasing its dividend by 6% per annum.

   George currently earns 10% on his investments and wishes to purchase 1% of Gorge plc's shares. What is the highest price he should pay per share?

7. How would George have valued the shares if he expected the dividends to increase by 12% per annum?

8. How would George have valued the shares if he was considering purchasing 51% of the company's shares?

9. Hull plc wishes to purchase Ipswich Ltd from Mr Jones who owns 100% of the shares in Ipswich. Ipswich Ltd makes a profit after tax of £100,000.

   Hull plc expects to make cost savings of £20,000 from combining its business with Ipswich Ltd's business. Hull plc would finance the purchase by issuing loan stock that yielded 8% per annum after tax. Mr Jones has not indicated a sale price.

   What would Hull plc's opening offer most likely be?

10. If Mr Jones needed to make the sale and there were no other buyers would he be wise to hold out for £1,600,000?

*(Answers are given in the Appendix.)*

## Suggested reading

*Accounting for banking students* by J.R. Edwards and H.J. Mellett, 4th Edition 1994, CIB Publications

# Unit 11

## Ratio Analysis

### Objectives

**After studying this Unit you should be able to:**

- outline the methods available to interpret the accounts of companies

- identify the information needed to prepare a full analysis of a company

- understand the principles of ratio analysis

- calculate, analyse and classify accounting ratios

- acknowledge the limitations of ratio analysis as a tool in interpreting accounts

- interpret the results of ratio analysis in full and identify trends.

## 1 Introduction

1.1 In previous Units you have been concerned mainly with the preparation of financial statements. As a banker, however, one of your key tasks will be to *interpret* financial information: to explain what the information means, what it tells you about the position of the company; its prospects in profitability and cash flow terms; its stability; its ability to repay debts and so on. These factors can be assessed both in absolute terms and more usefully in comparative terms. Comparisons are with previous years and with similar companies. Thus the *relative* performance of the company can be assessed.

1.2 The syllabus objectives include the requirement to be able to undertake a 'detailed study of financial accounts including traditional accounting ratios and cash flow analysis, and an appreciation of methods of predicting corporate success and failure.'

1.3 Thus the ability to interpret accounts is seen as a fundamental skill. Reflecting this, the examination will contain a compulsory 30 mark question on financial analysis and appraisal.

This question will require the student to display a range of calculative and analytical skills.

1.4 Interpretation of accounts is facilitated through employing some or all of the following techniques:

- 'desk top' review of the financial statements

FINANCIAL REPORTING, ANALYSIS AND PLANNING

- ratio analysis of the financial statements
- preparation of a cash flow statement.

1.5 In addition, preparation of the other primary statements and other analytical techniques may be used to interpret the accounts of an enterprise. It is unlikely that only one of the above methods would be necessary to come to a judgment about a company's performance and position. The skill in interpreting accounts is in the employment of the right methods of analysis and recognition of the limitations of the analysis performed.

1.6 For example, one could undertake a full financial analysis of a company utilising all the above techniques and comparing with previous years and industry standards. However, the analysis would probably not be complete without an examination of what might be called the human aspects of the company. Imagine, for instance, we were interpreting the position and future prospects of a company engaged in scientific research. Such factors as staff abilities, training, and morale, length of service contracts, relationships between employees and management and links to local centres of excellence would all be relevant in our analysis. Such information may not be included in the financial statements, but these factors would affect the financial statements and future prospects of the company.

1.7 This Unit will consider the mechanics of ratio analysis, together with guidance on interpreting the results. Units 12 and 13 will consider the preparation and interpretation of cash flow information.

## 2 Role of ratio analysis

2.1 It is important to reiterate that ratio analysis is a tool of interpretation not an end in itself. Time and again, a common failing noted by examiners is that students faithfully prepare accounting ratios and then neglect to interpret them meaningfully. You are unlikely to pass an interpretation question by merely calculating the appropriate ratios, however accurate your calculations are. Of equal importance is the initial selection of the appropriate ratios and subsequent interpretation of what the ratios mean, what they show about the company's position, performance and adaptability.

2.2 Before we look at the individual ratios that can be calculated, let us look at an interpretation method referred to earlier, the 'desk top review'.

## 3 Desk top review

3.1 A mistake commonly made by students is to rush into an accounts interpretation question, busily calculating ratios and cash flow statements without sitting back and asking the following questions.

- Why am I being asked to do this exercise?
- Who is requiring me to do this exercise?
- What exactly am I being asked to do?

# RATIO ANALYSIS

3.2 Once these questions have been answered satisfactorily look at the financial statements as a whole. In *general terms*, the following questions should be asked.

- How well is the company performing?
- Are profits increasing or decreasing?
- Is the company liquid? (That is, is there cash in the bank or a large overdraft?)
- What major changes have there been in the year? (for example, major increases in fixed assets/borrowings repaid/working capital changes/share capital raised etc.)
- Who is financing this company – mainly shareholders or loan creditors?

3.3 Finally, try and come to an initial 'gut feel' judgment:

- Would I lend money to this company?
- Would I invest in this company?
- Will this company be here in three years time?
- Is this company growing or contracting?
- Is this company a winner or a loser?

The above analysis may sound simplistic—it is necessarily so at this stage of the analysis.

## 4 Other information presented

4.1 The second stage is to consider any other information given in the question. The examiner is asking you, in approximately 50 minutes, to report on the prospects of a company with, possibly, a turnover of a million pounds. In order to help you in such an exercise, the examiner will often give clues as to the performance of the company in question. For instance, debtor and/or stock levels may be unusually high or have risen by more than expected. There may have been a substantial investment in fixed assets—how was that financed? Has it resulted in increased sales? A major loan might have been raised. How have the proceeds been utilised? What is the effect on borrowing costs in the profit and loss account?

## 5 Information needs

5.1 Non-financial information given may provide some clues. Narrative information about the state of the market or the company's plans are all relevant. At this stage also it is important to consider what information is needed to perform a full analysis but is *not* available in this question. Remember you can never have too much information, the data given in the question will always be insufficient to prepare a fully rounded out complete answer.

5.2 As part of your answer, which is usually prepared in report format, identify limitations in your analysis (see below) and extra information that you need

FINANCIAL REPORTING, ANALYSIS AND PLANNING

but have not been given. For example, comparative information is always useful, not just one year but longer periods are often necessary to see if any trends are being established. Information about competitors' performance or industry standards are valuable. Non-financial information is invariably useful. Information about off-balance sheet assets, e.g. inherent goodwill (see Unit 4); off balance sheet liabilities; potential contingencies; intangible assets which are difficult to measure and hence may have been excluded from the accounts, e.g. brands; company order book; loyal workforce and so on.

5.3 In addition, quite often the examiner will only present summary accounts—the notes to the financial statements are often omitted. Narrative information in the accounts such as the directors' report and chairman's statement are often not included.

5.4 In summary, at this stage begin to think what information you would like *but have not been given*. You should have a lengthy list by the end of the question.

## Student Activity 1

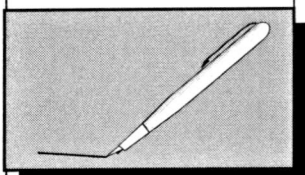

The Activities in this Unit will use the information given at the end of the Unit, before the Summary.

1. Undertake a 'desk top review' of the company. Note your preliminary findings and judgments about the company.

2. List information which would be useful in your analysis, but is not given.

## 6 Ratio analysis

**Overview**

6.1 As mentioned above, this is a tool of analysis not an end in itself. However, it is a very useful tool. Simply put, an accounting ratio is the relationship of one figure in the accounts to another. For example, the ratio of profits to assets, or stock levels to turnover. On its own the ratio is usually meaningless, although this is not always true. We have seen in previous units that the Companies Act and accounting standards set specified formats and methods for calculating and displaying accounts items. This standardisation of presentation and calculation gives us confidence in preparing ratio analysis using these accounts items.

6.2 Businesses do not usually include ratios in their accounts. It is left to outside analysts to look at the connections between the figures which are published. Banks, as lending institutions, may have the advantage of access to more detailed and regular information than other accounts users, so they may be placed to carry out a more thorough analysis.

6.3 Ratios are simply expressions of the relationship between two numbers or variables. In considering the wide number of different figures in a set of accounts, you can appreciate that the number of potential ratios between those figures is enormous. In order to produce a meaningful analysis, the ratios calculated should be based on figures which have a genuine connection. For example, linking net profit to sales makes sense because higher levels of sales are expected to generate higher levels of profits.

# RATIO ANALYSIS

However, a connection between share capital and stock levels would be pointless as there is no identifiable relationship between the figures.

## Types of ratio

6.4 Ratios are usually presented in one of four different forms, as follows.

- As a percentage, for example gross profit at 25% percent of sales.
- As a simple ratio, for example a ratio of 3 to 1, current assets to current liabilities.
- Or it can be shown as a number of times, for example the profits may be five times the level of interest payable.
- As a function of time, for example stock could be turned over (sold) every 35 days.

6.5 It is not the presentation of the ratio that is important, it is the interpretation of what the ratios mean and show about the company. Simple comments that the ratio has 'gone up' or is 'good' or 'bad' will of themselves not earn many marks.

## Interrelationships between ratios

6.6 A point to consider is any interrelationship between ratios. An unfavourable change in a ratio may be mitigated by a favourable change in another ratio. For instance, a company may embark on a strategic repositioning of its product line and image, perhaps taking the company 'up market' as it were. The company might then refocus on higher margin, luxury products and delete cheaper, poorer quality products from its sales portfolio. As a result overall sales may fall.

6.7 This could lead to a fall in the *asset turnover* ratio, the relationship between sales and net assets. In isolation, this could be seen to be a 'bad' thing. The company's net assets are generating fewer sales. However when considering the gross profitability of the firm, the relationship between gross profit and turnover, this should show an increase. Thus the overall effect of the policy should be looked at.

6.8 On the other hand, ratios may be complementary. The results of one ratio may herald problems shown by another ratio. One example could be where a slowdown in the rate of debtor collection, highlighted by ratio analysis, could be a precursor to liquidity problems, indicated by the quick ratio (see paragraph 9.9)

## Interpreting ratios

6.9 It is not always easy to interpret a ratio on its own. For instance, you may be told that a company earns a profit of 10% on its net assets. Your initial judgment may be that that seems a reasonable return. However other factors you would need to consider include:

- last year's return
- the return of other similar companies

# FINANCIAL REPORTING, ANALYSIS AND PLANNING

- alternative returns (for example the return available on a building society deposit).

6.10 Other factors such as the riskiness of the company, the volatility of the returns over recent years and the company's liquidity are all relevant.

6.11 In addition you would need to look behind the figure of 10%. It is composed of two main elements: profits and assets. Consider each of these in turn.

### *Profits*

- How have the profits been earned?
- What are the individual components of profit: gross profit, operating profit, etc.?
- What were the profits last year?
- Is there an identifiable trend in profitability?
- Did any one-off factors affect profit?
- What is the relationship between profits and sales?
- What change has there been in the industry's profitability?
- How have the new operations/deleted operations affected profits?

### *Assets*

- What is the composition of the net assets?
- How are the assets valued?
- Have any asset revaluations taken place in the year?
- Which accounting policies have been adopted?
- When did the asset additions/disposals take place?
- How does the asset base compare with previous years/comparative companies?

### Groups of ratios

6.12 Traditionally ratios have been grouped into the following categories.

- Profitability and return on capital.
- Liquidity and solvency.
- Gearing.
- Working capital.
- Asset utilisation.
- Shareholder ratios

6.13 In an exam question, the examiner will often ask you to report on particular aspects of a business; for instance, its profitability and liquidity. Thus the classification of ratios is useful in identifying which ratios to select. Sometimes the question will specify which ratios to calculate. More often, the examiner will leave it to your judgment to select appropriate ratios.

# RATIO ANALYSIS

6.14 Do not fall into the trap of calculating too many ratios, two or three per section will usually be sufficient. The mere calculation of the ratios is not enough, it is the interpretation of the results, especially the overall impression that the ratios and the desk top review give. Even if you are not asked to report on a particular area of the business, a ratio from within that classification can be calculated to help you form an overall impression of the business' performance. Consider the interrelationships between ratios, 'good' performance in one area masking 'poor' performance in another.

6.15 Occasionally, the examiner will set a very general question asking you to comment on the standing of a company. Little or no direction may be given as to which areas of the business you should focus on. In these circumstances it is best to concentrate on the company's profitability, particularly the return on capital employed (ROCE).

## 7 Profitability and return on capital

7.1 Profit is generally seen as the most important indicator of a company's performance. However, a profit figure in absolute terms can be meaningless. A profit of £1m may represent a great success for a sole trader, but for an international conglomerate it could be a disastrous performance.

7.2 Also remember the statement of total recognised gains and losses (SORG) in Unit 6. The ASB's *Statement of Principles* indicated that this too should be regarded as a primary statement in assessing a company's performance. However, it is likely that the major components of financial performance will be encompassed in the profit and loss account. The primary indicator of financial performance is usually calculated with reference to the size of the company, its net assets. Basically expressed, return on capital employed is calculated by dividing profits by assets.

7.3 The next question is how to define 'profit' and 'assets'.

The standard ratio is calculated as follows.

$$\frac{\text{Profit before interest and tax}}{\text{Capital, reserves and long term liabilities}} \times 100$$

7.4 Remember the accounting equation that net assets = capital. An alternative calculation therefore is using the definition of capital employed as being the *company's net assets*; i.e. *its capital and reserves*. To be consistent, our measure of profit in this case should be that profit available to the shareholders i.e. *profit after tax*:

$$\frac{\text{Profit after tax}}{\text{Capital and reserves}} \times 100$$

7.5 Either method is appropriate as a measure of return on capital employed. However, unless you are told otherwise, it is best to use the first method. The distinction between the two is quite simple. In the first method, 'capital employed' is defined as equity (shareholders' funds) and loan capital. In the second it is defined as shareholders' funds only (therefore if you are asked for return on shareholders funds you should use the second method).

# FINANCIAL REPORTING, ANALYSIS AND PLANNING

7.6 To be consistent, the choice of 'profit' definition used depends on the choice of 'capital employed' used. Thus, if we define capital employed as Equity and Loan capital, then the profits available to this group are 'profits before interest and taxation'. Conversely, if we define profits as shareholders' funds, then the profits available to this group are 'profits after taxation' (and after interest).

7.7 Other variations on the ROCE theme include *return on total or gross assets*. This is calculated as follows.

$$\frac{\text{Profit after tax (or profit before interest and tax)}}{\text{Fixed and current assets}} \times 100$$

7.8 Alternatively, you may be asked to calculate *return on average capital employed*. This is calculated as follows.

$$\frac{\text{Profit before interest and tax}}{\text{Average capital, reserves and long term liabilities *}} \times 100$$

*\* This is usually worked out by taking the capital employed at the start of the year added to the capital employed at the end of the year and dividing by two.*

7.9 The exact method you employ is not overly important. It is vital though to be consistent, from year to year and from company to company, when undertaking comparisons.

7.10 The ROCE ratio is often referred to as the primary accounting ratio because it looks at the most basic measure of success. In open-ended questions that ask you to assess a business this is often a good starting point. However, bear in the mind that this ratio is not the end of the story. What makes up this ratio, the components of profit and assets, their valuation and accounting treatment, are more important (see paragraph 6.11 above).

7.11 Following on from the primary ratio are two secondary ratios which can be used to analyse the information provided by the return on capital employed. These are the net profit ratio and the asset turnover ratio. The relationship between the three ratios is as follows.

| **ROCE** | | **Net profit ratio** | | **Asset turnover** |
|---|---|---|---|---|
| $\dfrac{\text{Net profit} \times 100}{\text{Assets}}$ | = | $\dfrac{\text{Net profit} \times 100}{\text{Sales}}$ | × | $\dfrac{\text{Sales}}{\text{Assets}}$ |

**Net profit ratio**

7.12 This shows the relationship between profit and sales. In general, you would expect there to be a relationship between these two figures. As turnover increases you would anticipate higher profits. However, the *rate* of increase may well not be the same.

7.13 Remember the example given above where a company decided to reposition itself in the market. Conversely, a company could decide to boost market share by cutting prices. The effect on the net profit percentage ratio would be likely to be downwards as gross profit fell. However asset turnover could be increased, extra sales being generated from the same assets. Thus the overall effect on ROCE could be balanced out.

# RATIO ANALYSIS

**Asset turnover**

7.14 In simple terms this is the level of sales that the company's (net) assets generate. It is sometimes referred to as asset utilisation. This figure will differ from industry to industry. Capital intensive industries such as heavy manufacturing businesses, are likely to have a much lower asset turnover than service industries, e.g. a travel agent with a smaller asset base. Again the companies' polices and strategies will affect this ratio. The example above of a company going down market, cutting prices to boost sales will, as a by product, show increased asset turnover.

7.15 In summary, in analysing the ROCE we can look at a business in two ways: how much turnover is generated from the assets and how much profit the sales generate.

7.16 Overall the ROCE is seen as indicator of the return the owner is generating from his investment. The ROCE can be compared to returns the investor may generate from alternative investments. However, there are a number of points to bear in mind. It may not be easy to withdraw from the business in question and reinvest somewhere else. The balance sheet values are expressed at historic cost which may not be the same as realisable values. The business often represents the employment and livelihood of the investor. Finally, there may be a difficulty in finding an alternative investment with which to compare the current return. If the return on an investment, in say a money market deposit, is used as a comparison, we are not comparing like with like. One is risk free, while the business investment carries an element of risk. It is likely that the business investor will require a higher return from the business to compensate for the extra risk involved.

# 8 Detailed profitability ratios

8.1 We have already considered the net profit ratio, which compared net profit to sales. The net profit is the end result after taking:

- profit from trading i.e. gross profit

less

- overheads
- financing costs and
- taxation.

8.2 Thus we can break down our analysis of profitability into subsections.

**Trading profitability**

$$\frac{\text{Gross profit}}{\text{Sales}} \times 100$$

8.3 This ratio indicates the profit margin earned on each £ of sales. The percentage is called the gross profit percentage or gross margin. If you are asked to calculate the *mark up* this refers to the gross profit as a percentage of cost of sales. Thus for instance a gross profit of 20% is the same as a mark up, on cost, of 25%.

# FINANCIAL REPORTING, ANALYSIS AND PLANNING

*Interpretation*

8.4 Once again we have difficulty in interpreting this ratio in absolute terms. For example, a gross margin of 30% may represent a reasonable return for a newsagent; however a jeweller may expect a much higher gross profit percentage. The reason is usually the volume of products sold. A newsagent, selling small items quickly may be satisfied with a lower gross margin; in comparison a jeweller will sell higher-priced products more slowly but at higher margins.

8.5 There is a linkage to the ROCE-net profit percentage-asset utilisation group of ratios seen above. Contrasting the sale of a large number of products quickly at low margins with the sale of a small number of products slowly but at high margins.

8.6 Once again it is important to look at changes in ratios rather than at the absolute figure. There are many possible reasons for a change in gross margin. For example:

- company policy to boost margins
- company policy to increase market share by cutting margins
- repositioning in market (see above)
- increased costs not passed on to customers
- fall in input costs not passed on to customers
- increased turnover leading to more buying power, and hence lower purchase prices
- increased competition leading to falls in selling prices.

8.7 Look for other indicators to try to explain what has happened. For instance, the change in overall sales, any change in market/industry margins.

**Operating profitability**

8.8 Following on from the gross profit margin, take away administration and distribution overheads to give operating profit. As can been seen in Unit 14, some of these costs (and indeed some of the costs of sales) will be 'fixed', i.e. they will not alter with changes in volumes of activity. However, generally one would expect overheads to change in line with activity, i.e. turnover. So more ratios can be prepared:

$$\frac{\text{Overheads}}{\text{Sales}} \times 100$$

8.9 This can be further broken down into:

$$\frac{\text{Administration expenses}}{\text{Sales}} \times 100$$

and

$$\frac{\text{Distribution costs}}{\text{Sales}} \times 100$$

# RATIO ANALYSIS

## *Interpretation*

8.10 Again look for any clues as to why the ratio of expenses to sales has changed. For example, more fixed assets might have been purchased which would imply higher depreciation charges. A pay increase might have been granted. The directors might have reduced their remuneration but increased their dividends. Overall activity may have decreased, therefore the proportion of fixed costs would have increased leading to higher expense/sales ratios.

8.11 Aggregating the results of these ratios we can calculate the relationship between operating profit and sales:

$$\frac{\text{Operating profit}}{\text{Sales}} \times 100$$

This is usually the same as:

$$\frac{\text{Profit before interest and tax}}{\text{Sales}} \times 100$$

## Interest payable and similar charges

8.12 Next in line in the profit and loss account is: interest payable and similar charges. Normally these are not compared to sales as there is no direct relationship. Instead the usual calculation is to look at the *interest cover*; the relationship between profit before interest and interest.

This is calculated as follows.

$$\frac{\text{Profit before interest and tax}}{\text{Interest payable}}$$

8.13 This gives a margin of safety, indicating how many times the current level of operating profits can cover the current level of interest payable. As an aside, remember we are talking here in profit terms. Even if we have the *profits* to cover the interest it does not follow that we necessarily have the *cash* to pay the interest and any repayments of capital due. To analyse our cash flow position we need to prepare a cash flow statement (see Units 12 and 13).

8.14 In general, the higher the ratio the greater the margin of safety. Interest payable is a charge on profits, payable whether the company makes a profit or not. Thus a lower or negative interest cover spells potential future problems for a company.

8.15 Again try and look for any explanations resulting in the change in interest cover. A change in overall profitability would obviously be one explanation, however the company may have raised/repaid finance in the year or interest rates may have changed.

8.16 In summary, after considering the overall position and changes in profitability look behind the scenes to examine in detail why the company's profitability has changed. There may be compensating factors, for instance, improved gross margins countered by increased interest charges; increased overheads in absolute terms mitigated by a proportionally greater increase in turnover.

# FINANCIAL REPORTING, ANALYSIS AND PLANNING

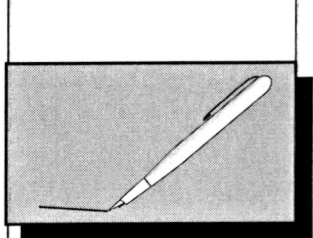

### Student Activity 2

Using the information given at the end of the Unit calculate the following ratios for 19X3 and 19X4.

1. Return on capital employed.
2. Return on shareholders equity.
3. Return on total assets.
4. Return on average capital employed (19X4 only).
5. Net profit ratio.
6. Asset turnover.
7. Gross profit percentage.
8. Overheads/Sales ratio.
9. Administration expenses/Sales ratio.
10. Selling and distribution costs/Sales ratio.
11. Operating profit/Sales ratio.
12. Interest cover.

## 9 Liquidity and solvency ratios

9.1 A company may be profitable, but it may not be liquid. This can occur in a fast growing company which is expanding so rapidly that it does not have sufficient cash to pay its debts as they fall due. This is sometimes referred to as overtrading. Using ratio analysis we can calculate a company's position in a number of ways. One way is to look at the company's cash operating cycle (see below). The other way is to look at the company's liquid assets in absolute and relative terms. Consider first the company's working capital movements. In general the company's operations will look like this diagram.

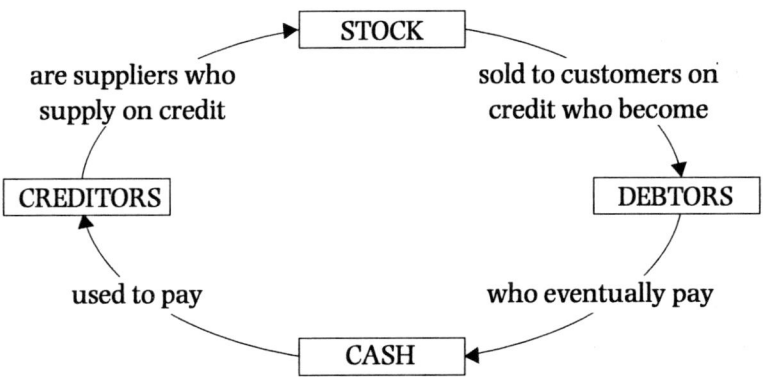

9.2 Time is involved from the original order from the supplier, to the delivery of the stock, to the sale of the stock, to the receipt of the cash from the debtor. All these delays are not in the business' favour. The only delay in the company's favour is the length of time taken to pay the supplier.

# RATIO ANALYSIS

9.3 For a formal calculation of how long this working capital cycle takes see below, paragraph 11.15.

9.4 However, initially we can look at the working capital items in absolute and relative terms. Two common ratios are normally calculated.

   a) *Working capital or Current ratio*

$$\frac{\text{Current assets}}{\text{Current liabilities}}$$

9.5 The rationale behind calculating this ratio is that the current assets will be used to finance the payment of the current liabilities. The current assets, stock and debtors, will be converted into cash and used to settle the liabilities due.

## *Interpretation*

9.6 A broad rule of thumb often quoted is that the ratio should be 2 to 1. That is, current assets should exceed current liabilities by a factor of 2. Treat this rule of thumb with caution. A 'high' ratio ostensibly is good, however it could be because stock levels are too high (perhaps old/obsolete stock is held) or it could indicate a debtor collection problem. Remember that any assets held need to be financed, think back to the accounting equation:

$$\text{Net assets} = \text{Capital}$$

9.7 The capital financing the business has an associated cost; either dividends for equity finance or interest for loan finance. Therefore businesses will, in general, try to minimise stock and debtor levels to reduce the level of net assets and hence financing costs.

9.8 Another point to consider is the type of business the company is in. A supermarket chain, for example, is likely to have little or no debtor levels because it is a cash business. Also because of its buying power, it is likely to be able to demand extended credit terms from its suppliers. In addition, supermarkets employ sophisticated stock management schemes to minimise the levels of stock held. All these factors mean that the current ratio, for a supermarket, could well be less than 1.

   b) *Acid test ratio*

9.9 A more stringent test is the acid test or quick ratio:

$$\frac{\text{Current assets less stock}}{\text{Current liabilities}}$$

9.10 The argument with this ratio is that stock is less liquid than other current assets, therefore it should not be incorporated when assessing the current assets available to pay current liabilities.

9.11 A rule of thumb is again quoted that this ratio should not be less than 1. The caveats noted above apply equally to interpretation of this ratio.

9.12 Once again the absolute level of the ratio is not as important as the change or trend in the ratio. A sudden deterioration in the ratio could mean that the company has cash flow problems. A ratio significantly higher than the industry average could imply, for example, that the company has problems in collecting its debts. It is important, as with all ratios, but especially with these ratios, that they are examined in conjunction with other accounting ratios and cash flow data.

## 10 Gearing

10.1 As mentioned earlier, all the net assets of a business have to be financed. We commented that businesses often attempt to reduce their holdings of non-earning assets, such as debtors, to reduce their financing costs. However, a business can be financed in two ways—either by shareholders (represented by share capital and reserves) or by loan creditors. It is not the purpose of this examination to evaluate the best methods of financing a business, but you should be aware, in general terms, of the advantages and disadvantages of the two main types of finance.

**General comparison of equity and loan finance**

10.2 *Equity finance* (share capital and retained profits) is perceived as being less risky than loan finance; mainly because the company is under no obligation to repay the capital.

10.3 This does not mean that the equity financiers can be ignored or that the finance is at no cost. The company is obliged to look after its shareholders' interests. First, the directors are appointed and can be removed by the shareholders. Secondly, the company is under pressure to pay a reasonable level of dividends to satisfy the shareholders. If inadequate levels of dividends are paid, the shareholders may divest and the company's share price may fall. This could make it more difficult for the company to raise equity finance in the future. In addition, a low share price could make the company vulnerable to takeover.

10.4 *Loan finance* is different. The company is legally obligated to pay interest and repay capital at the due dates. Whilst a company will pay a dividend only if it has the retained profits and cash available to do so, the company must pay its interest and capital when due. The loan creditors have sanctions to force the company to do so. Quite often the loan will be secured on the company's assets. This could take the form of a fixed charge on the company's fixed assets or a floating charge on its other assets. In the event of a default in payment of interest or capital the creditors can exercise their right to sell the secured assets and force the company to repay outstanding interest and capital.

10.5 Thus interest is said to be a *charge* on profits while dividends are an *appropriation* of profits. In interpreting the position of a business, one of the key indicators is the relationship between equity and loan finance. In general, the higher the debt element, the more risky it is for the company, because of the priority rights of loan creditors as seen above.

10.6 With the inherent increased risk, why do companies utilise loan finance in preference to equity capital? There are several reasons. For example, it may be easier to raise loan finance; the existing company shareholders may not want their existing level of control diluted by introducing more shareholders; finally it is likely that loan interest will be cheaper than equity finance. This is

# RATIO ANALYSIS

because loan interest, as a charge against profits, is allowable against corporation tax, while dividends are not.

### Gearing (or leverage) ratio

10.7 To calculate the relationship between equity and loan finance we use the following formula.

$$\frac{\text{Long term debt}}{\text{Shareholders funds}} \times 100$$

10.8 You may find variations on the above formula; sometimes long-term debt is added to the denominator to give a gearing percentage always less than 100%. However, consistency is important when comparing with previous years and other companies.

### *Interpretation*

10.9 No hard and fast rules can be given as to an ideal level of gearing; as mentioned earlier, higher gearing normally implies higher risk. The trend of gearing should be considered as well as the relative gearing in comparison to other similar companies. The industry in which the business operates is significant. Capital intensive industries tend to have a higher gearing levels because of the high amount and long-term nature of their asset base. Cash generative, stable businesses, such as utilities, often have high gearing levels.

10.10 Gearing levels should be relatively stable; however some of the following factors could mean a noticeable movement in the gearing ratio:

- equity capital raised
- loan capital raised
- redemption of share capital
- repayment of loan capital
- high levels of retained profits
- low levels of profit, or losses incurred.

10.11 Look again for the explanation behind the change in the gearing ratio. Major loan finance might have been raised—why? Share capital might have been redeemed—why?

## Student Activity 3

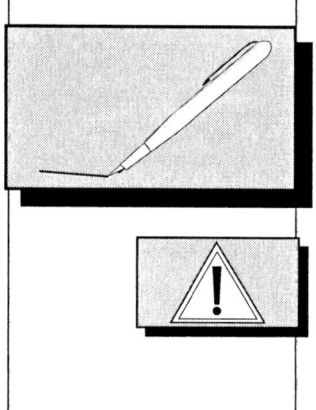

Using the information given at the end of the Unit calculate the following ratios for 19X3 and 19X4.

1. Current ratio.
2. Quick ratio.
3. Gearing.

FINANCIAL REPORTING, ANALYSIS AND PLANNING

## 11 Working capital

11.1 A useful division between assets is that of fixed and current assets. Generally, fixed assets are held on a continuing basis for the long term, while current assets are held for the short term (see Unit 4). Fixed assets are used to facilitate the productive capacity of the business. Current assets are sometimes referred to as operating assets, used in the day-to-day operations of the business, changing identity on a regular basis. As we saw above, the movement in these current assets (and liabilities) can be expressed as a diagram.

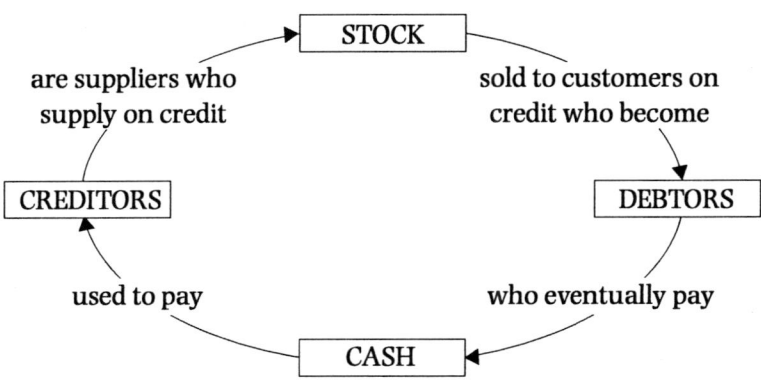

11.2 This is referred to as the working capital cycle. As a general rule, the company will want to keep its levels of working capital as low as possible. Chiefly to reduce the funding costs associated with holding such current assets. Ratios can be computed for each of the three main current assets and liabilities above.

**Stock turnover period**

11.3 This is calculated as follows.

$$\frac{\text{Average stock*}}{\text{Cost of sales}} \times 365$$

*Note: if average stock is not available for both years, use closing stock.*

This expresses in numbers of days, how long, on average, the company holds its stock. Note the consistency in the ratio – average stock (at cost price) compared with cost of sales (at cost price).

*Interpretation*

11.4 Once again there is no ideal period of time that a company should hold its stock. The relative performance of the company, in comparison to other similar companies and previous periods should be examined. In general, the quicker the company can sell its stock the better. The just-in-time philosophy promotes very low stock levels. The drawback in holding low levels of stock is the risk of stock-outs, where customer or production requests cannot be met.

11.5 As in other ratios above, the type of industry in which the business operates will determine what the likely/desired stock; turnover ratio should be. A construction firm is likely to have a much longer stock turnover than an ice-cream vendor.

# RATIO ANALYSIS

11.6 There may be a linkage to the gross profit percentage. A company might have increased its stock selling prices to boost gross margins. However the stock turnover might have suffered.

## Debtor collection period

11.7 This is calculated as follows:

$$\frac{\text{Average trade debtors *}}{\text{Credit sales \#}} \times 365$$

Note:
* If average debtors are not available for both years – use closing debtors
\# If credit sales are not available – use total sales

This ratio expresses in days, how long, on average, a company takes to collect its debts.

### *Interpretation*

11.8 In general, the quicker a company can collect its debts the better. The credit taken by its customers is a free source of finance for them and the tendency is for customers to delay as long as possible before settling trade debts. Once again, to interpret the effectiveness of the company's debt collection policy, compare the period with other companies, previous years and the company's stated credit period. Again, different industries traditionally may have different credit periods.

11.9 In attempting to explain why a collection period has changed, consider if the company has recently changed its policies, it may not previously have offered credit, it may have started offering discounts to customers to encourage early payment, it may have employed a debt collection agency, it may have decided to factor its debts.

## Creditor payment period

11.10 This is calculated as follows.

$$\frac{\text{Average trade creditors *}}{\text{Credit purchases \#}} \times 365$$

Note:
* If average creditors are not available for both years, use closing creditors.
\# If the purchases figure is not available, use cost of sales as a surrogate.

This ratio calculates, on average, how many days the company takes to pay its trade creditors.

### *Interpretation*

11.11 In general, the longer a company takes to settle its current liabilities the better. It is a free source of finance and helps to reduce the overall level of working capital. Once again, comparison needs to be made with previous periods, comparable companies and the official credit period granted by the suppliers.

# FINANCIAL REPORTING, ANALYSIS AND PLANNING

11.12 There are a few caveats when interpreting this ratio. On the surface, an increase in this period is a good thing; the company has increased its usage of this free source of finance. However, it may not have been a conscious policy to extend the average period of credit taken, it may be a necessity due to a cash flow problem. Perhaps the company does not have the available funds to settle its debts on time. The company's cash flow statement should be analysed in conjunction with this ratio.

11.13 In addition, deliberately extending the credit period may not be without cost. The company may have to forgo discounts for early settlement; if the credit period is extended too far, the supplier may refuse to supply; or the supplier may impose penalties such as demanding that the company pay a deposit up front before any supplies are made, or insisting on cash-on-delivery.

11.14 Recent government initiatives have sought to establish industry-wide codes of best practice in the settlement of trade debts. It recognises the considerable burden that late payment can mean for companies, especially smaller enterprises. Often large companies, in addition to their considerable bulk buying power have undue influence over the period of credit they take from smaller suppliers.

**Cash operating cycle**

11.15 If we aggregate the stock turnover ratio to the debtors collection period and take away the creditors' payment period it will give us the *cash operating cycle*. In essence, this estimates how long the period is from paying the supplier to eventual collection of cash from the customer. Evidently, the shorter the period the better. As implied earlier some businesses, especially cash businesses, may have a negative cash operating cycle. The relative performance in terms of previous periods and similar businesses in the important point of comparison.

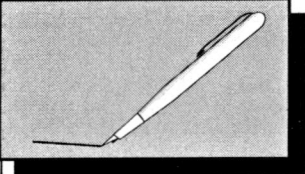

## Student Activity 4

Using the information given at the end of the Unit, calculate the following ratios for 19X3 and 19X4.

1. Stock turnover period.

2. Debtor collection period.

3. Creditor payment period.

4. Cash operating cycle.

## 12 Asset utilisation

12.1 We have already come across a ratio from this grouping earlier. Remember the ROCE ratio and its derivation from the net profit percentage and asset turnover ratios.

| ROCE | | Net profit ratio | | Asset turnover |
|---|---|---|---|---|
| $\dfrac{\text{Net profit} \times 100}{\text{Assets}}$ | = | $\dfrac{\text{Net profit} \times 100}{\text{Sales}}$ | × | $\dfrac{\text{Sales}}{\text{Assets}}$ |

# RATIO ANALYSIS

12.2 The last ratio was used to indicate how much sales the company generates from its asset base. Remember that different industries will have differing levels of asset utilisation. Capital intensive industries tend to have lower turnovers relative to assets than other industries.

12.3 Variations on the standard ratio include the following.

**Fixed asset turnover**

$$\frac{\text{Sales}}{\text{Fixed assets}}$$

**Current asset turnover**

$$\frac{\text{Sales}}{\text{Current assets}}$$

12.4 All the above ratios attempt to examine how efficiently the company is utilising the assets at its disposal; or how effective are the fixed, current or total assets in generating turnover.

*Interpretation*

12.5 This can be a difficult ratio to interpret. Always state the exact formula you have used and look out for major changes in assets which might have affected the ratio. For example, a significant investment in fixed assets, say a new factory, may not immediately lead to an increase in turnover. There may be a time lag while production is up and running and to capacity and marketing and distribution functions are undertaken.

12.6 Take care also when looking at the company's level of turnover: it may be due to one-off factors, seasonal or cyclical variations.

## Student Activity 5

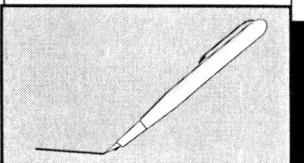

Using the information given at the end of the Unit, calculate the following ratios for 19X3 and 19X4.

1. Fixed asset turnover.
2. Current asset turnover.

## 13 Shareholder ratios

13.1 This category is a bit of a misnomer since all the above categories of ratio are of interest to shareholders. However there are certain ratios which are of particular concern to investors, both current and potential.

**Earnings per share**

13.2 This has already been considered in Unit 6. To repeat the earnings per share (EPS) is calculated as follows.

$$\frac{\text{Earnings}}{\text{Ordinary shares}}$$

# FINANCIAL REPORTING, ANALYSIS AND PLANNING

13.3 'Earnings' being defined as profits after:

- tax
- preference dividends and
- extraordinary items.

'Ordinary shares' being *equity* shares in issue ranking for dividend.

13.4 Earnings per share is a key indicator of the financial performance of the company. It expresses, in an amount per share, how much profit the company has earned in the last financial year. It is not necessarily the amount of dividend that is paid, nor is it the maximum dividend that could be paid, because the company can pay out a dividend from previous years' profits. However, the EPS is a good indicator of the performance of the company in profit terms.

## Price earnings ratio

13.5 The market uses the EPS to work out the key Price-Earnings (PE) ratio. This is calculated as follows.

$$\frac{\text{Market price per share}}{\text{Earnings per share}}$$

The PE ratio is an indication of the value the market places on a company's shares relative to its profitability.

## Dividend cover

13.6 Another pertinent shareholder ratio is the relationship between dividends and profits. This is calculated as follows.

$$\frac{\text{Profit available for distribution}}{\text{Dividends}}$$

13.7 The profit available for distribution is the profit after tax after preference dividends. 'Dividends' include ordinary dividends only, both those paid and proposed.

### *Interpretation*

13.8 The dividend cover is an indication of how 'safe' the dividend is. Generally, the higher the level of cover, the 'safer' the dividend. However, once again, there are a number of factors to take into account, in particular the company's dividend policy (if it has one).

13.9 A company may have a *progressive* dividend policy i.e. it is committed to increase its dividend every year. Alternatively, it could have a policy of paying out a set percentage of available profits every year, this would mean a constant dividend cover. A company's dividend is seen by some as a sign of company virility—such a company may pay a dividend out of retained profits if it does not have the current profits to pay a dividend.

13.10 Another possible constraint is the company's cash availability. The company may have available profits but no cash to pay a dividend.

# RATIO ANALYSIS

13.11 The level of dividend cover may indicate how prudent the company is. A low dividend cover may indicate that the company is perhaps paying out too high a dividend, possibly concerned more about short-term share price rather than long-term stability. Companies, particularly listed companies, are under great pressure from investors to maintain or increase the level of dividends.

13.12 Remember that the level of profits can fluctuate due to many factors as discussed previously. If you are given a historic summary of company results, say five years, you may be able to identify a dividend policy.

## Student Activity 6

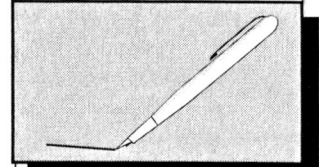

Using the information given at the end of the Unit, calculate the following ratios for 19X3 and 19X4.

1. Earnings per share.
2. Price earnings ratio.
3. Dividend cover.

## 14 Limitations of ratio analysis

14.1 Many statements and calculations performed by accountants tend to give an impression of precision and veracity. However, as you will have seen from previous units, financial statements, while purporting to show a true and fair view of a company's position and performance, may not be the unbiased representation that is expected. In particular, consider how the choice of the accounting policies and the effect of the numerous estimates contained within the accounts may affect the end result. For example, look at some of the following items and the possible effect on profit and asset levels:

- fixed asset revaluations
- depreciation: method, estimates of scrap value and useful lives
- leased assets: decision whether operating or finance leases
- research and development: write off or capitalise
- stock valuation: LIFO, FIFO etc., estimates of NRV
- long term work in progress: calculation of attributable profit
- debtors: estimates of bad debt provisions
- contingencies: estimates, disclose or provide
- post balance sheet events: adjust or not
- capital instruments: calculation of carrying value.

14.2 The ratio analyses will only be as good as the financial statements they are based on. Therefore great care should be taken in avoiding over reliance on the information contained in them. Remember that many of the figures in the accounts are only estimates. In addition, when comparing different companies, consider if the comparable company adopts similar or different accounting policies. Think about, for example, the effect on ROCE when a company exercises the option to revalue its fixed assets: profits fall (because of higher depreciation charges) and asset values increase. Thus the ROCE will be automatically less than it would have been had the company chosen not to revalue.

14.3 Another factor which may need to be taken into account is the effect of any one-off, non-recurring or unusual items which periodically affect the accounts. For example, a company may be hit by an exceptionally large bad debt, loss of a major order or other similar one-off event. It may be necessary to adjust the company's or comparative company's accounts for such items. One of the things you will be trying to ascertain is the company's *maintainable earnings*.

14.4 Other factors may be important. For example, when comparing two owner-run businesses, one may pay its directors a salary as remuneration while the other may decide to reward its directors through dividends. The former will show lower profits than the latter but the underlying earnings may be identical.

## 15 Trends

15.1 One year's figures in isolation are often not particularly useful. Previous years' figures are of more assistance, because one can examine whether any trends have been established. A long-term trend is likely to be more significant than a one-off 'blip'. The Companies Act 1985 only requires one year's figures with comparatives to be shown. Certain companies include a historical five-year summary of accounts. Consider too the requirements of FRS3 'Reporting Financial Performance'. Reporting entities are required to highlight the effect of new acquired operations, discontinued operations, 'exceptional' and 'extraordinary items'. For an explanation of the effects of FRS3, see Unit 6.

**Overview**

- Probably the most important quality you will need to make a reasonable interpretation of a set of company results is common sense. Remember the desk top review, getting a 'gut feeling' for the company you are analysing.

- Focus on the requirements of the question: to whom, on what and why are you reporting?

- Finally, you are likely to have to make a decision. To recommend that the company invests in Company A rather than Company B; that the bank lend the money or not; that the overdraft be extended or called in. So you will probably need to get off the fence and make a decision or recommendation. Do not be too dogmatic; you are more likely to have to give a qualified 'yes' or 'no' rather than be categoric in your decision.

- Calculate some appropriate ratios, make sensible comments based thereon, reflect on the non-financial data presented, include some advice from your business knowledge and finally come to a well rounded out conclusion, and you will do well in this type of question. Good performance in this compulsory question is vital to passing the Financial Reporting exam.

# RATIO ANALYSIS

## Student Activity information

The following details are taken from a question in the CIB 'Accountancy' paper, October 1994.

**Alexander Limited (as amended)**

The following draft accounts and other information are provided for Alexander Limited, a company which manufactures a single, standard product.

*Summarised profit and loss account: year to 30 September*

|  | 19X4 |  | 19X3 |  |
|---|---|---|---|---|
|  | units 000 | £000 | units 000 | £000 |
| Turnover |  | 1,500 |  | 1,800 |
| Less: Manufacturing costs: |  |  |  |  |
| Direct materials and labour |  | 700 |  | 600 |
| Factory overheads |  |  |  |  |
| Factory rent |  | 0 |  | 60 |
| Depreciation of plant |  | 180 |  | 180 |
| Other expenses |  | 660 |  | 660 |
| Quantity/cost of goods completed | 280 | 1,540 | 240 | 1,500 |
| Add: |  |  |  |  |
| Opening stock of finished goods | 40 | 250 | 40 | 250 |
| Deduct: |  |  |  |  |
| Closing stock of finished goods | (120) | (660) | (40) | (250) |
| Quantity/Cost of sales | 200 | 1,130 | 240 | 1,500 |
| Gross profit |  | 370 |  | 300 |
| Less: Directors' remuneration |  | (30) |  | (70) |
| Administration costs |  | (114) |  | (95) |
| Selling and distribution costs |  | (32) |  | (35) |
| Operating profit |  | 194 |  | 100 |
| Interest |  | (100) |  | 0 |
| Net profit |  | 94 |  | 100 |
| Proposed dividend |  | (70) |  | (30) |
| Retained profit |  | 24 |  | 70 |

FINANCIAL REPORTING, ANALYSIS AND PLANNING

| Balance sheet at 30 September | 19X4 £000 | 19X3 £000 |
|---|---|---|
| *Fixed assets* | | |
| Freehold buildings at cost | 1,000 | 0 |
| Plant and machinery at book value | 620 | 800 |
| | 1,620 | 800 |
| *Current assets* | | |
| Stock | 660 | 250 |
| Debtors | 250 | 300 |
| Cash in hand | 2 | 5 |
| | 912 | 555 |
| *Creditors: amounts falling due within one year* | | |
| Trade creditors | 190 | 100 |
| Proposed dividend | 70 | 30 |
| Bank overdrafts | 98 | 75 |
| | 358 | 205 |
| *Net current assets* | 554 | 350 |
| *Total assets less current liabilities* | 2,174 | 1,150 |
| *Creditors: amounts falling due after more than one year* | | |
| Debentures (secured on freehold building) | (1,000) | 0 |
| | 1,174 | 1,150 |
| *Capital and reserves* | | |
| Issued share capital (£1 shares) | 500 | 500 |
| Retained profit | 674 | 650 |
| | 1,174 | 1,150 |

## Additional information

- The company's share price at 31 December 19X3 and 19X4 is £2.00 and £1.50 respectively.

- The directors, who are also the major shareholders, have approached the bank requesting a continuation of overdraft facilities for the forthcoming twelve months and an increase in the maximum facility from £100,000 to £200,000.

- The directors inform you that the demand for their existing product is slowing down and that new equipment costing £120,000 is required to enable the manufacture of a new line for which strong demand is believed to exist.

- The directors point out that operating profit has increased and that the company now has a sound base for further expansion and diversification.

- The company values stock on a total cost basis.

- Ignore taxation.

# RATIO ANALYSIS

> **Summary**
>
> Now that you have completed this Unit you should be able to:
>
> - [ ] outline the methods available to interpret the accounts of companies and discuss their relative merits
> - [ ] identify the information needed to prepare a full analysis of a company and list required but unavailable information
> - [ ] calculate, analyse and classify accounting ratios
> - [ ] acknowledge the limitations of ratio analysis as a tool in interpreting accounts
> - [ ] interpret the results of ratio analysis in full and identify trends.

## Self-assessment questions

### Short-answer questions

1. Identify the information you would require to undertake a full analysis of a company's performance, in addition to the information contained within the financial statements.

2. What are the four ways in which accounting ratios are usually presented?

3. Discuss and illustrate why some ratios are interrelated and some are complementary.

4. Why is the ROCE referred to as the primary ratio?

5. What is the cash operating cycle?

6. Explain why the gearing figure is important, and outline the relative advantages and disadvantages of equity and loan finance.

7. What are the limitations of ratio analysis?

*(Answers are given in the Appendix)*

### Multiple choice questions

1. How is return on capital employed calculated?

    (a) Profit before interest and tax divided by shareholders' funds.

    (b) Profit before interest and tax divided by shareholders' funds and long term liabilities.

    (c) Profit after tax divided by shareholders' funds.

    (d) Profit after tax divided by shareholders' funds and long term liabilities.

2. How is return on shareholders funds calculated?

    (a) Profit before interest and tax divided by shareholders' funds.

    (b) Profit before interest and tax divided by shareholders' funds and long term liabilities.

    (c) Profit after tax divided by shareholders' funds.

(d) Profit after tax divided by shareholders' funds and long term liabilities.

3. What would be the likely effect of a cut in selling prices?

   | | *Gross margin* | *Stock turnover* |
   |---|---|---|
   | (a) | Decrease | Increase |
   | (b) | Decrease | Decrease |
   | (c) | Increase | Increase |
   | (d) | Increase | Decrease |

4. Which of the following would lead to a fall in the acid test ratio?

   (a) Increase in stock turnover.

   (b) Decrease in stock turnover.

   (c) Decrease in debtor collection period.

   (d) Increase in debtor collection period.

5. Gearing would increase if a company:

   1. made a profit
   2. made a loss
   3. repaid debt
   4. redeemed share capital.

   (a) 2 only

   (b) 1 or 3

   (c) 1, 3 or 4

   (d) 2 or 4

6. If a company's share price falls:

   (a) EPS would fall

   (b) EPS would rise

   (c) PE ratio would fall

   (d) PE ratio would rise.

*(Answers are given in the Appendix)*

# RATIO ANALYSIS

**Exam-style questions**

Taken from the CIB exam paper, October 1993.

The following financial information has been prepared in respect of the affairs of B. Page & Co., an advertising consultancy. The accounts are made up to 30 June each year.

### Profit and loss account: year to 30 June

|  | 1992 Actual £ | 1993 Budget £ | 1993 Actual £ |
|---|---|---|---|
| Turnover | 2,172,000 | 2,200,000 | 1,706,100 |
| Less: Cost of sub-contracted work | 1,496,510 | 1,474,000 | 1,177,210 |
| Staff salaries | 173,760 | 198,000 | 179,140 |
| Administration costs | 140,320 | 142,000 | 112,370 |
| Bad debts | 91,220 | 66,000 | 104,070 |
| Interest | 11,700 | 12,000 | 10,470 |
| Net profit | 258,490 | 308,000 | 122,840 |

### Balance sheet as at 30 June

|  | 1992 Actual £ | 1993 Budget £ | 1993 Actual £ |
|---|---|---|---|
| Premises at: cost | 120,000 | 120,000 | – |
| revalued amount | – | – | 320,000 |
| Other fixed assets at book value | 10,150 | 10,000 | 10,000 |
|  | 130,150 | 130,000 | 330,000 |
| *Current assets* |  |  |  |
| Work in progress | 272,100 | 275,000 | 220,000 |
| Debtors | 162,500 | 175,000 | 238,700 |
|  | 434,600 | 450,000 | 458,700 |
| *Current liabilities* |  |  |  |
| Trade creditors | 272,400 | 277,900 | 385,500 |
| PAYE and value added tax | 78,200 | 82,100 | 73,500 |
| Bank overdraft (secured) | 43,600 | 40,000 | 97,500 |
|  | 394,200 | 400,000 | 556,500 |
| Net current assets | 40,400 | 50,000 | (97,800) |
|  | 170,550 | 180,000 | 232,200 |
| Opening capital | 172,060 | 170,550 |  |
| Net profit | 258,490 | 308,000 |  |
| Drawings | (260,000) | (298,550) |  |
| Closing capital | 170,550 | 180,000 |  |

# FINANCIAL REPORTING, ANALYSIS AND PLANNING

B. Page has a mortgage of £170,000 on a house valued at £250,000 on 1 January 1991. The firm's overdraft facility has been £100,000 for the last three years.

**Required**

(a) Prepare the capital account of B. Page & Co. for the year to 30 June 1993.

[4]

(b) An examination of the financial performance and position of B. Page & Co. Your examination should include the calculations listed below and any others you consider relevant:

- individual expenses and profit expressed as a percentage of turnover
- current (working capital) ratio
- return on capital employed [20]

(c) Brief comments on B. Page's request for a continuation of the overdraft facility for a further twelve months. (6)

*Notes:* 1. The firm does not depreciate its premises.
2. Calculation of ratios to be made to one decimal place.

[Total marks for question 30]

# Unit 12

## Cash Flow Statement (1)

### Objectives

After studying this Unit, you should be able to:

- describe the background to cash flow reporting

- prepare cash flow statements using the standard format for cash flow statements per FRS 1(revised) 'Cash flow statements'

- list exemptions from FRS 1(revised).

## 1 Introduction

1.1 In July 1975, the Accounting Standards Committee (ASC) issued SSAP 10 'Source and application of funds' statement which, although not a cash flow statement, gave information about where funds had been earned and spent. On introduction there was some enthusiasm for this statement but it also attracted considerable criticism, not least because it failed to define 'funds' and did not lay down a format for the statement.

1.2 In September 1991, the Accounting Standards Board (ASB) issued its first financial reporting standard FRS 1 'Cash flow statements'. This superseded SSAP 10. The objective of the standard was to oblige reporting entities falling within its scope to report on a standard basis their cash generation and absorption for a period. It applied, with some exceptions, to all financial statements intended to give a true and fair view of the financial position and profit and loss (or income and expenditure) of the organisation.

1.3 FRS 1 was generally criticised for two reasons.

- It was based on cash and 'cash equivalents'. Cash included all deposits which were repayable *on demand*. Cash equivalents were defined as short term investments which were readily convertible to known amounts of cash *without notice* and which were *within three months of maturity* when acquired. This definition was criticised for being limited by the words 'without notice' and also for cash equivalents having to be within three months of maturity when acquired. Critics felt that the limited definition did not necessarily represent a company's liquidity. For example, if a company were to place surplus funds on deposit falling outside FRS 1's definition then the deposit would have to be classified as an investing activity – irrespective of the fact that it was not considered so by the company.

FINANCIAL REPORTING, ANALYSIS AND PLANNING

- It was felt that the format could be made easier to understand and could also be better supported by reconciliations back to the other financial statements.

1.4 The ASB addressed these criticisms quite radically by proposing, in FRED 10 'Revision of FRS 1 Cash Flow Statements' to make the cash flow statement a pure cash flow statement where cash equivalents would be dealt with in their own section titled 'management of liquid resources', and to make the format simpler and supported by more reconciliations.

1.5 In October 1996 FRS 1(revised) was issued. The main changes in the new cash flow statement are summarised below.

- Cash flows are only based on pure cash (cash in hand and deposits repayable on demand less overdrafts).
- Cash equivalents are in a new management of liquid resources section.
- Cash flows relating to investing activities are divided into two new categories: capital expenditure and financial investment; and acquisitions and disposals.
- A movement in cash to the movement in net debt (or net funds) shown in the opening and closing balance sheets reconciliation is now required.
- Exemption from preparing cash flow statements is extended to 90% owned subsidiaries (it was previously only available to 100% owned subsidiaries).

1.6 It is important for students to understand the need for cash flow reporting. Historical cash flow information may assist users of financial statements in making judgements on the amount, timing and degree of certainty of future cash flows. It gives some indication of the relationship between profitability and the ability to actually generate the cash necessary for survival – the two things do not always go hand in hand.

## 2  FRS 1 (revised) Cash flow statements

2.1 The objective of FRS 1 (revised) is to ensure that reporting entities falling within its scope:

(a) report their cash generation and cash absorption for a period by highlighting the significant components of cash flow in a way that facilitates comparison of the cash flow performance of different businesses; and

(b) provide information that assists in the assessment of their liquidity, solvency and financial adaptability.

The standard format included in Appendix 1 of FRS 1 revised is given below:

# CASH FLOW STATEMENT (1)

## Appendix 1 of FRS 1 (Revised)
(Example of cash flow)

### Example 12.1

*A cash flow statement for an individual company: XYZ Ltd*

Cash flow statement for the year ended 31 December 1996

| *Cash flow statement* | £000 | £000 |
|---|---:|---:|
| Net cash inflows from operating activities | | 6,889 |
| Returns on investments and servicing of finance (Note 1) | | 2,999 |
| Taxation | | (2,922) |
| Capital expenditure | | (1,525) |
| | | 5,441 |
| Equity dividends paid | | (2417) |
| | | 3024 |
| Management of liquid resources (Note 1) | | (450) |
| Financing (Note 1) | | 57 |
| Increase in cash | | 2,631 |

*Reconciliation of net cash flow to movement in net debt (Note 2)*

| | | |
|---|---:|---:|
| Increase in cash in the period | 2,631 | |
| Cash to repurchase debenture | 149 | |
| Cash used to increase liquid resources | 450 | |
| Change in net debt* | | 3,230 |
| Net debt at 1.1.96 | | (2,903) |
| Net funds at 31.12.96 | | 327 |

*Reconciliation of operating profit to net cash inflow from operating activities*

| | £000 |
|---|---:|
| Operating profit | 6,022 |
| Depreciation charges | 899 |
| Increase in stocks | (194) |
| Increase in debtors | (72) |
| Increase in creditors | 324 |
| Net cash inflow from operating activities | 6,889 |

Notes to the cash flow statement
Note 1 – gross cash flows

| | £000 | £000 |
|---|---:|---:|
| Returns on investments and servicing of finance | | |
|     Interest received | 3,011 | |
|     Interest paid | (12) | |
| | | 2,999 |

Capital expenditure
Payments to acquire intangible fixed assets (71)
Payments to acquire tangible fixed assets (1,496)
Receipts from sales of tangible fixed assets 42
                                                    (1,525)

Management of liquid resources
Purchase of treasury bills (650)
Sale of treasury bills 200
                                                    (450)

Financing
Issue of ordinary share capital 211
Repurchase of debenture loan (149)
Expenses paid in connection with share issues (5)
                                                    57

*Note 2 – Analysis of changes in net debt*

|  | At 1 Jan 1996 £000 | Cash flows £000 | Other changes £000 | At 31 Dec 1996 £000 |
|---|---|---|---|---|
| Cash in hand, at bank | 42 | 847 |  | 889 |
| Overdrafts | (1,784) | 1,784 |  |  |
|  |  | 2,631 |  |  |
| Debt due within 1 year | (149) | 149 | (230) | (230) |
| Debt due after 1 year | (1,262) |  | 230 | (1,032) |
| Current asset investments | 250 | 450 |  | 700 |
| Total | (2,903) | 3,230 | - | 327 |

2.2 You should note that the cash flow statement itself is quite brief, giving only totals for each heading. The detail behind the statement is given in Note 1 'Gross cash flows'. The reconciliation of net cash flow to movement in net debt and the analysis of changes in net debt facilitate user understanding by providing a link to the balance sheet.

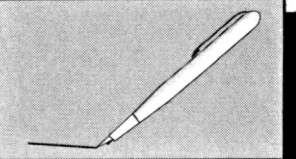

## Student Activity 1

Before reading the next section of the text, answer the following questions and then check your answers against the paragraphs indicated.

1. Why may cash flow information be important to users of accounts?
   *(paragraph 1.6)*

2. What is the objective of FRS 1 (revised)? *(paragraph 2.1)*

3. List the headings of the standard format of cash flow statements per FRS 1 (revised). *(paragraph 2.1)*

4. How does the revision to FRS 1 help users to relate the cash flow to other financial statements? *(paragraph 1.5)*

# CASH FLOW STATEMENT (1)

If your answers are basically correct, then proceed to the next section. If significant parts of your answers are wrong, then study the whole of the relevant sections again in detail. Note your areas of weakness, and be prepared for further questions on these areas in the self-assessment section at the end of this unit.

## Operating activities

2.3 Cash flows from operating activities are in general the cash effects of transactions and other events relating to operating or trading activities. Therefore the net cash flow from operating activities represents the net increase or decrease in cash and cash equivalent resulting from the operations shown in the profit and loss account arriving at operating profit. Operating activities may be presented using either the direct method or the indirect method of presentation.

## The direct method

2.4 This method shows operating cash receipts and payments (cash receipts from customers, cash payments to suppliers and cash payments to and on behalf of employees) aggregating to the net cash flow from operating activities.

2.5 A reconciliation between the operating profit recorded in the profit and loss account and the net cash flow statement is required whether the direct or indirect method is used. This reconciliation should disclose separately the movements in stocks, debtors and creditors related to operating activities and other differences between cash flows and profits.

### Example 12.2

**THE DIRECT METHOD – HELENA LTD**

The following information is available for Helena Ltd for the year ending 31 December 1995.

|  | £000 |
|---|---:|
| Operating profit | 20,200 |
| Cash received from customers | 195,000 |
| Cash payments to suppliers | (110,000) |
| Cash paid to/on behalf of employees | (56,000) |
| Other cash payments | (12,650) |
| Depreciation charges | 3,150 |
| Profit on sale of machine | 50 |
| Increase in stocks | 12,200 |
| Increase in debtors | 3,750 |
| Increase in creditors | 9,000 |

*Extract from the cash flow statement of Helena Ltd for the year ending 31 December 1995*

| Operating activities | £000 |
|---|---:|
| Cash received from customers | 195,000 |
| Cash payments to suppliers | (110,000) |
| Cash paid to/on behalf of employees | (56,000) |
| Other cash payments | (12,650) |
| Net cash inflow from continuing operating activities | 16,350 |

# FINANCIAL REPORTING, ANALYSIS AND PLANNING

*Notes to the cash flow statement*
1. Reconciliation of operating profit to net cash inflow from operating activities.

|  | £000 |
|---|---:|
| Operating profit | 20,200 |
| Depreciation charges | 3,150 |
| Profit on sale of machine | (50) |
| Increase in stocks | (12,200) |
| Increase in debtors | (3,750) |
| Increase in creditors | 9,000 |
| Net cash inflow from operating activities | 16,350 |

In this reconciliation you can see how we are trying to adjust the operating profit, which is prepared on the accruals basis, to a cash basis. Depreciation charges must be added back because they are purely a way of matching the cost of fixed assets to the benefit derived from them – depreciation does not relate to any cash outflow. Similarly profit on the sale of the machine will have been included in the operating profit but needs to be taken out because it does not relate to a cash inflow – the actual cash received will be included under capital expenditure later in the statement. Any increase in the amount of stock held or debtors outstanding will increase the amount of cash tied up in working capital, i.e. an effective reduction in cash available. On the other hand an increase in creditors means payments will be made later and more cash is available meantime.

2.6 The main advantage of the direct method is that it shows operating cash receipts and payments. Information about specific sources of cash receipts and the purposes for which cash payments were made in past periods may be useful in assessing future cash flows. However it is costly to provide such information.

### The indirect method

2.7 The indirect method starts with operating profit and adjusts it for non-cash charges and credits to reconcile it to the net cash flow from operating activities.

2.8 A reconciliation between the operating profit reported in the profit and loss account and the net cash flow from operating activities should again be given as a note to the cash flow statement. This reconciliation should disclose separately the movements in stocks, debtors and creditors related to operating activities and other differences between cash flows and profits.

**Example 12.3**

**THE INDIRECT METHOD – HELENA LTD**

If Helena Ltd's operating activities were prepared under the indirect method, much less information would be given:

# CASH FLOW STATEMENT (1)

*Extract from the cash flow statement of Helena Ltd for the year ending 31 December 1995:*

|  | £000 |
|---|---|
| Net cash inflow from continuing operating activities | 16,350 |

*Notes to the cash flow statement*
1. Reconciliation of operating profit to net cash inflow from operating activities.

|  | £000 |
|---|---|
| Operating profit | 20,200 |
| Depreciation charges | 3,150 |
| Profit on sale of machine | (50) |
| Increase in stocks | (12,200) |
| Increase in debtors | (3,750) |
| Increase in creditors | 9,000 |
| Net cash inflow from operating activities | 16,350 |

## Returns on investments and servicing of finance

2.9 Returns on investments and servicing of finance are receipts resulting from the ownership of an investment and payments to providers of finance, non-equity shareholders (for example, the holders of preference shares) and minority interests as shown by the examples in Table 12.1 below.

**Table 12.1**

| Cash inflows | Cash outflows |
|---|---|
| Interest received | Interest paid |
| Preference share dividend received | Preference share dividend paid |

**Example 12.4**

### MARIA LTD

The following extracts are taken from the financial statements of Maria Ltd for the year ending 30 June 1998.

*Profit and loss account*

|  | £ | £ |
|---|---|---|
| Interim preference dividend | 50,000 |  |
| Final preference dividend | 100,000 |  |

*Balance sheet*

|  | 30.06.1997 | 30.06.1998 |
|---|---|---|
| Dividends payable | 80,000 | 100,000 |

From this information it is possible to work out how much dividend has been paid in cash during the year ending 30 June 1998.

# FINANCIAL REPORTING, ANALYSIS AND PLANNING

|  | £ |
|---|---:|
| Outstanding at year end 30.06.97 | 80,000 |
| plus amount proposed during the year ending 30.06.98 | 150,000 |
| Total outstanding during the period | 230,000 |
| Amount outstanding at 30.06.98 | (100,000) |
| Therefore amount paid | 130,000 |

The same exercise can be repeated to work out how much interest has been paid.

**Taxation**

2.10 The cash flows included under this heading are cash flows to or from taxation authorities in respect of the reporting entity's revenue and capital profits. Examples are given in table 12.2 below.

**Table 12.2**

| Taxation cash inflows | Taxation cash outflows |
|---|---|
| Tax rebates | Corporation tax |
| Returns of overpayments | |

Cash flows in respect of other taxation, including sales taxes, property taxes and other taxes not assessed on the profits of the reporting entity should be shown under the most appropriate heading. For example where a fixed asset is purchased and the Value Added Tax (VAT) on it is irrecoverable the total cost (cost of the item plus the Value Added Tax) should be shown under capital expenditure. Cash flows should be shown net of any attributable Value Added Tax or other sales tax unless the tax is irrecoverable by the reporting entity.

**Example 12.5**

**ATHINNA LTD AND RATHINNA LTD**

Athinna Ltd is not registered for VAT and pays £10,000 plus £1,750 VAT for a fixed asset.

Rathinna Ltd is registered for VAT and pays £10,000 plus £1,750 VAT for a fixed asset.

*Extracts from the cash flow statements*

|  | Athinna Ltd £ | Rathinna Ltd £ |
|---|---:|---:|
| Capital expenditure | 11,750 | 10,000 |

**Capital expenditure and financial investment**

2.11 The cash flows included in this section may include the acquisition or disposal of any fixed asset (other than one required to be classified under 'acquisitions and disposals' described in Unit 13), or any current asset (other than ones included in the liquid resources section which is described later in this unit). If no cash flows relating to financial investment fall to be included

# CASH FLOW STATEMENT (1)

in this section, the heading may be reduced to 'capital expenditure'. Table 12.3 gives examples of entries in this section.

**Table 12.3**

| Cash inflows | Cash outflows |
|---|---|
| Receipts from sale of property | Payments to acquire property |
| Receipts from sale of plant & equipment | Payments to acquire plant & equipment |
| Receipts from the payment of loans to the reporting entity | Loans made by the reporting entity |

**Example 12.6**

**SOPHIA LTD**

Again we can use extracts from the financial statements to derive the cash flow information.

Sophia Ltd sold a machine during the year ending 31 July 1998; no purchases of fixed assets were made. Depreciation for the year amounted to £10,000.

*Extracts from the financial statements of Sophia Ltd for the year ending 31 July 1998.*

*Profit and loss account*

|  | £ | £ |
|---|---|---|
| Profit on sale of machine | 1,000 |  |

| Balance sheet | 31.07.97 | 31.07.98 |
|---|---|---|
| Fixed assets (nbv) | 100,000 | 80,000 |

We can work out the cash inflow for the machine by using the following information:

|  | £ |
|---|---|
| Fixed assets (nbv) 31.07.97 | 100,000 |
| Less depreciation | (10,000) |
|  | 90,000 |
| Fixed assets (nbv) 31.07.98 | 80,000 |

So if no assets had been sold the balance at 31.07.98 would have been £90,000, but it is actually £80,000 so a machine with a net book value (nbv) of £10,000 has been sold. The profit and loss account tells us that a £1,000 profit was made on the sale, therefore the machine must have been sold for £11,000 which is the cash flow.

|  | £ |
|---|---|
| Sale proceeds (cash inflow) | 11,000 |
| nbv at sale | 10,000 |
| Profit on sale | 1,000 |

2.12 Some purchases of fixed assets may be on credit terms; again, it is the actual cash flow which will be shown in the cash flow statement.

**Example 12.7**

**LUCIA LTD**

Lucia Ltd bought a new machine on credit terms. The machine cost £10,000. A deposit of £4,000 was payable on purchase, the remainder being split into three annual instalments.

The £10,000 asset will be included on the balance sheet from date of purchase (outstanding amounts are creditors). In the cash flow statement, the £4,000 will be included as a capital expenditure cash flow in the year of purchase and in the following three years there will be an annual cash outflow of £2,000 under the capital expenditure section.

**Equity dividends paid**

2.13 This section was introduced by the revision to FRS 1 and only includes the cash outflows of equity dividends paid by the reporting entity. Non-equity dividends should be included in the section 'Returns on investments and servicing of finance' as described in paragraph 2.9 above.

**Management of liquid resources**

2.14 This section was also introduced by the revision to FRS 1. Liquid resources are defined by FRS 1(revised) as current asset investments held as readily disposable stores of value. A readily disposable investment is one that is:

(a) disposable by the reporting entity without curtailing or disrupting its business;

and is either

(b) (i) readily convertible into known amounts of cash at or close to its carrying amount, or

(c) (ii) traded in an active market.

Each entity should explain what it includes as liquid resources and any changes in its policy.

Table 12.4 gives some examples of cash inflows and outflows of liquid resources.

**Table 12.4**

| Cash inflows | Cash outflows |
| --- | --- |
| Withdrawals from short term deposits not qualifying as cash* | Payments into short term deposits not qualifying as cash* |
| Inflows from disposal or redemption of any other investments held as liquid resources | Outflows to acquire any other investments held as liquid resources |

# CASH FLOW STATEMENT (1)

*Short term deposits may qualify as cash for the purposes of a cash flow statement where they are repayable on demand. Deposits are repayable on demand if they can be withdrawn at any time without notice and without penalty or if a maturity or period of notice of not more than 24 hours or one working day has been agreed.

**Financing**

2.15 Financing cash flows comprise receipts from, or repayments to, providers of finance in respect of the principal amounts of finance. In other words while returns on investments and servicing of finance deals with the 'day to day running costs' such as interest, this section focuses on the principal amounts of finance. Some examples of receipts and payments are given in Table 12.5 below.

**Table 12.5**

| Cash inflows | Cash outflows |
| --- | --- |
| Receipts from the issue of shares | Payments to reacquire or redeem the reporting entity's shares |
| Receipts from issuing loans | Repayments of amounts borrowed |

## Student Activity 2

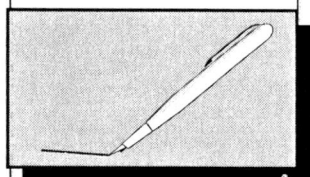

Before reading the next section of the text, answer the following questions and then check your answers against the paragraphs indicated.

1. How do the direct and indirect methods of preparing the operating activities section differ? *(paragraphs 2.3-2.8)*

2. Under which classification would you put any interest received? *(paragraph 2.9)*

3. Does VAT appear in the cash flow statement? *(paragraph 2.10)*

4. List two inflows and two outflows found under the financing section of the cash flow statement. *(paragraph 2.15)*

If your answers are basically correct, then proceed to the next section. If significant parts of your answers are wrong, then study the whole of the relevant sections again in detail. Note your areas of weakness and be prepared for further questions on these areas in the self-assessment section at the end of this Unit.

## 3 Preparation of a complete cash flow statement

3.1 The compilation of a cash flow statement is relatively straightforward once you have learnt the formats. The majority of exam questions are based on the indirect method for operating activities and this is the approach which will be taken in the remainder of this Unit. However students must be aware of how to prepare the direct method and be able to discuss the relative merits of each.

# FINANCIAL REPORTING, ANALYSIS AND PLANNING

## Example 12.8

### A FULL CASH FLOW STATEMENT

Jasmin Ltd has a year end of 30 June. We have been given the profit and loss account for the year ending 30 June 1996, together with the balance sheets as at 30 June 1995 and 1996 and asked to prepare a cash flow statement for the year ending 30 June 1996.

The depreciation charge for the year was £30,000 and no fixed assets were sold during the year.

*Profit and loss account for Jasmin Ltd for the year ending 30 June 1996*

|  | £000 |
|---|---:|
| Turnover | 1,200 |
| Cost of sales | (800) |
| Gross profit | 400 |
| Distribution costs | (50) |
| Administration costs | (110) |
| Operating profit | 240 |
| Interest received | 80 |
| Interest paid | (50) |
| Profit before tax | 270 |
| Taxation | (30) |
| Profit for the financial year | 240 |
| Equity dividends | (40) |
| Retained profit for year | 200 |

| *Balance sheet of Jasmin Ltd as at:* | 30 June 1995 £000 | 30 June 1996 £000 |
|---|---:|---:|
| Fixed assets | 230 | 470 |
| **Current assets** | | |
| Stocks | 100 | 110 |
| Debtors | 300 | 320 |
| Cash | 120 | 145 |
|  | 520 | 575 |
| **Current liabilities** | | |
| Creditors | 200 | 230 |
| Taxation | 25 | 30 |
| Dividend | 30 | 40 |
|  | (255) | (300) |
| Net current assets | 265 | 275 |
| Total assets less current liabilities | 495 | 745 |

# CASH FLOW STATEMENT (1)

Financed by:
|  |  |  |
|---|---:|---:|
| Share capital | 400 | 450 |
| Profit and loss | 95 | 295 |
|  | 495 | 745 |

The cash flow can be prepared by adjusting the operating profit to a cash figure and by comparing the balance sheet balances to find out where changes have occurred.

*Cash flow statement for Jasmin Ltd for the year ending 30 June 1996*

|  | £000 |
|---|---:|
| Net cash inflow from operating activities | 270 |
| Returns on investments and servicing of finance (note 1) | 30 |
| Taxation | (25) |
| Capital expenditure (Note 1) | (270) |
| Equity dividends paid | (30) |
| Management of liquid resources | – |
|  | (25) |
| Financing (Note 1) | 50 |
| Increase in cash | 25 |

*Notes to the cash flow statement*

*Note 1 Gross cash flows*

|  | £000 |
|---|---:|
| Returns on investments and servicing of finance: |  |
| Interest received | 80 |
| Interest paid | (50) |
|  | 30 |
| Capital expenditure: |  |
| Purchase of fixed assets (W1) | (270) |
| Financing |  |
| Issue of ordinary share capital | 50 |

*Reconciliation of operating profit to net cash inflow from operating activities.*

|  | £000 |
|---|---:|
| Operating profit | 240 |
| Depreciation | 30 |
| Increase in stocks | (10) |
| Increase in debtors | (20) |
| Increase in creditors | 30 |
|  | 270 |

The reconciliation of net cash flow to movement in net debt and the analysis of changes in net debt are not relevant here as there is no debt other than creditors.

*Workings*
*W1*

| Fixed assets | £000 |
|---|---|
| Opening balance of fixed assets (nbv) | 230 |
| Less depreciation | (30) |
| Balance if there were no additions | 200 |
| Actual closing balance | 470 |
| Therefore purchases must equal | 270 |

## 4 Exemptions from cash flow statement preparation

4.1 FRS 1(revised) applies to all financial statements intended to give a true and fair view of the financial position and profit or loss (or income and expenditure) except those of:

(a) subsidiary undertakings where 90% or more of the voting rights are controlled within the group, provided that consolidated financial statements in which the subsidiary undertakings are included are publicly available

(b) mutual life assurance companies

(c) pension funds

(d) certain open-ended investment funds

(e) certain building societies

(f) companies and other entities which qualify as 'small companies' under the Companies Act.

---

**Summary**

Now that you have completed this Unit you should be able to:

☐ describe the background to cash flow reporting

☐ prepare cash flow statements using the standard format for cash flow statements per FRS 1(revised) 'Cash flow statements'

☐ list exemptions from FRS 1(revised).

# CASH FLOW STATEMENT (1)

## Self-assessment questions

1. Prepare a reconciliation of operating profit to net cash flow from operating activities from the following information.

   |  | £ |
   |---|---:|
   | Operating profit | 200,000 |
   | Loss on sale of machine | 10,000 |
   | Increase in stocks | 10,000 |
   | Decrease in debtors | 2,000 |
   | Increase in creditors | 5,000 |
   | Depreciation | 50,000 |

2. List the classifications you would use for the following and indicate whether they represent a cash inflow or a cash outflow:

   equity dividends paid

   interest received

   tax rebate

   proceeds from the sale of a fixed asset

   preference dividend paid

   repayment of a loan to the bank.

3. List two entities which are exempt from the preparation of a cash flow statement under FRS 1(revised).

**Exam style question**

Thomas Ltd has a year end of 30 June You have been given the profit and loss account for the year ending 30 June 1996, together with the balance sheets as at 30 June 1995 and 1996 and asked to prepare a cash flow statement for the year ending 30 June 1996.

The depreciation charge for the year was £20,000 and a fixed asset with a net book value of £10,000 was sold during the year for a £2,000 profit.

*Profit and loss account for Thomas Ltd for the year ending 30 June 1996*

|  | £000 |
|---|---:|
| Turnover | 300 |
| Cost of sales | (160) |
| Gross profit | 140 |
| Distribution costs | (20) |
| Administration costs | (60) |
| Operating profit | 60 |
| Dividends received | 5 |
| Interest paid | (10) |
| Profit before tax | 55 |
| Taxation | (10) |
| Profit for the financial year | 45 |
| Equity Dividends | (25) |
| Retained profit for year | 20 |

## FINANCIAL REPORTING, ANALYSIS AND PLANNING

*Balance sheet of Thomas Ltd as at:*

|  | 30 June 1995 £000 | 30 June 1996 £000 |
|---|---:|---:|
| Fixed assets | 100 | 150 |
|  |  |  |
| Current assets |  |  |
| Stocks | 50 | 60 |
| Debtors | 100 | 120 |
| Cash | 70 | 80 |
|  | 220 | 260 |
|  |  |  |
| Current liabilities |  |  |
| Creditors | 80 | 70 |
| Taxation | 5 | 10 |
| Equity Dividends | 10 | 25 |
|  | 95 | 105 |
|  |  |  |
| Net current assets | 125 | 155 |
| Total assets less current liabilities | 225 | 305 |
| Less long-term loan | (50) | (60) |
|  | 175 | 245 |
|  |  |  |
| Financed by: |  |  |
| Share capital | 100 | 150 |
| Profit and loss | 75 | 95 |
|  | 175 | 245 |

You are not required to prepare either a reconciliation of net cash flow movement to movement in net debt or an analysis of changes in net debt.

# Unit 13

## Cash Flow Statement (2)

### Objectives

After studying this Unit you should be able to:

- appreciate how group cash flow statements are prepared and how they differ from single company statements
- analyse cash flow statements.

## 1 Introduction

1.1 Group cash flow is included in this Unit to give you an idea of how group cash flows are prepared and how they differ from single company statements.

1.2 Cash flow information is useful to users of accounts and in this Unit we will look at how best to analyse the cash flow statement.

## 2 Group cash flow statements

2.1 A group cash flow statement deals with flows of cash which are external to the group. Internal cash flows should be eliminated in the preparation of the cash flow statement.

2.2 The following example of a group cash flow statement is taken from Appendix 1 to FRS 1(revised).

**Example 13.1**

**A CASH FLOW STATEMENT FOR A GROUP: XYZ GROUP PLC**

*Cash flow statement for the year ended 31 December 1996*

|  | £000 | £000 |
|---|---:|---:|
| Cash flow from operating activities (note 1) |  | 16,022 |
| Returns on investments and servicing of finance (note 2)* |  | (2,239) |
| Taxation |  | (2,887) |
| Capital expenditure and financial investment (note 2) |  | (865) |
| Acquisitions and disposals (note 2) |  | (17,824) |
| Equity dividends paid |  | (2,606) |
| Cash outflow before use of liquid resources and financing |  | (10,399) |
| Management of liquid resources (note 2) |  | 700 |
| Financing (note 2) – issue of shares | 600 |  |
| Increase in debt | 2,347 |  |
|  |  | 2,947 |
| Decrease in cash in the period |  | (6,752) |

# FINANCIAL REPORTING, ANALYSIS AND PLANNING

*Notes to the cash flow statement*
*Note 1: Reconciliation of operating profit to operating cash flows*

|  | £'000 | Continuing £'000 | Discontinued £'000 | Total £'000 |
|---|---|---|---|---|
| Operating profit |  | 20,249 | (1,616) | 18,633 |
| Depreciation charges |  | 3,108 | 380 | 3,488 |
| Share of profit of associate | (1,420) |  |  |  |
| Dividend from associate | 350 |  |  |  |
| Profit of associate less dividends received |  | (1,070) |  | (1,070) |
| Cash flow relating to previous year restructuring provision |  |  | (560) | (560) |
| Increase in stocks |  | (11,193) | (87) | (11,280) |
| Increase in debtors |  | (3,754) | (20) | (3,774) |
| Increase in creditors |  | 9,672 | 913 | 10,585 |
| Net cash inflow from continuing operating activities |  | 17,012 |  |  |
| Net cash outflow in in respect of discontinued activities |  |  | (990) |  |
|  |  |  |  | 16,022 |

*Note 2: Headings netted in the cash flow statement*

|  | £000 | £000 |
|---|---|---|
| Returns on investments and servicing of finance |  |  |
| Interest received | 508 |  |
| Interest paid | (1,939) |  |
| Preference dividend paid | (450) |  |
| Interest element of finance lease rental payments | (358) |  |
| Net cash outflow for returns on investments and servicing of finance |  | (2,239) |
| Capital expenditure and financial investment |  |  |
| Purchase of tangible fixed assets | (3,512) |  |
| Sale of trade investment | 1,595 |  |
| Sale of plant and machinery | 1,052 |  |
| Net cash outflow for capital expenditure and financial investment |  | (865) |

## CASH FLOW STATEMENT (2)

| | | |
|---|---:|---:|
| Acquisitions and disposals | | |
| Purchase of subsidiary undertakings | (12,705) | |
| Net overdrafts acquired with subsidiary | (5,516) | |
| Sale of business | 4,208 | |
| Purchase of interest in a joint venture | (3,811) | |
| Net cash outflow for acquisitions and disposals | | 17,824 |
| | | |
| Management of liquid resources* | | |
| Cash withdrawn from 7 day deposit | 200 | |
| Purchase of government securities | (5,000) | |
| Sale of government securities | 4,300 | |
| Sale of corporate bonds | 1,200 | |
| Net cash inflow from management of liquid resources | | 700 |
| Financing | | |
| Issue of ordinary share capital | 600 | |
| Debt due within a year: | | |
| increase in short-term borrowings | 2,006 | |
| repayment of secured loan | (850) | |
| Debt due beyond a year: | | |
| new secured loan repayable in 2000 | 1,091 | |
| new unsecured loan repayable in 1998 | 1,442 | |
| Capital element of finance lease | | |
| Rental payments | (1,342) | |
| | | 2,347 |
| Net cash inflow from financing | | 2,947 |

* XYZ Group PLC includes as liquid resources term deposits of less than a year, government securities and AA rated corporate bonds.

*Note 3: Reconciliation of net cash flow to movement in net debt*

| | | |
|---|---:|---:|
| Decrease in cash in the period | (6,752) | |
| Cash inflow from increase in the debt and lease financing | (2,347) | |
| Cash inflow from decrease in liquid resources | (700) | |
| Change in net debt resulting from cash flows | | (9,799) |
| Loans and finance leases acquired with subsidiary | | (3,817) |
| New finance leases | | (2,845) |
| Translation difference | | 643 |
| Movement in net debt in the period | | (15,818) |
| Net debt at 1.1.96 | | (15,215) |
| Net debt at 31.12.96 | | (31,033) |

2.3 The section titled 'Acquisitions and disposals' relates to the acquisition or disposal of any trade or business, or of an investment in an entity that is now or, as a result of the transaction, becomes (or ceases to be) an associate, a joint venture or a subsidiary undertaking. Table 13.1 below gives examples of cash inflows and outflows under this section.

FINANCIAL REPORTING, ANALYSIS AND PLANNING

**Table 13.1**

| Cash inflows | Cash outflows |
|---|---|
| Receipts from sale of an investment in a subsidiary undertaking | Payments to acquire investments in subsidiary undertakings |
| Receipts from sale of associates and joint ventures | Payments to acquire investments in associates and joint ventures |

## 3 Analysis of cash flow statements

3.1 There are a number of benefits to be obtained from producing cash flow statements.

- Cash flow is vital to the ultimate survival of a business.
- Cash is more readily understandable to users than profit, which is dependent upon the accruals concept.
- Cash is more comparable than profit, which may be affected by different accounting policies.
- It is useful management information for decision-making.

3.2 The main disadvantage of the cash flow statement is that it may be costly to prepare, particularly if the direct method of reporting operating activities is used.

3.3 The cash flow statement actually provides some information which is not available elsewhere in the financial statements and provides useful reconciliations to other figures. In the analysis of cash flow statements it is important to regard the statement as 'part of the package'; to make a meaningful analysis the profit and loss account, balance sheet and supporting notes must also be considered, together with any other available information.

3.4 However, useful information can be gathered from analysing the statement itself. Over the following pages we will return to the exam style question presented in Unit 12.

*Thomas Ltd, cash flow statement for the year ended 30 June 1996*

|  | £000 |
|---|---:|
| Net cash flow from operating activities | 38 |
| Returns on investments and servicing of finance (Note 1) | (5) |
| Taxation | (5) |
| Capital expenditure (Note 1) | (68) |
| Equity dividends paid | (10) |
|  | (50) |
| Management of liquid resources | - |
| Financing | 60 |
| Increase in cash | 10 |

# CASH FLOW STATEMENT (2)

*Note 1: Gross Cash Flows*

|  | £000 |
|---|---:|
| **Returns on investments and servicing of finance** | |
|    dividends received | 5 |
|    interest paid | (10) |
| | |
| **Capital expenditure** | |
|    purchase of fixed asset (W1) | (80) |
|    sale of fixed asset (W1) | 12 |
| | |
| **Financing** | |
|    issue of ordinary share capital | 50 |
|    increase in loan | 10 |

*Reconciliation of operating profit to net cash inflow from operating activities*

|  | £000 |
|---|---:|
| Operating profit | 60 |
| Depreciation | 20 |
| Profit on sale of fixed asset | (2) |
| Increase in stocks | (10) |
| Increase in debtors | (20) |
| Increase in creditors | (10) |
| | 38 |

*Profit and Loss account for Thomas Ltd for the year ending 30 June 1996*

|  | £000 |
|---|---:|
| Turnover | 300 |
| Cost of sales | (160) |
| Gross profit | 140 |
| Distribution costs | (20) |
| Administration costs | (60) |
| Operating profit | 60 |
| Dividends received | 5 |
| Interest paid | (10) |
| Profit before tax | 55 |
| Taxation | (10) |
| Profit for the financial year | 45 |
| Dividends | (25) |
| Retained profit for year | 20 |

FINANCIAL REPORTING, ANALYSIS AND PLANNING

| Balance sheet of Thomas Ltd as at | 30 June 1995 £000 | 30 June 1996 £000 |
|---|---|---|
| Fixed assets | 100 | 150 |
| Current assets | | |
| Stocks | 50 | 60 |
| Debtors | 100 | 120 |
| Cash | 70 | 80 |
| | 220 | 260 |
| Current liabilities | | |
| Creditors | 80 | 70 |
| Taxation | 5 | 10 |
| Dividend | 10 | 25 |
| | 95 | 105 |
| Net current assets | 125 | 155 |
| Total assets less current liabilities | 225 | 305 |
| Less long-term loan | (50) | (60) |
| | 175 | 245 |
| Financed by: | | |
| Share capital | 100 | 150 |
| Profit and loss | 75 | 95 |
| | 175 | 245 |

3.5 The operating profit is £60,000 but is reduced significantly to £38,000 when adjusted to the cash flow figure. This is partly due to the depreciation figure but the changes to working capital are important. Working capital management is critical to the survival of a business and the reconciliation of operating profit to the cash flow from operating activities shows that it has deteriorated since last year. There may be valid reasons for this deterioration, for example a large one-off order leading to a temporary increase in stock and debtors, but it certainly needs further investigation.

3.6 It is useful to analyse how the cash generated has been used. For example, the interest paid may be compared with both profit and the loan, interest cover seems acceptable and the rate of interest paid is again reasonable. The fixed asset acquisition is quite significant and has been funded largely by the increase in debt and issue of share capital.

3.7 The following analysis shows the net amounts and percentages of funds spent/received in each of the cash flow classifications. It is useful to make comparisons on a percentage basis as this highlights what may not be apparent from looking at the financial statements. For example, the following analysis focuses on the significance of the fixed asset purchase and how it has been funded by the issue of shares and debt.

# CASH FLOW STATEMENT (2)

**Example 13.3**

## ANALYSIS OF THOMAS LTD'S CASH FLOW STATEMENT

|  | £000 | % |
|---|---:|---:|
| Returns on investments and servicing of finance | 5 | 6 |
| Taxation | 5 | 6 |
| Capital expenditure | 68 | 77 |
| Equity dividends paid | 10 | 11 |
|  | 88 | 100 |
|  |  |  |
| Funded by |  |  |
| Net cash inflow from operating activities | 38 | 39 |
| Financing | 60 | 61 |
|  | 98 | 100 |
|  |  |  |
| Increase in cash | 10 |  |

**Cash flow ratio**

3.8 A cash flow ratio may be calculated, comparing a business' net cash inflow from operating activities with its total debts. In the case of Thomas Ltd this would be:

$$\frac{£38,000}{(£70,000+£60,000)} = 29\%$$

This ratio needs to be compared with previous years and industry averages to decide whether it is acceptable or needs improving. It is designed to show whether a business is earning enough cash flow from its operation to be able to meet its debts. To get a full picture, analysis also needs to be made of the other financial statements, particularly with respect to liquidity and gearing.

## Student Activity 1

1. Which cash flows are reported in a group cash flow statement? *(paragraph 2.1)*
2. Why is cash flow information useful? *(paragraph 3.1)*
3. Define the cash flow ratio. *(paragraph 3.8)*

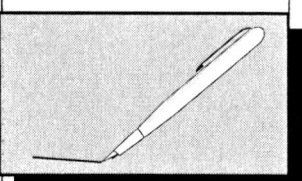

# FINANCIAL REPORTING, ANALYSIS AND PLANNING

## Summary

**You should now be able to:**

- [ ] **appreciate how group cash flow statements are prepared and how they differ from single company statements**
- [ ] **analyse cash flow statements.**

## Self-assessment questions

1. List three advantages of cash flow reporting.
2. When analysing a cash flow statement, what other sources of information should you also consider?

# Unit 14

## Cost Behaviour

### Objectives

**After studying this Unit you should be able to:**

- explain why knowledge of cost behaviour is essential to planning and control

- understand and explain the difference between historic cost, relevant cost, and opportunity cost

- identify and give examples of fixed costs and variable costs, and explain the significance of the concept of contribution

- calculate the effect of a change in activity level upon total costs, total fixed costs per unit, total contribution and profit

- calculate the break-even point, and margin of safety, and use this information to compare alternative production methods

- understand and explain the concept of limiting factors

- prepare production schedules to ensure maximum profit under conditions where limiting factors are present

- calculate an appropriate selling price for output when spare capacity is available

- prepare an income statement using the contribution approach to format.

## 1 Introduction

1.1 The material covered in this Unit, on cost behaviour and measurement, is essential to understanding some of the thinking which underlies management decisions. It is also essential to the examination, as questions are regularly set covering the topics of break-even analysis and contribution measurement.

1.2 So far in this text, you have viewed costs from the perspective of financial accounting, with costs being regarded as an item to be measured and recorded on the financial statements. In this Unit, we alter the perspective, and begin to look at cost data as a tool to aid management. Using a basic cost classification system the difference between these two viewpoints can be seen more clearly.

# FINANCIAL REPORTING, ANALYSIS AND PLANNING

1.3 Traditionally, many accounting texts split costs down into three classes:

- costs for stock valuation and profit measurement
- costs for decision-making
- costs for control.

1.4 Cost data for valuing stock and computing profit makes use of costs for financial reporting purposes. The other two uses of costs, decision-making and control, have an internal focus, in which cost information is used to help management.

1.5 Ideally, both private sector and public sector managers want to maximise the efficiency of their operations. In the private sector, financial efficiency can be measured in terms of profit. In the public sector, that efficiency is expressed in terms of costs per unit of activity. In both contexts, then, costs are important to assessing financial performance. This unit is concerned with how, exactly, costs can be measured, and how cost information can be used to make decisions which improve performance. We will start by considering the precise nature of the link between cost information and planning and control.

## 2 Costs for planning and control

2.1 If you have ever sat down to plan or budget for the future, you will have realised that actually being able to forecast some of your expenses or income accurately may be difficult. The growth of the market in fixed rate mortgages is evidence that many people prefer some certainty when it comes to planning for the future.

2.2 Business managers face this same problem, but on a larger scale. They need to be able to try and forecast sales volumes, cost levels and profit levels. These forecasts form the basis for the budgets which are discussed in Unit 16 of this book. Over the course of time, the actual sales, cost and profit levels achieved can then be compared with the budgeted figures, and corrective action taken as necessary. This cycle, of preparing a forecast, recording transactions and profit levels achieved, and adjusting the next year's forecast accordingly, is referred to as the planning and control cycle, Figure 14.1.

# COST BEHAVIOUR

*Figure 14.1: The planning and control cycle.*

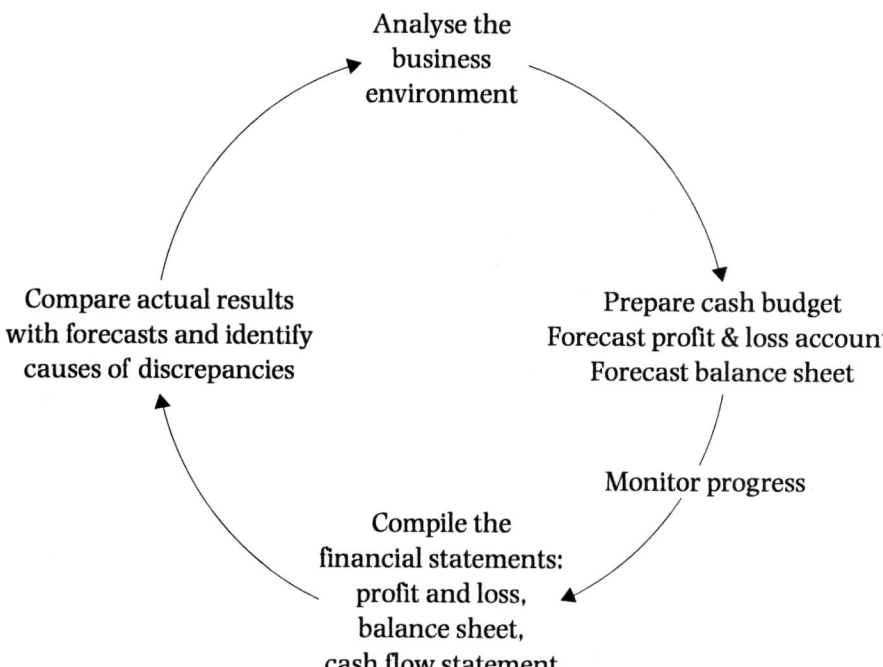

2.3 The diagram clearly shows that the hub of the cycle is decision-making. Plans are made, production is organised, managed, monitored and controlled, and then plans are rewritten in the light of recent experience. Managers need to have information which will help them produce their plans, monitor progress and make the correct decisions to see that targets are achieved.

2.4 The provision of this information is the role of the management accountant, and central to the information is a database of costs. The management accountant draws cost information from this database, according to need. It is fundamental to management accounting that there are different costs for different purposes. The first step towards understanding how costs behave is to differentiate the types of costs which are held in the database and understand their use for particular purposes.

# 3 Historic cost, relevant cost and opportunity cost

**What is cost?**

3.1 At first glance this may seem a ridiculously simple question. Surely cost is how much you have to pay to get something, i.e. purchase cost? On closer inspection, however, the answer may not be quite so straightforward. This is because if you compare management accounting with financial accounting, you realise that they have a different focus in terms of time.

FINANCIAL REPORTING, ANALYSIS AND PLANNING

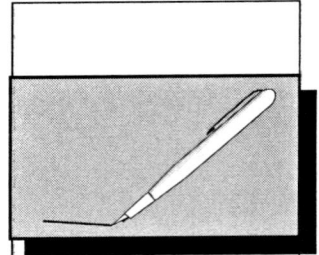

### Student Activity 1

Of the two types of accounting information, financial and management, which has a backward looking, and which has a forward looking focus?

3.2 Intuitively, you can perhaps see that the things that may influence your view of the future may differ from those in the past. In the same way, past costs are not always the same as future costs. What we must consider is how a measure of cost may change depending on the purpose to which the measure is being put. This is best illustrated by the use of a simple example.

**Example 14.1**

An antique dealer has purchased a Georgian bureau at a provincial auction at a cost of £1,500. The bureau needs some minor repair work on it, which the dealer estimates would cost him approximately £250. He estimates that he can sell the bureau, unrepaired, to a London dealer for £1,800. Alternatively, he can undertake the repairs and sell it retail for £2,300.

3.3 The *historic cost* of the bureau is the price which the dealer paid for it. This is also known as a *sunk cost*, indicating that regardless of what decision the dealer takes, he has already spent that money. Nothing can be done about money that has already been spent, and so sunk costs are irrelevant to future decisions. This is a very important principle, which, instinctively, many managers find hard to grasp.

**Relevant costs**

3.4 These are ones which influence the decision being made. In this case, the decision is 'repair or not repair?' To repair involves spending £250 in order to receive £2,300. The alternative is to spend nothing and receive £1,800. The comparative 'profit' of these two options can therefore be summarised as:

Repair 'profit'         = £2,300 – £250 = £2,050

Do not repair 'profit'  = £1,800

Notice that the historic or sunk cost has been irrelevant to the decision. The dealer should undertake the repairs and sell the bureau retail if he wishes to maximise his profit.

3.5 Your instinct might suggest to you that it cannot be 'irrelevant' that the dealer has paid out £1,500 in the first place to buy the bureau. You will see, however, that inserting the information about initial cost does not change the decision, because the price paid is identical in each case. Put another way,

£2,300 – £250 – £1,500 = £550

as opposed to

£1,800 – £1,500         = £300

still leads us to the same conclusion, that repairing the bureau leads to a higher profit.

# COST BEHAVIOUR

3.6 This simple example provides us with some basic but important rules about how to determine which costs are relevant to a decision.

Rule 1: Sunk costs are irrelevant to future decisions.

Rule 2: Costs which remain the same in the future, regardless of which decision is taken, are irrelevant.

Rule 3: The decision should be based on all the remaining costs.

## Opportunity cost

3.7 This is perhaps the most difficult cost concept to grasp. Such costs come from economic thinking, and refer to the cost of the benefit that is lost by being unable to exploit a competing economic opportunity. Opportunity costs affect decisions in that they tell us how much is lost by failing to exploit an opportunity.

**Example 14.2**

Suppose the dealer in Example 14.2 knows that if he has £2,000 to spend, he can buy a picture which he can sell on for £2,500. If he sells the bureau unrepaired, he would not have the cash to buy the picture, and so the opportunity cost of selling the bureau in this condition is zero. If, however, he can collect the repaired-bureau sum of £2,300 and so purchase the picture, he can make even more money. In this case, then, the benefit foregone by failing to sell the bureau in a repaired condition would equal £500, which represents the profit that he could have made from dealing in the picture.

3.8 You can now see that 'cost' has a number of different meanings in management accounting, and this contrasts with financial accounting where it simply equals historic cost: the price paid to obtain an asset. We can now extend the classification of costs a little further, by differentiating between them in terms of how the cost changes as output levels (activity levels) change.

3.9 Before moving on, however, it is a good idea to check your understanding of what has been said so far in this Unit, by working through a detailed example which involves the identification of relevant costs.

**Example 14.3**

The Fancy Furniture Company is trying to decide whether or not to invest in a new piece of production equipment. The new machine is a belt sander, which will reduce production time by 30 minutes per unit, and will give the product a finer finish, allowing a price premium of £0.50 per item to be charged. Current production equals 400 items per week, and the company works a 46 week year.

The machine costs £15,000 to purchase, and has an expected life of five years, and a salvage value of zero at the end of Year 5.

Instead of buying the new machine, Fancy Furniture could spend £15,000 on advertising, which it is expected would draw in additional sales totalling £200,000 over the next five years. The company anticipates that the extra profit generated from these sales will amount to £35,000 (before allowing for

# FINANCIAL REPORTING, ANALYSIS AND PLANNING

the additional advertising expense). These figures are expressed in present value terms, a concept which you will encounter in Unit 15.

- Based on relevant costs, which is the best option for Fancy Furniture?
- Following the rules for deciding the relevant costs:

(1) there are no sunk costs, all the costs under consideration are future costs

(2) the cost of the two alternatives is identical at £15,000, and so is irrelevant to the decision

(3) neither option has any residual value at the end of year 5, and so the salvage value in option 1 is irrelevant

(4) the facts which remain, and are relevant, are as follows:

- the extra profit earned from the purchase of the new sanding machine
- the extra profit generated from the new sales created by the advertising campaign.

Putting numbers against these two alternatives we get:

*Purchase of sander*
Extra profit = 400 × 46 × £0.50 × 5
= £46,000

*New advertising campaign*
Extra profit = £35,000

The conclusion is therefore that Fancy Furniture would be best to spend their money investing in the new sanding machine.

The opportunity cost of choosing to advertise instead of buy the machine, would be £11,000; i.e. the extra profit foregone by failing to take that opportunity.

## 4 Fixed costs and variable costs

**Fixed costs**

4.1 Fixed costs are distinguished from variable costs by the way in which the cost changes when the output/activity level changes. A fixed cost is one which remains constant regardless of changes in the activity level. For example, suppose office premises are rented at a rate of £10,000 per annum. If the office remains closed and unused for the whole year, that rent will still be payable. Equally, the same rent cost will be incurred if the office is fully occupied and utilised for 24 hours per day over the twelve month period.

4.2 It is useful to note that fixed costs are generally charged per time period, and for this reason most textbooks also call them 'period costs'. It is not strictly accurate to say, for example, 'the fixed cost of my employer's liability insurance is £6,000'. Instead, it should be said that ' the fixed cost of my employer's liability insurance is £6,000 per year'.

4.3 The relationship between cost and output is frequently represented by means of a diagram, with the axes marked out as in Figure 14.2.

# COST BEHAVIOUR

**Figure 14.2: Costs and output (framework)**

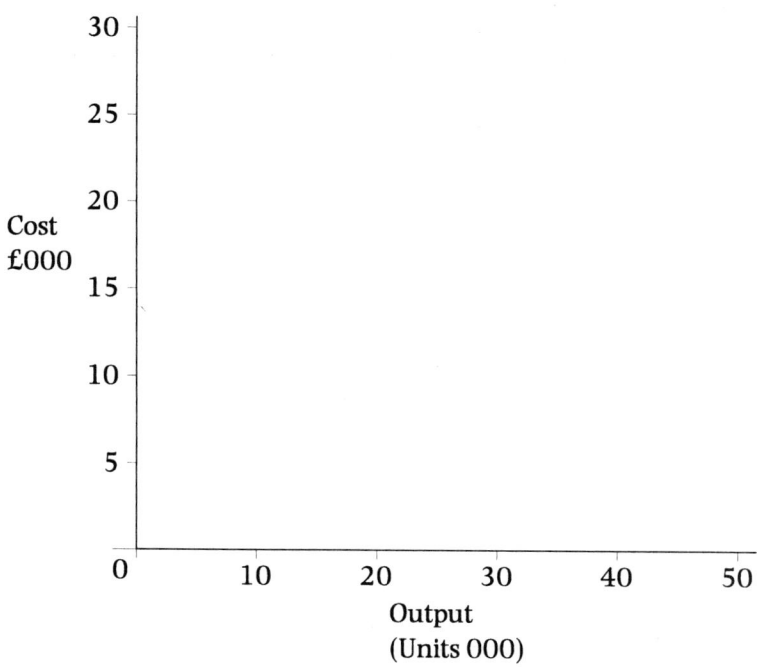

## Student Activity 2

Can you insert on to Figure 14.2 a line representing a fixed cost for office rental of £10,000 per year?

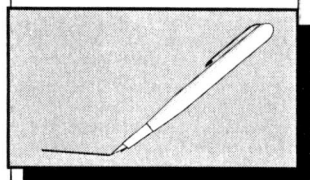

4.4 The idea that the level of output has absolutely no effect on the fixed cost is only true over a limited range of output. Suppose that the office being rented has space for just one occupant, and the business expands to a point where a second member of staff is needed if demand is to be met. The only option, if the orders are to be accepted, is to rent additional office space. At a certain level of turnover, which equals the capacity of the original office space, the fixed costs will rise as rent is paid on two offices. This situation is very common for costs which are related to space, or machinery usage. Plotting this type of fixed cost on to a graph gives us a stepped pattern as shown in Figure 14.3. Hence, such fixed costs are generally termed 'stepped' fixed costs.

FINANCIAL REPORTING, ANALYSIS AND PLANNING

*Figure 14.3: 'Stepped' fixed costs*

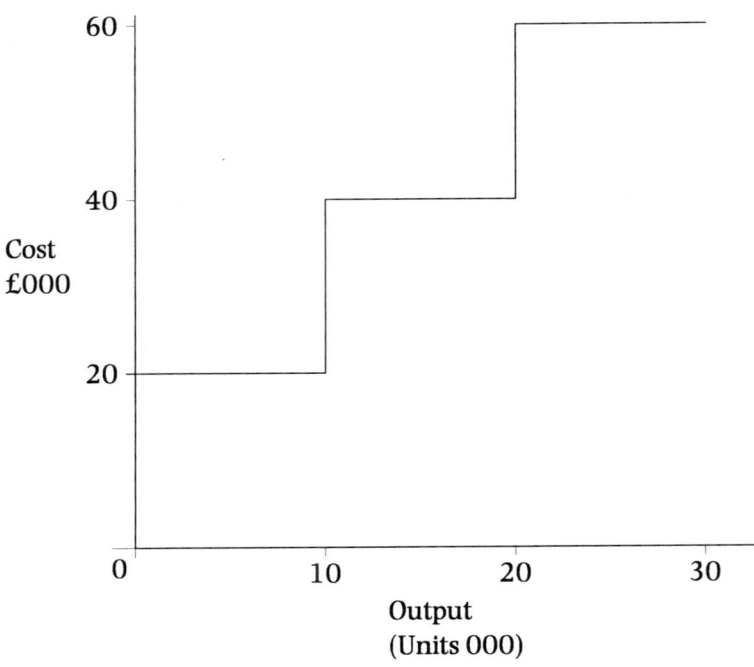

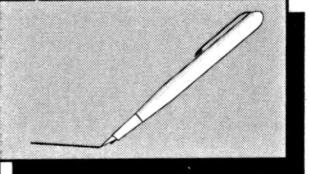

### Student Activity 3

Which of the following fixed costs are likely to follow a stepped pattern in relation to large changes in output levels?

- Packing machine in a CD manufacturing plant.
- Personal computer facilities in a bank.
- Public liability insurance premiums for a bank.
- Telephone line rental in an estate agency.

**Variable costs**

4.5  You can perhaps now guess the definition of variable cost. This is a cost which changes as the level of activity changes. In particular, if there is no output then the variable cost must, by definition, equal zero.

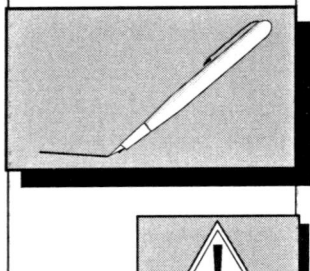

### Student Activity 4

List four costs which arise within the bank where you work, and which you would classify as variable costs.

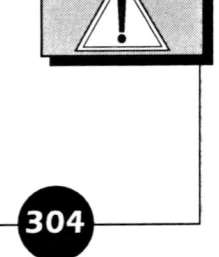

4.6  Variable costs can be expressed as £X,000 for a given output level, or they can be expressed as a cost per unit. The most important thing is that variable costs must always be linked to an output level, be it many units or a single unit.

# COST BEHAVIOUR

4.7 For example, suppose that processing 500 mortgage applications costs a lender an estimated £10,000 in staff costs, and these costs are seen as variable. This gives a cost per application processed of £20. Do not fall into the trap of being careless in your use of terminology. Make it clear which measure you are discussing. (For example, it is not sufficiently precise to say 'variable cost is £10,000'.)

4.8 The way in which variable costs change according to the level of activity will be explored in detail in the next section of this Unit. For the moment, we will assume that as output increases the total variable cost increases. In other words, in the case of the mortgage processing, the cost incurred in processing 1,000 applications will be twice that of processing 500 applications.

4.9 In graphical terms, this means that there is a linear relationship between variable cost and output, as shown in Figure 14.4.

*Figure 14.4: Linear variable costs*

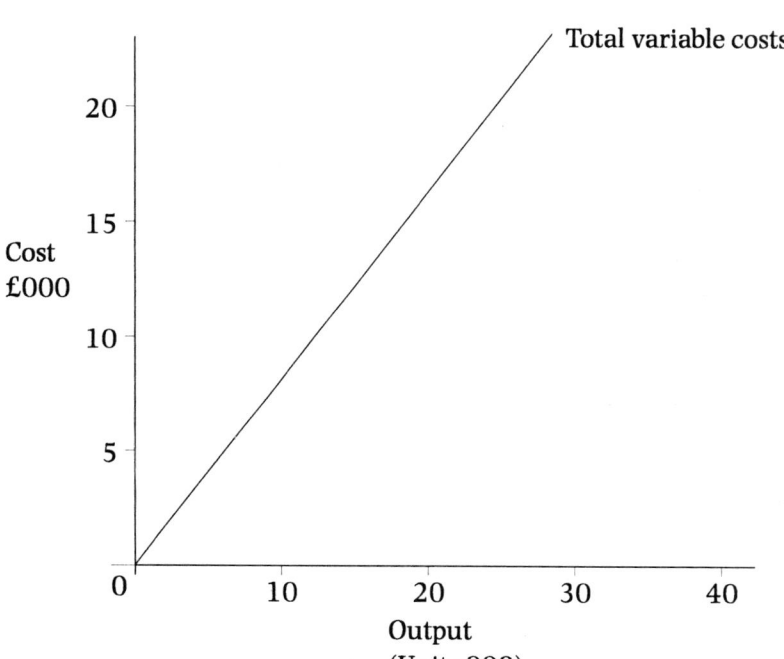

4.10 If a company wants to know what the total cost of producing a given level of output will be, it must combine the information available on fixed and total costs.

### Example 14.4

A mortgage lender estimates that it has total fixed costs of £3.5m per year. This figure covers the cost of office accommodation, business rates, insurance, telephone line rental and staff costs, and a contribution to head office overhead. As fixed costs do not change as output changes, the fixed cost line has an intercept of £3.5m.

In addition, variable costs are incurred as follows. Telephone call costs amounting to £150,000 per year; staff wages of £80,000 to employ temporary clerical help at busy times of the year; and £25,000 postage.

# FINANCIAL REPORTING, ANALYSIS AND PLANNING

Over the course of the year the company has processed 10,000 mortgage applications.

All this information can now be plotted on to a graph, as shown in Figure 14.5.

**Figure 14.5: Total costs**

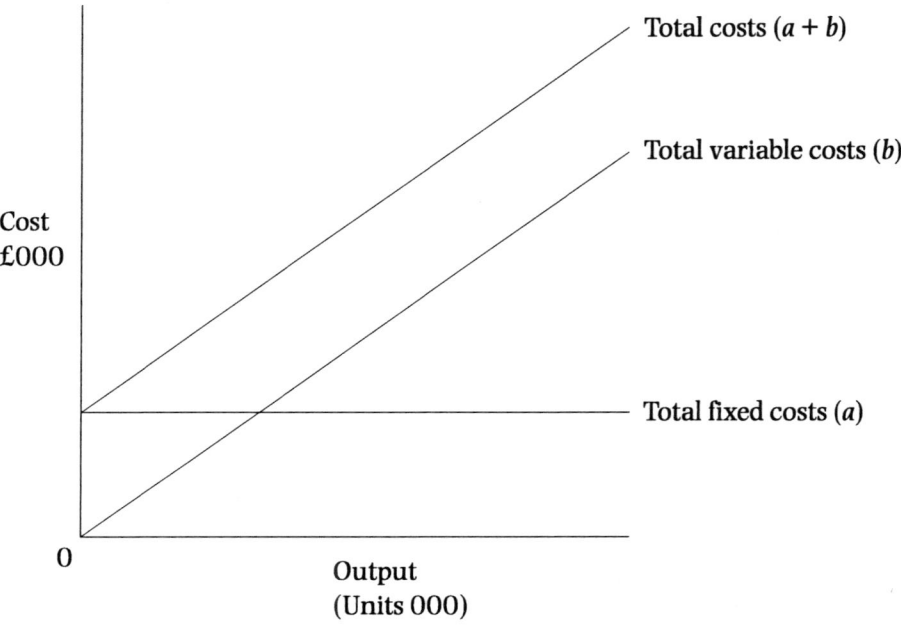

The diagram shows three cost lines:

- total fixed costs
- total variable costs
- total costs.

The total fixed costs, $a$, are shown as a horizontal line, as they do not change with output changes.

The total variable costs, $b$, rise in a linear pattern as output increases. This means that when there are no applications, the variable costs will be zero, but when applications equal 10,000 the sum of all the variable costs equals £255,000. This gives us two points on the graph which can be joined by a straight line, to form the total variable cost line $(a + b)$ in Figure 14.5.

The total cost line is computed by summing the fixed costs and variable costs for each level of activity. Hence at the level of zero applications, only fixed costs are incurred, equal to £3.5m. The intercept of the total cost line is therefore at £3.5m: it can never be less than this amount. When applications are at the level of 10,000, the variable costs are £255,000 and the fixed costs equal £3.5m, giving total costs of £3.755m.

You will see that the total cost line runs parallel with the variable cost line. This will always be the case.

This relationship between the three types of costs can also be expressed as follows:

# COST BEHAVIOUR

Total cost* = Total fixed costs + Total variable costs*

*\* At a specified level of output*

## Contribution

4.11 Cost information, if it is to be used effectively, needs to be linked to information on revenues, so that profit estimates can be made. The most important link is the use of the concept of contribution. If you think about how a bank operates, it is essentially seeking to charge more to customers for lending them money than it pays to depositors for borrowing money. The interest differential is the basis of the bank's profit.

4.12 A big problem for banks in recent years has been that of high fixed costs, associated with extensive branch networks. If a bank has fixed costs of £50m, then it has to find a way of covering them. This is where the concept of contribution comes in. Suppose that the bank generates revenue in interest income of £250m. Over the same period it incurs variable costs of £180m, which includes the interest paid on deposit accounts.

4.13 The contribution is defined as revenue less variable costs, i.e.:

£250m – £180m = £70m

This amounts to a form of profit, which the bank can then use to pay for its fixed costs.

Profit = Contribution – Fixed costs
= £70m – £50m
= £20m

It is easy to see why the term contribution is used: the money is a contribution towards fixed costs and eventual profit.

4.14 This simple idea is of very great importance. If fixed costs remain unchanged by definition, then it can be seen that profit can be increased by raising the contribution.

## Student Activity 5

Can you suggest two ways in which a bank may seek to raise its contribution level?

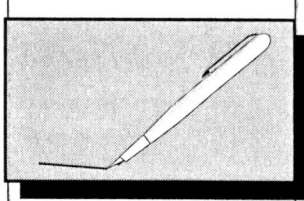

4.15 Looked at quite simply, contribution can be managed and increased either by raising revenue or by reducing variable costs. The increasing use of part-time staff in many companies, and the reduction in overall staffing levels in favour of automated processing are examples of ways in which variable costs can be cut. Bank revenue can be increased in a number of ways. One might be the use of a larger margin between interest paid and interest charged. The failure of institutions to cut the interest rates on credit cards in line with general interest rates is another example.

FINANCIAL REPORTING, ANALYSIS AND PLANNING

4.16 A very important aspect of contribution is that it is possible to predict losses. For example, if fixed costs are £10 million and the contribution is only £5 million then a huge loss is made. In other words, a minimal contribution level can be specified at which neither losses nor profits are made. This is known as the break-even point; it will be discussed in detail later in this unit.

4.17 At this point, we can move on to a more detailed discussion of how both costs and profit change as output increases, before discussing the calculation of break even and its associated computations.

## 5 The impact of changes in output on costs and profit

5.1 In the last section, you have learned that fixed costs do not change as output changes, but that variable costs will alter. We can now elaborate a little on these two key ideas. If costs per unit of production or service provided are being analysed, then the effect of an increase in activity can be dramatic in terms of fixed costs per unit.

**Example 14.5**

Suppose a paints factory had total fixed costs of £2.5m per year. Unit sales for 1996 equal 10m, but this figure is expected to rise to 15m in 1997. It is a straightforward calculation to compute a fixed cost per unit figure.

At 10m sales      = £2.5m/10m
Fixed cost per unit   = £0.25

At 15m sales      = £2.5m/15m
Fixed cost per unit   = £0.17 (rounded to the nearest penny).

In other words, it has been possible to cut the cost per unit by 8 pence or one third of the original fixed cost per unit, simply by increasing output. Of course, it is not easy to sell 50% more in practice but if the opportunity arises then it is a useful way of cutting costs per unit.

5.2 As we have already seen, the total cost per unit is made up of both a fixed and a variable component. So far, in plotting the relationship between the total variable cost and the level of activity as a straight line, we have assumed that the unit variable cost is unchanged regardless of volume. In practice, it is frequently the case that for items such as raw materials, managers will be able to negotiate bulk discounts as activity levels increase. For example, if a building contractor buys sand in 50kg bags, he may pay £6 per 100kg. If he has a job large enough to have sand bulk delivered by volume, he may pay by the cubic yard, which brings the price down to just £4 per 100kg. In this situation, the contractor is able to benefit from economies of scale in purchasing.

5.3 In contrast, some costs may escalate if activity levels rise dramatically. An example of this was the increase in the price of memory chips for PCs because of a shortage of supply relative to demand.

5.4 This leads us to conclude that there is no universal rule about how unit variable cost will change in response to increases in activity levels. The pattern of change will depend upon the specific item in question, and the

# COST BEHAVIOUR

current market conditions for that item. The conditions facing any individual business at any particular time will vary, and cost management involves understanding those conditions and what influences them.

5.5 If we have information about how fixed and variable costs behave in a business, then if this is combined with data relating to sales revenue, it is possible to plot how profit will change as output changes.

**Example 14.6**

Suppose that a fashion retailer has extracted the following information from her accounting records.

| | |
|---|---|
| Shop rental cost | £15,000 per year |
| Business rates | £4,000 per year |
| Business insurance premiums | £1,000 per year |
| Window dressing costs | £800 per year |
| Staff costs (permanent staff) | £26,000 per year |
| Losses by theft | 5% sales receipts |
| Temporary staff costs | 2% sales receipts |
| Packaging (bags) | £0.50 per customer |
| Advertising | 5% sales receipts |
| Purchase cost of clothes | 40% sales value |

The current level of sales in the shop is £150,000 per year, with an average spend of £100 per customer. Next year's sales are expected to equal £180,000, with no significant changes to cost or spending patterns, except for a rise in business rates of 12.5%.

Profit = Total revenue – Total fixed costs – Total variable costs

Armed with this information we can now calculate:

(a) the profit earned in the current year, (before depreciation or tax)

(b) the expected profit next year

(c) the impact on profit of a £1 increase in sales.

## Student Activity 6

Calculate (a), (b) and (c) above.

*Hint:* Before you start:

- classify each of the costs under the heading of fixed or variable
- calculate the total fixed cost
- find the relationship between total variable cost (TVC) and revenue, e.g. TVC = 0.6 revenue.

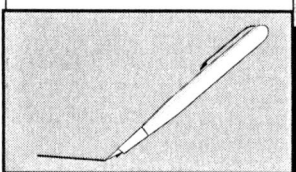

5.6 The relationship between changes in activity rates and profit is very important. It is the starting point for break-even analysis.

FINANCIAL REPORTING, ANALYSIS AND PLANNING

## 6 Break-even analysis

6.1 The shopkeeper in Student Activity 6 did not have too much of a problem, as she was in a marketplace in which she foresaw increasing sales. Many businesses, especially in the late 1980s and early 1990s faced the opposite: a future of declining sales. In such a situation it is very important to know the break-even value of sales. Break even is simply the sales level at which there is neither a loss nor a profit.

6.2 *If*     Profit = Total revenue − Total fixed costs − Total variable costs,

*then,*   Profit = Zero

*when*   Total revenue = Total fixed costs + Total variable costs

*or,*     Total revenue − Total variable costs = Total fixed costs

### Student Activity 7

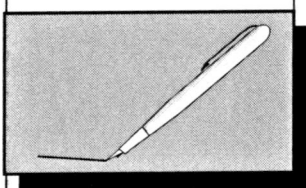

Can you recall the name given to the value of total revenue less total *variable* costs?

6.3 When contribution is just sufficient to meet the fixed costs, the business will break even.

**Example 14.7**

A sandwich shop estimates that it makes an average contribution of 20p on every £1 sandwich sold. The shop's fixed costs amount to £1,500 per month. How many sandwiches must be sold before the shop breaks even?

The answer can be calculated as follows:

Total revenue = £$x$, where $x$ is the unknown number of sandwiches, sold at £1 each

To break even, the shop must be in the following position,

£$x$ = £1,500 + £0.8$x$.
Or,
£$x$ − £0.8$x$ = £1,500.

Therefore,
£0.2$x$ = £1,500.

In other words,
£$x$ = £7,500.

At a selling price of £1 per sandwich, the shop must therefore sell 7,500 per month to break even.

6.4 The final equation in the example, i.e. 0.2$x$ = £1,500, can be rewritten in words as:

Unit contribution multiplied by volume equals fixed costs.

# COST BEHAVIOUR

The answer to the equation is then a monetary value, which represents the sales revenue needed to break even over the course of one month.

## Student Activity 8

Suppose the cost of sandwich fillings increases and the shop now finds that the contribution per sandwich is reduced to 12p.

What is the new break even level of sales, both in terms of value and number of sandwiches?

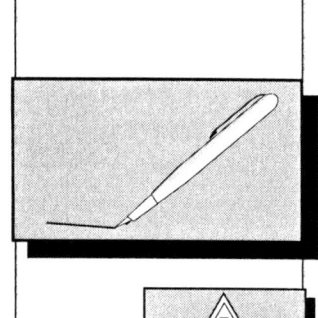

6.5  You should have found that the effect of the reduction in unit contribution was an increase in the break-even level of sales. This is a vitally important piece of information, and gives us an important rule of thumb: the higher the contribution per unit, all other things being equal, the lower the break-even level of sales.

6.6  Suppose, now, that the shop experiences an increase in its fixed costs to £2,000 per month. At a contribution level of 20p per sandwich, this will give a break-even level of sales equal to £10,000 per month. This gives us a second simple rule: the higher the fixed costs, all other things being equal, the higher the break-even point.

**Margin of safety**

6.7  If the shop is selling £15,000 worth of sandwiches per month, and has a break even of £10,000, then it can be said to be fairly certain of being able to maintain its profitability. If sales are only equal to £11,000, however, with the same break-even level, then it only needs a small drop in sales to be at risk of making losses.

6.8  The difference between the current (or anticipated) sales revenue and the break-even level can be expressed in terms of a margin of safety.

Total sales – Break-even sales = Margin of safety

This is commonly presented in percentage form, that is,

Total sales – Break-even sales/Total sales = % Margin of safety

6.9  Using the numbers given above, at sales of £15,000 per month,

Margin of safety = 15,000 – 10,000/15,000 = 33.33%.

In other words, the shop could experience a sales drop of one third before it risked making no profit at all.

## Student Activity 9

Calculate the margin of safety if the sales level is £11,000, with break even at £10,000.

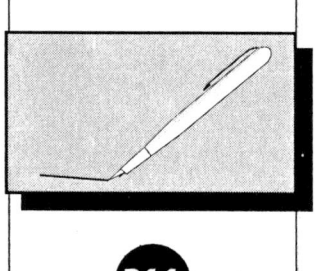

FINANCIAL REPORTING, ANALYSIS AND PLANNING

6.10 We can see that a high margin of safety is a good idea if possible! What is more, the greater the volatility of the marketplace, the greater the need for a high margin of safety.

**Uses of break-even analysis**

6.11 Apart from being a tool to measure the point at which a business might be at risk of making losses, break even is important as a tool for comparison of different opportunities, and so is an aid to decision making.

**Example 14.8**

An architect is trying to choose between purchasing some computer aided design software costing £2,000, or replacing his computer at a cost of £5,000. Assume a useful economic life of one year only for both items and zero salvage value at the end of the year.

The effect on sales (over the next 12 months) of the two options is as follows.

Purchase of new software: new contracts worth £1,000 each, with variable costs of £800 per contract.

Purchase of new computer: new contracts with an average value of £1,200 and contribution of £400.

Calculate the break-even number of new contracts needed for each of the two purchase options.

The formula for break even when buying the software is:

£0.2$x$ = £2,000
    £$x$ = £10,000
        = 10 contracts.

The formula for the computer is:

£400/1,200$x$ = £5,000
         £$x$ = £15,000
             = 12.5 contracts.

Assuming a world in which it was equally difficult to obtain either type of contract, the architect should opt to buy the software. He needs to generate less new business to break even than he does if he buys the computer. The lesson here is – select the option which has the lowest break even. Usually, the higher the capital cost, i.e. fixed cost, the higher the break even, as we have already seen.

6.12 If the architect is a pessimist, and wants to break even at the lowest possible level, he will opt to buy the software. Another way of viewing the decision, however, might be to ask 'at what level do the two alternatives generate equal profit?' This is a topic which has arisen in a number of past exam questions, and which you should feel confident to handle.

# COST BEHAVIOUR

## 7 The problem of limiting factors, or scarce resources

7.1 So far, we have assumed that businesses are making decisions in a world in which resources are freely available and the only point at issue is how to maximise profit. In practice, the world is more complex, and companies have to make decisions in the knowledge that a key resource, e.g. labour, may be in scarce supply. We need to extend the rules for financial decision making to encompass a world of scarce resources. Frequently, it is shortage of a factor of production which acts as a constraint on whether a business can sell, rather than the unwillingness of the market to buy.

7.2 Recalling basic economic theory, you may remember that the factors of supply are land, labour raw materials and capital. Any one of these resources may be available in limited supply, and so serve to restrict production levels. In such a situation, the company will maximise its profit by maximising the contribution *per unit* of the scarce resource. This is best illustrated using a simple numerical example.

**Example 14.9**

A brewery bottles three different types of beer, classified by strength, for which the cost, selling and contribution schedules are given below.

|  | Beer A (low alcohol) | Beer B (average) | Beer C (strong) |
|---|---|---|---|
| Selling price (per bottle) | £1.20 | £1.00 | £1.50 |
| Variable costs (per bottle) | £0.60 | £0.50 | £0.60 |
| Contribution (per bottle) | £0.60 | £0.50 | £0.90 |

If the company were to try and maximise its profit with unlimited resources, it would therefore concentrate on producing the strong beer, which offers the highest unit contribution. Suppose, however, that producing Beer C requires more brewing time, and the supply of fermenting casks is restricted.

Let us suppose that the relative time taken in casks by each of the three beers is as follows:

| Beer A | 8 days  | Annual demand = 500,000 units |
| Beer B | 7 days  | Annual demand = 800,000 units |
| Beer C | 14 days | Annual demand = 700,000 units |

One cask is sufficient to brew 500 units.

There is a total of 3,500 casks available per year. The company must now allocate the cask time between the beers in the most profitable manner, a process which involves a series of separate calculations.

The first step is to calculate the contribution per unit of the limited factor.

Beer A earns £0.6/8     = £0.075 per bottle per day in the cask
Beer B earns £0.50/7     = £0.071 per bottle per day in the cask
Beer C earns £0.90/14    = £0.064 per bottle per day in the cask

This means that the most profitable use of the scarce cask time lies in brewing the low alcohol beer, and not the strong beer as was originally indicated.

# FINANCIAL REPORTING, ANALYSIS AND PLANNING

The next step is then to apportion the available cask time in the most profitable manner, taking into account the demand for the product.

Total annual cask capacity = 3,500 × 500 units
= 1.75m units

Cask profitability ranking is as follows:

Beer A, Beer B, Beer C.

Production plan to maximise profit is thus,

Beer A    500,000 units
Beer B    800,000 units

The balance of the capacity, i.e. 450,000 units can then be used to brew Beer C. This means that in relation to market demand, Beer C will be in short supply, but at the same time the brewery will be maximising its total contribution, and hence maximising its profit.

Contribution at the optimal production levels:

500,000 × £0.075 + 800,000 × £0.071 + 450,000 × £0.064

Total contribution = £123,100.

Any other mix of brewing would generate a lower overall contribution.

7.3  The lesson to be learned from the above exercise is that good management requires an understanding of the relative scarcity of resources, and the decisions which make the best use of those scarce resources. Bottlenecks hold up production and lead to the loss of sales, so production schedules need to be designed in such a way as to avoid such stumbling blocks without putting profit in jeopardy.

## 8  Decision making under conditions of spare capacity

8.1  Understanding how to maximise contribution and profit when spare capacity is available requires the use of relevant costs. Suppose an upholsterer sells armchairs for £400 each, and the variable costs per chair are £200 each. A customer wants to buy one of the chairs but offers just £300. Should the upholsterer accept the offer? The answer is that it depends on his current level of production compared to his capacity production.

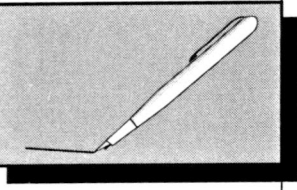

### Student Activity 10

In your place of work do you think that current activity levels are equal to, above or below capacity? Is the position constant throughout the year?

8.2  If the upholsterer has a waiting list of customers, all of whom are prepared to pay the full price, there is no reason for him to accept the order. On the

# COST BEHAVIOUR

other hand, if he is sitting idle with plenty of spare capacity, then accepting £300 will at least contribute £100 towards his fixed costs.

8.3 The lesson from this is that when there is spare capacity present, a business should accept orders which have a minimum selling price just above the variable costs of production. As long as variable costs are more than covered, then there is some contribution to fixed costs. If such orders are not accepted, that additional contribution is forfeited.

## Student Activity 11

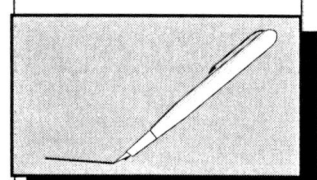

The day before its scheduled departure date, an airline has 10 seats available on a flight from London to New York. The normal ticket price is £399, and the associated variable costs are estimated at £220. A customer comes in to request a late booking 'bargain fare'. What is the lowest price which the airline should charge for the ticket?

## 9 Income statements: a contribution based approach

9.1 This Unit has shown you how to make decisions relating to volume of production and also product mix, which are based around the concept of contribution. Ultimately, the purpose of any business decision is to add to profit. This means that it is useful to know how to present the impact of any such decisions in terms of profit changes. The income statement which is easiest to use in this context, differs from the ordinary profit and loss account of financial accounting, because it focuses on contribution rather than total costs and revenues.

9.2 Let us continue the example of the brewery which we discussed in the context of limiting factors.

**Example 14.9 continued**

In section 7 we showed that the optimal production mix, given the limited cask brewing capacity, was as shown below:

Beer A 500,000 units
Beer B 800,000 units
Beer C 450,000 units

Let us now assume that the brewery faces fixed costs of £80,000 per year.

The decision was taken by ranking the products in terms of their contribution per unit of the limited cask facility. This means that the profit statement can be presented in terms of contribution, instead of a detailed cost breakdown.

The layout would look something like the one shown on the next page.

# FINANCIAL REPORTING, ANALYSIS AND PLANNING

|  | Beer A | Beer B | Beer C | Total |
|---|---|---|---|---|
| Contribution per unit | £0.075 | 0.071 | £0.064 | |
| Cask time per unit | 8 days | 7 days | 14 days | |
| Ranking (per unit of cask time) | 1 | 2 | 3 | |
| Market demand | 0.5m units | 0.8m units | 0.7m units | 2m units |
| Production scheduled | 0.5m units | 0.8m units | 0.45m units | 1.75m units |
| Contribution | £37,500 | £56,800 | £28,800 | £123,100 |
| *less* | | | | |
| Fixed costs | | | | £80,000 |
| Net profit | | | | £43,100 |

9.3 You should practise this form of presentation as it does occur quite frequently in exam questions. You also need to be able to make brief comments on the statement, e.g. on the differences in unit contribution per limiting factor. As part of this practice, try doing the past exam question at the end of the Unit.

9.4 This Unit has covered a great deal of material and you may well find that you will need to reread certain sections before you fully understand the linkages between all the topics. Exam questions may cover any mix of the topics covered in this Unit, but the most frequently examined area is break-even analysis. Make sure that you are competent at calculating break-even point and explaining what the results mean. Having read this Unit you are now in a much better position to understand how sensible are the decisions of some of the bank's commercial customers.

# COST BEHAVIOUR

> **Summary**
>
> Now you have studied this Unit you should be able to:
>
> - [ ] explain why knowledge of cost behaviour is essential to planning and control
> - [ ] understand and explain the difference between historic cost, relevant cost, and opportunity cost
> - [ ] identify and give examples of fixed costs and variable costs, and explain the significance of the concept of contribution
> - [ ] calculate the effect of a change in activity level upon total costs, total fixed costs per unit, total contribution and profit
> - [ ] calculate the break-even point, and margin of safety, and use this information to compare alternative production methods
> - [ ] understand and explain the concept of limiting factors
> - [ ] prepare production schedules to ensure maximum profit under conditions where limiting factors are present
> - [ ] calculate an appropriate selling price for output when spare capacity is available
> - [ ] prepare an income statement using the contribution approach to format.

## Self assessment questions

**Examination questions**

1. Zenith Ltd manufactures three products—A, B and C—in one of its departments.

   |                                   | A    | B    | C    |
   |-----------------------------------|------|------|------|
   | Sales price per unit              | £21  | £30  | £26  |
   | Variable cost per unit            | £11  | £12  | £21  |
   | Hours of skilled labour per unit  | 4    | 9    | 1    |
   | Machine hours per unit            | 8    | 3    | 5    |
   | Monthly sales capacity (units)    | 700  | 300  | 800  |

   The monthly fixed costs of the department amount to £3,000.

   **Required**

   (a) Explain what you understand by the terms:

   (i) contribution;

   (ii) limiting factor. [4]

   (b) Calculate the contribution per unit of limiting factor' for each of the products manufactured by Zenith Ltd assuming the limiting factor is:

(i) skilled labour;

(ii) machine hours. [6]

(c) Prepare a statement showing planned production and estimated profit for one month, assuming that the company is able to engage sufficient skilled labour to work 1,400 hours. [4]

(d) Prepare a statement showing planned production and estimated profit for one month, assuming the number of machine hours available is 1,140. [4]

(e) Comment briefly on the production plan prepared under (d). [2]

[Total-20]

2. The research department of Ohlson Ltd is going to develop a new product at a cost of £500,000. There is known to be a strong demand for the product and this demand will last for five years and then collapse because of forecast technological change. The product can be manufactured in either of two ways which would give rise to the following costs and related data:

|  | Method I | Method II |
|---|---|---|
| Plant: cost | £1,000,000 | £2,500,000 |
| physical life | 8 years | 7 years |
| expected residual value | zero | zero |
| Working capital requirements | £250,000 | £200,000 |
| Variable cost per unit | £800 | £700 |
| Fixed costs per annum, other than depreciation and development expenditure | £300,000 | £510,000 |
| Development expenditure (referred to above) | £500,000 | £500,000 |

The new product will be sold for £1,000 per unit. The maximum production capacity is 6,000 units per annum under either method. The sales director is confident that the company will be able to sell all the items produced. The finance director disagrees and points out that the company rarely manages to operate at more than 90% of total capacity and that, anyway, the company is unlikely to be able to sell more than 5,000 units per annum.

**Required**

(a) Outline the nature and purpose of break even analysis. [5]

(b) For Method I and Method II, separate calculations of:

(i) the annual break even point in units;

(ii) the annual level of sales, in units, required to produce a return of 20% per annum on the original investment;

(iii) the annual profit, assuming maximum production. [13]

(c) A full discussion of the alternative production methods, using your calculations under (b) and any others you consider appropriate. [12]

[Total 30]

# COST BEHAVIOUR

# Unit 15

## Capital Investment Appraisal

### Objectives

When you have completed your study of this Unit you should be able to:

- explain how investment appraisal forms part of the planning and control process

- identify the key characteristics of capital investment

- determine the payback period of an investment

- calculate the rate of return on an investment using the ARR formula

- explain the techniques of compounding and discounting

- use information on the cost of capital and the cash flows associated with an investment to calculate a net present value and an internal rate of return

- describe and explain the non-financial factors which influence investment decisions.

## 1 Introduction

1.1 In this Unit the concept of investment appraisal is introduced. Companies purchase new capital equipment on a regular basis, either to expand their operations or simply to replace outdated equipment. As with any investment, the new equipment must earn a return for the business, and the methods of investment appraisal outlined in this Unit offer alternative methods for the calculation of that return.

1.2 The Unit links back to topics covered in the financial reporting section of this manual.

All financial reports include a balance sheet which records the value of the fixed assets held by a business. Investment appraisal is concerned with the renewal and replacement of those fixed assets.

The financial reports also include a cash flow statement, and the purchase of any large item of equipment will result in a change in both inward and outward cash flows.

# FINANCIAL REPORTING, ANALYSIS AND PLANNING

1.3 We can therefore see that investment decisions have an effect on the financial reports. The appraisal process is an internal, management accounting issue, but it has external, financial reporting implications.

## 2 Investment appraisal and planning and control

2.1 You will recall that a fixed asset is defined as any asset that has a useful life that extends beyond a single accounting period. This definition is very broad, and can encompass anything from computer software, which has a life span of just a few years, to an office building which may have a useful life of several hundred. No business will wish to invest money in long life assets unless they can be fairly certain that they have a use for them. The purchase decision is therefore linked to the plans of the business. It is useful to look at this in terms of a pyramid of decisions.

**The decision pyramid**

2.2 Financial reports provide external investors (and others) with information on how well a business is performing in financial terms. Investors will be seeking a particular rate of return on their investment and, if it is not forthcoming, they have the option to sell their shares and invest elsewhere. The first element in the decision pyramid thus involves being able to answer the question: 'What return is required by our investors?'

2.3 A return for investors is earned by generating a profit on turnover and, all else remaining constant, it should be true that the higher the turnover the higher the profit available to investors. Armed with information on its gross and net profit margins, a company can work out the level of turnover required in order to generate a target profit figure. For example, Company X wants to earn a profit of £50,000 next year, and it knows that it earns a net margin of 12.5% on sales.

Next year's sales therefore need to equal £50,000/12.5% = £400,000

If tax at a rate of 40% was payable on those profits, and the company wanted to earn £50,000 post tax profit, the required sales figure would be £50,000/[(1 – 0.4) × 0.125] = £666,666.

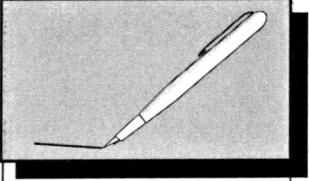

### Student Activity 1

The LMT Company knows that its shareholders expect it to report a figure of £1.25m for profit attributable to equity in the next financial year. LMT earns a net margin of 8% on sales, and has no debt in its capital structure. This means that all the net profit goes to shareholders, after payment of corporation tax at a rate of 40%.

*Required:*

Estimate the target turnover required for the shareholders to receive the desired £1.25 million.

# CAPITAL INVESTMENT APPRAISAL

2.4 At this stage in the planning process the company has a target level of sales. It now needs to answer another question in the decision pyramid: What assets (fixed and variable) are needed to generate the required sales level?

2.5 This involves capital asset planning. It is quite possible that the company finds that it needs to purchase more production equipment, or computers, or office space. In such a situation, the proposed capital purchase will be subjected to an investment appraisal. It is vital to ensure that assets purchased generate a return at least equal to the cost of the funds used to purchase them. Otherwise the business will lose money on the investment. This is easier to understand if you put some numbers into the story.

2.6 Suppose a bank invests in an ATM machine for inside the branch, and the machine is paid for by using short term loan finance at a cost of 7%. If the savings generated by the machine equate to earning a return of just 6%, then the equipment has 'cost' 1% more than it has earned. That cost will lead to a drop in the reported profit of the bank. It is vital to ensure that a system exists to compare the expected returns earned by a capital investment, with the expected costs of that investment. This is the purpose of investment appraisal analysis.

2.7 Of course, the expected returns on any individual investment may not be achieved, or they may be more than achieved. As part of the planning and control cycle, then, it is important to operate a system involving a regular review of current investments, which compares actual returns with both expected returns and costs. In this way, weak investments can be liquidated, and the resulting cash invested elsewhere in the business.

2.8 The way in which investment appraisal fits in to the planning and control process can be usefully summarised using a diagram such as Figure 15.1.

**Figure 15.1: Investment appraisal and the planning and control cycle**

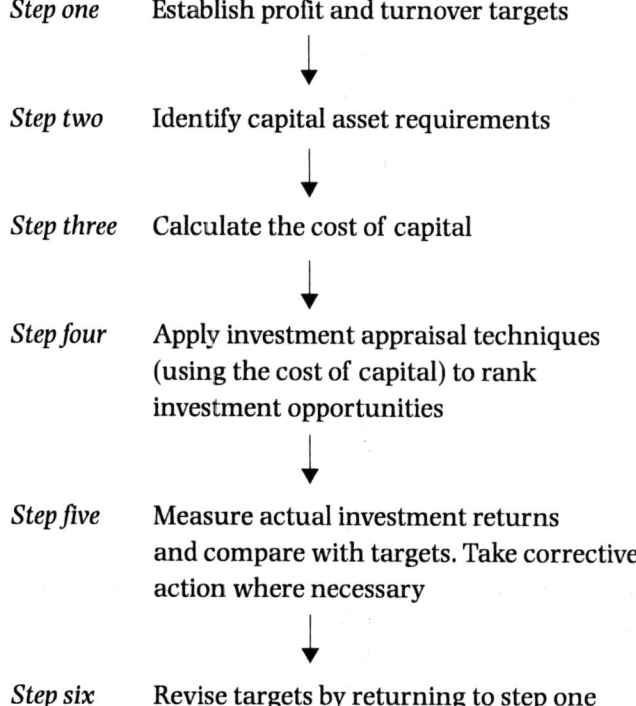

*Step one*     Establish profit and turnover targets

*Step two*     Identify capital asset requirements

*Step three*     Calculate the cost of capital

*Step four*     Apply investment appraisal techniques (using the cost of capital) to rank investment opportunities

*Step five*     Measure actual investment returns and compare with targets. Take corrective action where necessary

*Step six*     Revise targets by returning to step one

# FINANCIAL REPORTING, ANALYSIS AND PLANNING

## 3 Characteristics of capital investments

3.1 A common feature of all capital investment decisions is that they involve payment now for an asset which will generate returns in the future. There is thus a time difference between an investment being paid for, and when the returns are generated. What is more, the initial outlay is often very large, while the returns come in the form of smaller sums received regularly over an extended period of time. In making an investment decision, therefore, companies need to be able to take account of the effect of time on the value of money. Adjusting for changes in the value of money over time complicates the decision process and is dealt with via discounting, a topic which is covered later in this unit.

3.2 A second important characteristic of investment decisions is that they involve the purchase of assets which have a life extending beyond a single accounting period. You will recall that such fixed assets need to be valued for inclusion in the balance sheet, and the valuation process may include the computation of depreciation. Remember that not all assets (e.g. land) depreciate in value. The balance sheet value of any fixed asset is its value after deduction of depreciation, where appropriate. This means that investment appraisal techniques need to be capable of calculating the return on two types of investments:

- non-depreciable assets
- depreciable assets.

3.3 A third important characteristic is that the sums involved in capital investments tend to be large. This means that if a bad decision is made, the cash flow effects on the business could prove very serious, and affect its ability to continue trading. For this reason it is essential that a standardised procedure for assessing capital purchases is in place.

3.4 Lastly, it is not always easy for a company to 'escape' from a bad investment. Capital investments such as stocks or land and buildings may be easily saleable in the right market conditions. Other investments, such as specialised production or processing machinery may have very low or non-existent second hand values. In such instances, the investing company will incur huge writing-off losses if it pulls out of the investment.

3.5 Thus the characteristics of capital investments are such that it is vital that businesses take their investment decisions with care. The consequences of inappropriate investments can prove dire for the business.

3.6 Suppose, for example, that the central planning division of a major clearing bank decided that very substantial levels of new retail business could be attained by a major expansion of the branch network. As a result the bank invested in a huge number of new retail sites, while paying little attention to the choice of location. Within a few years it becomes clear that location is as important to generating business as the absolute number of branches, and that a high proportion of the newly opened branches are loss making. The bank therefore decides to close them again, and seeks to sell the sites. The net effect of this sequence of events is that in the year of sale there are large write offs in the profit and loss account. This is not dissimilar to the experience of recent years, where a number of banks and financial institutions have made large losses when investing heavily in the retail estate agency business, only to find that they are pulling out again a few years later.

# 4 Calculation of payback periods

4.1 The cautious investor will always be aware of how long it might take to get his or her money back, and it is this concern which underlies the calculation of a payback period. Taking into account the fact that 'a bird in the hand is worth two in the bush', then the sooner that the original sum invested is recouped the better. The payback period can therefore be defined as the length of time required before the investor receives back the full value of the sum invested.

**Example 15.1**

A new note-counting machine costs £5,000. The estimated savings in staff time from using the machine are as follows:

Year 1    £2,000

Year 2    £2,000

Year 3    £1,500

Year 4    £1,500

Year 5ff  £1,000

Assume that all cash flows are received evenly throughout the course of a year.

The payback period can be calculated by adding the yearly savings until the cumulative sum equals the value of the original investment, i.e. £5,000.

In this case, then, the bank has received back the value of its original investment sometime during Year 3. At the start of Year 3 returns to date equalled £4,000, but by the end of that year they equalled £5,500.

To find exactly when in the year the payback figure was reached we need to use the assumption that the Year 3 cash flows of £1,500 arrived evenly throughout the year. In other words, it would have taken two-thirds of Year 3, or eight months, to have earned an additional £1,000. This means that the cumulative return of £5,000 was reached after three years and eight months. Hence the payback period for this investment is three years and eight months.

**Payback formula**

4.2 You may find it easier to calculate payback using the simple formula:

$$\text{Payback period} = \frac{\text{Net sum invested}}{\text{Net annual cash inflow}}$$

This formula can only be used, however, when the annual cash flows are a constant amount.

# FINANCIAL REPORTING, ANALYSIS AND PLANNING

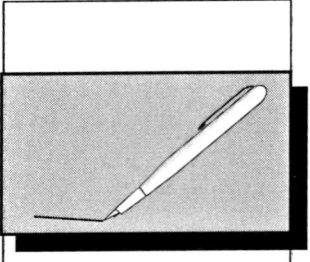

### Student Activity 2

Low Street Bank has found that in recent years its customer use of the branch network has been declining, as increasing use is made of ATM machines and the bank's telephone banking service. As a result the bank is considering alternative courses of action.

The first option is to reduce the opening hours of the branches by one hour per day. If this is done there will be cost savings of £4,000 per annum in each of the bank's 500 branches. To ensure no reduction in customer service level, however, the bank would need to invest in 45 ATM machines for installation at all those branches currently lacking this facility. ATM machines cost £100,000 each.

The second option is to maintain the existing opening hours, but make 10% of the counter staff redundant. This would generate a reduction in wage costs equal to £1.5m per annum. The resulting reduction in customer service provision would be compensated for by investing in 50 'in bank' ATM's at a cost of £100,000 each.

Using payback period as the criteria, which of the two options should be selected?

### The limitations of payback period as a basis for selection of investments

4.3  The illustration in Student Activity 2 demonstrates the simplicity of the payback approach to investment appraisal. Needless to say, however, the simplicity of the approach means that it also has some drawbacks.

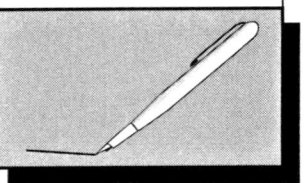

### Student Activity 3

Think about the sort of information that is contained in the payback period. Is it enough for you to decide whether an investment is worthwhile, and if not, what information is missing?

4.4  One of the problems of using payback periods to determine investment decisions can be seen by looking at the pattern of cash flows associated with each of the two options that faced Low Street Bank. Under option 1 the bank would receive cash inflows (savings) of £2m per year, compared with £1.5m under option 2. Of course, the actual investment required under the two options is not identical, but cash is recovered much quicker under the first alternative.

4.5  Unfortunately, payback period takes no account of the timing of cash flows, as it is only concerned with the cumulative speed of payback. This can mean that problems arise if cash flow patterns arising from two mutually exclusive investments are dissimilar. This is best illustrated by means of a specific example.

### Example 15.2

Jeronimo Bank is thinking of investing in a new risk management software system at a cost of £150,000. Estimated savings attributable to using the software are as follows.

# CAPITAL INVESTMENT APPRAISAL

| Year | Savings |
|---|---|
| 1 | £75,000 |
| 2 | £50,000 |
| 3 | £25,000 |
| 4 | £25,000 |
| 5–7 | £25,000 |

Instead of buying the risk management software, the bank could buy laptops for all its staff involved in dealing with investments by high net-worth clients. The laptops would cost a total of £150,000 and could be expected to generate commission earnings as follows.

| Year | Commission revenue |
|---|---|
| 1 | £95,000 |
| 2 | £35,000 |
| 3 | £20,000 |
| 4–9 | £15,000 |

In such a situation, the payback period for each of the two options is a follows:

### Purchase of risk management software

Payback period = Period required to generate £150,000
= 3 years

### Purchase of laptops

In this case the sum to be recouped is again £150,000.
The time taken to recoup this sum is also three years.

4.6 Using the payback period as the criterion for investment, therefore, an investor would be indifferent between the two choices. In practice, however, this is unlikely as the pattern of cash flows favours the laptop option. In this instance £95,000, or almost two thirds of the investment, is recovered within a year, as compared with just £75,000 under the software option.

4.7 In reality, if a finance director was asked if he or she would prefer to receive money sooner rather than later, the reply would inevitably be sooner. This means that an important shortcoming of the payback approach to investment is that it ignores the timing of cash flows during the payback period.

4.8 When you think that investment is undertaken to earn a return, it is easy to see that payback periods contain no information about net returns on an investment. Knowing how long you have to wait to get your money back is a very basic way of measuring the time period over which an investor is exposed to risk, but the overall final return on an investment is also of interest.

4.9 The payback period approach to investment appraisal totally ignores the cash flows that arise *after* the initial investment has been recouped. In this sense, it takes a very short term perspective on the problem of selecting investments. This is unfortunate as investments have potentially long term cash flow effects which are ignored when payback period is used.

FINANCIAL REPORTING, ANALYSIS AND PLANNING

4.10 This limitation of the payback period approach can again be illustrated by the use of an example.

**Example 15.2 continued**

Taking the figures given above for the Jeronimo Bank, we can see how the pattern of cash flows differs between the two investments once payback has been achieved.

As before, the payback period is exactly three years for each of the investment options, but *after* year three, the expected cash flows are as follows.

***Software option***

Years 4–7 inclusive, £25,000 per annum = £100,000 in total

***Laptop option***

Years 4–9 inclusive, £15,000 per annum = £90,000 in total

On this basis, the risk management alternative looks the more attractive.

4.11 Unfortunately, as already indicated, payback periods ignore all the post-payback cash flows and so the difference of £10,000 highlighted above would be irrelevant. This is despite the fact that such cash flows represent part of the return on the investment. Hence the payback approach cannot be regarded as a measure of the comparative profitability of different investments. Needless to say, this limits the usefulness of this method of investment appraisal.

4.12 The final problem associated with payback is one that has already been mentioned in passing: it ignores the timing of cash flows and so takes no account of the time value of money. In the case of Jeronimo Bank £25,000 received in Year 7 has the same value as £25,000 received in Year 4. Clearly, economic reality and the impact of inflation means that this is not true in practice. Instead, what is required is a method of selecting investments which takes account of the aggregate returns over the whole life of an investment and which adjusts for the time value of money.

## 5 Using accounting rate of return to make investment decisions

5.1 As indicated above, it is useful to be able to calculate the overall rate of return on an investment and this is the logic that underpins the accounting rate of return approach. In many ways it is analogous to the return on capital employed approach to the analysis of financial statements.

5.2 Given that an investment is expected to generate profits, the ARR calculates return by comparing the average profit on the investment with the average sum invested. This investment appraisal approach is unique in that it concentrates on profits rather than cash flows.

5.3 The ARR method of calculation is best expressed in algebraic form:

# CAPITAL INVESTMENT APPRAISAL

$$ARR = \frac{\text{Average profit per year } \textit{(after depreciation)} \times 100\%}{\text{Average sum invested}}$$

The ARR is made up of two component parts, each of which require separate calculation.

## Average profit per year

5.4 The average profit per year is calculated by taking the sum of the annual profits (after charging depreciation) and dividing it by the number of years in the investment's life. Note that we are only interested in the profit change which results from making this specific investment.

### Example 15.3

Initial investment cost equals £50,000 and the scrap value in Year 5 is zero.

| Year | Incremental revenues | Incremental costs | Profit |
|---|---|---|---|
| 1 | £60,000 | £45,000 | £15,000 |
| 2 | £65,000 | £40,000 | £25,000 |
| 3–5 | £55,000 | £40,000 | £15,000 |

Depreciation then needs to be deducted from these profit figures. In this case, assuming straight line depreciation is applied:

Annual depreciation charge = £50,000/5 = £10,000

This gives a profit profile as follows:

Year 1     £5,000
Year 2     £15,000
Year 3–5   £5,000

This gives a figure for annual average profit of (£5,000 + £15,000 + £15,000)/5 = £7,000

## Average sum invested

5.5 To compute the average investment figure, we need details of the balance sheet value of the investment year by year, after adjustment for depreciation. Using the depreciation charged above, this gives balance sheet values as follows.

| End of Year 1 | £40,000 |
| End of Year 2 | £30,000 |
| End of Year 3 | £20,000 |
| End of Year 4 | £10,000 |
| End of Year 5 | £0 |

The average balance sheet value is thus

(£40,000 + £30,000 + £20,000 + £10,000 + £0)/5 = £20,000

The ARR is therefore $\frac{£7,000}{£20,000} = 35\%$

There are several ways of defining the ARR but providing that the same method is used when comparing projects with one another this should not present a problem.

# FINANCIAL REPORTING, ANALYSIS AND PLANNING

5.6 A useful characteristic of the ARR method is that it seeks to compare the profit generated with the sum invested. A company can then compare the ARR on any new investment with the ARR currently earned elsewhere in the business. On a broader level, comparison can be made between the ARR and the ROCE. If a new capital purchase generates an ARR below the ROCE currently earned across the business as a whole, then the overall effect of that investment will be to reduce the ROCE in the business. This is not necessarily a bad thing per se, but the implications of going ahead with such an investment need to be carefully thought through.

**Limitations of the ARR approach**

5.7 In one important respect, ARR is superior to the payback approach, but it still has limitations. ARR is superior because it allows a business to compare investments in projects or pieces of equipment which have different economic lives. The ARR is based on profits expressed in relation to the length of the project life. This means that, as with Example 15.2, Jeronimo Bank, two investments could offer the same payback period, but the overall return on the investments (as measured by ARR) may differ.

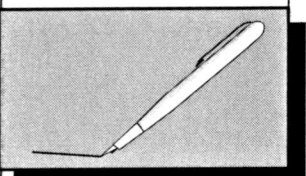

## Student Activity 4

It is useful to repeat the information on the investment choices open to Jeronimo Bank.

Jeronimo is thinking of investing in a new risk management software system at a cost of £150,000. Estimated savings attributable to using the software are as follows.

| Year | Savings |
|---|---|
| 1 | £75,000 |
| 2 | £50,000 |
| 3 | £25,000 |
| 4 | £25,000 |
| 5–7 | £25,000 |

Instead of buying the risk management software, the bank could buy laptops for all its staff involved in dealing with investments by high net worth clients. The lap tops would cost a total of £150,000 and could be expected to generate commission earnings as follows:

| Year | Commission revenue |
|---|---|
| 1 | £95,000 |
| 2 | £35,000 |
| 3 | £20,000 |
| 4–9 | £15,000 |

Assume that both the software system and the laptops have zero scrap value at the end of the project lives.

(1) Calculate the average profit after depreciation on each of the two investments.

(2) Calculate the average sum invested in each of the two projects.

# CAPITAL INVESTMENT APPRAISAL

(3) Calculate the ARR on each of the investments, and select the most profitable option.

*Complete this Activity before reading on.*

5.8 You should find that the ARR on the software purchase is significantly higher than that on the laptops. Using ARR, then, the two investments are not equally attractive, which is the case when payback period is used. The main advantage of ARR over payback is that it does take into account the returns earned throughout the whole life of an investment.

5.9 You may have noticed that, as with payback, the ARR approach ignores the time value of money. This is the major limitation of the approach to investment appraisal. Cash flows throughout the life of an investment are taken into account, but a receipt of £10,000 in year 5 is deemed equivalent to £10,000 received in year 1. In an inflationary environment, spending power will clearly change over time, and two such receipts are not equivalent. As a result, ARR is a useful but limited approach to investment appraisal.

5.10 More sophisticated approaches, which take account of the fact that the value of money changes over time, are therefore outlined below. First, however, we need to look at how to use discounting to calculate the present value of a sum of money received at some future point in time.

## 6 Discounting and compounding

6.1 Have you ever been tempted by those advertisements in the financial press, suggesting that if you invest a fixed amount every month you can collect a huge sum of money in twenty years time? The appeal lies in the apparent size of the capital you can get back. You might, for example, be offered £50,000 in twenty years time in return for investing £50 per month. On the surface this appears to be a very good deal, because the sum invested by you amounts to just £12,000: so your money has more than quadrupled in value. Even better, you can start dreaming about how you might spend the money. When the changes in the value of money over time are taken into account, however, the deal is not as good as it first appears. In fact, £50,000 received in twenty years has a relatively low present value.

6.2 As a general rule, most people regard £100 received in one year's time as being worth less than £100 received today. The value of money reduces over time, and the further into the future we go the lower the value of any given sum. The reasons usually given to explain our preference for money now rather than later are threefold:

- risk
- investment interest forgone
- inflation.

6.3 Risk is important because we can be certain of the spending power of money received today, but not of that received in the future. Even worse, we cannot be certain of getting the cash in the future, and so having it now is much less risky.

FINANCIAL REPORTING, ANALYSIS AND PLANNING

6.4 Cash invested today will earn interest, but that interest may be lost if there is a delay in receiving the cash. The value of the forfeited interest means that we value future receipts lower than current receipts.

6.5 Inflation erodes spending power and so, if we have to wait to receive cash, we will find that any given sum of money will buy less for us in the future.

6.6 Adjusting for changes in the value of money over time can be done via either discounting or compounding. Discounting converts future values into present values, and so it is the exact reverse of compounding, a procedure which most of us remember from school. We will start by looking at compounding, before moving on to present value calculations.

**Example 15.4 COMPOUNDING**

If £1,000 is placed on deposit in a bank and the annual interest payable is compounded at a rate of 5%, the value of the deposit increase over time as follows.

End of year 1: Value = (£1,000 × 1.05)
= £1,050

End of year 2: Value = (£1,050 × 1.05)
= £1,102.5

End of year 3: Value = (£1,102.5 × 1.05)
= £1,157.625

and so on.

6.7 It is possible to work out the value of the sum on deposit at the end of any future year by using this long hand approach to the calculation. The disadvantage of the approach is that it is increasingly time consuming the further into the future we wish to go.

6.8 An alternative way of computing the future value is to use the formula for compound interest which is shown below.

Sum receivable in year $n$ = (Sum deposited in Year 1) $(1 + \text{interest rate})^n$
Here, $n$ denotes the future year for which the value is sought.

*Example:*
Deposit £1,000 in Year 1
Interest received is 5% per annum
Value in year 10 = (£1,000)$(1.05)^{10}$
= £1,000 × 1.629
= £1,629

6.9 If you have never used power functions before except for squaring a number, the process is quite simple. On your calculator you should have a function button marked $x^y$. The '$y$' denotes the power level to which you wish the number to be raised, so if you want to know the value of $(1.05)^5$, then the '$y$' value is 5. You need to be confident at using your calculator to obtain such values, if you wish to fully understand compounding and discounting.

6.10 You can perhaps now see that if the formula for the future value using compounding is re-arranged, the value of the present sum placed on deposit can be calculated, provided we know the future value and the interest rate.

# CAPITAL INVESTMENT APPRAISAL

As with any maths equation, if we know the value of two out of three of the components, it is possible to derive the value of the third, unknown element.

6.11 Re-arranging the formula is a test of basic algebra skills, and gives the following:

$$\text{Sum deposited in Year 1} = \frac{\text{Sum receivable in Year } n}{(1 + \text{Interest rate})^n}$$

Using the figures from the example above,

$$\text{Sum placed on deposit} = \frac{£1,629}{1.629}$$

$$= £1,000$$

6.12 In the context of investment decisions, the 'sum placed on deposit' in the equation above is generally referred to as the *present value* of the investment. When the net cash flows from an investment are known, the discounting formula can be used to revalue them in terms of present day prices. The present value can then be directly compared with the present day cost of the investment.

6.13 If the present value of the sums received is less than the present day cost of the investment, then a company is earning a negative return, and so would choose not to invest. Conversely, if the present value of the benefits exceeds the present cost, then there is a net gain from investing. This gives us a general rule which you must be able to explain:

if present value exceeds costs – *invest*; net present value is positive;
if present value is below costs – *do not invest*; net present value is negative.

6.14 This principle can be used to rank alternative investment choices. If a company has the opportunity to select from several different investments, all of which have a present value which exceeds costs, then it would be logical to select the one which generates the greatest surplus of benefits over costs, i.e. the one with the highest net present value. This method of investment appraisal, referred to as the net present value approach, is a form of discounted cash flow analysis.

## Student Activity 5

(1) What is the major advantage of the net present value technique over the payback and ARR methods of appraisal?

(2) What is the value at the end of year 15 of £10,000 deposited in an investment account which guarantees an annual interest rate of 6%?

## 7 Calculating net present values

**Net present value**

7.1 As indicated above, the present value is nothing more than the current day worth of the future benefits generated by an investment The net present value is the current value of the future benefits *after* all the costs associated

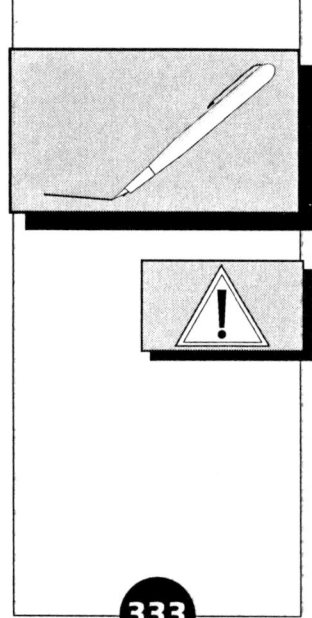

with the investment have been deducted. This can be illustrated using the investment opportunity cited in Example 15.1.

**Example 15.5**

A new note counting machine costs £5,000. The estimated savings in staff time from using the machine are as follows:

Year 1    £2,000
Year 2    £2,000
Year 3    £1,500
Year 4    £1,500
Year 5ff  £1,000

Assume that all cash flows are received evenly throughout the course of a year.

Let us start by recalling the formula for present value:

$$\text{Present value} = \frac{(\text{Sum receivable in year } n)}{(1+r)^n}$$

The formula shows that we need the following information in order to be able to calculate the present value:

- the value of $n$
- the sum receivable in the future
- a value for $r$, which we have so far called the interest rate.

We need to deal with each of these in turn.

*The value of n*

In the case of a bank deposit account, we saw that $n$ represented the future year under consideration when seeking a value for the deposit. It is much the same for an investment in an item of capital equipment. The example shows that the investment generates benefits for the bank every year, up to and beyond Year 5. In practice, most items of equipment have a predetermined useful life. Let us assume, in this case, that the machine can be used until the end of Year 7, by which time it has a value of zero.

We can now see that the benefits coming from the investment, in lasting a total of seven years give us seven values for $n$, i.e. one through to seven. We want to be able to obtain a present value for the benefit that has been earned in any or all of the years of the investment.

*The sum receivable in the future*

The sum receivable in the future is the net cash which is generated by the investment, at any particular point in time. From the example we can see that in each of the first two years, cash benefits of £2,000 are obtained. One very important point to note here is that we are interested in net cash flows, i.e. benefits less costs at any point in time. In some years, of course, costs may exceed benefits, in which case the net cash flow becomes negative.

We can now plot a simple table of values for net sums receivable against values for $n$, for the example in question.

# CAPITAL INVESTMENT APPRAISAL

| Net cash receivable | Value of n |
|---|---|
| £2,000 | 1 |
| £2,000 | 2 |
| £1,500 | 3 |
| £1,500 | 4 |
| £1,000 | 5 |
| £1,000 | 6 |
| £1,000 | 7 |

The *aggregate* value of the benefits arising from the investment is, of course, the sum of all the cash received through Years 1 to 7, and this must be discounted back to a present value. Expressed in algebraic form, this is:

$$\text{Present value} = \sum_{1}^{n} \frac{(B_1)}{(1+r)} + \frac{(B_2)}{(1+r)^2} + \frac{(B_3)}{(1+r)^3} + \ldots + \frac{(B_n)}{(1+r)^n}$$

Where:

$B_1$ = Benefits arising in year 1, etc.

$r$ = Discount rate

This is a very important formula which you need to be able to explain and apply.

*A value for r*

This is the hardest figure to obtain. If we are compounding a present value forward, we can simply use the interest rate received on the investment, to obtain a future value. In the case of discounting it is not quite so simple. Instead of the interest rate received, $r$ (the discount rate), represents the cost of the capital which has been used to fund the investment.

Businesses will sometimes spend a great deal of time selecting the correct discount rate to use for a particular investment. The cost of capital is not easy to calculate, as you may have seen in Unit 3, because it involves consideration of all the sources of funding used by a business. The mechanism for deriving a cost of capital/discount rate is outside the scope of this syllabus. For the purposes of this course, you can assume that the figure for cost of capital, will be given in the exam question.

In many cases in practice, firms choose to simplify their own decision making process by using what is termed a hurdle rate for investment decisions. The hurdle rate is the discount rate which is applied to all investment decisions in the business, and represents the rate of return sought by the company. As indicated earlier in this Unit, the rate of return must be at least equal to the cost of capital if the company is not to lose money on an investment.

For the purposes of working through our example, we therefore need to assume a cost of capital or discount rate for the investment. Let us assume that it is 8%.

We now have all the information necessary in order to calculate the present value of the benefits arising from purchasing the new note counting machine. All we need is to slot it into the formula. It is easier to see how this works if we have in front of us the table of cash benefits year by year.

# FINANCIAL REPORTING, ANALYSIS AND PLANNING

| Net cash receivable | Value of n |
|---|---|
| £2,000 | 1 |
| £2,000 | 2 |
| £1,500 | 3 |
| £1,500 | 4 |
| £1,000 | 5 |
| £1,000 | 6 |
| £1,000 | 7 |

Applying the formula given above, this gives us:

$$\text{Present value} = \sum \frac{£2,000}{(1.08)} + \frac{£2,000}{(1.08)^2} + \frac{£1,500}{(1.08)^3} + \frac{£1,500}{(1.08)^4} + \frac{£1,000}{(1.08)^5} + \frac{£1,000}{(1.08)^6} + \frac{£1,000}{(1.08)^7}$$

$$\text{Present value} = \sum \frac{£2,000}{1.08} + \frac{£2,000}{1.1664} + \frac{£1,500}{1.2597} + \frac{£1,500}{1.3605} + \frac{£1,000}{1.4693} + \frac{£1,000}{1.5868} + \frac{£1,000}{1.7138}$$

Rounding to the nearest pound

$$= £1,852 + £1,201 + £1,191 + £1,102 + £681 + £630 + £583$$

$$= £7,240$$

In other words, purchase of the note counting machine has resulted in cash benefits (savings) of £7240 at today's prices. This figure can now be compared with the cost of the investment to determine the *net present value*.

7.2 *Note* It is possible to speed up the calculation of the present value by using discount tables instead of calculating values for $(1 + r)^n$. In the tables, for example, the factor for the present value of £1 at a discount rate of 10% is 0.909 for year 1. This means that £1 received in year 1 has a value of £0.909 when discounted back to a present value. Simply multiplying the relevant cash flow by the relevant factor eradicates the need for the longhand calculations of the value of the denominator.

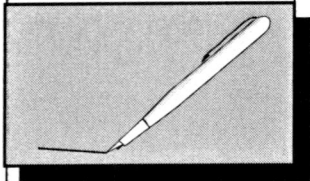

## Student Activity 6

Using the discount tables provided at the end of Unit 16, calculate the present value of the following sets of cash flows:

(1) Year 1 £2,000
    Year 2 £2,500
    Year 3 £3,000

Assume a discount rate of 10%.

(2) Year 1 £1,500
    Year 2 £4,000
    Year 3 £5,000
    Years 4–6 £1,000

Assume a discount rate of 7%.

*Complete this Activity before reading on.*

# CAPITAL INVESTMENT APPRAISAL

7.3 The net present value is equal to the present value of the total net cash benefits, less the initial cost of the investment. In Example 15.5 the note counting machine had a cost of £5,000, and so

Net present value = £7,240 – £5,000

= £2,240

The bank, by making the investment, obtained a net gain of £2,240 at today's prices. Using the net present value criteria, then, the note counting machine is a good investment.

7.4 You will perhaps have noticed that the final figure for the net present value is well below the figure for the benefits less cost *before* discounting. Before discounting, the sum of the benefits over the seven year period was £10,000, and so after deducting the cost of £5,000, the *apparent* benefit was £5,000. By recognising that the value of money declines over time, and applying a discount rate to those future benefits, the value of the net gain has been more than halved. This is very important, and links back to the illustration which started this Section 7.

7.5 Knowing that you will receive £50,000 in twenty years time in return for investing just £12,000 sounds good, but the present day value of that £50,000 may be quite small.

### Student Activity 7

Applying a discount rate of 8%, what is the value of £50,000 received in 20 years time? What does this tell you about the attractiveness of the proposed investment?

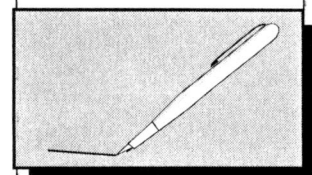

7.6 Understanding the logic of how to calculate a net present value (NPV) leads us to the conclusion that the NPV approach to investment decisions is superior to either payback or ARR. The one drawback of using NPV in practice is its complexity. It is not easy to obtain the figures on annual cash flows resulting from an investment, and finding a suitable discount rate is also problematic. For this reason, many of the smaller firms stick to the more basic approaches to investment appraisal, which take no account of the time value of money.

## 8 The internal rate of return approach

8.1 The internal rate of return (IRR) approach to investment appraisal, like the use of NPV, recognises changes in the value of money over time. The internal rate of return can be defined as the discount rate at which the net present value of an investment is zero. To calculate this requires an understanding of how changes in the discount rate affect the net present value.

8.2 Suppose that your bank has a customer who runs a small manufacturing business, for which a loan is being sought to purchase new production

# FINANCIAL REPORTING, ANALYSIS AND PLANNING

equipment. The business has projected the following change in cash flows arising from the investment:

| Year | Cash in | Cash out | Net cash flow |
|---|---|---|---|
| 1 | 0 | £12,000 | (£12,000) |
| 2 | £2,500 | £500 | £2,000 |
| 3 | £4,000 | £500 | £3,500 |
| 4 | £4,000 | £500 | £3,500 |
| 5 | £4,000 | £500 | £3,500 |
| 6 | £4,000 | £500 | £3,500 |
| 7 | £3,000 | 0 | £3,000 |

If the company borrows from the bank in order to purchase the equipment, it will mean that its current cost of capital will become 8%.

8.3 The first step towards computing the IRR is to calculate the net present value at the current cost of capital. You should now be able to do this calculation in full, and it is a good idea to attempt it on your own first, before looking at the solution given below.

NPV = Sum of the present value of the benefits *less* costs

Note that the cash out in Year 1 represents the cost of purchasing the equipment.

$$\text{NPV} = \frac{£2,000}{1.166} + \frac{£3,500}{1.260} + \frac{£3,500}{1.360} + \frac{£3,500}{1.469} + \frac{£3,500}{1.587} + \frac{£3,000}{1.714}, -£12,000$$

NPV = £1,409.

8.4 The investment has a positive net present value and so is attractive, but if we change the discount rate we can see that the size of the net gain changes. Most importantly, the higher the discount rate, the lower the NPV, if all other factors remain constant. This means that if the NPV calculation is repeated, using a discount rate of 10% instead of 8%, the NPV becomes just £361.

8.5 It is easy to see that if the discount rate rises much above 10% then the NPV will become negative. In fact, at a rate of 13%, the NPV equals (£1,006). The internal rate of return was defined as the rate at which the NPV equalled zero, and so if we have both positive and negative NPV figures, and the relevant discount rates, it is possible to use iteration (repeated trials) to derive the IRR. The position is perhaps best expressed in a diagram such as figure 15.2.

# CAPITAL INVESTMENT APPRAISAL

**Figure 15.2 The impact of changes in the discount rate on NPV**

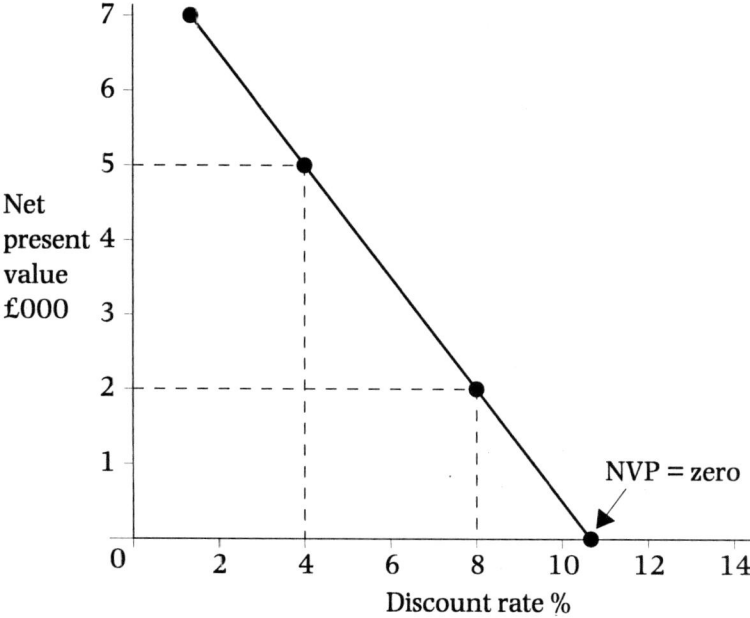

At a discount rate of 4%, the NPV equals £5,000.

At a discount rate of 8%, the NPV equals £2,000.

When the discount rate rises to approximately 11%, the NPV equals zero. The discount rate at this point is termed the internal rate of return.

8.6 Summarising the information obtained so far:

NPV = £361 when *r* equals 10%

NPV = (£1006) when *r* equals 13%

This means that a 3% change in the discount rate has led to a change of £1,367 in the NPV. So a 1% change in the discount rate would result in a change in NPV = £1,367/3 = £456.

8.7 Starting from an NPV of £361, to get to a figure of zero we need the NPV to fall by exactly £361, and this can only happen if the discount rate increases. The exact amount by which the discount rate needs to increase can be calculated as: 361/456 = 0.79 expressed as a percentage.

8.8 In other words, if the discount rate rises from 10% to 10.79%, we will find that the NPV of the project equals exactly zero. 10.79% is the internal rate of return on this particular investment. You can prove this if you wish by calculating long-hand the NPV at the suggested discount rate of 10.79%.

## Student Activity 8

Assume that a proposed investment project has yielded the following results in terms of NPV values:

NPV = £1,800 when *r* is 7%

NPV = (£400) when *r* is 11%

What is the IRR for this investment?

# FINANCIAL REPORTING, ANALYSIS AND PLANNING

## Uses of IRR

8.9 The most useful aspect of the IRR calculation is as an aid to forecasting what might happen if the cost of capital changes. Interest rates have been very volatile in recent years, and businesses like to have an idea of whether a project will remain viable even if the cost of capital rises. In this sense, the IRR figure acts as a form of break-even, whereby a company can say 'if the interest rate rises above the IRR, it is no longer viable'. This means that the lower the IRR, the less attractive the project. By the use of economic forecasting, it is possible to assess the probability of interest rates reaching the IRR level.

8.10 There is one major drawback to the IRR approach, however: it ignores the scale of an investment and so it does not always rank projects in the same way as they would be ranked using NPV. The reasons for this are essentially mathematical, and are beyond the scope of this syllabus, but the practical effect can be significant.

8.11 Suppose a company wishes to choose between Projects A, B and C. Using the NPV criteria, C is the preferred option. Using IRR Project A has the most appeal, however, as it has the highest IRR. Which decision criterion is correct, NPV or IRR? Most writers would suggest that NPV is preferable because of the mathematical sensitivity of IRR. In such an instance, then, NPV is seen as the superior appraisal technique.

## 9 Non-financial aspects of investment decisions

9.1 So far in this Unit the investment appraisal techniques outlined have all emphasised the role of financial viability as the criterion for an investment decision. This would seem to be sensible for companies which are in the business of generating profits. Investing in loss-making projects would not help the market reputation of a business. Nevertheless, even when companies view financial viability as essential, there will often be non-financial considerations which may influence an investment decision.

### Student Activity 9

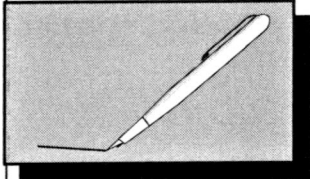

Can you think of any investments made recently in your business which have had non-financial effects on the workplace or marketplace?

*Complete this Activity before reading on.*

9.2 Here are some ideas on the way in which there are non-financial effects arising from investment decisions:

- working conditions are improved by investing in a staff restaurant facility
- the removal of asbestos from buildings reduces the health hazards for people working there

- tighter quality controls in chemical production can reduce environmentally damaging effluent levels
- enhanced public image from the corporate sponsorship of a local youth football team.

9.3 By using some subjective judgment, it might be possible to attach monetary values to some of these non-financial issues, but the process would be difficult, and the resulting numbers non-verifiable. This raises the question of how companies can incorporate such factors into their investment decision making. The answer lies in trade-off.

9.4 The recent Olympic Games in Atlanta is a good example of how companies trade off the multitude of effects that come from investments. Coca Cola allowed its staff from Atlanta paid time off to work as helpers/officials at the games, and they provided free drinks facilities for competitors and team officials. The cost of this 'investment' must have been very substantial. At the same time, it would be impossible to compile an accurate cash flow forecast of the impact on Coca Cola sales world-wide. The event was covered by the world's media and the company was recognised as a sponsor of the games. Presumably, the non-financial effects in terms of publicity, community goodwill etc. were of value within Coca Cola, and the trade-off in terms of cash paid out in 1996 was offset by contributions from future sales revenue arising from the additional customer goodwill.

9.5 In a similar way, if a company installs a staff restaurant, it will spend money for no immediate financial return. The NPV on the investment would look negative at first sight. That negative figure, however, could well be offset by the savings on staff time involved in staff staying on the premises over lunch, or the reduced costs of staff leaving in search of better working conditions.

9.6 We can therefore conclude that there are no specific rules on how to deal with non-financial aspects of investment decisions. Instead, the party making the investment must subjectively compare financial losses with non-financial gains. This puts subjectivity back into a process which should, ideally, be standardised but then it is the non-standard aspects of life that make it interesting!

# FINANCIAL REPORTING, ANALYSIS AND PLANNING

## Summary

**Now that you have completed this unit you should be able to:**

- explain how investment appraisal forms part of the planning and control process
- identify the key characteristics of capital investment
- determine the payback period of an investment
- calculate the rate of return on an investment using the ARR formula
- explain the techniques of compounding and discounting
- use information on the cost of capital and the cash flows associated with an investment, to calculate a net present value and an internal rate of return
- describe and explain the non-financial factors which influence investment decisions.

## Self assessment questions

### Exam-style question

The directors of Iwata Ltd are considering two mutually exclusive investment projects in respect of which the following information is provided:

|  | Project A £000 | Project B £000 |
|---|---|---|
| Initial capital investment | 1,000 | 1,000 |
| Net cash inflows: Year 1 | 700 | 400 |
| 2 | 300 | 500 |
| 3 | 100 | 800 |
| 4 | – | 600 |

The initial outlay will occur immediately and you may assume that the net cash inflows will arise at the year end.

Iwata's estimated cost of capital over the four year period is 10%.

*Required:*

(a) Outline the main advantages and disadvantages of the 'payback' method of capital investment appraisal. [6]

(b) State the way in which the net present value (NPV) method of investment appraisal overcomes the criticisms made of payback. [4]

(c) Numerical assessments of the two projects above based on the following methods of capital project appraisal:

(i) payback;

(ii) net present value (NPV). [6]

# CAPITAL INVESTMENT APPRAISAL

(4) Your advice on which project should be adopted, giving reasons for your choice.

[4]

*Note:* Factors for the present value of £1 applying a discount rate of 10%:

| Year | Factor |
|------|--------|
| 1 | 0.909 |
| 2 | 0.826 |
| 3 | 0.751 |
| 4 | 0.683 |

[Total-20]

# Unit 16

## Plans, Forecasts and Budgets

> **Objectives**
>
> When you have completed this Unit you should be able to:
>
> - explain the links between plans, forecasts and budgets
> - define budgeting and explain its role in management control
> - explain the term 'master budget' and illustrate the link between the various component budgets
> - draft a simple cash budget using relevant data
> - construct a budgeted income statement and balance sheet.

## 1 Introduction

1.1 As we have already seen in Unit 6, businesses are concerned with achieving financial goals. Investors require companies to meet profit targets which will ensure that they receive the required dividends, and see the share price rise over time. If goals are to be achieved, planning needs to be detailed, and the performance monitored and controlled. This Unit deals with the planning and control process, and specifically with how budgets are used as a tool to assist management. The need to exercise caution in using budgets for control and performance measurement is also discussed.

## 2 The link between plans, forecasts and budgets

**Definitions**

2.1 it is useful to begin by defining each of the relevant terms, to clarify the subtle differences in meaning. A *forecast* is a prediction of what is thought likely to happen; a *plan* is a means by which a set objective (or what should happen) will be achieved. A *budget* is a tool which is used in the planning process, to translate physical plans into financial terms. We will now look at these definitions in more detail.

2.2 Looking to the future, most businesses specify objectives for what they hope to have achieved by a particular date. These will usually relate to sales figures, production volumes and profit levels. Objectives alone, however, are of little value, unless they are accompanied by clear ideas on how they might be accomplished. A *plan* is the document which plots the way to achieve a given objective.

# FINANCIAL REPORTING, ANALYSIS AND PLANNING

2.3 For example, suppose a major clearing bank has decided to set targets for an increased share of the small business market. The aim is to have a market share (in terms of customer numbers) of 12% in five year's time. The bank's current market share is just 5%. A plan needs to be devised which shows in detail how the additional market share will be acquired, and details the yearly progress needed so that the five year target is met. The resulting plan might take the following simple form.

| Year | Target market share |
|---|---|
| 1 | 6% |
| 2 | 8% |
| 3 | 9% |
| 4 | 10% |
| 5 | 12% |

The five-year overall objective is thus sub-divided into subsidiary targets for each year.

2.4 The next stage of the planning process is to look at the detail of how each subsidiary target can be met. This requires the preparation of *operating plans* and budgets. For example, the aim is to have achieved a 1% rise in market share by the end of the first year, and the operating plan details the resources needed to achieve that aim. Clearly, a given market share can be converted into a sales value, which in turn can be used to calculate the required level of sales personnel. A staffing cost can then be computed and a recruitment plan drawn up. Alongside details of staffing requirements, the operating plan may identify other needs, e.g. computing facilities, credit checking facilities, and so on. The revenue generated from the new customers can also be calculated and, by matching costs and revenues, a profit forecast compiled.

2.5 The difference between an *operating plan* and a *budget* is that an operating plan is generally expressed in terms of physical requirements, whereas a budget expresses the requirements in financial terms. The operating plan may suggest that five new staff need to be recruited. The budget will then translate that requirement into monetary terms, e.g. two staff at salaries of £15,000 p.a. per head, plus three staff at a cost of £9,000 p.a. per head. A budget of £57,000 thus needs to be provided for new staff costs if the plan is to be put into effect.

2.6 In practice, the annual operating budgets usually will be further broken down into monthly budgets. This has the advantage that the budget can then cope with seasonal sales or cost patterns, and control is tightened if budget performance is monitored more frequently.

2.7 The relationship between the five-year plan (strategic plan) which sets general long-term objectives and the shorter term operating plans and budgets, is illustrated in figure 16.1 below.

# PLANS, FORECASTS AND BUDGETS

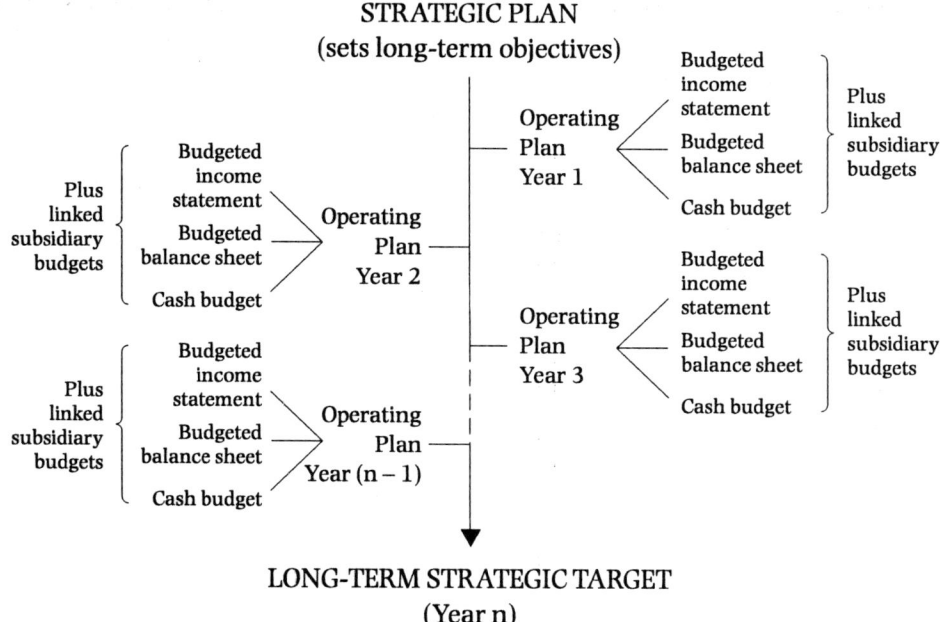

**Figure 16.1** *The relationship between strategic plans, operating plans and budgets*

## 3 Budgeting and management control

3.1 In the sections above we saw that planning involves looking at how a future objective will be achieved, and how budgets add financial detail to the plan. CIMA, the Institute of Management Accountants, defines a budget as follows.

> **'A budget is a plan quantified in monetary terms, prepared and approved prior to a defined period of time, usually showing planned income to be generated and/or expenditure to be incurred during that period and the capital to be employed to attain a given objective.'**

The budget may therefore relate to costs, revenues, cash movements, profits or asset values.

3.2 Budgets also have another important function, and that is as part of the control process. Take the earlier example of a staffing budget of £57,000 p.a. Let us suppose that the bank manager was able to recruit staff at lower than expected salaries. He therefore spends only £50,000 in Year 1, thus saving the bank £7,000. By being asked to comply with a set salary target, the manager has been subjected to a financial control, and if he overspends he can be penalised, or alternatively he can be rewarded if he underspends. The budget becomes a target against which actual performance can be compared, and control exercised accordingly.

### Limitations of budgets as control mechanisms

3.3 It is important that caution is applied when using budgets as a tool of control. Perhaps most importantly, managers should not be required to be answerable for budget results which are outside their span of control. For

# FINANCIAL REPORTING, ANALYSIS AND PLANNING

example, suppose that a chocolate manufacturer is faced with a sudden massive increase in the price of cocoa beans, and fails to achieve the specified profit target. The purchasing manager should not be held responsible for the failure to achieve the budget, as he has been the victim of price movements over which he had no control. If budgets are to be used for control purposes, then it is important that the reasons for any variation between the actual results and the budgeted results are identified. It will then be possible to see if variation was inside or outside the manager's control.

3.4 A second aspect of budgeting which often causes concern arises when unrealistic budget targets are set. In such circumstances managers know that they can never achieve what is being asked of them and this has a demotivating effect. Budgets should be used to establish challenging but attainable targets. This is most effectively achieved by using a budgetary process which directly involves managers in setting their own budget targets, rather than having them imposed from above.

3.5 Used with care, however, budgets can be a very useful part of the planning and control process. Budgeting can be viewed as advantageous from the angle of both the company and the manager for the following reasons.

- Managers are required to think through a plan in great detail in order to prepare a budget. This serves to formalise the planning process.
- Preparing budgets encourages managers to be forward thinking.
- Potential short-term problems are identified before they arise.
- Budgets encourage managers to exercise self control.
- By quantifying targets, budgets clarify the basis for comparison when appraising future performance.
- Budgets are a useful way of co-ordinating and linking the operations in different parts of a business. The sales budget, for example, cannot be set completely independently of the production budget; the link between budgets is discussed in detail in the next section.

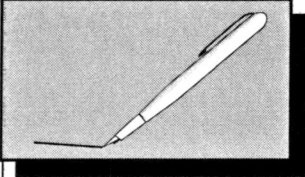

## Student Activity 1

1. Find out the types of budgets which are prepared in the department where you work, and over what time periods they are monitored.

2. Find out how budget targets are set at your place of work. Are managers asked to set their own targets, which are then the subject of negotiation with senior management, or are the budgets imposed from above?

*(See Appendix for answers.)*

## 4 The master budget

4.1 It is perhaps easiest to understand the various stages involved in the budget process by looking at an example of a manufacturing operation. Let us assume that a five-year profit target has already been set, and that this has been converted into a sales target, based on current operating margins. The

# PLANS, FORECASTS AND BUDGETS

five-year sales target has then been broken down into staged annual targets for both profit and sales.

4.2 For each year of the plan, the manufacturer will then produce the following:
- budgeted profit and loss account
- budgeted balance sheet
- cash budget
- sales budget
- production budget
- stock budget (raw materials, WIP and finished goods)
- materials budget
- direct labour budget
- manufacturing overhead budget
- selling and distribution costs budget.

4.3 The first three items in the above list constitute the *master budget*, and we can see that they are very similar to the contents of the published financial statements. Note that they are *similar* but not *identical* because the published statements relate to *historic* information, whereas the budgets relate to *forecast* information.

4.4 The profit and loss account, balance sheet and cash flow statement are all dependent upon the revenues generated and costs incurred and paid over the course of a specified period. If we are planning for the future instead of recording the past, what the business wants to achieve in the profit and loss account—and the associated changes in the balance sheet—will determine what sales, production, materials and labour, etc. are required over the next twelve months. Hence the use of the term 'master budgets', because those three forecasts dictate what must happen elsewhere in the business if the plans are to be fulfilled. We will now look more closely at the budget system.

4.5 Assuming that all the goods sold are manufactured by the business, then the level of sales that can be achieved in any one year depends upon two things:

1) finished goods stocks
2) production levels.

4.6 Production levels are dictated by the availability of raw materials and direct labour, as well as access to the required overhead facilities. At the same time, cash costs will be incurred in the form of selling and distribution expenses. The ability to pay all these direct and indirect costs depends upon cash being generated from sales via the collection of the trade debts.

4.7 In other words, the opportunity to hit the original sales and profit target depends upon a collection of related targets being achieved. This maze is headed by the master budget which is composed from information contained in various *subsidiary budgets*.

4.8 You may find this easier to follow by looking at the links shown in figure 16.2 below.

# FINANCIAL REPORTING, ANALYSIS AND PLANNING

## Example 16.1

### LARGESSE PLC

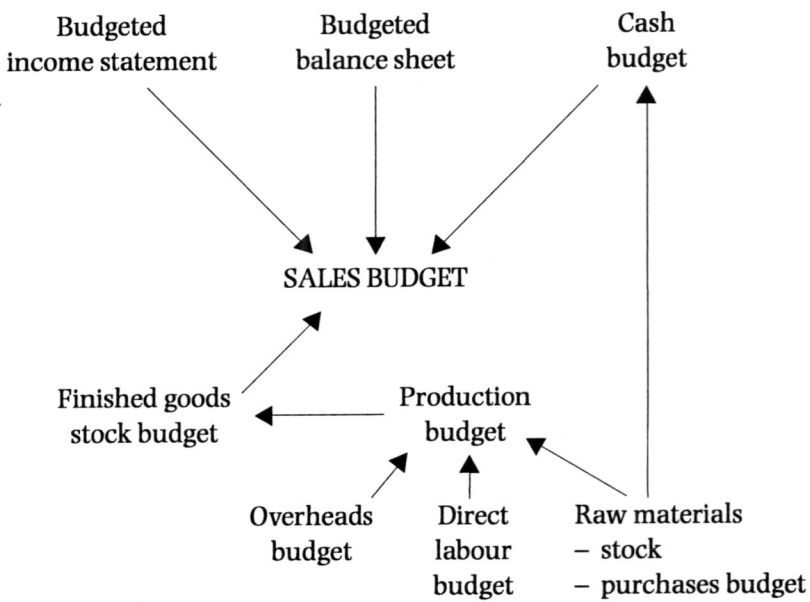

*Figure 16.2: Master budgets and subsidiary budgets: Largesse Plc*

The budgeted profit and loss account for Largesse plc shows a forecast profit of £10 million at the end of next year. The company knows that it earns a gross margin of 25% on sales and that sales volumes vary throughout the year as follows.

January—May 5% of annual sales per month
June—August 15% of annual sales per month
September—December 7.5% of annual sales per month

Largesse produces a single product which has a selling price of £20 per unit.

We can use this information to draft a simple sales budget for the coming twelve-month period. The first step is to convert the forecast profit into a sales target.

If Q is the unknown sales figure, then,

Profit = £10 million = £0.25Q

Q = £40 million

A basic sales budget can now be prepared showing sales volumes and values on a monthly basis.

## PLANS, FORECASTS AND BUDGETS

| Month | Sales (£m) | Sales (Units) |
|---|---|---|
| Jan | 2 | 100,000 |
| Feb | 2 | 100,000 |
| Mar | 2 | 100,000 |
| Apr | 2 | 100,000 |
| May | 2 | 100,000 |
| Jun | 6 | 300,000 |
| Jul | 6 | 300,000 |
| Aug | 6 | 300,000 |
| Sep | 3 | 150,000 |
| Oct | 3 | 150,000 |
| Nov | 3 | 150,000 |
| Dec | 3 | 150,000 |
| Total | 40 | 2 million |

The sales budget can then be used as the basis to prepare a production budget, which records opening stock levels, expected sales levels and required final stock figures for each month. For example:

Opening stock   January £1m
Sales budget    January £2m

Closing stock target (end January) £1.5 m

The level of production thus required in January, if stock and sales targets are to be achieved, equals:

£2m + £1.5m – £1m = £2.5m.

Or, expressed in words,

Sales + closing stock – opening stock = production required

Note: these amounts are all expenses in terms of selling values.

4.9 We have now seen that the forecast profit plan has generated a sales budget which has in turn created a production budget, and so the process continues. In this way, all the component elements of the business are brought together, so that sales staff will not sell goods that cannot be made and producers will not demand raw material stocks which are not available.

4.10 Each month, the business sees cash being paid out in direct costs and expenses and also receives cash in from its debtors. A cash budget thus flows out of the other budgets. We can now turn, then, to a detailed consideration of the *cash budget*. For the banks and other providers of finance for business, this is perhaps the most important single budget to consider. For this reason read the next section with great care and be prepared to answer an examination question on cash budgeting.

## Student Activity 2

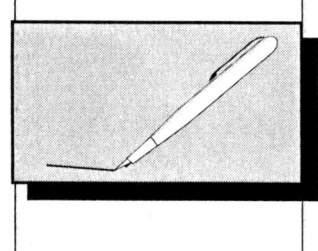

Think about the following questions before looking at the discussion that follows.

If a company decides to run down its final stock levels, what implications does this have for production, assuming that sales levels are constant from month to month? What effect do you think this will this have on the cash requirements of the business?

FINANCIAL REPORTING, ANALYSIS AND PLANNING

*Discussion*

You may have noticed that the production budget level depends upon the budgeted stock levels at the end of the period. Planning stock levels is an important aspect of control, because if they are excessive then money is tied up unnecessarily and this has an effect on profits. Equally, if stocks are too low, custom may be lost.

## 5 Cash budgets

5.1 A cash budget is a schedule of cash payments and receipts which covers a defined future period of time and the aim in preparing it is to ensure that the business always has the necessary cash available to it to continue trading. If the budget shows an excess of payments over receipts, then overdraft or other financing can be arranged accordingly. Similarly, if there is evidence that cash holdings will be accumulating, the business can look for suitable short-term investment opportunities.

5.2 As with the other budgets, it is common practice to prepare the figures on a monthly basis, but the frequency of budgets must be in line with the nature of the business. In businesses where long-term contracts are the norm, then a longer time scale of, say, three months may be more appropriate.

5.3 The primary advantage of cash budgeting is that, by forcing the company to plan, it ensures the maintenance of necessary, but not surplus, cash balances. From the banker's standpoint, then, a well-prepared cash budget should mean that the customer will not require sudden unauthorised overdraft facilities. Where requests for these facilities are made even when a cash budget has been prepared, the most likely cause is an unexpected event, e.g. failure of a major customer.

5.4 Not surprisingly, the key determinant of the cash budget is the level of sales, and hence the volume of production. As sales are paid for by debtors, the cash receipts can be entered into the cash budget. Similarly, as materials suppliers, staff salaries and other production costs are paid, these are entered as cash disbursements on the budget. The exact timing and amounts may be difficult to assess at times but, if a margin for error is incorporated, then the business should never find itself at the limits of its cash availability.

**Components of a cash budget**

5.5 All cash budgets will contain details of the following.

- Opening cash balance
- Cash in (sub-divided by source)
- Cash out (sub-divided by category)
- Net surplus/deficit
- Closing cash balance.

The budget will be presented in columnar format, with each column representing one time period and line-by-line entries to indicate the relevant values of each of the items above. This format is clearly demonstrated in Example 16.2 below, for a twelve-month cash budget drawn up on a quarterly basis.

# PLANS, FORECASTS AND BUDGETS

**Example 16.2**

|  | 1st quarter | 2nd quarter | 3rd quarter | 4th quarter |
|---|---|---|---|---|
| £000 | | | | |
| Opening balance | 15 | 30 | | |
| Cash in (debtors) | 125 | 145 | 180 | 135 |
| | 140 | 175 | | |
| Cash out: | | | | |
| Materials | 40 | 65 | 80 | 85 |
| Wages | 65 | 65 | 65 | 65 |
| Other expenses | 5 | 5 | 5 | 5 |
| | 110 | 135 | | |
| Cash surplus | 15 | 10 | | |
| Cash balance | 30 | 40 | | |

## Student Activity 3

Complete the cash budget given above, filling in the missing entries, before you move on to the Discussion below.

### Discussion

If we look at the cash budget on a line-by-line basis, we can see how the information is obtained to make the entries.

The first line deals with cash in (receipts from debtors) and will be determined by the terms on which the company trades. Commonly, if trading on credit, payment will be received for goods at least one month in arrears. At the same time, a certain proportion of debts may go bad and this must be allowed for in the budget.

For example, suppose that we take the sales figure of £2 million for the month of January for Largesse plc in Example 16.1. If the company receives payment on thirty days net, then it should collect £2 million in February before any allowance for bad debts. If a 5% bad debt allowance is made, the entry for February in the cash budget would read £1.9 million. The sales budget, along with information on debt collection policy, therefore forms the basis of the receivables entry in the cash budget.

Sales receipts may not be the only source of cash for the company. Other sources might include rental income, investment dividends or loans. These will each be recorded under separate categories, under the general heading of 'cash in'.

The second section of the budget deals with cash out, categorised by the reason for the payment. Clearly, the materials purchased will be determined by the production budget, which has been set in accordance with the sales budget. The entries under production expenses here are obtained by reference back to the production budget. In the case of other, non-production, expenses they will be drawn from an overheads budget(s).

# FINANCIAL REPORTING, ANALYSIS AND PLANNING

The cash surplus/deficit entry is calculated by deducting cash out from cash in for the relevant time period. The line is intended to make clear the times when the business is a net user or generator of cash.

The final entry shows the balance to be carried forward into the next period. This is calculated as:

Opening balance + cash in − cash out = closing balance.

In the many businesses which are subject to seasonal demand patterns, this balance will be fairly volatile. For bankers, the thing to look out for is a steadily declining balance, or one which is frequently at the limit of the agreed loan facility. In such circumstances, it would be wise to call the management in and ask them why they are trading under such tight cash conditions and what they are going to do about it.

## Student Activity 4

Panache Catering Ltd is a wholesaler of chilled food products, selling to the restaurant and hotel trade. It has prepared a sales budget for the first six months of 1996 which shows the following.

| Jan | £45,000 |
|-----|---------|
| Feb | £40,000 |
| Mar | £45,000 |
| Apr | £60,000 |
| May | £60,000 |
| Jun | £70,000 |

Payment for sales is received one month in arrears. Sales for December 1995 equalled £85,000, and the closing cash balance at the end of December was £15,000. A monthly bad debt allowance of 5% is estimated as necessary.

The company estimates that food preparation costs amount to 35% of the selling price. Payment to suppliers is made one month in arrears. In addition, the company faces a staff wages bill of £15,000. Factory rental costs £3,000 per month and delivery costs add a further £3,000 to costs. In April, a major customer goes into liquidation, resulting in the non-receipt of half of that month's expected sales receipts.

### Required

Prepare a cash budget for Panache Catering Ltd, covering the period Jan – Jun 1996

*(The answer is given in the Appendix)*

### Benefits of cash budgeting

5.6   If you look at your answer for Panache Catering, we can see some of the benefits of cash budgeting.

- The cash balance at the start of the year was relatively low, but accumulated quite rapidly as the year progressed. The company is clearly a good cash generator. At the same time, however, the cash surplus is reaching levels which are perhaps inappropriate for the volume of trade. By the end of June the cash in the bank is almost equivalent to the sales

# PLANS, FORECASTS AND BUDGETS

figure for that month. At this stage, the company should consider using its cash more effectively.

- The sales figures for Panache are fairly volatile, ranging from a high in December of £85,000, to a low of £40,000 in February. In order to meet the sudden upsurges in sales at certain times of year, it is fair to assume that there will be several months when the company is operating with significant levels of surplus capacity. Questions need to be asked about this. It is easy to be complacent if the cash budget looks healthy, but it would also indicate that there is scope for further expansion.

- The failure of the key customer was an unexpected event, which could have caused the failure of Panache itself, if it had been in a weak cash position. Cash budgets should always make some allowance for the unexpected. Nonetheless, the company could perhaps have saved itself cash by using debtor management to monitor key customers. In this way, it might have seen that trouble was brewing and refused to issue further supplies without cash up front.

5.7 As already suggested, all cash budgets emanate from information which is contained in the sales, production and overhead budgets. It is still true, however, that a company can be very poor at generating cash in the short term and still be very profitable. The reverse is also possible. It therefore makes sense to view the cash budget as just part of the story. The budgeted profit and loss account and balance sheet also contain vital pointers as to the viability of a business. We will therefore now look at how to draft a budgeted profit and loss account and balance sheet.

## 6 Budgeted income statements and balance sheets

6.1 This section assumes that you have fully understood the material contained in Units 4 to 8 of this book, which covered the preparation of financial statements. In the examination, if you are asked to prepare a forecast profit and loss account, you must use the standard procedures and layout in its preparation. A number of examiners' comments have related to the poor quality of layout in students' solutions. The fact that the statement is just a forecast and will be used only by management is irrelevant; issues such as depreciation must still be dealt with correctly. If you need to review some of these basic facts, work through those Units again before starting work on this section.

6.2 A problem frequently encountered by bank managers is that of companies which are trading with excessively high overdraft levels. The directors may be asked to reduce the level of overdraft to a specified amount. As we have already seen, however, the cash balance in the cash budget is inextricably linked to the figures contained in other budgets. This means that a request for a reduction in the overdraft will require the directors to rethink the production and sales targets, and possibly undertake a fundamental review of production methods.

6.3 Faced with alternative scenarios, it is possible to produce forecast profit and loss accounts which show what profit will be earned under each separate circumstance. As might be expected, managers will select the option which

# FINANCIAL REPORTING, ANALYSIS AND PLANNING

generates the greatest profit, and a cash budget can then be drafted to accompany the forecast profit and loss account. The resulting cash balance can then be compared with the target overdraft figure set by the bank.

6.4 Before looking at this type of exercise in some detail, it is worthwhile considering the options that might be identified by the managers as a way of reducing the overdraft level.

## Student Activity 5

Imagine that you are a director of a small company which manufactures office furniture. Your current overdraft level is £45,000 on a turnover of £700,000, and the bank has asked you to reduce the overdraft to £30,000. Suggest three strategies which you might adopt to meet the bank's request.

Think about the above problem before looking at the solutions which follow.

- Reducing stock levels is a fairly standard solution to cutting an overdraft. In essence, the need is to reduce the working capital requirements of the business. This means that investment in debtors or stock must be reduced, since the cash balance is already negative. The risk that accompanies stock cutting is one of lost custom caused by stock outs. The likely lost sales can often be quantified.

- A similar risk exists if debtor levels are cut. If debtor figures are high simply because poor collection procedures are in operation, then it is a low-cost exercise to reduce the debtor figure. If, however, credit control is already tight, then leaning on customers to pay sooner might cause some loss of custom.

- The alternative is to sacrifice some profit by offering discounts in return for early payment.

**Profit forecasts**

6.5 The starting point for understanding how to tackle examination questions in this area is the ability to amend an existing forecast. Let us start with the following example.

### Example 16.3

Six-month forecast profit and loss account for Greene Ltd for the period ending 30th June 1997.

|  | £000 |
|---|---:|
| Turnover | 650,000 |
| Less: | |
| Cost of goods sold | 400,000 |
| Operating expenses | 190,000 |
| Depreciation | 22,000 |
|  | 612,000 |
| Net profit | 38,000 |

*Notes:*

1. Sales are not subject to seasonal variations.

# PLANS, FORECASTS AND BUDGETS

2. Payments are received and made one month in arrears, with the exception of operating expenses, which are paid as incurred.

Let us now assume that the directors have decided that they want to reduce the risk of bad debts by offering discounts for early payment. A discount of 5% is offered in return for payment in the month of invoicing, instead of a month in arrears. It is estimated that 10% of customers will take up the discount, but at the same time debt collection costs will fall by £400 per month. The directors are unsure as to what effect that the policy will have upon profits.

We can re-draft the forecast, using the new policy, and compute the profit impact as follows.

Step 1

Calculate the adjusted figure for sales receipts, following the introduction of the discount.

Current forecast £650,000 of which £65,000 (10%) will seek the discount.

This gives:

Non-discounted sales £585,000
Discounted sales £65,000 × 0.95 = £61,750
Total sales under discount scheme = £646,750

Step 2

Adjust costs for any changes caused by the new policy.

Debt collection costs would be classified as an operating expense, and this is reduced by £2400 i.e. £400 × 6

New operating costs = £190,000 – £2400 = £187,600

Step 3

Combine the revenue and cost effects to draft the new profit and loss account.

|  | £000 |
|---|---:|
| Turnover | 646,750 |
| Less |  |
| Cost of goods sold | 400,000 |
| Operating expenses | 187,600 |
| Depreciation | 22,000 |
|  | 609,000 |
| Net profit | 37,750 |

We can see that the proposed policy would reduce profits by just £250. On the other hand, the reduced profit might be compensated for by improved cash flow. We can see the possible cash flow effects by preparing a cash budget under the original policy and comparing it with the equivalent budget under the new policy. Note that depreciation charges do *not* represent a cash movement.

For the purposes of the budget we will assume that the opening cash balance on 1st January 1997 is an overdraft of £25,000 and sales in December 1996 were £108,333.

*Cash budget adjustments*

*Greene Ltd. Cash Budget January 1997 – June 1997 (Existing Credit Collection system)*

|  | January | February | March | April | May | June |
|---|---|---|---|---|---|---|
| Opening Balance | (25,000) | (14,999) | (4,998) | 5,003 | 15,004 | 25,005 |
| *Cash in* | | | | | | |
| Last month's sales | 108,333 | 108,333 | 108,333 | 108,333 | 108,333 | 108,333 |
| Current Month's sales | | | | | | |
| *Cash out* | | | | | | |
| Cost of goods sold | 66,666 | 66,666 | 66,666 | 66,666 | 66,666 | 66,666 |
| Operating Expenses | 31,666 | 31,666 | 31,666 | 31,666 | 31,666 | 31,666 |
| Cash Surplus | 10,001 | 10,001 | 10,001 | 10,001 | 10,001 | 10,001 |
| *Cash balance* | (14,999) | (4,998) | 5,003 | 15,004 | 25,005 | 35,006 |

*Greene Ltd cash budget January 1997 – June 1997 (with new discount policy)*

|  | January | February | March | April | May | June |
|---|---|---|---|---|---|---|
| Opening balance | (25,000) | (4,707) | 5,152 | 15,011 | 24,870 | 34,789 |
| *Cash In* | | | | | | |
| Last month's sales | 108,333 | 97,500 | 97,500 | 97,500 | 97,500 | 97,500 |
| Current month's sales | 10,292 | 10,292 | 10,292 | 10,292 | 10,292 | 10,292 |
| Total sales | 118,625 | 107,792 | 107,792 | 107,792 | 107,792 | 107,792 |
| *Cash out* | | | | | | |
| Cost of goods sold | 66,666 | 66,666 | 66,666 | 66,666 | 66,666 | 66,666 |
| Operating expenses | 31,666 | 31,267 | 31,267 | 31,267 | 31,267 | 31,267 |
| Cash Surplus | 20,293 | 9,859 | 9,859 | 9,859 | 9,859 | 9,859 |
| *Cash balance* | (4,707) | 5,152 | 15,011 | 24,870 | 34,729 | 44,588 |

The cash budget shows that offering the discount has enabled the company to see a rise in its cash balance of nearly £10,000 by the end of the six-month period. The directors now need to weigh up the relative merits of a marginally higher profit versus a definite improvement in cash flow in order to select the most appropriate policy.

## Budgeted balance sheets

6.6 The preparation of a budgeted balance sheet is the final stage in the drafting of the master budget. The closing balances on the last period's balance sheet represent the opening balances on the forecast sheet. The closing balance sheet position (at the end of the forecast period) will depend upon the sales, costs and cash movements recorded in the profit and loss and cash budgets. Hence:

Forecast stock level = opening stock +
    purchases less stock used in production

Forecast debtors = opening debtors +
    credit sales less cash received from sales

Forecast creditors = opening creditors +
    purchases less cash paid to trade creditors

and so on.

# PLANS, FORECASTS AND BUDGETS

## Student Activity 6

If the discount scheme (detailed above) was introduced, which balance sheet items would be affected?

### Cash balances

6.7 The opening cash figure for Greene Ltd on 1st January 1997 is (£25,000). The closing figure, as at 30th June 1997, with the new policy in place, is £44,588. Both these numbers come from the cash budget. The forecast balance sheet figure for cash is thus easily derived.

6.8 Fixed asset figures in a forecast balance sheet must take account of the depreciation charged through the forecast profit and loss account. One-off changes in debtor collection policies or stock levels will have no effect on fixed asset values.

6.9 The forecast income statement will contain details on turnover which may in turn affect stock levels. Care must be taken to adjust the balance sheet accordingly. Debtor figures will often change over a time period. If discounts are offered, debtor balances will be reduced, because a greater proportion of sales are cash sales. For example, in the case of Greene Ltd, the new debtors' figure would equal £97,500 instead of £108,333 as it would have been if the discounts were not introduced. Again, this figure can be obtained from the cash budget and profit and loss forecasts.

6.10 Exactly the same basic rules apply to changing balance sheet values, as those that apply to adjustment of a profit and loss account. The main thing to remember is to check that you have identified *all* the affected elements and adjusted them accordingly. If you end up in a position in which fixed assets plus current assets equal short-term plus long-term liabilities, then it is likely that you have completed the corrections in full.

### Examination questions

6.11 It is usual for examination questions to ask you to comment on the budgets that you have prepared, as well as simply perform the computations correctly. Examiners' comments suggest that the quality of the commentaries is often quite poor. Things to remember when commenting on policy changes, and their impact on profit, cash and the balance sheet, include the following.

- Overdrafts per se are not bad; they are only a matter of concern if they are rising rapidly, or regularly close to the limit.

- High cash balances are undesirable. They represent a waste of valuable resources.

- Directors will choose between policies on the basis of their profit impact. Banks should also look at the cash effects.

- Policy changes which increase the volatility of cash balances are undesirable.

# FINANCIAL REPORTING, ANALYSIS AND PLANNING

- Policy changes which involve investment in fixed assets funded out of short-term loans are undesirable, unless they have a rapid cash payback.

## Summary

☐ Talk of budgets often draws a negative reaction from managers, who view them as a means of control, over which they have little influence. You should now appreciate that budgets are very useful tools to both managers and their superiors.

☐ Budgets offer the opportunity for companies to plan the financial detail which will ensure that the broader strategic objectives are fulfilled.

☐ Planning forces people into forward, instead of backward, thinking. In this way, managers can foresee problems before they ever arise, and in so doing they can devise plans for overcoming problems.

☐ Budgets must not be viewed rigidly as a tool of control, but more as an aid to effective planning. The figures contained in budgets are not written in tablets of stone, but simply represent best estimates of costs and revenues. As a consequence, there will be many occasions on which budget targets remain unfulfilled, for reasons outside the control of the manager in charge. In such circumstances when hard, but attainable, targets are set, managers will be motivated to improve their performance. When this happens budgets and plans are performing their true function, as tools which help raise the effectiveness of management.

## Self-assessment question

**Exam-style question**

Taken from the Autumn 1995 examination paper.

Cox Ltd's bank overdraft facility at present amounts to £350,000. The company's bank has recently requested the directors to take steps to reduce the level of the overdraft to £200,000 by 30 April 1996.

The forecast accounts for the six months to 31 October 1995 contain the following information:

*Profit and Loss Account: Six Months to 31 October 1995*

|  | £ |
|---|---:|
| Turnover | 1,200,000 |
| Less: Cost of goods sold (variable) | 720,000 |
| Operating expenses | 360,000 |
| Depreciation (straight line) | 40,000 |
|  | 1,120,000 |

# PLANS, FORECASTS AND BUDGETS

| | |
|---|---:|
| Net profit | 80,000 |

*Balance Sheet at 31 October 1995*

| | £ |
|---|---:|
| Fixed assets at cost | 500,000 |
| *Less:* Accumulated depreciation | 200,000 |
| | 300,000 |
| Stock in trade | 240,000 |
| Trade debtors | 200,000 |
| | 440,000 |
| Trade creditors | 120,000 |
| Bank overdraft | 350,000 |
| | 470,000 |
| Net current liabilities | (30,000) |
| | 270,000 |
| Issued share capital | 100,000 |
| Retained profit | 170,000 |
| | 270,000 |

Trading transactions take place at a constant rate during the year. All payments are made to trade creditors and received from trade debtors in the month following the date on which the purchase or sale takes place. Payments for operating expenses are made immediately they are incurred. The profit and loss account for the six months to April 1996 is expected to contain the same information as the forecast statement set out above, except for the financial effect of the alternative plans set out below.

The company's directors are considering the following ways of achieving the required reduction in the bank overdraft.

**Plan A:** A reduction in stock of £50,000 which would mean that, with effect from 1 November 1995, monthly sales would fall by 5%, as a result of having fewer goods available for customers. Operating expenses would fall by £2,000 per month.

**Plan B:** A discount of 3% to be allowed to customers who agree to pay immediately goods are supplied to them. It is estimated that half the customers would take the discount and the remainder would continue to take one month's credit.

Either alternative (A or B) would be put into effect on 1 November 1995.

That is:

- stock would be reduced by £50,000 in November by reducing purchases (Plan A); or
- sales in the month of November would be eligible for the 3% discount (Plan B).

# FINANCIAL REPORTING, ANALYSIS AND PLANNING

**Required**

(a) Separate forecast profit and loss accounts (monthly figures not required) for the six months to 30 April 1996 as a result of implementing:

  (i)  Plan A

  (ii) Plan B [7]

(b) Identify the forecast decrease in profit, compared with the expected results for the six months to 31 October 1995, which would result from the implementation of:

  (i)  Plan A

  (ii) Plan B [2]

(c) Select the plan (A or B) which would achieve the required reduction in the overdraft at the lower cost, and prepare:

  (i)  a monthly cash budget for the six months to 30 April 1996.

  (ii) a balance sheet at 30 April 1996. [15]

(d) The directors have asked the bank to consider allowing a longer period to achieve the required reduction in the level of the overdraft. Assuming the company is not obliged to implement either Plan A or Plan B, calculate how long it will take to achieve the required reduction and state whether this repayment period seems reasonable. [6]

*Notes:* Ignore bank interest.

Assume each month consists of 30 days.

[Total-30]

# Unit 17

## FRS 8 'Related Party Disclosures'

### Objectives

**When you have completed this Unit you should be able to:**

- define a related party according to FRS 8
- understand the disclosure of related party transactions
- list the exemptions in FRS 8.

## 1 Introduction

1.1 The Companies Act requires companies to disclose the name and country of incorporation of their ultimate holding company and, if relevant, the share interests of both directors and 'connected persons'. FRS 8 goes further: it requires disclosure of any controlling party, whether it is a company, a trust, a director, another individual or group acting in concert. FRS 8 also requires the disclosure of information on related party transactions.

## 2 Related parties

2.1 We need to consider at this point exactly what a related party is.

According to FRS 8, two or more parties are related parties if **one** of the following applies at any time during the financial period.

(i) One party has direct or indirect control of the other party.

(ii) The parties are subject to common control from the same source.

(iii) One party has influence over the financial and operating policies of the other party to an extent that that other party might be inhibited from pursuing at all times its own separate interests.

(iv) The parties, in entering a transaction, are subject to influence from the same source to such an extent that one of the parties to the transaction has subordinated its own separate interests.

### Student Activity 1

Tick from the following list any parties you consider to be related.

i) a company's parent undertaking

ii) a company's fellow subsidiary undertaking

# FINANCIAL REPORTING, ANALYSIS AND PLANNING

iii) a company's supplier

iv) a company's associated undertaking

> You should have ticked: i), ii), iv)
>
> iii) is not necessarily a related party simply by virtue of being a supplier

2.2 Certain parties are presumed to be related parties of a reporting entity unless it can be demonstrated that neither party has influenced the financial and operating polices of the other in such a way as to inhibit the pursuit of separate interests. For example, the key management of the reporting entity and key management of its parent undertaking would be presumed to be related parties.

## 3 Related party transactions

3.1 Financial statements should disclose material transactions undertaken by the reporting entity with a related party. Disclosure should be made irrespective of whether a price is charged. Table 17.1 lists the disclosures to be made.

**Table 17.1 Disclosures**

- the names of the transacting related parties
- a description of the relationship between the parties
- a description of the transactions
- the amounts involved
- any other elements of the transactions necessary for an understanding of the financial statements
- the amounts due to/from related parties at the balance sheet date and provisions for doubtful debts due from such parties at that date
- amounts written off in the period in respect of debts due to/from related parties

Transactions may be aggregated unless individual disclosure is necessary for the user to understand the impact of the transactions on the financial statements of the reporting entity.

**Exemptions**

3.2 FRS 8 applies to all financial statements that are intended to give a true and fair view of a reporting entity's financial position and profit or loss (or income and expenditure) for a period. The FRS does not, however, require disclosure:

(a) in consolidated financial statements, of any transactions or balance between group entities that have been eliminated on consolidation;

(b) in a parent's own financial statements when those statements are present together with its consolidated financial statements;

# FRS 8 'RELATED PARTY DISCLOSURES'

(c) in the financial statements of subsidiary undertakings, 90% or more of whose voting rights are controlled within the group, of transactions with entities that are part of the group (or investees of the group) qualifying as related parties, provided that the consolidated financial statements in which that subsidiary is included are publicly available;

(d) of pension contributions paid to a pension fund; and

(e) of emoluments in respect of services as an employee of the reporting entity.

FRS 8 does not require disclosure of the relationship and transactions between the reporting entity and the parties listed below simply as a result of their role as:

(a) providers of finance in the course of their business in that regard;

(b) utility companies

(c) government departments and their sponsored bodies;

(d) a customer, supplier, franchiser, distributor or general agent with whom an entity transacts a significant volume of business.

## Summary

**You should now be able to:**

- define a related party according to FRS 8
- understand the disclosure of related party transactions
- list the exemptions in FRS 8.

## Self-assessment questions

1. Define a 'related party' per FRS 8.
2. Do all related party transactions have to be disclosed?
3. List three disclosures which have to be made with respect to related party transactions.

FINANCIAL REPORTING, ANALYSIS AND PLANNING

# Appendix – Answers

# Unit 1

## Student Activities

2  You should have obtained the following answer:

Year 1: Y = 2,000 + (3,471 – 4,974) = £497
Year 2: Y = 2,000 + (1,818 – 3,471) = £347
Year 3: Y = 2,000 + (0 – 1,818) = £182

In order to maintain his capital and therefore his income in Year 1 Alan will have to save and reinvest (presumably at 10% interest) £1,503 i.e. £2,000 – £497.

4.  1. FALSE
    2. FALSE
    4. Substance over form

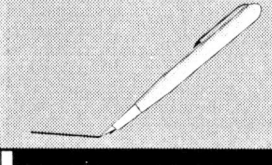

## Self-assessment questions

1.  'The Corporate Report' stated that:

    **'the fundamental objective of corporate reports is to communicate economic measurements of and information about resources and performance of the reporting entity useful to those having reasonable rights to such information.'**

    The ASB's *Statement of Principles* states that:

    **'The objective of financial statements is to provide information about the financial position, performance and financial adaptability of an enterprise that is useful to a wide range of users for assessing the stewardship of management and for making economic decisions.'**

2.  The ASB gave the following as its main reasons for developing the *Statement of Principles*.

    - To assist the ASB by providing a basis for reducing the number of alternative accounting treatments permitted by accounting standards and company law.

    - To provide a framework for the future development of accounting standards.

    - To assist auditors in forming an opinion as to whether financial statements conform with accounting standards.

    - To assist users of accounts in interpreting the information contained in them.

    - To provide guidance in applying accounting standards.

    - To give guidance on areas which are not yet covered by accounting standards.

- To inform interested parties of the ASB's approach in formulating accounting standards.

3. Gains are increases in ownership interest, other than those relating to contributions from owners.

   Losses are decreases in ownership interest, other than those relating to distributions from owners.

4. The primary financial statements are:
   - profit and loss account;
   - statement of total recognised gains and losses
   - balance sheet
   - cash flow statement.

5. The *Statement of Principles* defines financial adaptability as:

   **'the ability of an entity to take effective action to alter the amounts and timing of cash flows so that it can respond to unexpected needs or opportunities.'**

6. The operating gain is calculated as follows:

   |  |  | £ |
   |---|---:|---:|
   | Sale proceeds |  | 600 |
   | Less historic cost |  | 300 |
   | Historic cost profit |  | 300 |
   | Less holding gain: |  |  |
   | Replacement cost | 350 |  |
   | Historic cost | 300 |  |
   |  |  | 50 |
   | Operating gain |  | 250 |

7. A company's capital could be measured as follows:

   (a) historic cost

   (b) adjusted historic cost

   (c) replacement costs (entry values)

   (d) net realisable value (exit values)

   (e) the present value of future receipts from an asset.

8. False.

9. The disadvantages of using replacement costs are:
   - the replacement costs can be subjective
   - technological change may mean that the asset is obsolete
   - the business may not intend to replace the asset
   - replacement cost accounts are difficult for users to understand.

10. False.

APPENDIX

# Unit 2

## Student Activities

4   (a) £60,000 – accumulated realised profits less accumulated realised losses.

   (b) £10,000 – the distributable profits are further restricted by the unrealised losses of £50,000.

## Self-assessment questions

1. The four bodies are:

   (a) The Financial Reporting Council (FRC)

   (b) The Accounting Standards Board (ASB)

   (c) The Urgent Issues Task Force (UITF)

   (d) The Review Panel.

2. See paragraph 3.10.

3. The Review Panel only looks at a company's accounts when they have been brought to its attention by another party, e.g. press comment.

4. To date every company has amended its accounts when requested to do so by the Review Panel. This is probably due to the Companies Act provisions which allow the Review Panel to take recalcitrant companies to court to force them to comply. If the court finds in the Review Panel's favour the directors of the company face harsh penalties.

5. There is no precise definition of the 'true and fair' view; however, for practical purposes, a company's financial statements give a true and fair view when:

   (a) the requirements of the Companies Act are complied with;

   (b) all applicable accounting standards have been complied with;

   (c) if no accounting standard is available, accepted industry accounting principles are followed;

   (d) all material items have been adequately disclosed; and

   (e) the presentation of the accounts is appropriate with regard to the information needed by the user of those accounts.

6. The auditors provide the shareholders with an external objective check on the directors' financial statements.

7. False. The directors provide the statement.

8. The duties of the audit committee should include:

   (a) making recommendations to the board on the appointment, resignation or dismissal of the auditor and on the audit fee;

   (b) reviewing the interim and annual statements before they are submitted to the board;

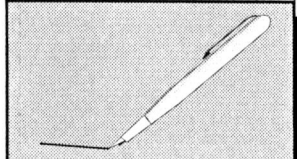

(c) undertaking discussions with the auditors, without the presence of executive directors, at least once a year;

(d) reviewing the internal audit programme and any significant findings;

(e) reviewing the external auditors' management letter and the company's statement on the internal control system.

9. The directors must explain their responsibility for preparing the accounts next to a statement by the auditors about their reporting responsibilities.

10. Section 263 of the Companies Act defines distributable profits as accumulated realised profits, so far as they have not been distributed or capitalised, less accumulated realised losses, so far as they have not been previously written off in a reduction or reorganisation of capital.

In addition a public company cannot make a distribution if at the time:

(a) the amount of its net assets is less than the combined total of its called up share capital plus its undistributable reserves; or

(b) the distribution will reduce the amount of its net assets to below the combined total of its called up share capital plus its undistributable reserves.

APPENDIX

# Unit 3

## Self-assessment questions

1. FALSE. It contains two balance sheet formats and four profit and loss account formats.

2. True, unless they have nil value for the current and previous year.

3. False

4. The following must not be treated as assets in the company's balance sheet:

   (a) preliminary expenses;

   (b) expenses of and commission on any issue of shares or debentures;

   (c) research costs.

5. False

6. False

7. The Companies Act requires that the accounts are accompanied by notes on the following:

   (a) Particulars of turnover

   (b) Particulars of staff

   (c) Directors' emoluments

   (d) Charges which must be disclosed

   (e) Income from listed investments

   (f) Rents receivable from land after deducting outgoings

   (g) Taxation

   (h) Extraordinary and exceptional items and prior year adjustments

   (i) Redemption of shares and loans

   (j) Earnings per share (listed companies only)

   (k) Statement showing movement on reserves.

8. The following particulars of staff must be disclosed.

   (a) Average number employed by the company (or by the group in consolidated accounts), divided between categories of workers, i.e. between manufacturing and administration.

   (b) (i) Wages and salaries paid to staff.

   (ii) Social security costs of staff.

   (iii) Other pension costs for employers.

   (c) Number of employees (excluding those working wholly or mainly overseas) earning over £30,000 per annum, analysed under successive multiples of £5,000 excluding pension contributions.

9. The following details of directors' emoluments must be disclosed.

(a) The aggregate amounts of:

   (i) emoluments, including pension contributions and benefits in kind (distinction should be made between those emoluments paid as fees and those for executive duties);

   (ii) pensions for past directors;

   (iii) compensation for loss of office.

(b) The chairman's emoluments and those of the highest paid director, if paid more than the chairman, excluding the pension contributions in both cases.

(c) The number of directors whose emoluments, excluding pension contributions, fall within each bracket of £5,000.

(d) Total amounts waived by directors and numbers concerned.

10. The relevant European Directives are as follows:

(a) 7th

(b) 8th

(c) 4th

APPENDIX

# Unit 4

## Self-assessment questions

**Short-answer questions**

1. The company's choice of depreciation rate can have a material effect on its reported profits. For example, if the reducing balance method is used it is likely in the earlier years to give a higher depreciation charge, and consequently lower profits, than if the straight line method is used. However, in the later years of the asset's life the reverse will be true. Over the whole of the asset's life the total charge to the profit and loss account will be identical regardless of which depreciation method has been employed.

2. The chief merit in regular revaluations of fixed assets is that the balance sheet more accurately reflects the true worth of the business. Fixed assets may comprise the majority of an enterprise's net worth. If these assets are materially understated (if, for example, the fixed assets comprise land and buildings stated at historic cost) the net book value of the business will not correlate with the true worth of the business.

   The effect of revaluations then is likely to be an uplift in the net book value, the reported net assets of the business. Under the rules of SSAP12, if a building is revalued then depreciation must be charged on the revalued amount. Thus reported profits are likely to be lower as the depreciation charge will be higher.

   Hence a revaluation will reduce reported ROCE, reduce reported gearing levels and reduce other reported profitability ratios. (See Unit 11)

3. See 3.17 – 3.27

4. A deficit on IRR, unless a temporary one, should be written off to the profit and loss account.

5. There are three methods for valuing purchased stock: LIFO (last in first out); FIFO (first in first out) and AVCO (average cost). Generally, in times of rising prices, LIFO will give the lowest stock values and lowest profits; FIFO will give the highest stock values and highest profits; AVCO will give stock valuations and profits somewhere in between. For an illustration of the effects of each of the three methods see Example 4.5.

6. An intangible fixed asset purchased separately from a business should be capitalised at its cost. An intangible asset acquired as part of the acquisition of a business should be capitalised separately from goodwill if its value can be measured reliably on initial recognition.

   According to FRS 10, intangible fixed assets should be amortised over their useful economic life. Where it is felt that the useful economic life exceeds 20 years or is indefinite, it should be subject to impairment reviews (described earlier in this book).

# FINANCIAL REPORTING, ANALYSIS AND PLANNING

**Multiple choice questions**

1. (d)
2. (d)

they should be valued annually, but by whom is not stated.

3. (d)
4. (c) see workings
5. (d) see workings
6. (d) see workings

*Workings for 4., 5., 6.*

## Hound

|  | £000 |
|---|---:|
| *Sales* | |
| 1200/1800 × 2000 | 1,333 |
| | |
| *Cost of sales* | |
| 1200/1800 × 1800 | (1200) |
| | |
| *Anticipated profit* | 133 |

|  | £000 |
|---|---:|
| *Debtors* | |
| P/L sales | 1333 |
| less cash received | (500) |
| | 833 |

|  | £000 |
|---|---:|
| WIP | |
| Costs to date | 1200 |
| Transfer to P/L | (1200) |
| | 0 |

## Racquet

|  | £000 | £000 |
|---|---:|---:|
| *Sales* | | |
| 750/1200 × 1000 | | 625 |
| | | |
| Cost of sales | | |
| 750/1200 × 1200 | 750 | |
| | | |
| plus anticipated loss not accounted for 450/1200 × 200 | 75 | |
| | | (825) |
| | | |
| (Whole of loss) | | (200) |

# APPENDIX

| Debtors | £000 |
|---|---|
| P/L sales | 625 |
| less cash received | (500) |
| | 125 |

| WIP | £000 |
|---|---|
| Costs to date | 750 |
| Transfer to P/L | (825) |
| Provisions | (75) |

*Totals*
Cost of sales (1200 + 825) = 2025
Debtors (833 + 125) = 958
WIP (nil + nil) = 0
Provisions (nil + 75) = 75

**Exam-style questions**

1. Despite the imposition of numerous accounting standards, there remains considerable scope for the adoption of different accounting policies when preparing published financial reports. This question required students to calculate and discuss the impact on the profit and loss account and balance sheet of the adoption of different accounting policies in three key areas, namely the valuation of plant, goodwill and stock.

(a) That accounting policies to be adopted in order to produce, respectively, the lowest and highest possible profit figure based on the information provided here as follows.

   (i) Plant and machinery: the reducing balance basis.

   Goodwill: capitalise and amortise over the expected useful life. Under SSAP 22, the goodwill could have been written off immediately against reserves; this has now been superseded by FRS 10 which does not allow this option.

   Stock: average cost basis gives a lower figure for costs, £2.77m, to be carried forward to future years and a correspondingly increased amount of expenses to be charged against the profit for this year.

(b) *Profit and Loss Account for year to 30 September 1995*

|  | Lowest | | Highest | |
|---|---:|---:|---:|---:|
|  | £000 | £000 | £000 | £000 |
| Sales |  | 11,470 |  | 11,470 |
| Less: |  |  |  |  |
| Opening stock | 1,850 |  | 2,050 |  |
| Cost of goods produced | 6,260 |  | 6,260 |  |
| Closing stock | (2,770) |  | (3,010) |  |
|  | 5,340 |  | 5,300 |  |
| Depreciation | 1,500 W1 |  | 950 W2 |  |
| Goodwill | 320 W3 |  | 320 W3 |  |
| Administration and selling expenses | 2,850 | (10,010) | 2,850 | 9,420 |
| Net profit |  | 1,460 |  | 2,050 |
| Retained profit, 1 October |  | 3,470 |  | 3,470 |
| Prior year adjustment – stock |  | – |  | 200 |
| Retained profit, 30 September |  | 4,930 |  | 5,720 |

*Balance Sheets at 30 September 1995*

|  | Lowest | Highest |
|---|---:|---:|
|  | £000 | £000 |
| **Intangible fixed assets** |  |  |
| Positive goodwill | 1,280 | 1,280 |
| **Tangible fixed assets** |  |  |
| Plant and machinery at cost | 5,000 | 5,000 |
| Less: Depreciation | 1,500 | 950 |
|  | 3,500 | 4,050 |
| **Current Assets** |  |  |
| Stock | 2,770 | 3,010 |
| Debtors | 1,500 | 1,500 |
|  | 4,270 | 4,510 |
| **Less: Current liabilities** |  |  |
| Trade creditors | 1,070 | 1,070 |
| Bank overdraft | 50 | 50 |
|  | 1,120 | 1,120 |
| Net current assets | 3,150 | 3,390 |
|  | 7,930 | 8,720 |
| **Financed by:** |  |  |
| Share capital | 3,000 | 3,000 |
| Retained profit | 4,930 | 5,720 |
|  | 7,930 | 8,720 |

W1  £5m × 30% = £1.5m
W2  £5m − £1.2m = £3.8m/4 = £0.95m
W3  £1.6m/5 = £0.32m

(c) Main points for discussion:

1. Rate of return on shareholders' equity

   Lowest: $(1460/7930) \times 100 = 18.4\%$

   Highest: $(2050/8720) \times 100 = 23.5\%$

2. The events measured are the same in each case.

3. The large difference in the rate of return is caused entirely by the use of different valuation bases; valuation procedures used under (b) (i) result in higher write-offs in the year to 30 September 1995 and smaller balances carried forward to be written off in future.

4. Over the entire life of an asset or business, the total amount written off is the same whichever valuation basis is used, but the allocation of the total charge (and profit) between different years varies.

*Areas of weakness in answers submitted to this question.*

- The application of the reducing balance percentage of 30% to cost less residual value (5m – 1.2m) rather than to the original cost of £5m.

- The omission of the prior year adjustment required in the case of stock where the first in first out basis is to be used,

- The failure to link comments under (c) (ii) with the rates of return reported for shareholders as a result of adopting different accounting policies.

2. This question tested students' understanding of the rules relating to the valuation of stocks.

   (a) Both SSAP 9 and the Companies Act 1985 require companies to value stock at cost, except where cost exceeds net realisable value (i.e. market price less further cost to completion, and less all costs to be incurred in marketing, selling and distributing stock), in which case the latter figure should be used.

   To ensure that full provision is made for foreseeable losses, SSAP 9 requires the comparison between cost and net realisable value to be based on individual items of stock, with the proviso that groups of similar items may be compared where the comparison of individual items is impracticable.

   Companies are required to use the total cost basis for external reporting purposes. Total cost is defined as those costs incurred 'in bringing the product or service to its present location and condition'.

   In the case of a manufacturing company, the total cost basis of valuation requires the inclusion of a share of factory overheads but not distribution costs or administrative expenses.

   The overheads included should be based on the normal level of activity in order to avoid fluctuations in stock values brought about simply by the fact that production has been abnormally high or low during a particular year.

# FINANCIAL REPORTING, ANALYSIS AND PLANNING

(b) (i)

1.  
          £  
A   3,600  (cost)  
B   2,500  (cost)  
C   5,000  (NRV)  
     11,100

2. 50,000/50 = 1.000 units  
NRV (£60 – £2) × 1,000   = £58,000

3. Cost                     £50,000  
NRV £40 – £2 = £38 × 1,000  £38,000

4.

|  | £ | per unit |
|---|---:|---:|
| Materials | 10,000 | 20 |
| Direct labour | 8,000 | 16 |
| Overheads 20,000/800 × 500 | 12,500 | 25 |
|  | 30,500 | 61 |
| Stock £30,500/500 × 100 | 6,100 |  |

(ii)

1. Stock is valued at the lower of cost and net realisable value, treating each item separately for the purpose of the comparison.

2. Net realisable value exceeds cost and, therefore, the figure to appear in the accounts will be £50,000.

3. This is a post-balance sheet event which requires an adjustment to re-state the stock at the net realisable value of £38,000.

4. Administrative overheads are not included in stock valuation. The factory overheads are included based on the normal level of production. This means that closing stock should include £25 per unit for overheads, and unrecovered overheads of £7,500 (£20,000-£12,500) will need to be written off in the profit and loss account.

**Areas of weakness in answers submitted to this question:**

- Few candidates drew attention to the fact that companies are required to use the total cost basis for external reporting purposes, or discussed the way in which total costs should be computed.

- Many candidates misunderstood requirement (b) and attempted to calculate profit figures in respect of Product D by comparing its cost with its net realisable value.

- A common error was for candidates to add the distribution cost for Product D to its selling price rather than deduct it.

- Few candidates were able to account properly for overheads in the valuation of the 'cambers'.

APPENDIX

# Unit 5

## Self-assessment questions

**Short-answer questions**

1. The three main principles in accounting for capital instruments are:
   - debt should be recorded at its fair value; the carrying amount of the debt will be reduced by any repayments of the principal and increased by any finance charges
   - the finance cost of the debt is, broadly speaking, the difference between the proceeds of the debt and the aggregation of the total repayments
   - the finance cost is allocated to accounting periods so as to produce a constant rate of interest on the carrying amount.

2. Events after the balance sheet date may either affect the items in the year end accounts or the future prospects of the company. Thus they need to be examined to see if the year end accounts need to be adjusted; or if the events, while not requiring an adjustment of the accounts, should be brought to the attention of the accounts' user through appropriate disclosure.

3. Prudence dictates that potential gains should not be anticipated while potential losses should be accounted for. Thus, in the case of contingencies a probable gain should not be accounted for and a probable loss should be accrued for.

4. Accounting for pension costs is an especially problematic area because of:
   - the long time scale involved
   - the large sums involved
   - the inherent uncertainties involved—necessitating numerous estimates as to future events. For example, future pay levels, average service length of employees, anticipated lifetimes, future inflation rates, future economic factors, etc.

5. Normally a fund surplus or deficit should be spread over the remaining service lives of the pension fund employees. There are two exceptions to this rule where the deficit may be spread over a shorter period: a material deficit or a significant reduction in the number of scheme employees.

   When a fund surplus is spread it leads to lower future pension cost charges in the accounts over the spreading period. Vice versa for a fund deficit.

**Multiple choice questions**

1. (d)
2. (d)
3. (a)
4. (d)
5. (b)
6. (a)

# FINANCIAL REPORTING, ANALYSIS AND PLANNING

**Exam-style question**

1. This question was based on section 2 of the syllabus, 'Accounting Practice'. Candidates were provided with a trial balance for Moonitz Plc as at 31 March 1995 and also informed of a number of post trial balance adjustments required for the purpose of preparing the company's final accounts. This was the least popular question in section B and answers were generally of a low standard.

   (i) *Profit and Loss Account of Moonitz plc, for the year ended 31 March 1995*

   |  | £000 | £000 |  |
   |---|---:|---:|---|
   | Turnover |  | 49,100 |  |
   | Cost of goods sold |  | 38,531 | W1 |
   | Gross profit |  | 10,569 |  |
   | Administrative, selling and distribution costs |  | (4,335) | W2 |
   | Profit on sale of freehold property |  | 400 | W3 |
   | Operating profit |  | 6,634 |  |
   | Interest payable |  | 600 | W4 |
   | Profit on ordinary activities before taxation |  | 6,034 |  |
   | Tax on profit on ordinary activities: |  |  |  |
   | charge for year | 2,120 |  |  |
   | transfer from DTA | (124) | 1,996 |  |
   | Profit after taxation |  | 4,038 |  |
   | Dividends: Paid | 400 |  |  |
   | Proposed | 600 | 1,000 |  |
   | Retained profit for the year |  | 3,038 |  |

   W1 £37,000 + £87 (loss on sale of widgets) – £506 (overstatement of opening stock) + £1,750 (depreciation) + £200 (goodwill written off).
   W2 £4,375 – £40 (insurance claim)
   W3 £3,150 – £2,750
   W4 £300 + £300 (accrual)

   (ii) *Statement of Movement on Reserves year ended 31 March 1995*

   |  | Retained profit | Revaluation reserve | Debenture redemption reserve |
   |---|---:|---:|---:|
   |  | £000 | £000 | £000 |
   | Balance at 1 April 1994 | 2,726 | 2,200 | 3,250 |
   | Retained profit for year | 3,038 |  |  |
   | Prior year adjustment | (506) |  |  |
   | Realised profit on property sold | 750 | (750) |  |
   | Revaluation of property |  | 4,200 W5 |  |
   | Transfer to debenture redemption reserve | (250) |  | 250 |
   |  | 5,758 | 5,650 | 3,500 |

   W5 £9,650 – (£8,200 – £2,750)

APPENDIX

*(iii) Balance Sheet at 31 March 1995*

|  | £000 | £000 |  |
|---|---:|---:|---|
| *Fixed assets* | | | |
| *Tangible* | | | |
| Freehold properties at valuation | | 9,650 | |
| Plant and machinery at cost less depreciation | | 8,340 | W6 |
| *Intangible* | | | |
| goodwill | | 1,200 | W7 |
| | | 19,190 | |
| Current assets | | | |
| Stocks | 3,598 W8 | | |
| Debtors and prepayments | 5,234 W9 | | |
| Cash in hand | 5 | | |
| | 8,837 | | |
| *Creditors: amounts falling due within one year* | | | |
| Trade creditors and accruals | 2,902 W10 | | |
| Corporation tax | 2,120 | | |
| Proposed dividend | 600 | | |
| ACT | 150 | | |
| Bank overdraft | 216 | | |
| | 5,988 | | |
| Net current assets (liabilities) | | 2,849 | |
| Total assets less current liabilities | | 22,039 | |
| *Creditors: amount falling due after more than one year* | | | |
| 12 debentures redeemable 2001 | 5,000 | | |
| Deferred tax account | 131 W11 | 5,131 | |
| | | 16,908 | |
| *Capital and Reserves* | | | |
| Called up share capital | | 2,000 | |
| Profit and loss account | | 5,758 | |
| Revaluation reserve | | 5,650 | |
| Debenture redemption reserve | | 3,500 | |
| | | 16,908 | |

W6 £12,240 - (£2,150 + £1,750)
W7 £1,400 - £200
W8 £3,685 - £150 + £63
W9 £5,194 + £40
W10 £2,602 + £300
W11 £405 - £124 - £150

(b)

*Note:* 4. The sale of the stock is a post balance sheet event but it provides information concerning conditions which existed at the balance sheet date, namely that the stock had declined in value due to water damage. The stock must therefore be restated at its realisable value and the

# FINANCIAL REPORTING, ANALYSIS AND PLANNING

difference (£150,000 - £63,000: £87,000) must be added to cost of sales.

*Note: 5.* It is almost certain that the £40,000 will be received and this may be offset against the cost of the repairs and treated as a debtor in the balance sheet. There is also a contingent gain of £12,000 but, as it is improbable that it will materialise, it should not be disclosed.

*Note: 6.* This is a post balance sheet event comprising new information which does not relate to conditions existing at the balance sheet date. No adjustment to the accounts is required but the event should be disclosed by way of note as it is relevant to a proper appreciation of a company's financial position.

## *Areas of weakness in answers submitted to this question*

- Failure to show workings.
- Many candidates included no more than two or three of the eight adjustments required to be made to figures included in the profit and loss account.
- Few candidates treated the fundamental error as a prior year adjustment requiring the cost of goods sold and the retained profit brought forward to be reduced by £506,000. Indeed, many candidates reduced the figure for stock at 31 March 1995 by that amount.
- In the balance sheet, only a small minority of candidates made the necessary adjustment to closing stock and relatively few included the interest accrual amongst 'Creditors: amounts falling due within one year'.
- Hardly any candidates succeeded in calculating correctly the balance on deferred tax account.
- Many candidates either ignored or guessed at answers to requirement (b).

2. This question required candidates to assemble a number of balances in the form of a balance sheet, to identify two categories of business asset which are typically omitted from this financial statement and to discuss certain aspects of the content of FRS5.

   (a) part (i) Balance sheet at 30 April 1995

   |  | £000 | £000 |
   |---|---|---|
   | *Fixed assets* | | |
   | Tangible assets | | 3,850,000 |
   | Investment in Armstrong Ltd | | 750,000 |
   | | | 4,600,000 |
   | *Current assets* | | |
   | Stocks | 375,400 | |
   | Cash at bank and in hand | 12,600 | |
   | | 388,000 | |

# APPENDIX

*Creditors: amounts falling due within one year*

| | | |
|---|---:|---:|
| Trade creditors | 262,100 | |
| MCT payable | 153,700 | |
| Proposed dividend | 80,000 | |
| VAT payable | 37,500 | |
| ACT payable | 20,000 | |
| | 553,300 | |
| Net current assets (liabilities) | | (165,300) |
| Total assets less current liabilities | | 4,434,700 |

*Creditors: amounts falling due after more than one year*

| | |
|---|---:|
| Provision for deferred taxation | (75,100) |
| | 4,359,600 |
| Capital and Reserves | |
| Called up share capital | 1,000,000 |
| Share premium account | 220,000 |
| Profit and loss account (balance figure) | 2,189,600 |
| Revaluation reserve | 950,000 |
| | 4,359,600 |

(a) part (ii) Two business assets which commonly exist but are excluded from the balance sheet are as follows.

*Research expenditure.* The Companies Act and SSAP13 require research expenditure to be written off as soon as it is incurred. The justification for this approach is that the future benefits are extremely difficult to identify and value and so are best ignored.

*Non-purchased goodwill.* This is goodwill built up over time as a result of the development of good trading relationships. FRS 10 and the Companies Act both make it clear that only purchased goodwill should be recognised in the accounts. The main reason for excluding non-purchased goodwill is that its value is subject to wide fluctuation due to both internal and external circumstances, making any assessment of its worth highly subjective. In essence, the problem is that its value has not been evidenced by an arm's length transaction.

Other items which candidates might discuss include development expenditure and purchased goodwill where the company has chosen to write these off immediately they are incurred.

(b) FRS5 attempts to ensure that the published accounts reflect the 'substance' of an entity's transactions and are not merely confined to reporting the strict legal form of business transactions, i.e. the statement is a determined attempt to establish truth and fairness as the principal test of the adequacy of financial reporting practices.

One example of a special purpose transaction, designed principally to achieve the objective of removing 'off balance sheet finance' (where the reported debt is less than the effective debt), is a sale and repurchase agreement. This involves arrangements for the sale of stock to, say, a finance company, and for the repurchase of the stock at some later date.

FINANCIAL REPORTING, ANALYSIS AND PLANNING

The objective of this scheme has been to raise temporary finance, but avoid disclosure in the accounts (the company receives cash and stock is reduced - the finance does not appear in the balance sheet). The repurchase price covers the amount of the loan plus an agreed rate of interest.

FRS5 believes that the substance of such a transaction is a loan rather than a sale, and that it should be reported as the former rather than the latter, and the 'loan' raised disclosed in the balance sheet.

Other examples of special purpose transactions which students might discuss are:

- loan transfers, e.g. SPVs
- consignment stock
- factoring
- securitised assets.

*Areas of weakness in answers submitted to this question*

- The only common error in the balance sheet was to mis-classify the investment in Armstrong Ltd under 'capital and reserves'.
- Many candidates appeared to attempt this question as a 'last resort' in Section B, and a significant number guessed at the answers to (a) (ii) and (b), although a very small number were fully familiar with the provisions of FRS5.

APPENDIX

# Unit 6

## Self-assessment questions

**Short-answer questions**

1. FRS3 was introduced to improve the quality of reporting enterprises' financial performance. This was facilitated by:
   - splitting the components of profit and expenditure into those derived from ongoing, newly acquired and discontinued activities;
   - prevention of abuse and misrepresentation of company results through classifying items as extraordinary when in fact they were not;
   - highlighting the range of financial performance including non-operating and unrealised gains presented in the SORG;
   - focusing users' attention on a range of performance indicators.

2. Probably yes. The abuse of the old SSAP6 regarding extraordinary items has ceased. Users are given more information on the face of the profit and loss account to enable them to ascertain maintainable earnings. Conversely the extra information and new primary statements have possibly resulted in information overload and user confusion. Also the virtual abolition of 'extraordinary' items has led to more volatile earnings and arguably made it harder to identify the underlying performance of the company.

3. A prior period adjustment is necessary in the event of a material situation arising where previous years' financial accounts have been misstated either due to:
   - a fundamental error or
   - a change in accounting policy.

   To effect the prior period adjustment the opening balance sheet should be amended, in the current year the correct/new policy should be applied and the comparative figures amended if necessary. The adjustment, its nature, justification and effect should be disclosed in the financial statements.

4. The requirement of the Companies Act 1985 is that the financial statements should show a 'true and fair' view of the company's performance and position. It may be necessary for certain items in the accounts to be accounted for in line with their economic substance rather than their strict legal form. One example is an asset leased under a finance lease. Legally the asset is that of the lessor. In substance, looking at the length of hire period, the obligation of the hirer and the total payments of the hirer, it may well, in substance, be the asset of the lessee.

5. According to the *Statement of Principles* an asset is 'The right or access to future economic benefits, controlled by an entity, as a result of past transactions or events'. The definition is significant in the context of FRS5 because the definition is used to identify whether a transaction gives rise to an asset or not. The party with access to the benefits, for example, will probably be the party that has to account for the resulting asset (and any associated liability) in its books.

# FINANCIAL REPORTING, ANALYSIS AND PLANNING

6. EPS is of interest because it is a fundamental indicator of company performance. It expresses, in an amount per share, how much the current year's earnings of the company amount to. The EPS is used to calculate the key PE ratio, an indication of the worth of a share in profit terms.

7. Often, in attempting to interpret the results of an enterprise, one year's figures together with comparatives is insufficient, particularly if one is trying to establish whether any trends have been set. Other factors may be hard to spot if only one or two years' figures are available. For example, a business may operate in a cyclical industry; or the year in question may be unusually good or bad in comparison to the long-term average. One-off factors may affect one of the years in question.

8. Generally, according to SSAP4, a government grant is spread over the period to which the grant relates. For example, if a grant is given against the cost of capital plant, the grant will be released to the profit and loss account over the useful economic life of the asset. Or in the case of a revenue grant, released to the profit and loss account over the period of the qualifying expenditure, for example the required employment of a certain number of employees to qualify for the grant. If some of the grant conditions have been breached, for example the asset had been sold or the qualifying number of employees are no longer employed, then potentially all or part of the grant may be repayable. In this instance, the prudence concept would dictate that a provision be made in the accounts for the amount potentially repayable.

## Multiple choice questions

1. (d)
2. (c)
3. (a)
4. (d). If the accounts are prepared correctly, economic substance usually, but not always, equates with the legal form.
5. (b)
6. (c)

## Exam-style question

Students were required to define and calculate earnings per share for Brownlee Plc based on information provided for 1994. They were also required to demonstrate their understanding of a bonus (capitalisation) issue of shares and to assess its effect on the calculation of the earnings per share for the current and preceding year.

(a) Earnings per share may be defined as earnings for the period after deducting tax, minority interest and preference dividends, in pence, attributable to each equity share ranking for dividends in the period under consideration.

Its purpose is to discover the amount of profit per share used for comparison with a previous year or another company.

(b) $$\text{EPS} \frac{(3{,}920{,}000 - 800{,}000) \times 100}{5{,}000{,}000} = 62.4\text{p}$$

# APPENDIX

(c) (i) A bonus issue occurs when a company allots fully paid equity shares to existing members and capitalises a corresponding value from its reserves, including any credit balance on its profit and loss account. The company does not receive any consideration for the issue. Every shareholder receives bonus shares in proportion to their existing stake in the company, e.g. the holder of 10% equity shares would receive 10% of any bonus issue.

Profit earned and retained within a business remains legally available for distribution, though in practice this is normally impossible as re-investment in business assets is likely to have taken place, i.e. the resources which have been retained are used to finance expansion. A bonus issue recognises this fact and is accounted for by making a transfer from distributable reserves to the (permanent) share capital account

(ii) Balance sheet extracts 31 December 1994

|  | £000 |
|---|---|
| Issued share capital (£ shares) | 30,000 |
| Retained profit | 1,100 |
|  | 31,000 |
| 8% Preference shares | 10,000 |

(d) EPS $\dfrac{(3{,}920{,}000 - 800{,}000) \times 100}{30{,}000{,}000} = 10.4p$

1993 comparative EPS $\dfrac{54}{6} = 9p$

A comparison of the EPS for 1994, 10.4p, with the unadjusted figure for 1993, 54p, would suggest that performance has declined significantly. However, each shareholder who previously held one share, now holds six shares. The EPS for 1993 must therefore be divided by six to allow a valid comparison with 1994's results.

## Areas of weakness in answers submitted to this question:

- The definition of earnings per share simply as earnings for the period after deducting tax.

- The failure to deduct the dividend on preference shares from after tax profit for the purpose of calculating EPS.

- Bonus issue of five fully paid ordinary shares made instead of the one already held rather than in addition to the one held, resulting in an issue a share capital of £25,000.

- Many candidates, although aware of the mechanics of the bonus issue, were unaware of the purpose of this adjustment.

- The failure to calculate the adjusted EPS for 1993 and/or explain its purpose.

# Unit 7

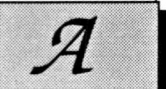

## Self-assessment questions

### Short answer questions

1. Timing differences arise because the tax treatment of fixed assets differs from the accounting treatment. Capital allowances are given by the Inland Revenue against the cost of fixed assets; while in the financial accounts depreciation is charged against the cost of the assets.

   Calculating depreciation is a subjective exercise with several different methods allowed. Further, estimates are made regarding assets' useful lives and residual values. This degree of latitude is unacceptable to the Inland Revenue who set strict rules on qualifying assets and rates of capital allowances.

2. ACT is advance corporation tax paid following a qualifying distribution (usually a dividend) by a company. It is paid fourteen days after the quarter end in which the dividend is paid. It is not an extra tax because any ACT paid is deducted from the mainstream corporation tax liability due in the following accounting period.

3. Dividend income should be shown gross (the tax element is added to the corporation tax charge in the profit and loss account). Dividends paid should be shown net.

4. Strictly a deferred tax provision is not a liability. There is no current obligation to pay the Inland Revenue, apart from the corporation tax liability. However deferred tax represents the tax potentially payable in the future, therefore it is classified as a provision.

5. A company will only provide for deferred taxation when there is reasonable anticipation that the tax will be payable in the future. When a timing difference arises but there is no likelihood of its reversing in the foreseeable future (e.g. a revaluation of a fixed asset when the company does not intend to sell the asset) then the amount of unprovided tax should be disclosed.

### Multiple choice questions

1. (c) Working:

|  | £000 | £000 |
|---|---|---|
| C tax liability | | 1,000 |
| less ACT paid | | |
| Dividend paid | 228 | |
| dividend received | (72) | |
| | 156 × 20/80ths | (39) |
| ACT on proposed dividend | 344 × 20/80ths | 86 |
| | | 1,047 |

2. (d)
3. (b)
4. (d)

# APPENDIX

5. (a) Working:

|  | £000 |
|---|---|
| Balance at 1 January 19X1 | 300 |
| Transfer from P/L a/c | 60 |
| less ACT on proposed dividend | |
| 20/80ths × £200,000 | (50) |
| | 310 |

**Exam-style question**

Candidates were first required to define the following terms:

- **Exceptional items.** Broadly speaking. these are items which are abnormal as regards their size but which result from the ordinary activities of the business. An example is an abnormal charge for bad debts.

- **Extraordinary items.** These arise as a result of events outside normal trading activities: they are material in amount and not expected to recur. Because of the extreme rarity of such items. no examples are provided in FRS3.

- **Prior year adjustments.** These consist of:
  - Material adjustments applicable to prior years arising from changes in accounting policies, e.g. where a company changes from FIFO to AVCO.
  - The correction of fundamental errors made when preparing earlier years' accounts. e.g. where the directors forget to count the stocks in one of the warehouses and, as a result. materially understate profits.

The final accounts of Pavin Ltd are in the process of being prepared and candidates were required to prepare the following financial statements.

*Profit and loss account for the year ended 31 December 1995*

|  | £000 | £000 |
|---|---|---|
| Turnover | | 3,620 |
| Cost of goods sold | | 2,533 |
| Gross profit | | 1,087 |
| Administrative expenses | | 526 |
| Distribution costs (317+90) | | 407 |
| Operating profit | | 154 |
| Investment income | | 110 |
| Interest payable | | (12) |
| Profit on ordinary activities before taxation | | 252 |
| Tax charge | 40 | |
| Tax credits reinvestment income | 22 | 62 |
| Profit after taxation | | 190 |
| Dividends: ordinary | | 80 |
| Retained profit for the year | | 110 |

*Statement of movement on reserves, 1995*

|  | Retained profit £000 | Redemption reserve £000 |
|---|---|---|
| Balance brought forward | 560 | |

# FINANCIAL REPORTING, ANALYSIS AND PLANNING

| | | |
|---|---:|---:|
| Prior year adjustments: | | |
|    Development expenditure written off | (88) | |
|    Change in method of stock valuation | (24) | |
| Transfer to redemption reserve | (12) | 12 |
| Retained profit for the year | 110 | |
| | 546 | 12 |

Workings. £000

W1 2,105 + 102 (development expenditure) + 6 (change in method of stock valuation) + 320 (depreciation).

*Balance sheet at 31 December 1995*

| | £000 | £000 |
|---|---:|---:|
| **Fixed assets** | | |
| Tangible assets | | |
| Plant and machinery at cost | 2,108 | |
| Less: accumulated depreciation | 1,320 | |
| | | 788 |
| Advance corporation tax recoverable | | 20 |
| **Current assets** | | |
| Stocks | 321 | |
| Debtors and prepayments | 320 | |
| Cash at bank and in hand | 7 | |
| | 648 | |
| **Creditors: amounts falling due within one year** | | |
| Trade creditors | 126 | |
| Current corporation tax | 40 | |
| Proposed dividend | 80 | |
| Advance corporation tax | 20 | |
| Interest payable | 12 | |
| | 278 | |
| Net current assets | | 370 |
| Total assets less current liabilities | | 1,178 |
| **Creditors: amounts falling due after more than one year** | | |
| 10% Debentures | | 120 |
| | | 1,058 |
| **Capital and reserves** | | |
| Called-up share capital | | 500 |
| Debenture redemption reserve | | 12 |
| Profit and loss account | | 546 |
| | | 1,058 |

### Areas of weakness in answers submitted to this question:

- The classifications of exceptional item and extraordinary item confused with one another.
  - The conviction that prior year adjustments covered all revisions or valuation estimates made in earlier years.
  - The treatment of the entire development expenditure cost, £190,000. as a write-off in 1995.

# APPENDIX

- Difficulties in making the adjustments required to change from FIFO to AVCO.

- Failure to recognise that no depreciation had been charged for 1995 and, therefore, the inclusion of only the difference between the original charge of £200,000 and the revised charge of £320,000 in the accounts for 1995.

- Failure to show accruals for interest. corporation tax, and proposed dividend amongst current liabilities.

- The omission of the debit and credit entries in the balance sheet relating to advance corporation tax on the final dividend.

FINANCIAL REPORTING, ANALYSIS AND PLANNING

# Unit 8

## Self-assessment questions

**Short-answer questions**

1. Either by acquiring more assets itself, or by acquiring the assets of another company, or by buying shares in another company. In the third instance the investment could take the form of a trade investment, an associate or a subsidiary.

2. Consolidated accounts are necessary to show the performance and position of the whole entity: the entity comprising the group of companies over which the holding company has control.

3. We account for *all* the subsidiary's assets and liabilities (and indeed all the subsidiary's income and expenditure) because the holding company has control over *all* those items. Even if the holding company only owns 75% of the subsidiary's share capital it in fact can buy/sell/use those assets as it chooses, regardless of the wishes of the minority shareholders.

4. We account for the assets and liabilities of the group. Thus intercompany items are not assets or liabilities due from or to parties outside the group.

5. Dividends straddling the acquisition date should be split – the portion before acquisition is deducted from the cost of acquisition (in the cost of control account). The post acquisition element should be accounted for in the consolidated profit and loss account.

6. Monetary assets and liabilities should be valued at the amount expected to be received or paid, possibly adjusted for their timing. For example, long-term receivables may need to be discounted to give a fair value of that asset. Market values are often a useful source for establishing fair values of monetary assets/liabilities.

7. One of the likely effects of the introduction of FRS7 is that provisions on acquisition against the subsidiary's assets will become rarer. Therefore it is likely that the effect of FRS7 will be to reduce post acquisition ROCE. This is because post acquisition profits will probably be lower than before FRS7, while assets values will very probably be higher.

8. Merger accounting is usually preferable because the 'goodwill on acquisition' termed 'premium on merger' is likely to be lower. Also, group reserves are merged since incorporation, not since merger. Finally, the fair value exercise does not have to be undertaken.

9. Goodwill on acquisition is calculated on a fair value basis; premium on merger is calculated on a nominal basis. Goodwill is the difference between the fair value of the consideration and the fair value of separable net assets acquired. Premium on merger is the difference between the nominal value of shares issued and the nominal value of shares acquired.

10. FRS2 was introduced to update UK accounting standards to bring them in line with the Companies Act 1989. It introduced the principle that a Parent –

# APPENDIX

Subsidiary relationship exists as a result of control not necessarily ownership. The notion of an unincorporated subsidiary undertaking was also introduced.

## Multiple choice questions

1. (d)
2. (a)
3. (b)
4. (a) Working:

|  | £m |
|---|---|
| Holding company reserves (£130m + £40m) | 170 |
| Holding company's share of post-acquisition reserves (60% × [£140m − £60m]) | 48 |
|  | 218 |

5. (c)

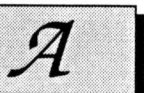

## Exam-style questions

1.

| **Workings** | Total equity £000 | At Acquis. £000 | Since £000 | Minority Interest £000 |
|---|---|---|---|---|
| Toye (60%) | | | | |
| Share capital | 800 | 480 | | 320 |
| Profit and loss account: | | | | |
|   At acquisition | 460 | 276 | | 184 |
|   Since acquisition | 640 | – | 384 | 256 |
| | 1,900 | 756 | 384 | 760 |

|  | Total Equity £000 | At Acquis. £000 | Since £000 | Minority Interest £000 |
|---|---|---|---|---|
| <u>Brown</u> 75% |  |  |  |  |
| Share capital | 300 | 225 |  | 75 |
| Profit and loss account |  |  |  |  |
|   At acquisition | 264 | 198 |  | 66 |
|   Since acquisition | 36 |  | 27 | 9 |
|  | 600 | 423 | 27 | 150 |
| Totals Toye & Brown |  | 1,179 | 411 | 910 |
| Price paid |  | 1,303 |  |  |
| Positive goodwill |  | 124 |  |  |
|  |  |  | 1,220 |  |
| Profit and loss account. Lyle |  |  | 1,631 |  |

*Consolidated balance sheet of Lyle Ltd and its subsidiaries at 31 December 1995*

|  | £000 |
|---|---|
| Positive goodwill | 124 |
| Sundry assets less current liabilities | 4,217 |
| 13% debenture stock | (1,300) |
|  | 3,041 |
| Share capital | 500 |
| Retained profit | 1,631 |
|  | 2,131 |
| Minority interest | 910 |
|  | 3,041 |

Requirement (b) called for an examination of the gearing position of each of the companies separately and the group as a whole at 31 December 1995.

Debt: equity ratios

| Lyle | 500:1720 | 0.29:1 |
|---|---|---|
| Toye | 600:1900 | 0.32.1 |
| Brown | 200:600 | 0.33:1 |
| Group | 1,300:2,131 | 0.61.1 |

It will be noticed that the gearing ratios of the three companies taken individually is significantly less than that of the group. The reason for this is that inter-company share holdings cancel out on consolidation whereas debentures all held outside the group must be aggregated. Consequently the consolidation statement reveals a much higher level of gearing than is evident from the examination of the individual balance sheet of each of the component companies within the group. It is therefore evident that the group as a whole is rather more vulnerable in terms of the level of gearing and the related legal obligation to make interest payments than is evident from an examination of the balance sheets of any single company.

# APPENDIX

## Areas of weakness in answers submitted to this question:

- An inability to properly allocate profits between the preacquisition period and the post-acquisition period for the purpose of computing goodwill and the retained profit of the group.

- Aggregation of the share capital of all three companies.

- Basing the calculation of minority interest only on equity at the date of acquisition.

- An inability to explain why the computed gearing of the group is higher than that of the individual companies comprising the group.

2. Candidates were required to prepare consolidated balance sheets for Rowland plc and Coase Ltd complying separately with the requirements of FRS2 and SSAP 23, and to advise the directors of Rowland plc how the financial information appearing in the published accounts would differ depending upon the method adopted.

(a) **Consolidated Balance Sheet**

|  | Acquisition Method £000 | Merger Method £000 |
|---|---|---|
| Positive goodwill arising on consolidation | 420 W2 | – |
| Fixed assets at book value | 15,700 | 15,700 |
|  | 16,120 | 15,700 |
| Current assets: Stocks | 2,610 | 2,610 |
| Debtors | 1,137 | 1,137 |
| Cash | 60 | 60 |
|  | 3,807 | 3,807 |
| Trade creditors | 1,109 | 1,109 |
| Net current assets | 2,698 | 2,698 |
| Total assets *less* current liabilities | 18,818 | 18,398 |
| 12% debentures | 1,800 | 1,800 |
|  | 17,018 | 16,598 |
| Issued share capital | 9,200 W3 | 9,200 W3 |
| Share premium account | 3,000 W7 | – |
| Retained profit at 30 Sept 1993 | 4,466 | 6,906 W4 |
| Profit, year to 30 Sept 1994 | 352 W1 | 492 W5 |
|  | 17,018 | 16,598 |

# FINANCIAL REPORTING, ANALYSIS AND PLANNING

| W1 | Total equity £000 | At Acquisition £000 | Since Acquisition £000 |
|---|---|---|---|
| Share capital | 1,000 | 1,000 | |
| Retained profit: at acq. | 2,640 | 2,640 | |
| since acq. | 296 | | 296 |
| | 3,936 | 3,640 | 296 |
| Price paid 1,200,000 × 3.50 | | 4,200 | |
| Goodwill | | 560 | |
| Profit of Rowland | | | 196 |
| | | | 492 |
| Less: Goodwill written off | | | 140 |
| | | | 352 |

W2  560 – 140                W5  196+296
W3  8,000+1,200              W6  1,200 – 1,000
W4  4,466 + 2,640 – 200 (W6) W7  4,200 – 1,200

(b) Under the acquisition method. it is necessary to calculate goodwill as the difference between the price paid (with shares issued valued at their market price) and the fair value of assets acquired. In this instance, goodwill amounts to £560,000.

Goodwill is recorded in the balance sheet and amortised over its expected useful economic life as has been done above. The result is to report a stronger asset base but the reported profits for the current year and the following three years will be lower than under the merger method due to the need to write off goodwill at the rate of £140,000 per annum

The requirement to value shares issued at market price gives rise to a share premium of £3m if the acquisition method is used

Under the merger method, past profits remain distributable thus providing, theoretically, a substantial basis for future dividend payments should the directors so choose

### *Areas of weakness in answers submitted to this is question*

- The failure to capitalise pre acquisition profits under the acquisition method.
- The failure to compute the premium arising on the issue of shares under the acquisition method.
- The failure to calculate the merger reserve under the merger method.
- The inclusion of issued share capital at £9m instead £9.2m under each method.

# APPENDIX

# Unit 9

## Self-assessment questions

1. The statement is false.

2. 
| | |
|---|---:|
| The premium on the new issue is | £5,000 |
| The premium paid on redemption is | £10,000 |
| The balance on the share premium account after the new issue is | £25,000 |
| The premium on the original issue was | £10,000 |

Thus £5,000, being the lowest amount, can be written off to the share premium account.

The distributable profits will be reduced by:

| | £ | £ |
|---|---:|---:|
| Cost of shares redeemed | | 60,000 |
| less: nominal value of shares issued | 20,000 | |
| written off to share premium | 5,000 | |
| | | 25,000 |
| | | 35,000 |

3. The capital redemption reserve will be:

| | |
|---|---:|
| Nominal value of shares redeemed | 50,000 |
| less nominal value of shares issued | 20,000 |
| Capital redemption reserve | 30,000 |

The £5,000 premium paid on redemption not written off to the share premium account is written off against distributable reserves.

4. Before a private company can make such a payment out of capital the following conditions must be met under sections 171–177 of the Companies Act.

    (a) It must be authorised by the company's articles;

    (b) The payment must not exceed the 'permissible capital payment'. (The permissible capital payment is the amount required to purchase the shares less the company's available profits and any proceeds from a new issue of shares.)

    (c) The directors must make a statutory declaration specifying the amount of the permissible capital payment and also that they are of the opinion that the company will be able to pay its debts:

    (i) immediately following the purchase or redemption; and

    (ii) also for one year immediately following.

    (d) A report by the company's auditors must be annexed to the statutory declaration stating that:

    - they have enquired into the company's affairs
    - the permissible capital payment has been properly determined

- they are not aware of anything to indicate that the opinion expressed by the directors is unreasonable.

(e) The payment must be approved by a special resolution. The special resolution is invalid if it is passed only because the shares being purchased were voted.

(f) The payments out of capital must be made not earlier than five weeks nor later than seven weeks after the date of the resolution.

5. False, see paragraph 2.6.

6. Under section 135 of the Companies Act 1985 a company may:
   - write off unpaid share capital
   - write off any share capital which is lost or not represented by available assets
   - write off any paid up share capital which is in excess of requirements.

   Under section 425 a company may:
   - write off debenture interest arrears
   - replace existing debentures with a lower interest debenture
   - write off preference dividend arrears
   - write off amounts owing to trade creditors.

7. Individual stakeholders have the right to dissent, and can apply to receive the cash equivalent of their holding or to insist that the sale to the new company is abandoned.

8. (a) If the capital reduction is less than the accumulated losses the scheme must be revised as the raison d'être of the scheme would be to eliminate the accumulated losses.

   (b) The amount by which the capital reduction exceeds the accumulated losses should be transferred to a capital reserve.

9. The proceeds available to the shareholders are:

   |  | £000 | £000 |
   |---|---|---|
   | Net proceeds |  | 200 |
   | less Creditors | 80 |  |
   | Bank overdraft | 85 |  |
   |  |  | 165 |
   | Available to shareholders |  | 35 |

   Therefore in (a) the preference shareholders would receive £30,000.

   In (b) where they did not receive priority in the repayment of capital they would receive:

   £35,000 × 30/80 = £13,125

10. The preference shareholders would have all their capital returned in a liquidation. They would not accept a capital reduction without gaining in some other respect.

    This would entail increasing the possible return on the preference shares. This could be achieved by:

# APPENDIX

- increasing the dividend rate
- having a high redemption value at some future date, or
- providing the preference shares with an option whereby they could be converted into ordinary shares at a fixed price at some future date.

FINANCIAL REPORTING, ANALYSIS AND PLANNING

# Unit 10

## Self-assessment questions

1. False. The value of a business is based upon its earnings and the investors' circumstances.

2. Delta plc's valuation is as follows:

   |  | £000 |
   |---|---|
   | Profit after tax | 1,000 |
   | Return on capital employed £5m × 12% = | 600 |
   | Return on goodwill | 400 |

   The goodwill is worth £400,000/0.18 = £2,222,222

   The company is therefore worth
   £5,000,000 + £2,222,222 = £7,222,222.

3. The current share price is £50,000/100,000 × 12 = £6.

4. The company's shares have a PE ratio of 100/12.5 = 8.

5. 
   |  | £m |
   |---|---|
   | Fox plc's free cashflow would be £175m/10 = | 17.5 |
   | Less depreciation | (3.5) |
   | Plus replacement of fixed assets | 2.0 |
   |  | 16.0 |
   | Less retained profits | 12.0 |
   | Dividends paid | 4.0 |

6. The highest price George should pay is:

   $$\frac{25p \times 1.06}{0.10 - 0.06} = £6.625$$

7. The model used to answer 6 would not work as the dividend growth exceeds George's required return. He would have had to construct a schedule of the dividends he expects to receive in the future and discount them using his required rate of return to obtain the net present value of the dividend stream.

8. If George was considering purchasing 51% of the company's shares he would be able to control the company's dividend policy. He would therefore discount the company's future earnings stream as opposed to the expected dividends unless this was lower than the company's value on liquidation.

9. Hull plc's opening offer would probably be based on Ipswich Ltd's current profits of £100,000. The finance for the purchase costs 8% and the deal would only be economic if the profits covered this.

   Therefore the opening offer would be at or slightly below:

   £100,000/0.08 = £1,250,000

## APPENDIX

10. The maximum Hull plc could pay would be:

|  | £000 |
|---|---:|
| Current profits | 100 |
| Potential cost savings | 20 |
| | 120 |

$$£120,000/.08 = £1,500,000$$

If Mr Jones needed to make the sale he would be unwise to insist upon £1,600,000 as Hull plc cannot pay more than £1,500,000.

# Unit 11

## Student Activities

1. 1. Desk top review and preliminary findings.

    - Question requires a report to the bank – overdraft continuation and increase. Focus on cash flow and profitability.
    - Profits virtually unchanged.
    - Operating profits virtually doubled.
    - Company currently reliant on one single product – 'sales slowing down'.
    - Turnover down 17% – why? Is market down?
    - Volume of sales 240,000 down to 200,000, down 17%.
    - Therefore average selling price unchanged.
    - Production up 240,000 to 280,000 – why, when sales are down?
    - High element of fixed costs- plant depreciation and 'other expenses'.
    - Closing stock up three fold.
    - No factory rent in 19X4.
    - Directors' remuneration down £40,000 – why?
    - Administration costs up 20%, when sales down – why?
    - Interest charge for first time – over half of operating profits.
    - Dividends more than doubled (probably to compensate directors' for remuneration cut).
    - Major purchase of freehold buildings – explains no factory rent, part explains increase in profit.
    - Depreciation of freehold buildings?
    - Stocks up 264%. Obsolete, NRV?
    - Trade creditors nearly doubled – will need to be settled in 19X5
    - Bank overdraft at limit.
    - Proposed dividends – will need to be settled in 19X5.
    - New debenture in year – secured on freehold property – 100% security.
    - No change in share capital
    - New equipment required £120,000. Effect on production/cash flow.

# APPENDIX

- Estimate of overdraft facility:

|  | £000 |
|---|---|
| Currently | 98 |
| New equipment | 120 |
| Pay dividend | 70 |
| Settle creditors to, say, 19X3 levels | 90 |
| Required overdraft | 378 vs. 200 requested |

- Gut feeling – problem company with severe cash flow/product difficulties. Don't extend overdraft – call it in.

2. Other information required

    - Previous years figures.
    - Industry averages.
    - Size of Alexander in comparison to competitors.
    - Explanation of state of market – why sales volume down? – extra competition, old or unfashionable product?
    - State of economy in general.
    - Effects of cutting prices to reduce stock levels?
    - Breakdown of production costs – fixed and variable.
    - NRV of stocks.
    - Analysis of administration expenses.
    - Is interest on debentures fixed?
    - Why no overdraft interest in 19X3?
    - Current valuation of freehold buildings.
    - Value of plant and machinery (especially in light of declining market for company's sole product).
    - Collectability of debts – vs. company terms.
    - Terms of repayment of trade creditors – state of relationship.
    - Proof of demand for new product – any market research?
    - How long to get new product on line – existing or new market/any competition?. Is new product as profitable as old?

**2.** 1. Return on capital employed.

$$\frac{\text{Profit before interest and tax}}{\text{Capital, reserves and long term liabilities}} \times 100$$

| **19X4** | **19X3** |
|---|---|
| $\dfrac{194}{1{,}174 + 1{,}000}$ | $\dfrac{100}{1{,}150 + 0}$ |
| **= 8.9%** | **= 8.7%** |

# FINANCIAL REPORTING, ANALYSIS AND PLANNING

2. Return on shareholders' equity

$$\frac{\text{Profit after tax}}{\text{Capital and reserves}} \times 100$$

| **19X4** | **19X3** |
|---|---|
| $\dfrac{94}{1,174}$ | $\dfrac{100}{1,150}$ |
| = **8.0%** | = **8.7%** |

3. Return on gross assets.

$$\frac{\text{Profit before interest and tax}}{\text{Fixed and current assets}} \times 100$$

| **19X4** | **19X3** |
|---|---|
| $\dfrac{194}{1,620 + 912}$ | $\dfrac{100}{800 + 555}$ |
| = **7.7%** | = **7.4%** |

4. Return on *average* capital employed.

$$\frac{\text{Profit before interest and tax}}{\text{Average capital, reserves and long term liabilities}} \times 100$$

**19X4 only**

$$\frac{194}{(1,150 + 0) + (1,174 + 1,000) / 2}$$

= **11.7%**

5. Net profit percentage

$$\frac{\text{Net profit}}{\text{Sales}} \times 100$$

| **19X4** | **19X3** |
|---|---|
| $\dfrac{94}{1,500}$ | $\dfrac{100}{1,800}$ |
| = **6.3%** | = **5.6%** |

6. Asset turnover

$$\frac{\text{Sales}}{\text{Net assets}} \times 100$$

| **19X4** | **19X3** |
|---|---|
| $\dfrac{1,500}{1,174}$ | $\dfrac{1,800}{1,150}$ |
| = **1.28 times** | = **1.57 times** |

# APPENDIX

Linkage

| ROCE | | Net profit ratio | | Asset turnover |
|---|---|---|---|---|
| $\dfrac{\text{Net profit}}{\text{Assets}} \times 100$ | = | $\dfrac{\text{Net profit}}{\text{Sales}} \times 100$ | × | $\dfrac{\text{Sales}}{\text{Assets}}$ |

**19X4**

$$\dfrac{94}{1,174} \qquad\qquad \dfrac{94}{1,500} \qquad\qquad \dfrac{1,500}{1,174}$$

**8.0%** = **6.3%** × **1.28 times**

**19X3**

$$\dfrac{100}{1,150} \qquad\qquad \dfrac{100}{1,800} \qquad\qquad \dfrac{1,800}{1,150}$$

**8.7%** = **5.6%** × **1.57 times**

7. Gross profit percentage

$$\dfrac{\text{Gross profit}}{\text{Sales}} \times 100$$

**19X4**      **19X3**

$$\dfrac{370}{1,500} \qquad\qquad \dfrac{300}{1,800}$$

= **24.7%**      = **16.7%**

8. Overheads / sales ratio

$$\dfrac{\text{Overheads}}{\text{Sales}} \times 100$$

**19X4**      **19X3**

$$\dfrac{30 + 114 + 32}{1,500} \qquad\qquad \dfrac{70 + 95 + 35}{1,800}$$

= **11.7%**      = **11.1%**

9. Administration expenses/sales ratio

$$\dfrac{\text{Administration expenses}}{\text{Sales}} \times 100$$

**19X4**      **19X3**

$$\dfrac{114}{1,500} \qquad\qquad \dfrac{95}{1,800}$$

= **7.6%**      = **5.3%**

10. Selling and distribution costs/sales ratio

$$\dfrac{\text{Distribution costs}}{\text{Sales}} \times 100$$

| 19X4 | 19X3 |
|---|---|
| $\dfrac{32}{1{,}500}$ | $\dfrac{35}{1{,}800}$ |
| = **2.1%** | = **1.9%** |

11. Operating profit/sales ratio

$$\dfrac{\text{Operating profit}}{\text{Sales}} \times 100$$

| 19X4 | 19X3 |
|---|---|
| $\dfrac{194}{1{,}500}$ | $\dfrac{100}{1{,}800}$ |
| = **12.9%** | = **5.6%** |

12. Interest cover

$$\dfrac{\text{Profit before interest and tax}}{\text{Interest payable}}$$

| 19X4 | 19X3 |
|---|---|
| $\dfrac{194}{100}$ | $\dfrac{100}{0}$ |
| = **1.9 times** | = **N/A** |

3.  1. Working capital or Current ratio

$$\dfrac{\text{Current assets}}{\text{Current liabilities}}$$

| 19X4 | 19X3 |
|---|---|
| $\dfrac{912}{358}$ | $\dfrac{555}{205}$ |
| = **2.6 times** | = **2.7 times** |

2. Quick ratio (Acid test ratio)

$$\dfrac{\text{Current assets less stock}}{\text{Current liabilities}}$$

| 19X4 | 19X3 |
|---|---|
| $\dfrac{912-660}{358}$ | $\dfrac{555-250}{205}$ |
| = **0.7 times** | = **1.5 times** |

# APPENDIX

3. Gearing (or leverage) ratio

$$\frac{\text{Long-term debt}}{\text{Shareholders funds}} \times 100$$

| **19X4** | **19X3** |
|---|---|
| $\dfrac{1{,}000}{1{,}174}$ | $\dfrac{0}{1{,}150}$ |
| = **85.2%** | = **0%** |

4. 1. Stock turnover period

$$\frac{\text{Closing stock}}{\text{Cost of sales}} \times 365$$

| **19X4** | **19X3** |
|---|---|
| $\dfrac{660}{1{,}130} \times 365$ | $\dfrac{250}{1{,}500} \times 365$ |
| = **213 days** | = **61 days** |

2. Debtor collection period

$$\frac{\text{Closing trade debtors}}{\text{Sales}} \times 365$$

| **19X4** | **19X3** |
|---|---|
| $\dfrac{250}{1{,}500} \times 365$ | $\dfrac{300}{1{,}800} \times 365$ |
| = **61 days** | = **61 days** |

3. Creditor payment period

$$\frac{\text{Trade creditors}}{\text{Direct materials \& labour and other expenses *}} \times 365$$

*The purchases figure is not available from the question hence this has been used as a surrogate.*

| **19X4** | **19X3** |
|---|---|
| $\dfrac{190}{700 + 660} \times 365$ | $\dfrac{100}{600 + 660} \times 365$ |
| = **51 days** | = **29 days** |

4. Cash operating cycle

|  | **19X4** days | **19X3** days |
|---|---|---|
| Stock turnover period | 213 | 61 |
| Debtor collection period | 61 | 61 |
| Creditors payment period | (51) | (29) |
| Total | 223 | 93 |

**5.** 1. Fixed asset turnover

$$\frac{\text{Sales}}{\text{Fixed assets}}$$

| *19X4* | *19X3* |
|---|---|
| $\dfrac{1{,}500}{1{,}620}$ | $\dfrac{1{,}800}{800}$ |
| **= 0.93 times** | **= 2.25 times** |

2. Current asset turnover

$$\frac{\text{Sales}}{\text{Current assets}}$$

| *19X4* | *19X3* |
|---|---|
| $\dfrac{1{,}500}{912}$ | $\dfrac{1{,}800}{555}$ |
| **= 1.65 times** | **= 3.24 times** |

**6.** 1. Earnings per share

$$\frac{\text{Earnings}}{\text{Ordinary shares}}$$

| *19X4* | *19X3* |
|---|---|
| $\dfrac{£94{,}000}{500{,}000}$ | $\dfrac{£100{,}000}{500{,}000}$ |
| **= 18.8p per share** | **= 20p per share** |

2. Price earnings ratio

$$\frac{\text{Market price per share}}{\text{Earnings per share}}$$

| *19X4* | *19X3* |
|---|---|
| $\dfrac{150\text{p}}{18.8\text{p}}$ | $\dfrac{200\text{p}}{20\text{p}}$ |
| **= 8.0** | **= 10.0** |

3. Dividend cover

$$\frac{\text{Profit available for distribution}}{\text{Dividends}}$$

| *19X4* | *19X3* |
|---|---|
| $\dfrac{94}{70}$ | $\dfrac{100}{30}$ |
| **= 1.3 times** | **= 3.3 times** |

# APPENDIX

**Short answer questions**

1. Additional information required could include: previous periods results; information (financial and non-financial) on competitors, industry averages; explanatory information e.g. notes to accounts, directors report, Chairman's statement, other company data, economic data re state of industry/economy; management accounts, forecasts, costing data; information on value of company assets e.g. nrv of stock, value of fixed assets, value of identifiable intangibles etc.

2. 
   - As a percentage
   - As a simple ratio x:y
   - As a number of times
   - As a function of time

3. See 6.6 to 6.8

4. ROCE is the primary ratio because it shows the return (in profit terms) the company's owners are getting on their net investment in the business. It highlights whether, in general terms, the business is a viable entity or whether in fact the investors would be better off investing their capital elsewhere.

5. The cash operating cycle is an estimate of the length of time taken for cash to circulate within the business. In essence, it is the gap (in time terms) between the payment of suppliers and receipt of cash from customers. It is calculated by adding the stock turnover period to the debtor collection period and taking away the creditor payment period.

6. The gearing figure is important because it is an indication of the inherent riskiness of the company. The higher the gearing ratio, the more dependent the company is on loan finance as opposed to shareholder finance. In times of low profits or losses, this makes the company vulnerable because interest is a priority charge on profits, and the loan creditors often have priority rights to the company's assets through the security attached to the loans. The long-term viability is in jeopardy if loan creditors charge over company assets is crystallised.

   The absolute level of gearing may not of itself be a reliable indicator of the company's riskiness. However, relative levels of gearing and trends in gearing should be examined. Specified gearing ratios are often included within loan covenants.

   For an overview of the relative advantages of equity and loan finance see 10.2 to 10.6

7. Ratio analysis is only a tool of interpretation. Other methods of analysis may need to be employed. In addition, ratio analysis relies heavily on the quality of the financial statements. The financial statements themselves are inherently subjective. Factors such as the company's accounting policies, cut-off date, one-off unusual items, judgment on fixed assets, stock and debtor valuation, are all potential areas where the financial statements can be manipulated to present an over-favourable or indeed overly unfavourable view of the company.

   Finally ratio analysis utilises only the financial statements, which by their nature are historic. Forecast data and non-financial information may be more relevant in assessing a company.

# FINANCIAL REPORTING, ANALYSIS AND PLANNING

**Multiple choice questions**

1. (b) usually although (c) is sometimes used.
2. (c)
3. (a)
4. Probably (b)

    If stock turnover increased then debtors would probably also increase leading to a rise in the acid test ratio. If however stock turnover decreased likely debtors would also fall leading to a fall in the acid test ratio.

    If the debtor collection period increased or decreased it would be matched by an increase or decrease in cash, thus in either instance the acid test ratio would be unaffected.

5. (d)
6. (c)

**Exam-style question**

In this question students were provided with actual results for 1992 and budgeted and actual results for 1993. Students were therefore expected to assess the actual performance in 1993 in the light of both the budget and achievements during the previous year.

(a)

|  | £ |
|---|---:|
| Opening capital | 170,550 |
| Net profit | 122,840 |
| Revaluation of premises | 200,000 |
| Drawings (by difference) | (261,190) |
| Closing capital | 232,200 |

(b) The following are points which were appropriate for inclusion in the report:

- The company budgeted for a level of turnover approximately equal to that of the previous year and expected to achieve reductions in the cost of goods sold and bad debts (each expressed as a percentage of turnover) enabling it to increase the net profit margin from 11.9% to 14%.

- The company suffered a down-turn in the level of turnover of approximately 22.5% which was mainly responsible for the collapse in net profit to £122,840.

- There were some modest increases in expense levels, as a percentage of sales, which would not have been damaging if the budgeted level of activity had been achieved but, at the lower level of activity, these increases produced further significant inroads to profitability. In particular, there were the following increases compared with budget; cost of goods sold 2%; staff salaries 1.5%; and bad debts 3.1%

- The company's working capital ratio has fallen from 1.1:1 to 0,8:1 (compared with both actual and budget). We have no information concerning what is appropriate for this kind of business but the significant decline is a further cause for concern

# APPENDIX

- The rate of collection of debts has slowed down dramatically at 50.9 days compared with 27.3 days in the previous year and a budgeted collection period of 29 days. A significant increase in the bad debt write-off has already been made but the lengthening credit period raises the possibility that the reported figure for debtors includes further bad debts which have not yet been recognised.

- The return on capital employed was extremely healthy in 1992. The firm was obviously doing well and the very high percentage also reflects the nature of its activities with very little 'tied up' in fixed assets other than the cost of the premises. Presumably most other fixed assets are leased.

- The return on capital employed has fallen dramatically in 1993 to 52.6%. However, this is partly attributable to the upward revaluation of fixed assets which has significantly increased the level of capital employed.

- If the fixed assets had not been revalued, the return on capital employed would have come out at a spurious 540% (122,84/22,750 × 100) due to the fact that drawings have significantly exceeded profit for the year.

- Drawings by Page during the year to June 1993 are below budget, but are excessive in relation to rssults achieved. Drawings are more than double net profit and have been financed by the increase in bank overdraft and non-payment of creditors.

- The overdraft has increased by £57,500 over the last 12 months and, in the absence of an upturn in trading conditions a further increase might be expected during the forthcoming year.

- We are not told how the bank overdraft is secured. If based on the business premises, the new information concerning its value will be a 'comfort factor' but the bank is unlikely to be happy about a continuation of facilities unless drawings are limited to profits earned.

- Page's house is unlikely to be of use as possible further security. House prices have fallen significantly since January 1991 and might not even cover his personal mortgage.

| *Profit and Loss Account* | 1992 Actual % | 1993 Budget % | 1993 Actual % |
|---|---|---|---|
| Turnover | 100.0 | 100.0 | 100.0 |
| Less: Cost of goods sold | 68.9 | 67.0 | 69.0 |
| Staff salaries | 8.0 | 9.0 | 10.5 |
| Administration costs | 6.5 | 6.5 | 6.6 |
| Bad debts | 4.2 | 3.0 | 6.1 |
| Interest | 0.5 | 0.5 | 0.6 |
| Net profit | 11.9 | 14.0 | 7.2 |
| | | | |
| Current ratio | 1.1:1 (W1) | 1.1:1 (Q4) | 0.8:1 (W7) |
| Return on capital employed | 151% (W2) | 171% (W5) | 52.6% (W8) |
| *Other possible ratios include:* | | | |
| Rate of debt collection, days | 27.3 (W3) | 29 (W6) | 51 (W9) |

| | | |
|---|---|---|
| W1 434.6:394.2 = 1.1:1 | W4 450:400 = 1.1 | W7 458.7:556.5 = 0.8:1 |
| W2 258.49/170.55 × 100 = 151% | W5 308/180 × 100 = 171% | W8 122/232.2 × 100 = 52.6% |
| W3 162.5/2172 × 365 = 27.3 days | W6 175/2200 × 365 = 29 | W9 238.7/170 6.1 × 365 = 51 |

(c) 
- B. Page & Co. has had a poor year by comparison with 1992, but a profit of £122,840 has nevertheless been generated, subject to the above concern regarding the adequacy of the bad debt write-off.

- The levels of expenses have been kept under reasonable control so far as one can judge from the information provided.

- The essential problem is the excessive drawings by B. Page, indicating that he has made no attempt to reduce private expenditure in line with weaker trading results.

- Page's house was valued at £250,000 at the beginning of 1991, but is now likely to be worth much less and, quite possibly, is insufficient to cover his existing mortgage.

- The business premises provide adequate security for Page's business overdraft and the facility might be continued provided Page can be convinced that his personal expenditure should be brought in line with his business income.

### Areas of weakness in answers submitted for this question

- Requirement (a): the inclusion of £180,000 (the budgeted closing capital for 1993) as the opening capital.

- Requirement (a): the failure to account for the revaluation of premises

- Requirement (b) the failure to include calculations of ratios based on budgeted performance for 1993.

- Requirement (c): comments often confined to a statement of whether particular ratios went up or down, without exploring the reasons for these changes. For example, the impact of the reduction in turnover on expense and profit ratios was rarely explored.

- Requirement (c): relatively few candidates recognised the impact of the revaluation of fixed assets on calculations of the rate of return on capital employed and, where calculated, the gearing ratio.

# APPENDIX

# Unit 12

## Self-assessment questions

1.

| Reconciliation of operating profit to net cash inflow from operating activities: | £ |
|---|---|
| Operating profit | 200,000 |
| Depreciation | 50,000 |
| Loss on sale of machine | 10,000 |
| Increase in stocks | (10,000) |
| Decrease in debtors | 2,000 |
| Increase in creditors | 5,000 |
| Net cash inflow from operating activities | 257,000 |

2.

| Item | Cash inflow/ outflow | Section |
|---|---|---|
| Equity dividends paid | outflow | Equity dividends paid |
| Interest received | inflow | Returns on investments and servicing of finance |
| Tax rebate | inflow | Taxation |
| Proceeds from sale of fixed asset | inflow | Capital expenditure |
| Preference dividend paid | outflow | Returns on investments and servicing of finance |
| Repayment of loan to the bank | outflow | Financing |

3. You should have selected two entities from the following list.
   (a) Subsidiary undertakings where 90% or more of the voting rights are controlled within the group, provided that consolidated financial statements in which the subsidiary undertakings are included are publicly available.
   (b) Mutual life assurance companies.
   (c) Pension funds.
   (d) Certain open-ended investment funds.
   (e) Certain building societies.
   (f) Companies and other entities which qualify as 'small companies' under the Companies Act.

**Exam style question**

*Thomas Ltd, cash flow statement for the year ended 30 June 1996*

|  | £000 |
|---|---:|
| Net cash flow from operating activities | 38 |
| Returns on investments and servicing of finance (Note 1) | (5) |
| Taxation | (5) |
| Capital expenditure (Note 1) | (68) |
| Equity dividends paid | (10) |
|  | (50) |
| Management of liquid resources | - |
| Financing | 60 |
| Increase in cash | 10 |

*Note 1: Gross Cash Flows*

|  | £000 |
|---|---:|
| Returns on investments and servicing of finance |  |
| dividends received | 5 |
| interest paid | (10) |
|  |  |
| Capital expenditure |  |
| purchase of fixed asset (W1) | (80) |
| sale of fixed asset (W1) | 12 |
|  |  |
| Financing |  |
| issue of ordinary share capital | 50 |
| increase in loan | 10 |

*Reconciliation of operating profit to net cash inflow from operating activities*

|  | £000 |
|---|---:|
| Operating profit | 60 |
| Depreciation | 20 |
| Profit on sale of fixed asset | (2) |
| Increase in stocks | (10) |
| Increase in debtors | (20) |
| Decrease in creditors | (10) |
|  | 38 |

*Working 1 (W1)*

|  | £ |
|---|---:|
| Sale of fixed assets |  |
| Net book value | 10,000 |
| Profit on sale | 2,000 |
|  |  |
| therefore cash inflow | 12,000 |

# APPENDIX

Purchase of fixed assets

| | |
|---|---:|
| opening balance of fixed assets (nbv) | 100,000 |
| less fixed asset which was sold (nbv) | (10,000) |
| less depreciation | (20,000) |
| balance if there were no additions | 70,000 |
| actual closing balance | 150,000 |
| therefore purchases must equal | 80,000 |

# Unit 13

## Self-assessment questions

1. There are a number of advantages to be obtained from producing cash flow statements. You may have suggested some of the following:

   - cash flow is vital to the ultimate survival of a business
   - cash is more readily understandable to users than profit, which is dependent upon the accruals concept
   - cash is more comparable than profit, which may be affected by different accounting policies; it is useful management information for decision-making.

2. When analysing a cash flow statement, you also need to consider:

   the profit and loss account
   the balance sheet
   the statement of total recognised gains and losses
   supporting notes
   any other available information.

# Unit 14

## Student Activities

1. Financial accounting is concerned with the maintenance of accounting records, hence it is backward looking. Management accounting is used for decision making and is forward looking.

2.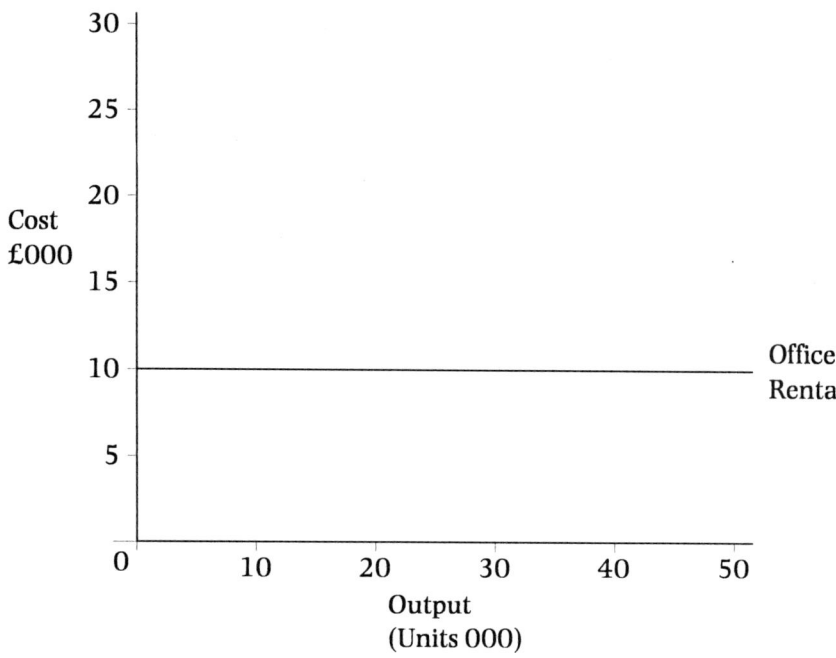

3. All but the public liability insurance are likely to have a stepped pattern.

4. Examples might include:
   - office consumables e.g. paper, pens etc.
   - postage
   - telephone charges (excluding line rental)
   - travelling expenses for managers visiting commercial customers etc.
   - printing costs for statements, promotional literature etc.
   - staff training costs.

5. Contribution could be raised by increasing bank revenue e.g. by raising the interest rate charged on personal loans. Alternatively, contribution could also be increased via a reduction in variable costs, such as those detailed in Activity 4.

6. (a) Profit = Total Revenue – Total Fixed Costs – Total Variable Costs

   Total revenue = £150,000

   Total fixed costs = £15,000 + £4000 + £1000 + £800 + £26000
   = £46,800

   Total variable costs = £150,000 × (0.52) + (£0.5 × £150,000/£100)
   = £78000 + £750
   = £78,750

Profit = £150,000 − (£46,800 + £78,750)
= £24,450

(b) Total revenue = £180,000

Total fixed costs = £46,800 + (£4000 × 0.125)
= £47,300

Total variable costs = £180,000 × 0.52 + (0.5 × £180,000/100)
= £93,600 + £900
= £94,500

(c) Every £1 increase in revenue will add to profit only if all fixed and variable costs are already covered. Once the fixed costs are paid for, then every extra sale will add to profit an amount equal to the contribution per £1 i.e. revenue less variable costs

In this case variable costs amount to 52% plus the cost of the packaging at £0.50 per £100 revenue. This gives a total variable cost level of 52.5%. In other words, a contribution rate of 47.5%. In other words, every £1 increase in sales will, once fixed costs have been covered, lead to a rise in profit of £0.475.

7. Contribution.

8. Let break even sales equal $x$, then

$£x - £0.88x = £1500$
$£0.12x = £1500$
$x = £12,500$

This equals 12,500 sandwiches sold per month.

9. Margin of safety = (11,000 − 10,000)/ 11,000
= 9.09%

10. There is clearly no single solution to this Activity. The answer will be dependent upon individual circumstance. Nonetheless, it is true to say that activity levels in both corporate and retail banking are not constant throughout the year.

11. The airline can earn a contribution towards its fixed costs as long as it charges a fare in excess of the marginal cost of providing the seat. A minimum price of £221 should therefore be charged.

### Exam-style questions

1. Zenith Ltd manufactures three products in one of its departments. The question involved two basic features. It tested the understanding of the nature and calculation of the 'contribution'. It also required candidates to consider the impact on production planning of the 'contribution'. Finally, it required candidates to consider the impact on production planning of the existence of limiting factors.

    (a) The contribution is the surplus of sales proceeds over and above variable cost. The term obtains its name because it represents that part of the proceeds from each item sold which is available to meet fixed costs and, once these are covered, contributes to an increase in profit of an equivalent amount.

# APPENDIX

The term limiting factor refers to the scarce resource which places an effective limit on the scale of operations, e.g. the lack of skilled labour or materials, or shortage of production facilities. In such circumstances profit is maximised by concentrating production on those products which produce the greater contribution per unit of limiting factor.

(b) **Contribution per unit of limiting factor**

|  | A<br>£ | B<br>£ | C<br>£ |
|---|---|---|---|
| Selling price | 21 | 30 | 26 |
| Variable cost | 11 | 12 | 21 |
| Contribution | 10 | 18 | 5 |
| (i) skilled labour | 10/4 = £2.5 | 18/9 = £2 | 5/1 = £5 |
| (ii) machine hours | 10/8 = £1.25 | 18/3 = £6 | 5/5 = £1 |

(c)

|  | A | B | C | Total |
|---|---|---|---|---|
| Contribution per unit | £2.5 | £2 | £5 |  |
| Ranking | 2 | 3 | 1 |  |
| Labour hours per unit | 4 | 9 | 1 |  |
| Labour hours, sales capacity | 2,800 | 2,700 | 800 |  |
| Production allocated hours | 600 |  | 800 | 1,400 |
| Contribution, £ | 1,500 |  | 4,000 | 5,500 |
| Fixed costs |  |  |  | 3,000 |
| Net profit |  |  |  | £2,500 |

(d)

|  | A | B | C | Total |
|---|---|---|---|---|
| Contribution per unit | £1.25 | £6 | £1 |  |
| Ranking | 2 | 1 | 3 |  |
| Machine hours per unit | 8 | 3 | 5 |  |
| Machine hours, sales capacity | 5,600 | 900 | 4,000 |  |
| Production allocated hours | 240 | 900 |  | 1,140 |
| Contribution, £ | 300 | 5,400 |  | 5,700 |
| Fixed costs |  |  |  | 3,000 |
| Net profit |  |  |  | £2,700 |

(e) Any reasonable comment based on calculations made was acceptable.

*Areas of weakness in answers submitted to this question:*

- The inability to translate correct calculations of the contribution per unit of limiting factor, made under (b) into the apportionment of available skilled labour and machine hours between the relevant product lines.

- Inability to convert allocation of hours between products into the profitability of each option.

# FINANCIAL REPORTING, ANALYSIS AND PLANNING

- Failure to elaborate on the statement that the contribution is sales proceeds minus variable cost.

2. This question was based on section 8 of the syllabus, 'Cost analysis'. It is the kind of question which has proved popular in this examination and is based on the concept of 'break-even analysis'.

   (a) Break-even analysis examines the behaviour of costs in response to changes in the level of output. The point at which the firm breaks even is when it makes neither profit nor loss as total costs are exactly equal to sales revenue.

   The essence of break-even analysis is the calculation of the contribution. The contribution is the difference between selling price and variable cost, and the company breaks even where enough units are sold to generate contributions sufficient to cover fixed costs.

   Break-even analysis is useful both to discover the level of output required to achieve various profit targets and also to compare the likely results of different techniques of production. It is often possible to interchange fixed and variable costs; for example, a method of production can be capital intensive or labour intensive.

   (b) (i) Break-even point

   |  | Method I £ | Method II £ |
   |---|---|---|
   | Sales price | 1,000 | 1,000 |
   | Less variable costs | 800 | 700 |
   | Contribution | 200 | 300 |
   | Fixed costs: Depreciation * | 200,000 | 500,000 |
   | Development expenditure * | 100,000 | 100,000 |
   | Other fixed costs | 300,000 | 510,000 |
   |  | 600,000 | 1,110,000 |
   | Break-even point in units: 600,000/200 | 3,000 |  |
   | 1,110,000/300 |  | 3,700 |

   * Amortised over five years.

   (ii) Sales to achieve 20% return

   |  | £ | £ |
   |---|---|---|
   | Original investment: Plant | 1,000,000 | 2,500,000 |
   | Working capital | 250,000 | 200,000 |
   | Development expenditure | 500,000 | 500,000 |
   |  | 1,750,000 | 3,200,000 |
   | 20% return | 350,000 | 640,000 |
   | Sales required in units: |  |  |
   | (600,000 + 350,000)/200 | 4,750 |  |
   | (1,110,000 + 640,000)/300 |  | 5,833 |

## APPENDIX

(iii) Profit at maximum production

|  | £ | £ |
|---|---|---|
| Contribution (6,000 units) | 1,200,000 | 1,800,000 |
| Fixed costs | 600,000 | 1,110,000 |
| Profit | 600,000 | 690,000 |

(c) Other calculations

Point of equal profit: $600,000 + 800Q = 1,110,000 + 700Q$
$$100Q = 510,000$$
$$Q = 5,100 \text{ units}$$

Normal capacity: 5,400 units
FD's forecast sales: 5,000 units

Margin of safety: Method I (6,000 – 3,000)/6,000 = 50%
Method II (6,000-3,700)/6,000 = 38.3%

- Method I has a relatively higher variable cost (possibly indicating the fact that it is relatively labour intensive) while Method II is relatively more capital intensive. This is reflected in both the cost structure and forecast profit margins at different levels of activity.

- Method I breaks even at a much lower level of activity: 3,000 units as compared with 3,700 under Method II. The result is that the margin of safety under Method I is 50% and under Method II it is 38.3%.

- To make an investment worthwhile, a company will require a rate of return sufficient to compensate for capital sunk into the project and risk. This is put at 20% by Ohlson Ltd. The level of sales required to produce a 20% return under the much more capital intensive Method II is 5,833 units compared with 4,750 units under Method I. In view of the fact that maximum sales are 6,000 units, this leaves very little leeway under Method II.

- At maximum production Method II produces £90,000 more profit than Method I but it must be remembered that almost twice the investment is required under Method II compared with Method I.

- The level of sales at which both methods produce identical profit is 5,100 units; below this level of activity Method I produces the higher profit and above it Method II.

- Assuming the normal level of activity indicated by the financial director is achieved, sales will be 5,400 units which will mean that the larger profit is achieved under Method II but not the required 20% return on investment.

- The financial director's sales forecast of 5,000 units would favour Method I in view of the fact that, at this level, it produces the higher profit and is the only option which achieves the 20% return.

- Weighing up all the facts provided, it would seem that Method I is both the safer option and the one likely to prove more remunerative.

### Areas of weakness in answers submitted to this question

- Under part (a) most candidates were able to identify the fact that break even analysis helps to identify the point at which total costs are covered by total

# FINANCIAL REPORTING, ANALYSIS AND PLANNING

revenues but relatively few candidates outlined the nature of the break even calculation or explored its purpose in greater depth.

- When computing fixed costs for the purpose of calculating the break even point under requirement (b) (i), the most common errors were to include only 'other fixed costs', to include working capital requirements and to base the depreciation charge on the useful physical life rather than the 'effective' life of the assets.

- Calculations of the original investment under (b) (ii), were often based only on the investment in plant, and in other cases included also 'other fixed costs'.

- Only a minority of candidates were able to compute the 'point of equal profit', which is of crucial significance in this kind of question.

# Unit 15

## Student Activities

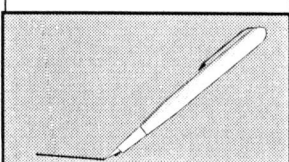

1. Required turnover = £1.25 million / ((1 − 0.4) × 0.08) = £26,041,667

2. Option 1:

   Savings = £4000 × 500 pa
          = £2 million pa

   Investment cost = 45 × £100,000
                     = £4.5 million

   Payback period = 4.5/2 years
                     = 2.25 years

   Option 2:

   Savings = £1.5 million pa

   Investment cost = 50 × £100,000
                       = £5 million

   Payback period = 5/1.5 years
                     = 3.33 years

   Using the payback criterion, the first option should be selected.

3. Information about the length of time over which the benefits will flow is not considered, nor is the absolute size of the investment. You might find one project pays back much quicker but also costs ten times as much. Payback systems ignore changes in the value of money over time.

4. It is easiest to compute the average profit, average investment and ARR on each project separately.

   *Purchase of software*

   The profit profile before depreciation is the same as the savings profile. The annual depreciation charge, calculated on a straight line basis will equal: £150,000/7 = £21,429

   Post depreciation profit profile is thus:

   | Year | Profit |
   |------|--------|
   | 1 | £75,000 − £21,429 = £53,571 |
   | 2 | £50,000 − £21,429 = £28,571 |
   | 3 | £25,000 − £21,429 = £3,571 |
   | 4 | £25,000 − £21,429 = £3,571 |
   | 5-7 | £25,000 − £21,429 = £3,571 |

   Average annual profit = £99,997/7
                                 = £14,285

   Average sum invested is determined by the end of year balance sheet values as follows:

| End of Year | Value |
|---|---|
| 1 | £128,571 |
| 2 | £107,142 |
| 3 | £85,713 |
| 4 | £64,284 |
| 5 | £42,855 |
| 6 | £21,426 |
| 7 | £0 |

This gives an average balance sheet value of £64,284

The ARR on the investment is therefore:

£14,285/£64,284 expressed as a percentage
That is, 22.22%

*Purchase of laptops*

Annual depreciation charge, using straight line, equals £150,000/9 = £16,667 pa

Post depreciation profit profile is thus:

| Year | Profit |
|---|---|
| 1 | £95,000 – £16,667 = £78,333 |
| 2 | £35,000 – £16,667 = £18,333 |
| 3 | £20,000 – £16,667 = £3333 |
| 4-9 | £15,000 – £16,667 = (£1667) |

Average profit (taking into account all the negative years) is thus equal to £89,997/9 =£10,000

Average sum invested is based on balance sheet values:

| End of Year | Value |
|---|---|
| 1 | £133,333 |
| 2 | £116,666 |
| 3 | £99,999 |
| 4 | £83,332 |
| 5 | £66,665 |
| 6 | £49,998 |
| 7 | £33,331 |
| 8 | £16,664 |
| 9 | £0 |

This gives an average sum invested equal to:

£599,988/9 =£66,665

The ARR on the investment is therefore:

£10,000/£66,665 expressed as a percentage.
That is, 15%.

The purchase of the software thus offers the highest ARR and so should be the chosen option.

5. (1) It takes account of *all* cashflows, but adjusts for changes in the value of money over time.

# APPENDIX

(2) £23,965. This is based on using a pocket calculator to determine the value. If tables are used a slightly different figure may result due to the effects of rounding in the calculation.

6. (1) £6,136 = (£2000 × 0.909) + (£2500 × 0.826) + (£3000 × 0.751)

   (2) £11,116 = (£1500 × 0.935) + (£4000 × 0.873) + (£5000 × 0.816) + £1000 × 0.763) + (£1000 × 0.713) + (£1000 × 0.666)

7. Value = £50,000 × 0.215
         = £10,750

   When this is compared with the current investment cost of £12,000 it shows a bad investment, which has a negative NPV.

8. Difference in NPV is equal to £2200, for a 4% difference in the discount rate. The change per 1% move in the discount rate is thus £2200/4 = £550

   Adjusting from the negative value for NPV ie (£400), we need to discount *less* heavily to reach an NPV of zero. The change in discount rate required to give an NPV of zero equals:

   400/550 = 0.727

   In other words, if the discount rate is reduced by 0.727% we will reach the ARR.

   ARR = 11% – 0.727%
       = 10.273%

   Working in the other direction should lead to a similar solution,
   Adjustment required equals 1800/550% = 3.27%
   In other words, we need to discount 3.27% more heavily than the current 7% to get an NPV of zero.

   ARR = 7 + 3.27
       = 10.27%

   Exactly the same answer as the one arrived at by working from the other direction.

9. There is no single answer to this activity, it will depend upon individual circumstance.

**Exam-style question**

This question focused on section 9 of the syllabus, 'Capital investment appraisal', paying particular attention to the payback and net present value methods.

(a) The advantages claimed for payback are:

- It involves simple calculations and is easy to understand.

- The project selected, because it is chosen to recover its cost rapidly, leaves the company at risk for the shortest period of time.

- The initial capital investment reduces the company's cash resources, and so the selection of a project with a short payback period ensures a prompt restoration of liquidity which may be of critical importance to a company with liquidity problems.

- The technique implicitly acknowledges that the further into the future predictions are made the less reliable they are.

# FINANCIAL REPORTING, ANALYSIS AND PLANNING

The criticisms of payback are:

- It ignores receipts expected to arise after the end of the payback period.
- No account is taken of the timing of the receipts, despite the fact that the further into the future cash is expected to arise, the lower is its present value.
- The selection of the time period within which an acceptable project must recover its cost is entirely arbitrary.
- The technique does not take profitability into consideration.
- Payback cannot be used to reach decisions where there are no cash inflows, for example when deciding whether to leave or buy an asset.

(b) NPV is designed to overcome some of the major disadvantages of payback by:

- Taking account of cash receipts over the entire life of the project.
- Recognising that cash received earlier is worth more than cash received later by applying the time value of money.
- Avoids the need to specify a payback period.
- Can be applied in circumstances where there is no cash inflow, in which case the lower negative present value will be favoured.

(c)

(i) **Payback**  Project A: 2 years  
Project B: within 3 years

(ii) **Net present value**

| Year | Cash Flows Project A £000 | Cash Flows Project B £000 | Discount factors | Present Values Project A £000 | Present Values Project B £000 |
|---|---|---|---|---|---|
| 0 | 1,000 | 1,000 | 1,000 | (1,000.0) | (1,000.0) |
| 1 | 700 | 400 | 0.909 | 636.3 | 363.6 |
| 2 | 300 | 500 | 0.826 | 247.8 | 413.0 |
| 3 | 100 | 800 | 0.751 | 75.1 | 600.8 |
| 4 | - | 600 | 0.683 |  | 409.8 |
|  |  |  |  | (40.8) | 787.2 |

(d) The two methods of capital investment appraisal produce different results: payback favours Project A and NPV favours Project B.

Project B should be selected for the following reasons:

- Although Project A pays back more quickly, it never recovers the original cost when taking account of cost of capital.
- There are substantial cash inflows under Project B after the end of the payback period, producing an impressive positive NPV compared with a negative NPV for Project A.

# APPENDIX

## Areas of weakness in answers submitted to this question

- Failure to read the question carefully was evident in answers to requirement (a), with a number of candidates describing the ways in which the two systems operated rather than outlining their main advantages and disadvantages.

- Most candidates were able to identify a number of advantages and disadvantages of the payback method, although a number devoted attention to a description of how the system operates.

- Most candidates coped well with requirement (c), although a small minority omitted the cost of the initial investment in the calculation of NPV.

- Comments under requirement (d) often suggested that Project A should be selected applying payback and Project B applying NPV. Candidates were informed that the two projects were mutually exclusive and further analysis was required in order to make an informed choice between them.

FINANCIAL REPORTING, ANALYSIS AND PLANNING

# Unit 16

## Student Activities

1. Clearly this question will have company specific answers, but amongst the budgets that might be identified are:

   - Temporary Contract staff
   - Liabilities budget
   - Capital purchases budget
   - Commission earnings budget
   - Interest receivable budget
   - Cash budget

   In the majority of cases the answer to this question will be that a mix of top down and bottom up planning is used. Management may be asked to set their own budget levels and priorities, and these will then be amended and adjusted after discussion with senior management.

2. A stock reduction will mean that demand is being met out of stock and production levels can thus be reduced. This should serve to lower the cash requirements of the business on the grounds that:

   less working capital will be tied up in finished goods stock and
   less working capital is needed to fund production.

3. Missing entries are as follows:

   3rd Quarter:

   Opening balance = 40
   Opening balance plus cash in = 220
   cash out = 150
   Cash surplus = 30
   Cash balance = 70

   4th Quarter

   Opening balance = 70
   Opening balance plus cash in = 205
   Total cash out = 155
   Cash surplus = (20)
   Cash balance = 50

4. 

|  | Jan | Feb | Mar | Apr | May | Jun |
|---|---|---|---|---|---|---|
| Opening balance | 15000 | 45000 | 51,000 | 54000 | 38625 | 53625 |
| Cash in | 80750 | 42750 | 38000 | 21375 | 57000 | 57000 |
| Cash out | 50750 | 36750 | 35000 | 36750 | 42000 | 42000 |
| Cash surplus | 30000 | 6000 | 3000 | (15375) | 15000 | 15000 |
| Closing balance | 45000 | 51000 | 54000 | 38625 | 53625 | 68625 |

5. Solutions are built in to the text

# APPENDIX

**6.** The cash balance would increase, as cash would be coming in sooner. The debtor balance would be reduced as cash was being collected quicker.

**Exam-style question**

Cox Ltd is up against its overdraft facility and the directors are considering two ways of satisfying the bank's instruction to reduce the level of the overdraft by £150,000 over the forthcoming six months. Candidates were required to prepare forecast accounts setting out the financial implications of each of these plans in the light of the bank's requirement.

(a) *Profit and Loss Account: 6 months to 30 April 1996 (£000)*

|  | Plan A | Plan B |
|---|---|---|
| Sales (1,200 – 60) | 1,140 | 1,200 |
| Cost of goods sold (720 – 36) | 684 | 720 |
| Operating expenses (360 – 12) | 348 | 360 |
| Depreciation | 40 | 40 |
| Discount (1,200 × 3% /2) | – | 18 |
|  | 1,072 | 1,138 |
| Net profit | 68 | 62 |

(b)

|  | Plan A | Plan B |
|---|---|---|
| Six months to October 1995 | 80 | 80 |
| Six months to April 1996 | 68 | 62 |
| Reduction in profit | 12 | 18 |

(c) *Cash budget: 6 months to 30 April 1996 (£000) – Plan A*

|  | Opening balance | Sales | Purchases | Expenses | Closing balance |
|---|---|---|---|---|---|
| Nov | (350) | 200 | 120 | 58 | (328) |
| Dec | (328) | 190 | 64 W1 | 58 | (260) |
| Jan | (260) | 190 | 114 | 58 | (242) |
| Feb | (242) | 190 | 114 | 58 | (224) |
| Mar | (224) | 190 | 114 | 58 | (206) |
| Apr | (206) | 190 | 114 | 58 | (188) |

W1   684/6=114-50

*Balance sheet at 30 April 1996 (£000)*

| | |
|---|---|
| Fixed assets at cost | 500 |
| Less: Accumulated depreciation | 240 |
| | 260 |
| Stock in trade | 190 |
| Trade debtors | 190 |
| | 380 |
| Bank | 188 |
| Trade creditors | 114 |
| | 302 |
| Net current assets | 78 |

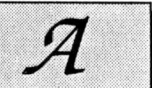

# FINANCIAL REPORTING, ANALYSIS AND PLANNING

|  |  |
|---|---|
|  | 338 |
| Issued share capital | 100 |
| Retained profit | 238 |
|  | 338 |

(d) Funds flow, 6 months to October 1995: £80,000 (profit) + £40,000 (depreciation) = £120,000. Assuming no additional investment, this will be the cash flow for the six months to April 1996. Monthly cash flow therefore £120,000/6 = £20,000. Period to achieve required reduction in overdraft, £150,000/£20,000 = 7.5 months. This appears reasonable and will be financially beneficial to the company.

**Areas of weakness in answers submitted to this question:**

- Operating expenses under Plan A reduced by just £2,000 for the entire six months instead of £2,000 per month.

- The failure to adjust cost of goods sold under Plan A in line with the reduced level of sales activity.

- The deduction of the reduction in stock, £50,000, from cost of goods sold, £720,000 to produce a balancing figure of £670,000 under Plan A.

- In the preparation of the cash budget, the most common error was the failure to adjust purchase payments for December to take account of the reduced stock requirements.

- Inclusion of figures for sales, £190,000 and purchases, £114,000 for November in the cash budget, i.e. candidates failed to realise that the receipts and payments in that month would be the debtors and creditors in the balance sheet at 31 October 1995.

- The omission of the additional depreciation charge for the six months to 30 April 1996 from figure for accumulated depreciation in the balance sheet at that date.

- Many candidates failed to attempt to answer requirement (d).

# APPENDIX

Present value of £1 received $n$ years hence, at a discount rate of $x\%$ per year

| Years (n) | 1% | 2% | 3% | 4% | 5% | 6% | 7% | 8% | 10% | 12% | 14% | 15% | 16% | 18% | 20% |
|---|---|---|---|---|---|---|---|---|---|---|---|---|---|---|---|
| 1 | 0.990 | 0.980 | 0.971 | 0.962 | 0.952 | 0.943 | 0.935 | 0.926 | 0.909 | 0.893 | 0.877 | 0.870 | 0.862 | 0.847 | 0.833 |
| 2 | 0.980 | 0.961 | 0.943 | 0.925 | 0.907 | 0.890 | 0.873 | 0.857 | 0.826 | 0.797 | 0.769 | 0.756 | 0.743 | 0.718 | 0.694 |
| 3 | 0.971 | 0.942 | 0.915 | 0.889 | 0.864 | 0.840 | 0.816 | 0.794 | 0.751 | 0.712 | 0.675 | 0.658 | 0.641 | 0.609 | 0.579 |
| 4 | 0.961 | 0.924 | 0.888 | 0.855 | 0.823 | 0.792 | 0.763 | 0.735 | 0.683 | 0.636 | 0.592 | 0.572 | 0.552 | 0.516 | 0.482 |
| 5 | 0.951 | 0.906 | 0.863 | 0.822 | 0.784 | 0.747 | 0.713 | 0.681 | 0.621 | 0.567 | 0.519 | 0.497 | 0.476 | 0.437 | 0.402 |
| 6 | 0.942 | 0.888 | 0.837 | 0.790 | 0.746 | 0.705 | 0.666 | 0.630 | 0.564 | 0.507 | 0.456 | 0.432 | 0.410 | 0.370 | 0.335 |
| 7 | 0.933 | 0.871 | 0.813 | 0.760 | 0.711 | 0.665 | 0.623 | 0.583 | 0.513 | 0.452 | 0.400 | 0.376 | 0.354 | 0.314 | 0.279 |
| 8 | 0.923 | 0.853 | 0.789 | 0.731 | 0.677 | 0.627 | 0.582 | 0.540 | 0.467 | 0.404 | 0.351 | 0.327 | 0.305 | 0.266 | 0.233 |
| 9 | 0.914 | 0.837 | 0.766 | 0.703 | 0.645 | 0.592 | 0.544 | 0.500 | 0.424 | 0.361 | 0.308 | 0.284 | 0.263 | 0.225 | 0.194 |
| 10 | 0.905 | 0.820 | 0.744 | 0.676 | 0.614 | 0.558 | 0.508 | 0.463 | 0.386 | 0.322 | 0.270 | 0.247 | 0.227 | 0.191 | 0.162 |
| 11 | 0.896 | 0.804 | 0.722 | 0.650 | 0.585 | 0.527 | 0.475 | 0.429 | 0.350 | 0.287 | 0.237 | 0.215 | 0.195 | 0.162 | 0.135 |
| 12 | 0.887 | 0.788 | 0.701 | 0.625 | 0.577 | 0.497 | 0.444 | 0.397 | 0.319 | 0.257 | 0.208 | 0.187 | 0.168 | 0.137 | 0.112 |
| 13 | 0.879 | 0.773 | 0.681 | 0.601 | 0.530 | 0.469 | 0.415 | 0.368 | 0.290 | 0.229 | 0.182 | 0.163 | 0.145 | 0.116 | 0.093 |
| 14 | 0.870 | 0.758 | 0.661 | 0.577 | 0.505 | 0.442 | 0.388 | 0.340 | 0.263 | 0.205 | 0.160 | 0.141 | 0.125 | 0.099 | 0.078 |
| 15 | 0.861 | 0.743 | 0.642 | 0.555 | 0.481 | 0.417 | 0.362 | 0.315 | 0.239 | 0.183 | 0.140 | 0.123 | 0.108 | 0.084 | 0.065 |
| 16 | 0.853 | 0.728 | 0.623 | 0.534 | 0.458 | 0.394 | 0.339 | 0.292 | 0.218 | 0.163 | 0.123 | 0.107 | 0.093 | 0.071 | 0.054 |
| 17 | 0.844 | 0.714 | 0.605 | 0.513 | 0.436 | 0.371 | 0.317 | 0.270 | 0.198 | 0.146 | 0.108 | 0.093 | 0.080 | 0.060 | 0.045 |
| 18 | 0.836 | 0.700 | 0.587 | 0.494 | 0.416 | 0.350 | 0.296 | 0.250 | 0.180 | 0.130 | 0.095 | 0.081 | 0.069 | 0.051 | 0.038 |
| 19 | 0.828 | 0.686 | 0.570 | 0.475 | 0.396 | 0.331 | 0.277 | 0.232 | 0.164 | 0.116 | 0.083 | 0.070 | 0.060 | 0.043 | 0.031 |
| 20 | 0.820 | 0.673 | 0.554 | 0.456 | 0.377 | 0.312 | 0.258 | 0.215 | 0.149 | 0.104 | 0.073 | 0.061 | 0.051 | 0.037 | 0.026 |

**Example** £1 received in 10 years' time, discounted at a rate of 8%, has a value of £0.463.

# Unit 17

## Self-assessment questions

1. According to FRS 8, two or more parties are related parties when at any time during the financial period:

    (i) one party has direct or indirect control of the other party; or

    (ii) the parties are subject to common control from the same source; or

    (iii) one party has influence over the financial and operating policies of the other party to an extent that that other party might be inhibited from pursuing at all times its own separate interests; or

    (iv) the parties, in entering a transaction, are subject to influence from the same source to such an extent that one of the parties to the transaction has subordinated its own separate interests.

2. Yes, all material related party transactions, even those where no price is charged.

3. You should have listed three disclosures from the following list:

    - the names of the transacting related parties
    - a description of the relationship between the parties
    - a description of the transactions
    - the amounts involved
    - any other elements of the transactions necessary for an understanding of the financial statements
    - the amounts due to/from related parties at the balance sheet date and provisions for doubtful debts due from such parties at that date
    - amounts written off in the period in respect of debts due to/from related parties.

# Glossary

**Accounting rate of return (ARR)**

An approach to making investment decisions based on calculating profits rather than cash flows.

**Accruals concept**

Assumes that revenue and costs are recognised as they are earned and incurred and not as money is paid or received. Revenues and costs are matched with one another so far as their relationship can be established or justifiably assumed. They are dealt with in the profit and loss account of the period to which they relate.

**Advance corporation tax (ACT)**

If a company makes a qualifying distribution (usually a dividend), it is required to pay some of its corporation tax earlier than usual – in advance.

**Asset turnover**

The level of sales that the company's (net) assets generate.

**Asset-turnover ratio**

The relationship between sales and net assets.

**Assets**

Rights or other access to future economic benefits controlled by an entity as a result of past transactions or events.

**Assets – fixed**

Those intended to be held on a 'continuing basis' – it is not the nature of the asset that is important, but the intended use of that asset.

**AVCO**

Average Cost.

**Bonds – deep discounted**

Variation on zero-coupon bonds. The bonds (usually) carry no interest, rather they are issued at a substantial discount and redeemed at par.

**Break even**

The sales level at which there is neither a loss nor a profit.

**Budget**

A plan quantified in monetary terms, prepared and approved prior to a defined period of time, usually showing planned income to be generated and/or expenditure to be incurred during that period and the capital to be employed to attain a given objective.

## Budget – cash

A schedule of cash payments and receipts which covers a defined future period of time.

## Capital allowances

Amounts allowed by the Inland Revenue against the cost of purchasing certain qualifying fixed assets.

## Capital employed

The company's net assets; i.e. its capital and reserves.

## Capital instruments

Instruments used to raise finance, including shares, loans, warrants etc.

## Cash flow statement

Shows an entity's cash inflows and outflows during a period, distinguishing between those that are the result of operations and those that result from other activities. This assists users in assessing the entity's liquidity, solvency, financial adaptability and the relationship between profits and cash flow.

## Compounding

Calculating the interest eventually to be paid on a principal sum which is periodically increased by adding the interest remaining unpaid.

## Consistency concept

Requires that there is consistency of accounting treatment of like items within each accounting period and from one period to the next.

## Contingency

A condition existing at the balance sheet date, where the outcome will be confirmed only on the occurrence or non-occurrence of one or more uncertain future events. A contingent gain or loss is a gain or loss dependant on a contingency.

## Contributions

Revenue less variable costs.

## Contributions from owners

Increases in ownership interest resulting from investments made by owners in their capacity as owners.

## Corporate report

Publication that communicates economic measurements of and information about resources and performance of the reporting entity, useful to those having reasonable rights to such information.

## Current cost

The lower of net current replacement cost and recoverable amount.

# GLOSSARY

**Depreciation**

The measure of the wearing out, consumption, or other reduction in the useful life of a fixed asset whether arising from use, effluxion of time or obsolescence through technological or market changes.

**Derecognition**

From the financial statements e.g. following a disposal. The item should cease to be recognised if there is no longer sufficient evidence that the entity has access to future economic benefits or an obligation to transfer economic benefit.

**Development expenditure**

Expenditure encompassing the use of knowledge acquired, directed towards a specific commercial end product/service.

**Discounting**

Converts future values into present values.

**Distributions to owners**

Decreases in ownership interest resulting from transfers made to owners in their capacity as owners.

**Earnings per share**

Expresses in an amount per share, how much profit the company has earned in the last financial year; it is given by dividing total earnings available for distribution by the total number of equity shares.

**Events – adjusting**

Those PBSEs which provide additional evidence about conditions existing at the balance sheet date.

**Events – non-adjusting**

Those PBSEs which do not relate to a condition existing at the year end.

**Events – post balance sheet (PBSE)**

Incidents that occur between the company's year end and the publication of the company's accounts.

**Exceptional items**

Items which are: material; derive from the company's ordinary course of business; and are exceptional due to size or incidence.

**External capital reorganisation**

Eliminating a negative profit and loss balance against a company's non-distributable capital, by closing the books of the old company and opening books for a new company with the new asset values.

## Extraordinary items

Items which are: material; derive from outside the ordinary course of business; are not expected to recur and are highly abnormal in nature.

## FIFO

First In First Out.

## Financial statements – primary

The balance sheet, profit and loss account, cash flow statement and statement of total recognised gains and losses (SORG).

## Fixed costs

Those which remain the same regardless of the output level (i.e. number of items manufactured or amount of services delivered), as opposed to Variable costs.

## Forecast

A prediction of what is thought likely to happen.

## Gains

Increases in ownership interest, other than those relating to contributions from owners.

## Going concern concept

Assumes that an enterprise will continue in operational existence for the foreseeable future.

## Historic cost

The price paid for an item. See also Opportunity cost and Relevant cost.

## Historic cost accounts

Maintain a business capital in nominal pounds.

## Historic cost accounts (adjusted)

Recognise the change in the level of prices.

## Internal rate of return (IRR)

The discount rate at which the net present value of an investment is zero.

## Liabilities

Obligations to transfer future economic benefits as a result of past transactions or events.

## Liabilities – convertible

Carry the right (not necessarily an obligation) to convert to shareholders funds at some point in the future.

# GLOSSARY

**LIFO**

Last In First Out.

**Limiting factor**

A constraint put on decision making due to the scarcity of some resource (e.g. labour or materials).

**Losses**

Decreases in ownership interest, other than those relating to distributions from owners.

**Market value – open**

The best price which might be obtained on a sale assuming a willing buyer and seller.

**Materiality**

The magnitude of an omission or misstatement of accounting information that, in the light of surrounding circumstances, makes it probable that the judgment of a reasonable person relying on the information would have been changed or influenced by the omission or misstatement.

**Net book value**

Cost of an asset less accumulated depreciation to date.

**Net present value (NPV)**

The current day worth of future benefits generated by an investment.

**Net profit ratio**

The relationship between profit and sales.

**Net realisable value (NRV)**

The cash which would be obtained if an asset were sold. In other words, the sale proceeds less the costs incurred in making the sale.

**Opportunity cost**

The benefit lost when, by buying an item, money is not available for some other more profitable use.

**Ownership interest**

Residual amount found by deducting all the entity's liabilities from all the entity's assets.

**Plan**

A means by which a set objective (or what should happen) will be achieved.

**Primary accounting ratio**

The return on capital employed (ROCE).

### Profits – distributable

Accumulated realised profits, so far as they have not been distributed or capitalised, less accumulated realised losses, so far as they have not been previously written off in a reduction or reorganisation of capital.

### Prudence concept

Requires that revenue and profits are not anticipated, but are recognised by inclusion in the profit and loss account only when realised in the form of either cash or other assets of which the ultimate cash realisation can be assessed with reasonable certainty. It also requires that provision is made for all known liabilities (expenses and losses) whether the amount of these is known with certainty or is a best estimate in the light of the information available.

### Ratio – accounting

The relationship of one figure in the accounts to another.

### Recognition – initial

An element should be recognised if there is sufficient evidence that the change in assets or liabilities inherent in the element has occurred. This includes, where appropriate, evidence that a future inflow or outflow of benefit will occur and that it can be measured at a monetary amount with sufficient reliability.

### Recoverable amount

The higher of net realisable value and value in use.

### Relevant costs

Arise from making a decision to do or not to do something.

### Reserves – capitalisation of

A bonus issue of free shares.

### Reserves – undistributable

The share premium account; the capital redemption reserve; any accumulated surplus of unrealised profits over unrealised losses; and any other reserve which cannot be distributed, whether by statute, or the company's memorandum or articles of association.

### Statement of total recognised gains and losses (SORG)

Shows the profit for the period together with other movements on reserves which reflect recognised gains and losses attributable to shareholders.

### Subsidiary

If an investing company holds more than 50% of the (voting) shares in another company it has a subsidiary.

### Substance over form

Requires that the economic substance of a transaction is reported as opposed to its legal form.

# GLOSSARY

**Sunk cost**

Another name for Historic cost.

**Variable costs**

Those which do not vary according to output levels, as opposed to fixed costs.

**Window dressing**

An attempt by accounts preparers to deliberately alter the impression of a business by changing certain features just before the balance sheet date.

**Zero coupon bond**

A capital instrument that carries no interest.

# Index

## A
Accounting policy
  changes 116
Accounting rate of return 328
  average profit per year 329
Accounting Standards Board (ASB) 26
  guidelines 27
  Statement of Principles 9, 251
Accounting Standards Committee (ASC) 25
Accounts
  notes to 45
Accruals 37
Accruals concept 16
Acid test ratio 257
Acquisition accounting 200
Actuary 102
Administration expenses/Sales ratio 256
Advance Corporation Tax (ACT) 132, 151
  set off 152
ARR 328
Asset turnover 253, 256, 262
Asset turnover ratio 249
Assets 39
  fixed 260
  non-pool 149
  operating 260
  disposals 149
Associated company 168
Attributable profit 72
Auditing Practices Board 29

## B
Balance sheet 39
  vertical format 39
Bills of exchange
  discounting 126
Bonds
  deep discounted 93
Bonus issue 134
Borrowings 242
Brands 81
Break-even analysis 310
Break-even point 297, 308
Budgets 345-346, 348
  adjustments 358
  balance sheets 358
  benefits 354
  cash 351-352, 355
  master 348
  production 348, 351
  sales 348

## C
Cadbury Committee 30
  Code of Practice 31
Cadbury Report 25, 30
Capital allowances 148
Capital instruments 89, 91
Capital investment appraisal 321
  accounting rate of return 328
  compounding 331
  discounting 324, 331
  hurdle rate 335
  internal rate of return 337
  net present value 333
  non-financial considerations 340
  payback 325
  present value 333
Capital investments
  characteristics 324
Capital reduction 218
Capitalised interest 56
Cash flow statement 14, 237, 255, 273, 289
Cash operating cycle 256, 262
Changes in output on costs and profits 308
Commission 39
Companies Act 37, 47
  section 221 38
  section 263 32
Compounding 331
Conglomerate 235
Consignment stock 127
Consistency 37
  concept 16
Consolidation
  exemptions from 202
Contingencies 99, 127
  government grants 141
Contribution 307
Control mechanisms 347
Corporate governance 30
Corporate reports 7
  comparability 9
  completeness 9
  comprehensibility 9
  objectivity 9

relevance 9
reliability 9
timeliness 9
Corporation tax 148
Cost behaviour 297
Cost classification 297
Costs for planning and control 298
Court approval 217
Credit payment period 261
Credit-rating agencies 8
Current cost 63
Current Purchasing Power 20

**D**

Database of costs 299
Debt
   convertible 90, 92
   non-convertible 90
   perpetual 95
Decision making under spare capacity 314
Deferred tax
   flow through approach 159
   full provision approach 159
   partial provision approach 159
Depreciated replacement cost 64
Depreciation 58, 236
   adjustments 60
   definition 58
   methods 58
   useful economic life 59
Derecognition 12
Development expenditure 78
Directors' emoluments 46
Directors' Report 47
Discontinued operations 119
Discounting 331
Dividend cover 264-265
Dividends
   proposed 152
Dual capitalisation method 232

**E**

Earnings
   definition 131
Earnings per share (EPS) 115, 122, 131, 263, 265
   effect of issue at full market price 133
   effect of changes in capital structure 133
   net basis 132
Employee reports 138
Entity concept 20
Equity finance 258
Errors
   fundamental 117
European Directives 48
Exceptional items 116
Exit value 20

Exposure Draft (ED) 14, 51, 52, 56, 57, 63
External capital reduction 221
Extraordinary items 264
   definition 115

**F**

Factoring 126
FIFO 265
Financial information
   qualitative characters 11
Financial Reporting Council (FRC) 26
Financial statements 113, 355
   elements 12
   measurement in 13
   objective 10
   presentation 13
   recognition of assets and liabilities 12
Finished goods 68
Fixed assets
   enhancement costs 57
   intangible 77
   tangible 56
   valuation 56
   valuers 64
   worn out 237
Fixed costs 302
Forecasts 345, 349
   profit 356
   profit and loss 355, 359
Forte Hotels 28
FRS 1 revised 'Cash flow statements' 273
FRS 2 'Accounting for Subsidiary Undertakings' 48, 125, 201
FRS 3 'Reporting financial performance' 47, 98, 105, 113, 114, 266
FRS 4 'Capital Instruments' 89
FRS 5 'Reporting the substance of transactions' 22, 99, 123
FRS 6 'Acquisitions and mergers' 200
FRS 7 'Fair Value accounting' 185, 188-190
FRS 8 'Related party disclosures' 365

**G**

Gearing 258-259
   effect of FRS5 124
Gearing (or leverage) ratio 22, 259
Geographical analysis 51
Going concern 37
   concept 16
Goodwill 77, 232
   write off to SORG 121
Gordon's Growth Model 239
Government grants 139
Gross profit percentage 256

# INDEX

## H
Historic cost 19, 299
   adjusted 19
   modified 19
Historic cost accounts
   limitations 7, 21, 23
   net profit 252
Historic profits and losses note 122
Historical summaries 138
Hurdle rate 335

## I
Income statements 315
Institute of Management Accountants (CIMA) 347
Interest cover 256
Internal rate of return (IRR) 337
Investment income 154
Investment properties 64
Investments 62

## L
Leases
   accounting 129
   finance 128
   operating 128
Leasing 127
Liabilities 39, 89-90
   convertible 90
   non-convertible 90
LIFO 265
Limiting factors 297, 313
'Linked presentation' 127
Liquidation claims 224
Liquidation value 239
Loan covenants 242
Loan finance 258
Loans
   index linked 96
   variable rate 96
Local Authority Superannuation Scheme 102
Losses written off 219

## M
Market purchases 211
Matching concept 103, 139
Materiality 16
Merger accounting 200

## N
Net present value 333
Net profit percentage 262
Net profit ratio 256
Net realisable value (NRV) 20, 63
   stock 68

## O
Off balance sheet financing 123
Off-market purchases 211
Open Market value 62
Operating capacity, 20
Operating profit/Sales ratio 256
Opportunity cost 299, 301
Ordinary shares 264
Overdraft 355
Overheads/Sales ratio 256

## P
Par 213
Payback formula 325
PE ratio 243
Pension contributions 46
Pension costs 100
Pension funds 101
Pension schemes 100
Planning 360
Planning and control 322
   cycle 299
Plans 345
   operating 346
   strategic 346
Post balance sheet events (PBSE) 97
Preference dividends 131, 264
Present value 333
   discount tables 336
Price earnings (PE) ratio 131, 234, 264, 265
Price fixing 231, 242-243
Primary period 95
Prior period adjustments 116, 138
Profit
   operating 52
Profit and loss account
   formats 42
   FRS3 format 118
Profit forecast 346
Profit measurement 17
Profits
   accounting 147
   taxable 147
Proprietary concept 20
Prudence 37
   concept 16, 68, 77, 79, 99, 105, 141

## R
Ratios
   interpretation 249
   net profit 253
Ratio analysis 246, 248, 256
   limitations 265
Raw materials 68
Realised gains and losses 64
Redeemable ordinary shares 210
Redeemable preference shares 210
Regulatory regime 48

Relevant cost 299
Replacement cost accounting 20
Reporting entity 15
Research
   applied 78
   pure 77
Research & development expenditure 77
Reserves
   undistributable 33
Residual value 58
Return
   on capital employed (ROCE) 21, 251, 252, 256, 262, 265
   on shareholders' equity 256
   on total assets 256
Review Panel 26, 28
Rights issues 135

## S
Sale and repurchase of assets 126
Schemes of capital reduction 217
Secondary period 95
Selling and distribution costs/Sales ratio 256
Shareholder ratios 263
Shareholders' funds 89, 90, 251
   reconciliation on 121
Shares
   company purchases own 212
   company's capital to purchase own 215
   equity 90
   non-equity 90
SORG 251
SSAP2 15, 37
SSAP3 'Earnings per share' 47, 131
SSAP4 'Accounting for government grants' 139, 141
SSAP6 115
SSAP8 'The treatment of taxation under the imputation system in the accounts of companies.' 151
SSAP9 67, 72
SSAP 10 'Source and application of funds' 273
SSAP12 28, 58, 122
SSAP13 77-78
SSAP15 'Accounting for deferred tax' 157, 159
SSAP16 21
SSAP17 'Accounting for post balance sheet events' 89, 97
SSAP18 'Accounting for contingencies' 89, 99
SSAP19 64
SSAP20 'Accounting for foreign currencies' 120
SSAP21 'Accounting for leases and hire purchase contracts' 22, 125, 127
SSAP24 'Accounting for pension costs' 89, 100, 103
SSAP25 'Segmental Reporting' 137
Statement of Principles 9, 121
   definition of assets and liabilities 125
Statement of total recognised gains and losses 65, 114, 120
Stock 67
   long term work in progress 72
   turnover period 260
   turnover ratio 260
Stock turnover ratio 262
Stock valuation
   LIFO, FIFO, AVCO 69-70
Subsidiary companies 173
Substance over form 16, 123
Sunk cost 300
'Super-exceptional items' 119

## T
Tax treatments
   differences 156
Taxation
   deferred 155
'The Corporate Report' 10
Total costs 306
Trade investment 168
Turnover 45, 51

## U
Urgent Issues Task Force (UITF) 26
Uses of break-even analysis 312

## V
Valuations 242
   of assets 55
   balance sheet 231
   break-up 235
   cash flow 236
   dividend 238
   earnings 233
   fixed assets 62
   majority interest 239
   minority interest 239
Variable costs 302
Voluntary liquidation 218

## W
Warrants 94
Window dressing 98
Work in progress 68
Working capital 260

## Z
Zero coupon bonds 92, 93